INSIDE THE LAW

VIKKI PETRAITIS

Clan Destine
P R E S S

TRUE CRIME

First published in 2019
by Clan Destine Press
 PO Box 121, Bittern
 Victoria 3918 Australia

National Library of Australia Cataloguing-In-Publication data:

Petraitis, Vikki

INSIDE THE LAW: 25 years of true crime writing

ISBN: 978-0-6482937-1-2 (paperback)

ISBN: 978-0-6482937-2-9 (eBook)

Cover Photo: Darren McNamara
Cover Design © Willsin Rowe
Design & Typesetting: Clan Destine Press

Clan Destine Press

www.clandestinepress.com.au

This book is dedicated to my dad, John Burke,
whose dinner-table stories throughout my childhood
taught me how to be a storyteller.

1

In the Beginning

I'VE NEVER BEEN INSIDE MY OWN BOOKS. SOME TRUE CRIME WRITERS include themselves in the story, but I never have. I never felt the story was about me. The stories I've written for 25 years are about other people, their suffering, their triumph. I was just the storyteller. But a funny thing happens with storytellers. We spend time with people who have been through the worst life has to offer and we absorb their wisdom.

I'm not sure why I've kept in the background. With some books I've written, I've even left most of the publicity to the subject of the story, figuring it was their story to tell. But over the years, I've realised that my writing has changed people. Not just the story, but *my* writing, *my* lens. Increasingly, when I do talks, people come up to me and tell me that after reading my books, they decided to be an investigator or join the police force or become a criminal psychologist.

To hear that my books have changed people's lives, is a feeling that defies description.

It's taken me nearly 25 years to realise that the story is what it is; the magic is in the telling.

A student journalist once asked me how I remained unbiased in my stories. I laughed. Not for one minute am I unbiased. Every word, every sentence I write, takes the reader on the journey I planned for them. If my writing *looks* unbiased, don't be fooled.

Writing true crime has helped me learn about the world. Listening to people who've lost a loved one to a serial killer, or who've been the victim of a crime and have survived – they are my teachers. And then, in turn, I teach. Sometimes, I feel like a bee, hovering from flower to flower, taking with me what I learn from one person to the next.

As a child, I devoured books from the moment I could read. Reading transported me to other worlds. A childhood full of siblings and noise, vanished as soon as a book was open. I trawled the house like a reading junkie, hunting out my next hit; books I hadn't read yet, encyclopaedias, anything was fair game. Birthday money was spent on Enid Blyton books and I imagined myself climbing the Faraway Tree or flying in the Wishing Chair. My primary school library proved disappointing because it had books with boys and aeroplanes on the covers with titles like Biggles, while I hankered for girls' adventures and mysteries.

By Year 7, I'd grown too old for the Famous Five and Nancy Drew. I prowled the aisles of the Kilbreda College library and spied a cluster of Agatha Christies. My fate was sealed the moment I reached up and selected *Sparkling Cyanide*. Death by dinner party was followed by clues and finally, the reveal – the person I least expected. The books were the ultimate in crime and mystery for a kid already addicted. (So many crime writers I've spoken to over the years list Famous Five, Nancy Drew, and Agatha Christie as the gateway reading that led to crime writing. Just a friendly warning.)

A couple of years after that – in 1980 – Australia was mesmerised when baby Azaria Chamberlain was taken by a dingo while her family were holidaying at Uluru. Her mother, Lindy was 'different' in the eyes of 'regular' Aussies. She was a member of a religion most folks hadn't really heard of, and she didn't cry for the cameras. Those pretty much were her main crimes. As a 15-year-old, I watched the media wield its power and listened to people voice their opinions.

She'd have to be guilty; just look at her!

It was a heady time and the first in my short life where people felt part of a case. From the outset, I didn't believe Lindy Chamberlain killed her baby. I felt the wrongness of what was done to her. I remember reading the book, *Evil Angels* by John Bryson and a few years later, taking my nan to see the movie. I laid out the case for the defence to Nan. I'm not sure I moved her from her guilty leanings, but I did my best.

When I began to fancy myself a budding author in my early 20s, I naturally wanted to write crime. I tried writing a murder mystery set in Melbourne, but immediately hit the limits of my knowledge of crime and criminal behaviour. At that age, I knew very little of life, having been to primary and secondary school, teachers' college, then back to primary school as a teacher. My world was small, narrow, and sheltered.

A friend and I planned to write a novel. We made index cards, wrote a couple of chapters, and naturally, our first roadblock was that we had no idea why people killed. I remembered Agatha Christie alluding to it in one of her books. She said some people simply couldn't apply the brakes. Did that mean we could all kill? I didn't think I could.

I went on a quest to find out why people killed so I could write a believable fictional character who killed. The logical searching ground was my local book store. It was there I found a book called: *Myra Hindley: Inside the Mind of a Murderess* by Jean Ritchie.

Two things happened.

Firstly, I ditched any notion of writing fiction because true crime was so raw and it told the story of real people, real grief, real loss, real horror. Suddenly, the body-in-the-library fiction paled in comparison to the truth.

I became hooked on reading true crime – which in the early 1990s was nearly all from the United States or the United Kingdom. To me, it was human nature to the extreme; people pushed beyond the limits. It had death, loss and suffering, but at the heart of it lay human resilience and triumph.

Author Lisa Cron in her book *Story Genius* writes: 'We don't turn to story to escape reality. We turn to story to navigate reality.'

I think this explains how true crime helps people confront reality. Perhaps true crime is compelling because we want to know how people survive it. Or how we might survive if it happened to us.

At its heart is a core of profound humanity: the victim's family survived and became advocates; the dogged detective never gave up; the community marched for safer streets or tougher sentences. People came together to rise up. Good usually won, and evil ended up in a cell or – in the old days – at the end of a noose.

My urge to write soon became the urge to write true crime.

I found a book in Kill City – a wonderful crime book shop (now closed down) in Greville Street, Prahran. The book, by Gary Provost, was called *How to Write and Sell True Crime*. The step-by-step guide to researching, interviewing, and writing helped me formulate a plan. It also gave me the parameters to choose a case to write about.

Provost spoke of the need to find a case that had lots of *and thens*. It was not enough to find a fascinating crime, but it had to have *and then* moments. A woman befriends the old woman next door and then the old woman vanishes. And then the neighbour tries to withdraw money from the missing woman's bank account. And then… you get the drift.

I entered the true-crime writing world, a babe in the woods, ignorant of almost every aspect of book writing. But every writer begins with the self-belief – despite any supporting evidence – that they can write, and that people will want to read what they write. I was no exception. Writing looked easy enough. Just words on a page, right?

Lucky for me, I had no idea how much I didn't know.

Provost's advice helped me choose my first project. The origins came from an unlikely place – a teacher professional development day which began with a story.

The speaker addressed a room full of teachers and spoke about the need to support children from broken families. The new program we were learning about was sponsored by the family of a woman called Vivienne, the speaker told us solemnly.

Vivienne came from a broken home; her parents divorced when she was young and Vivienne never really got over it. When Vivienne grew up, she married a man called Fergus, and when Fergus began having an affair, Vivienne 'snapped'.

According to the speaker, all the hidden rage and sorrow from her parents' failed marriage came crashing down on her, and she broke into the home of the woman her husband was having the affair with and killed her. Vivienne then jumped to her death off the Phillip Island Bridge.

As the speaker spoke about the case, a kernel of an idea formed. This story was perfect. A woman who'd never gotten over her parents' divorce... *and then* she found out her husband was having an affair... *and then* she drove to the mistress's house in the dead of night... *and then* she vanished off the face of the earth.

Of course, back then, I thought it was a simple story of love, betrayal, and murder. But nothing is ever as simple as it seems.

The first port of call was a newspaper search which in those days meant that you rang the newspapers and asked them to do a search and then they found what you were after and sent you the photocopies of the articles. That, or microfiche which I never really mastered. It turned out that there were only two articles published in major newspapers about the case.

This was the first odd thing: such a sensational crime and an almost total newspaper blackout.

The next step was to contact the Coroner's Court and try to gain access to the file. It wasn't long before I was staring down at crime scene photos of a young woman called Beth Barnard who'd suffered a terrible death.

The photos were confronting. Stab wounds in movies look like thin red lines; in real life they gape open and show the yellow subcutaneous fat. A cut throat is a dark cavern of sinew. Dead eyes stare blankly.

Most striking was the huge letter A carved into her chest. I think they forgot to mention that at the Catholic primary teacher professional development day.

Perhaps in that moment more than any other, I realised that to be a crime writer, I would have to put aside my horror and distress, lock it in a box, so that I could get on with the job of documenting the story. The story had to rule over all else.

Back at home, with copies of all the documents and photos I began writing the story. That turned out to be the relatively easy part. It was when I organised to interview actual people, things became real.

I had a weird crisis as I stood in my wardrobe, wondering what real writers wore. I was scheduled to do my first police interview with Detective Rory O'Connor at the Russell Street Police Headquarters, and I wanted to look the part. Nowadays it would be called #Imposter-Syndrome – a label which would have made the whole wardrobe moment easier. I would have realised what I was suffering from, taken a deep breath, off-loaded on my Twitter feed, received 37 replies to reassure me, then I would have donned a pair of jeans and be done with it.

But my crisis was in 1991 and hashtags hadn't been invented. I also had no online community to consult because online communities hadn't been invented yet either. In fact, I had never even met another writer.

I arrived at Russell Street wearing a writerly jacket and a headband which quite possibly made me look more Alice in Wonderland than author. I was 25 years old and felt like a pretender. It's an unavoidable thing, but when I had yet to publish a book, I was just a girl with a notepad on a steep learning curve.

Back then, I taped all my interviews on a little voice recorder with tiny cassette tapes. I dutifully transcribed each one which was really helpful because listening to myself butt-in on questions, my transcribing-self kept telling my interviewing-self to SHUT UP.

Listening, I learnt, was the key.

It's worth putting my writing into a broader context. In a nutshell, I got married at 20, baby at 22, Diploma of Teaching at 23. Full-time teaching job at 24. Writing time was carved out in between all my other commitments. Was it hard to write and teach? I don't remember it being hard. Writing was something I prioritised. Like all working mothers, I juggled to fit it in. I wrote my first book at a desk in my kitchen.

I would come to understand that I always needed something *extra,* something other than family and a regular job. Writing was my extra. Something I did just for me.

In *How to Write and Sell True Crime*, Gary Provost suggested writing three chapters then sending them to publishers who published similar books. At that time, there were hardly any books published in Australia about local crime. I had read Tom Nobel's *Untold Violence*, and Andrew Rule's *Cuckoo*, but that was about all I could find. Tom's book was published by John Kerr, and it was to him that I sent my first attempts at writing – typed on a typewriter.

John read my three chapters and invited me to his office in Richmond to discuss my book. He had one concern about the story;

From typewriter to big desktop computer: the fledgling writer at work in her kitchen.

he said it didn't have a satisfactory ending. What neither of us realised was that this was the story's greatest strength. It was precisely *because* it didn't have a satisfactory ending, that it invited the reader to play detective.

John agreed to publish the book but on one condition.

'Since you're not a writer,' he said, 'I want to pair you up with a journalist to do this story.'

I was so excited. I'd never met a journalist before; nor a writer of any kind. He first suggested Tom Nobel, but Tom was busy on another project. The next name he mentioned was Paul Daley, a feature writer for *The Sunday Age*.

Paul agreed to do it, and for the next year, we took turns to drive to each other's houses every couple of weeks to write. By then I had obtained an early computer, and the book began to take shape. I sat at Paul's side and soaked up his knowledge of writing. I learnt words like tautology and added them to my vocabulary. Lessons of grammar, so dry at school, took on new and wonderful meaning when you were using them to craft sentences. I learnt more about the beauty and power of words sitting at Paul's side than I had in all of my education.

Slowly, but surely, I became a writer.

Beth Barnard, holidaying in the Maldives in 1985,
a year before her murder.

2

Murder on Phillip Island

THERE ARE A NUMBER OF ACCOUNTS OF WHAT HAPPENED ON PHILLIP Island on the night of Monday 22 September 1986 – some were later believed by detectives, some were not. But suffice to say, by the Tuesday morning, when a woman's mutilated body was discovered in a farmhouse on the Island, events were set in motion that would shatter several local families forever, and send ripples through the peaceful community.

Sergeant Cliff Ashe had just returned from leave and was working a morning shift at the Cowes police station on Tuesday 23 September. Two well-known locals, brothers-in-law Ian Cairns and Donald Cameron opened the creaking wire door and came over to the counter. Don Cameron had been on the shire council for some years. His family were respected in the small community. Ashe was busy with paperwork, and listened as the two men spoke of some family difficulties.

'There's been a domestic argument,' said Don Cameron, before beginning a long rambling explanation. Ashe reckoned it took Don about 10 minutes talking about family fights and family conferences before the police officer interrupted him.

'Donald, exactly what are you trying to tell me?'

'Um, it's Beth,' Don said, leaning over the counter and looking at Ashe. 'I think she's not well.'

It was a strange way of putting it.

Beth's lifeless body lay on the floor of her bedroom in her family's house in McFees Road, Rhyll. Don finally said as much to the police officer. 'We were just at her place and she was lying on the floor with blood everywhere.'

Galvanised into action, Sergeant Ashe called detectives at the Wonthaggi Criminal Investigation Branch and told them to meet him at the McFees Road house. Ashe and one of his juniors from the station, Senior Constable Peter McHenry, drove behind Don Cameron and Ian Cairns to the house down the lonely country road where homes were secluded and set apart from each other.

A crime scene needed to be preserved. Ashe and McHenry were responsible for securing the scene and limiting entry. Even so, given the vague descriptions from Cairns and Cameron, Ashe thought it best to enter the house to make sure that the young woman inside was actually dead.

The sergeant walked carefully up the side driveway until he got to the back of the house – retracing the route that Don and Ian said they took earlier. He saw that both the screen door and the back door were slightly ajar. He opened them carefully and went inside; the house was dark and silent. It took only a couple of steps along the hallway to get to the first bedroom door.

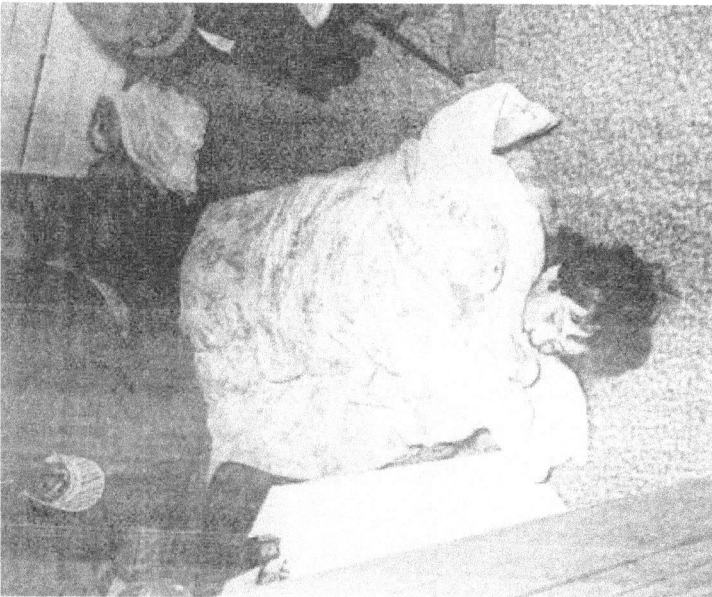

Beth Barnard's body, as it was found on Tuesday 23 September 1986.

Beth Barnard lay on the floor of the bedroom. Even though a quilt covered her from the nose down, Ashe could see her blue eyes, vacant and staring. A large pool of congealed blood on the carpet around her head made it obvious to the police officer that Beth was dead even though he could see no injuries.

Ashe carefully lifted a corner of the quilt and pulled it up and saw something that he would remember forever; the young woman's throat had been sliced to the bone, nearly beheading her. In what was clearly a savage attack, a knife blow to her upper lip had smashed out one of her top front teeth. Ashe gently placed the quilt in its original position, and backed out of the room, shocked.

While Ashe was in the house, young Senior Constable Peter McHenry stood outside with Don and Ian. Not having seen the carnage inside, nor heard anything but a second-hand account on the drive from the police station, McHenry listened as Don and Ian laughed and chatted as they waited for Ashe to re-emerge.

McHenry didn't think much of it at the time.

Ashe radioed detectives from the Homicide Squad; it would take them over an hour to get to the Island. Minutes later, three local CIB detectives arrived from Wonthaggi – Sergeant Ron Cooper, Senior Constable Alan (Jack) McFayden and Senior Detective Alan Lowe.

The house had officially become a crime scene.

Detective Jack McFayden was a no-nonsense country copper and when he wasn't involved in the business of fighting crime, he loved nothing better than to hang a *Gone Fishing* sign on his door and disappear to his favourite fishing hole. He'd seen a lot of bodies in his long career, and it never got any easier.

As McFayden entered the house, he was conscious of the intrusion of a homicide investigation. He knew that the dead woman's secrets would be poured over by the detectives, and her dignity and privacy would fall victim to the urgency of catching whoever killed her.

While the body on the floor gave a chilling aspect to the bedroom, the rest of it was achingly normal. Two single beds flanked opposite walls, piles of discarded clothes lay around, and stuffed animals fought for space on top of the chest-of-drawers with photos and bottles of perfume. Next to the clutter were some cold and flu tablets and a bottle of cough medicine. There was also a glass of water and some pain-killers. One of the beds was unmade, while the other was ruffled and blood-stained.

McFayden took in the bedroom and its contents and made a cursory search of the rest of the house – just in case there were further victims. But everything else seemed in order and there was no sign that the struggle had continued anywhere else, although there was some blood around the bathroom taps. Perhaps the killer had washed afterwards.

Back into the bright September day, McFayden noticed a couple of drops of blood on the concrete path outside the back door. Did that mean that the killer was injured as well? At this early stage, everything was mere conjecture.

First things first. Jack McFayden went with Ian Cairns and Donald Cameron to the police station where he would take their statements. He wanted to know how the two farmers came to discover the young woman's body. From their initial conversations, it seemed Beth was a friend of their family. It also seemed that she had been having an affair with Don Cameron's brother, Fergus.

While local cops stood outside guarding the crime scene, Beth's body lay undisturbed inside. She would not be moved until the crime scene had been fully examined and processed.

Having made the drive from Melbourne, Homicide detectives Rory O'Connor and Garry Hunter arrived on Phillip Island. In their wake, came crime scene examiners Sergeant Hughie Peters and Senior Constable Brian Gamble along with a police photographer and fingerprint expert to examine the house to try and make sense of what had occurred.

O'Connor and Hunter got the gist of the story from Don and Ian.

The previous evening, Fergus had apparently admitted to his wife Vivienne that he was having an affair with Beth. Vivienne and Fergus fought, and Vivienne had stabbed her husband with a broken wine glass, then taken him to the hospital to get stitched up. Ian Cairns, who was married to Fergus' sister, Marnie, said that Fergus had spent the rest of the night at their farm just up the road from his. Don Cameron said that Vivienne had called friends in the middle of the night, after she'd dropped Fergus at Marnie and Ian's, and asked them to come and collect her two young boys.

According to Don and Ian, the family hadn't known about this until the babysitter rang them earlier that morning to ask what she should do with the children since she had to go to work. It was then that they realised that both Vivienne and the family's Toyota Land Cruiser were missing.

And so, right from the get-go, the suggestion was that Vivienne rang the babysitter in the middle of the night, then drove out to Beth's place and killed her. And there was something the Homicide detectives were about to discover that would add weight to that theory.

In the bedroom of the dead woman, Cliff Ashe and Jack McFayden had lifted the doona just enough to see the vicious wounds to Beth's throat. It wasn't until Rory O'Connor, and Garry Hunter lifted the doona off completely that they saw something they could hardly fathom.

Carved deeply and clearly into Beth's chest and abdomen, was a giant letter 'A'.

Nathaniel Hawthorne's novel, *The Scarlet Letter*, written in 1850, told the story of a woman called Hester Prynne who was censured by her Puritan community for having a child out of wedlock. Her punishment was to wear a scarlet letter – A for adulteress – on all her clothing.

Did the A carved into Beth's chest brand her an adulteress?

And if that was the case, who would have more reason to do so than Vivienne Cameron?

It was the job of crime scene examiners Sergeant Hughie Peters and Senior Constable Brian Gamble to examine the house for evidence. While Homicide detectives look for motives and listen to people's stories, crime scene examiners look for physical evidence that will create a connection between the victim and the offender.

Gamble and Peters were told that a local woman, Vivienne Cameron had attacked her husband at their farmhouse in Ventnor over an affair with the dead woman, and had then vanished. This meant two things – there could be a possible offender to link to the scene, and also, there was a second scene they would have to examine – the Camerons' farmhouse where the wine glass attack had taken place.

Crime scene examination was painstaking work and while it was being carried out, the body had to remain *in situ* – exactly where it was found. No matter who she was in life, in death, Beth Barnard had essentially become a piece of evidence to be photographed, examined, and swabbed.

Beth's body was the starting point. She was photographed from different angles while Gamble made sketches of her bedroom and noted the position of the beds and furniture in relation to her body. Once that was done, the doona was removed and bagged as evidence. Next to the body, lay a bloodied wooden-handled knife which could be the murder weapon.

Beth was clothed in a pink nightie which was pulled up to expose her chest and the hideous letter A. There were only a few patches of the pink nightie that hadn't turned dark-red with blood. Interestingly, one of the parts of the nightie that wasn't stained was directly underneath the right side of the letter A. This suggested that the carving may have been a post-mortem addition, made after her heart was no longer pumping blood.

Beth Barnard's house in Rhyll, Phillip Island.

Beth still had her underpants on which suggested the attack did not include rape.

Gamble was interested in the circular smears of dried blood on Beth's legs. Did the killer rub their hands over the body as she bled? Another interesting fact was the damage to Beth's face. She had been stabbed in the chin, and her upper lip. One of her front teeth had been knocked out in the attack; Gamble found it on the carpet next to the body. While this kind of damage might have been part of a frenzied attack, there was a possibility it could have been a deliberate effort to disfigure the pretty young victim.

Gamble collected anything he considered evidence to be bagged and tagged and logged for examination at the Forensic Science Laboratory. After many hours of meticulous examination, he would collect over 70 items.

To those who are trained to see it, every crime scene tells the story of what happened. Even though Beth's body was found on the floor, it appeared that the initial assault had taken place in her bed. Blood stained the sheets, and there was a bloodied handprint on the wall next to the bed. It looked like Beth either got out of bed or was dragged out, and the attack continued on the floor. Gamble could tell that it wasn't a prolonged or particularly physical struggle because small ornaments on the nearby chest of drawers were still standing, and little else in the bedroom had been disturbed. Even the small lamp next to Beth's bed was still upright.

Beth died defending herself. Her body bore perhaps the most heart-breaking of injuries. Stab wounds to her elbows and forearms showed she had held her arms in front of her in a futile attempt to ward off the knife, and a particularly nasty slice in the webbing of her right thumb suggested she had tried to grab the knife to stop it.

After he'd finished processing the bedroom, Gamble continued his work in the rest of the house. It looked like the doona that covered the body had been taken from another bedroom, not Beth's. Little else was disturbed, but the bathroom showed evidence that the killer had washed up in the basin, leaving traces of blood around the taps. There were also cigarette butts in an ashtray. Did they belong to the killer?

There was no sign that the killer had been anywhere else in the house. All the doors except the back door were locked, and dust around the secured windows eliminated them as possible points of entry. It seemed that the killer had entered through the back door and gone straight into Beth's bedroom. Unless the killer had already been inside the house. And perhaps in Beth's bedroom. Most homicide victims are killed by people they know. Had she been entertaining someone in her bedroom? All of these questions would need to be considered later by the Homicide detectives.

Outside the back door, a concrete path led from the house to the yard. There were two tiny drops of blood on the concrete. Brian Gamble took scrapings of these and labelled them for analysis.

Meanwhile the fingerprint expert dusted the crime scene, as well as the knife found near the body. They found no distinguishable prints. The team would work well into the night. An eerie quiet settled over the scene as darkness fell on the lonely farmhouse.

While Gamble and Peters examined the crime scene, the Homicide detectives began canvassing the neighbours. Beth's closest neighbour remembered seeing a car drive up McFees Road the previous evening at 7.50pm which turned into Beth's driveway and had sat for several minutes with its headlights on. Another woman further up the road, recalled hearing a car come up past her place at 3.30am. She said that the car had sounded like her son's Toyota tray truck.

Detectives O'Connor and Hunter considered that piece of information. If Vivienne Cameron had called a babysitter in the middle of the night, could it have been her Toyota Land Cruiser that the neighbour heard?

Crime scene examiner
Senior Constable Brian Gamble

At the Cowes police station, Detective Jack McFayden took a statement from Donald Cameron. He wrote while Don spoke.

'At approximately 7.45 this morning, I received a phone call from Mrs Robyn Dixon, who is a close family friend. She was concerned because she hadn't heard from Fergus and Viv, and she couldn't get them on the phone. She said she had the children with her. As she had to go to work, she said she'd put the school-aged child on the bus with her two boys, and I told her not to worry, I would come to pick up the other child.'

He collected the younger boy, Hugh, then drove past Fergus' house and noticed Vivienne's Holden sedan was still in the driveway. 'I got home and my wife Pam rang my sister Marnie, and Fergus answered the phone. He seemed really distressed and didn't want to talk to us, so he handed the phone to Marnie's husband, Ian. Ian diplomatically told Pam that something had happened and he would talk to us later. Pam insisted that we know what had happened because we had their child with us.

'Fergus then got back on the phone and told Pam that there had been a row the night before and he had been injured and had to be treated at the hospital. We gathered that the row had been of a domestic nature and it had involved Beth Barnard. But other than that, Fergus was pretty uncommunicative.'

Don explained that Ian had telephoned a short time later and told him that Fergus' Land Cruiser was missing. Fergus had asked Ian and Don to drive to Beth's house to tell her what had happened. Don said that he had driven to Ian's house to pick up his brother-in-law. The two had then driven to Fergus' house, walked around it and called out to Vivienne but she was nowhere to be found.

Then they drove to Beth's house.

Detective Jack McFayden

Don described what happened next. 'We drove up the driveway and saw Beth's farm ute and her own car parked in their usual spots. I walked to the back door and knocked but there was no answer. The porch light was on and I saw that the door was open about six inches. I called out but there was no answer.

'I took a step inside and saw the door to my left. Just beyond the door, I saw Beth lying there on the floor covered with a quilt. Her face was almost covered but I recognised her and she appeared to be dead.

'I yelled out to Ian: "Come here quick, the worst has happened." We immediately left to report what we'd found at the Cowes police station. That's really all I can tell you.'

Don Cameron signed his statement at 12.50pm.

Like Senior Constable Peter McHenry earlier, Jack McFayden was struck by Don Cameron's demeanour. He would later say, 'I've never seen a bunch of people so cool, calm and collected. You'd think these blokes discovered bodies every day of their lives.'

Jack McFayden wanted to speak to the woman who had collected the Cameron children in the middle of the night. Was she the last person to speak to Vivienne Cameron? Was there a link between Vivienne organising for the children to be picked up at 3am, and the neighbours hearing a car driving in Beth's street at 3.30am? Hoping she could shed some light on matters, the detective tracked Robyn Dixon down at work.

According to Robyn, it was her husband, John, who had answered the phone in the middle of the night. Vivienne said she was calling from the hospital, and asked John to go and get her children and take them home for the night. Robyn explained that she and her husband had driven to the Cameron's house where they woke the children and took them home.

Robyn noticed that Vivienne's Holden sedan was in the garage, and wondered if perhaps Fergus and Viv had gone to the hospital in an ambulance. Inside the house, the Dixons saw Vivienne's handbag and thought she must have left in a hurry.

That morning, when Robyn had to go to work, she had tried to call Viv and got no answer. When she tried to ring Don Cameron, it took her 15 minutes to get through because their line was engaged. When she finally did, Don said he knew nothing about what had gone on the night before. He agreed to collect Hugh so that Robyn could go to work. The older child was sent to school.

McFayden wondered who Donald Cameron or his wife, Pam, had been speaking to for the 15 minutes that morning when Robyn Dixon was trying to call them.

For most of Tuesday 23 September, both Vivienne Cameron and the family's Land Cruiser were missing. In the afternoon, Don Cameron's wife, Pam, discovered the Land Cruiser on her way home from work.

She had heard that Beth had been murdered and that Viv and the Land Cruiser was missing, and when she drove home across the Phillip Island bridge, she saw the vehicle parked on a wide nature strip adjoining a playground on the Phillip Island end of the bridge.

Detectives, McFayden, O'Connor and Hunter headed to Forrest Avenue, Newhaven, to find the vehicle parked and locked. Later Pam would tell them that she had found it unlocked and she had taken the keys out of the ignition and gathered Vivienne's purse from the seat, then locked it.

If the car had been parked

Vivienne Cameron

Vivienne Cameron's vehicle, as found.

there all day, that meant that despite knowing it was missing, all of the detectives, local and city, had driven past it on their way to the Island.

There was one piece of evidence that McFayden noted. Robyn Dixon said she saw Vivienne's handbag at the house when she picked up the children, meaning that Viv didn't take it with her when she left the house in the middle of the night. If it was found in the Land Cruiser, did that mean that Vivienne drove to kill Beth, then returned home for her handbag only to dump the car with her handbag in it?

While the detectives checked the Land Cruiser, they wondered about the fate of Vivienne Cameron. The car was parked several hundred metres from the start of the bridge.

McFayden immediately searched the bridge for any signs that Vivienne could have jumped off it. He walked slowly along both sides looking for any break in the salty film on the guard rail. He found nothing to suggest that Viv might have jumped the 10 metres into the icy water below.

And, while the car was parked within a short walk to the bridge, it was also only metres from a bus stop. Had Vivienne caught a bus off the Island?

Later, a local baker would give a statement that he had seen a vehicle parked on the nature strip at 5am. Even though the baker wrote in his statement: *I cannot say what type of car it was or colour, all I can say is that there was a car parked there.*

This vague declaration would form the basis of a very specific Coronial finding. But that would come later.

The detectives spoke to a friend of Beth's, called Maree, who had spent several hours with Beth on the day she died. They had met at Maree's house and Beth was still feeling the effects of the flu and had antibiotics in her handbag. Part of their conversation that afternoon was about Beth's relationship with Fergus. He was coming over that evening and Beth said she planned to give Fergus an ultimatum; she was tired of having a relationship with a married man who wouldn't leave his wife. Beth had been deeply in love with Fergus and had always believed the Cameron marriage was over in all but name before her affair with Fergus had begun.

According to Maree, Beth had every intention of telling Fergus that he would have to resolve his marital difficulties – one way or another. Beth saw no future in their relationship continuing with the way things were.

Maree knew how hard the situation had been for Beth. She could remember how upset her friend had been after Vivienne had caught Fergus hugging her in the shearing shed. Maree also knew that Beth would never intentionally break-up a marriage.

Beth told Maree that her brother had intended to make the drive from Melbourne to Phillip Island where he would spend the night with her at the house in McFees Road. However, Beth's brother had broken his arm in an accident and had cancelled the trip. Maree said that Beth had assured her mother by phone that because her brother was not coming, she would bring the dogs inside as usual for extra protection.

Maree stated that Beth left her house early in the afternoon to return to McFees Road, so that she could prepare dinner for Fergus.

It was the last time Maree would see her best friend.

The job of performing the post-mortem examination of Elizabeth Katherine Barnard was given to Dr G R Anderson, a medical practitioner from Warragul, by order of the Coroner. The post-mortem examination was carried out in the mortuary of the

Korumburra District Hospital, in the early afternoon of Wednesday 24 September 1986.

Beth's body had been brought to the mortuary cool-room after it had been photographed, videoed and examined.

At 3pm, detectives Rory O'Connor, Alan McFayden, Brian Gamble, and photographer Peter Gates attended the post-mortem to view Dr Andersen's examination. Throughout the examination, Gates took nine graphic photographs.

The doctor placed a measuring tape gently around the woman's neck.

'The throat wound is 11cm wide and 6.5cm deep in the fold between the chin and the upper part of the neck.' The doctor walked over to the bench near the sink and took a notebook and a pen from his pocket and rested it there. He wrote down the measurements with his hand clad in its surgical glove. Traces of blood were left on the page. He walked back to the body and probed within the folds of the jagged neck wound.

'The pharynx has been completely severed just above the larynx, as has the right carotid artery, but not the left. Mmm, that's interesting,' the doctor murmured.

'Why?' asked O'Connor bending closer to take a look.

'Well,' replied Dr Anderson, 'one carotid artery is situated on each side of the neck.' He indicated to the detectives their approximate location. 'And when one is severed and the other one isn't, that suggests that her head has been turned or held to the side when her throat was cut.'

'Would the killer need much strength to do that?'

'Depends if the woman was struggling or not I suppose.'

The doctor continued probing while the detectives took notes.

'See this line along the lower border of the neck wound?' The detectives again leaned forward for a closer look. 'It's intermittently jagged. That suggests multiple cuts rather than a single slash. Cutting a throat isn't as easy as you might imagine.'

McFayden shuddered inwardly.

The doctor turned his attention to the wounds on the dead woman's face, as his gloved hands manipulated the tape measure.

'The upper lip shows a thick slash wound which is 3cm long,

extending from the mouth towards, but not reaching, the right nostril. The left corner of the mouth also has a 3cm slash wound running towards the angle of the jaw and there's a further slash wound under the point of the chin. It is 2.5cm long. The left front tooth has been completely knocked out.'

'By the knife blow?'

'Looks like it.'

McFayden and O'Connor exchanged glances. Seeing this kind of damage inflicted on a young woman was awful.

Dr Anderson turned his attention to the chest. 'The upper chest showed a gaping stab wound 4.5cm long in the midclavicular line, and there is a smaller gaping wound 2cm x 1.5cm, near the third rib.'

The detectives readied their pens as the doctor went on to measure and describe the A.

'The right side of the A shape consists of a deep slash that measures 25cm long. Two shorter and much more shallow slashes, which have not completely penetrated the skin, run parallel to the deep slash. The left side of the A consists of a slash that measures 29cm long which has penetrated into subcutaneous fat. As you can see here, it's quite deep.' The doctor indicated the exposed fat and then continued once the detectives had taken a closer look.

'Three shorter, much more shallow slashes run parallel and adjacent to it. The centre bar of the A consists of an 18cm horizontal slash. I've never seen anything like this.'

McFayden reflected darkly to himself that the likelihood of Dr Anderson, a country hospital pathologist seeing other bodies with huge letters of the alphabet carved into them was minimal.

Dr Anderson turned his attention to the defence wounds.

'Looks like your victim put up a bit of a fight,' he observed. Beth's body had plenty of these wounds. The doctor held up her left arm and measured the deep knife gash in her elbow. The police photographer snapped a photograph of the uplifted arm and captured on film the trickles of bloodied water running down the white surface of her skin. Also captured on film were the hands – the left hand had deep gash wounds in all the fingers and another deep wound in the web between the thumb and the index finger and the right hand had similar wounds.

Further examination revealed a small slash on Beth's left ankle. 'There's enough of these cuts,' muttered the doctor, who paused after each measurement to make a record in his note book. 'Let's hope this is the last one.'

Once Dr Anderson had described the external wounds, and they had been extensively photographed by police photographer Peter Gates, it was time to open the body to see the internal effects of these external assaults.

Using his scalpel, he opened the body from the neck down over the stomach. With a rib knife he removed the ribs and measured the length to which the knife had penetrated into vital internal organs and arteries.

'Ah,' he said, 'the right lung, the pericardium – that's the sack around the heart,' he explained for the benefit of the detectives, 'and the vena cava, have all been pierced with the long knife blade, which has entered in downwards thrusts. Your victim has bled large volumes of blood into her chest cavity. The right pleural cavity here, is completely filled with blood.'

The detectives could see for themselves without the benefit of a degree in medicine.

'Death by internal bleeding would have occurred some minutes after the upper chest wound was inflicted.'

McFayden murmured to O'Connor, 'From what we could tell from the crime scene, I reckon that the chest wounds would have been inflicted first. Looked like she'd been attacked while she was asleep. Murderer probably got the first strike in pretty cleanly.'

'Thank God,' said O'Connor.

Dr Anderson examined other major organs which he found were all normal and free of disease.

'There's no sign of pregnancy, if that's an issue,' offered the doctor.

Dr Anderson then took specimens: finger nail scrapings, a lock of hair, vaginal and anal swabs, a piece of thigh muscle and 10mls of blood. He carefully labelled the specimens and handed them to the detectives. Other samples including the stomach contents and additional blood were also given to Brian Gamble, to be taken for analysis at the Forensic Science Laboratory in Melbourne.

O'Connor fingerprinted the body so they had a set of prints to compare with any found at the crime scene.

McFayden walked over to the doctor who was removing his bloodied gown. 'What's the verdict, doctor?' he asked.

'I think she was alive when the chest wounds occurred because there is evidence of extensive internal bleeding around these wounds.'

'How long would it have taken her to die?'

'It could have taken five minutes or so, but she probably would have been unconscious earlier than that.'

'How about the "A"?'

'I can't say for certain whether she was alive then, but I think not.'

'Anything else you can add?'

'Only that prior to the attack she was a healthy young woman with every chance of living till she was 80.'

With the possibility that Vivienne had suicided off the Phillip Island bridge, members from the Search and Rescue Squad searched Western Port Bay. If she had jumped, there was a good possibility police divers would find her.

After an initial drifting period where air is expired from a body, it becomes a dead weight and sinks. But, as the body decomposes, it fills with gases and floats again. It was believed, in the early days, that if Vivienne had jumped, she should be located relatively close to the bridge. Or at least her glasses or shoes might be there.

Divers searching the sea bed in sweeping arcs designed to cover the area under the bridge thoroughly, failed to find any trace of Vivienne.

Even though Search and Rescue were optimistic that if she had jumped, they would find her, there had been cases of people drowning in Westernport Bay who had never been recovered. Since their search turned up nothing, it left them with two possible scenarios: either she jumped and drifted away, or she didn't jump at all.

At 10am the morning after Beth Barnard was murdered, a local woman called Glenda Frost received a phone call that would haunt her for years to come, although, at the time, she didn't think anything of it.

Her friend Pam arrived to stay at Glenda's house in the afternoon of Monday 22 September, after working an early shift as a nurse at a Melbourne hospital. Glenda had been at work all day too, and the two friends spent the evening chatting.

It was 10 o'clock on Tuesday morning when the phone rang in the kitchen. Pam, who was elbow-deep in soapy water washing the breakfast dishes, called to Glenda, who was getting dressed, to answer the phone.

'Pam, I'm so busy today – I haven't got time to chat to anyone. Can you answer it?'

'It won't be for me – answer it yourself!' laughed Pam.

Glenda hurried out from her bedroom and reluctantly picked up the phone: 'Hello?'

'It's Viv Cameron here, Glenda.'

'Hi Viv, you're lucky to catch me, I'm normally at work by now but I'm hand-sewing at home today for the fashion parade,' Glenda said.

'Have you found out where to buy the patchwork house gift for Isobel?'

Glenda remembered meeting Vivienne outside the post office the previous week and Vivienne had asked her where she could buy the patchwork house.

'Call Dianne. Her sister makes the patchwork houses. Do you want her number? I have it right here,' said Glenda. 'Have you got a pencil?'

When Vivienne went silent, Glenda assumed she was writing the number down. Vivienne's side of the conversation was interrupted by voices – voices that Glenda assumed were Vivienne's two young boys talking in the background. Vivienne asked Glenda to 'hold on a sec', before she left the phone. As the background noise stopped, Glenda covered the mouthpiece and whispered to Pam that it was Vivienne on the line.

'I won't be long.' She turned her attention back to the phone as Vivienne returned.

'Boys playing up?' Glenda joked.

'It's okay now,' said Vivienne.

From her experience with dozens of phone conversations over the years, Glenda knew that Vivienne was a bit awkward on the telephone. Glenda always felt it her role to make the conversation. But today she didn't have time.

'Is there anything else you want, Viv?'

'Why no... I don't think so.'

Just before hanging up, Glenda remembered the list of materials they both needed for patterns they were working on. She asked if Vivienne wanted her to read it out.

'Oh, don't bother now. Bring the list with you to patchwork lessons next week and I'll get it then,' Vivienne said.

There was another awkward silence.

'Well I'd better get back to my sewing now, Viv. See you next week at class.'

'Goodbye,' said Vivienne Cameron.

As news of the murder swept the small Island community, people were shocked by Beth Barnard's murder. Glenda and Pam went for a coffee at one of the local cafes in Cowes. It was there they learnt the terrible news. Neither of them knew Beth, but like most residents of the small community, they knew *of* her. It made Glenda think of her own safety – a woman living alone.

Glenda and Pam made no connection between Beth's murder and Vivienne Cameron. That wasn't until the 6 o'clock news when Glenda turned on the television to see if the crime had made the news. It was one of the leading items.

The reporter said that police were searching for a missing Phillip Island woman, Mrs Vivienne Cameron, in connection with the savage murder of a 23-year-old farm worker, Elizabeth Katherine Barnard. Vivienne Cameron's car had been found on the Phillip

Island side of the San Remo bridge, according to the news, and it was believed Vivienne had jumped from the same bridge to her death.

The reporter said the car had first been seen at 5am on Tuesday although it wasn't positively identified by police until about 4pm the same day. It was Vivienne's sister-in-law, Pamela Cameron, who identified the car for detectives.

Glenda froze in horror when she realised she had spoken to Vivienne some five hours *after* the car was first seen parked near the bridge. She was staring at the news report when the phone rang.

'Glenda? It's Pam. Have you seen the news?'

Glenda could hardly speak: 'Yes...'

'Wasn't it Vivienne Cameron who you spoke to this morning on the phone? How could she be jumping off the bridge at 5 o'clock in the morning when you spoke to her at 10? It doesn't make sense.'

'No. What am I going to do?' Finding herself suddenly caught up in a murder investigation, Glenda was scared.

'You've got to ring the police,' Pam told her firmly.

'No. I can't.' Her voice trembled.

'Glenda, this is vital to the police. You *have* to tell them now. They think Vivienne has got something to do with Beth's murder, but she can't have – not if she was talking to you on the phone about... what was it?'

'Patchwork patterns,' said Glenda, lost in thought.

'Let's face it,' said Pam, 'nobody's going to discuss patchwork if they've just killed somebody. Are they?'

'Oh my God, Pam! I can't believe this.'

Once off the phone to Pam, Glenda called the police immediately. She gave a statement to Jack McFayden, and then later to the Homicide detectives who arrived to double-check her story. Glenda assured the police officers that it was Vivienne on the phone, but she felt their doubt. They tried to suggest that it might have been Monday when she called, not Tuesday. But Glenda was certain. And Pam was a witness. Pam wasn't even there on the Monday morning.

Glenda's information was explosive. Was Vivienne alive at 10am? Was she still alive now? And, more importantly, if there were voices in the background, who else knew where she was? While Glenda assumed it was Vivienne's children in the background, it couldn't have been her older child as he had been taken to school. The younger one was picked up by Don Cameron on Tuesday morning.

Detective O'Connor had spoken briefly to Fergus Cameron before giving time to regain his composure. It was also his decision that Jack McFayden should conduct the formal interview on Thursday – two days after Beth's murder and Vivienne's disappearance.

When Jack McFayden visited him to take his statement, he found Fergus propped up in bed in his pyjamas, saying that he was feeling the after-effects of his injuries. He had been staying with his sister, Marnie, and her husband, Ian, since Monday night.

Despite losing both his wife and his girlfriend, Fergus was calm and able to give his account of what happened.

He and Vivienne had been married 10 years, he explained, and had two children. They had been having marital difficulties, compounded by Fergus' affair with Beth Barnard. He had met Beth when they both worked at the Penguin Parade and he had then employed her as a farmhand. It wasn't long before the two began having an affair that had lasted until her death.

Fergus described his strained relationship with his wife. He said Vivienne had noticed he gave Beth favoured treatment. He told the detective that several times in their relationship, he and Beth had decided to stop seeing each other, but their resolutions had never lasted.

In December of 1985, Vivienne had caught Fergus in the shearing shed with his arm around Beth. That, according to Fergus, was the first time his wife had accused him of having an affair. He told her that he and Beth were just good mates. Nonetheless, Beth had been shaken by the confrontation, and quit working at the Cameron farm.

A short while after that, Fergus explained that he'd come home in the early hours of the morning from a Christmas party at Beth's. He said that Vivienne had attacked him, punching him in the face and back.

Despite Beth's resolve to leave the Penguin Parade job and the job at the Cameron farm, Fergus said that the pull of their relationship was stronger and she was soon back working at both jobs. He said that Vivienne had questioned the wisdom of having Beth working on the farm.

The tension between Vivienne and Fergus culminated in a fight around shearing time.

'We had all been drinking, including myself, and when we'd gone up to the house, Vivienne became violent with me over Beth. She said that Beth was a scheming little bitch and in general criticising her to the point of hatred. She was very disparaging as to my admiration for Beth, but did not to my knowledge accuse me of having an affair with her but I think she assumed I was.

'During this argument, she punched me half a dozen to a dozen times around the face, arms and chest and at that time I was sitting on a stool in the back porch. I feel that she had every right to do what she was doing, not because of my association with Beth but because she deserved some answers and I wasn't giving her any. Although Vivienne was drinking on this occasion, she wasn't drunk but probably had enough to drink to say what she had wanted to say for a long while.'

McFayden reflected that this was the second time in several hours that Fergus had spoken about his wife's allegedly violent nature. He wondered too, how Fergus

23-year-old Beth Barnard

could have sat on that stool without falling off or protecting himself, while his wife beat him about the head.

From about May 1986, Fergus told McFayden he had become less concerned about protecting his family. Vivienne and Fergus had discussed their marriage and its problems and Vivienne had asked him to see a marriage counsellor. Fergus had told her that he didn't see what good it would do.

Around this time, Fergus explained, Vivienne had received a $5000 inheritance and asked Fergus to quit his job at the Penguin Parade and spend more time with her and the children. Fergus said that he was 'totally opposed' to quitting his part-time job, knowing it would mean that he'd see less of Beth.

At this point Fergus interrupted himself and said, 'I forgot to include earlier, I first told her [Beth] I loved her in December 1985 and she was immediately reciprocal.' McFayden duly recorded this fact.

According to Fergus, Beth was willing to wait until the end of the year to see what happened with his marriage. However, Fergus was anticipating that he would be leaving Vivienne and the children to live on another part of the Island. He wouldn't contemplate living with Beth because, he said, it would not be fair on her family.

'It had got to the point that if I had any sexual relations with Vivienne it would have been an enormous feeling of guilt towards Beth. Although Vivienne didn't say anything, I could tell that she felt rejected and I tried to compensate by doing all the things a loving husband should do, such as making her comfortable and making her wanted and needed in other ways and I used to confer with her in everything but our own personal relationship.'

About seven weeks before Beth's murder, on a Monday morning, Fergus recalled, he was late picking up his younger son to take him to kindergarten. Fergus said Vivienne was furious and had abused him for spending his time with Beth. 'She said she had had enough.'

He recalled that Vivienne had, once again, asked him to get help to save the marriage, to which he had replied: 'Don't be stupid'. Driving her own car, Vivienne had then followed Fergus to the Phillip Island Race Track where they had another heated discussion.

Asked by McFayden what it was about, Fergus said, 'I have no idea'.

McFayden thought it odd that, while Fergus could remember the time and date of the argument, he couldn't remember what was said.

Now that he had the background, McFayden needed Fergus' account of the night Beth died. Fergus said Beth had been sick with the flu and feeling down, but on Monday night, she seemed more cheerful. She had met him at the back door after he'd finished his shift at 8pm at the Penguin Parade. Fergus commented on the fact that the security door wasn't locked when he got there. 'I told her to be more security conscious and keep the door locked.'

Fergus said that he and Beth had discussed their relationship optimistically. He said that he left around 9.05pm and said that while they had 'kissed and cuddled' each other, they hadn't made love. He admitted having sex with her on the Sunday night, but not the Monday night.

Fergus left Beth promising to visit again the next morning. When he got home, he found Vivienne sitting at their kitchen table with his sister, Marnie. He described Marnie as being 'very agitated' and Vivienne was 'visibly trembling'. Apparently, the two women had rung the Penguin Parade looking for him at 8pm only to be told that he'd left for the evening.

Marnie left a short time later and Fergus said that Vivienne had launched into him as soon as his sister was gone, screaming at him, 'Where have you been?'

'I just said, "I've been talking to Beth." She then raced at me with the glass of wine and screamed, "I knew you were with the little bitch." I think she hit me with the wine glass which broke on the left side of my head and cut my left ear. I turned my back away from her and she hit me two or three times with the broken glass.'

Fergus said he had been standing in the doorway between his dining room and the hall. He then turned and walked to a bedroom at the top of the house, where he sat on the bed. Blood was later found on and around the bed. However, forensic tests later showed it wasn't his.

He told McFayden that Vivienne had followed him to the bedroom. 'She was screaming out things including, "I knew what was going on. I've been watching the number of hours you've been working. I suppose everyone out there knew what was going on." She said a lot of other things but I can't remember what they were.'

Fergus said Vivienne's rage had quickly changed to concern, 'as there was blood everywhere and she wanted to take me to hospital

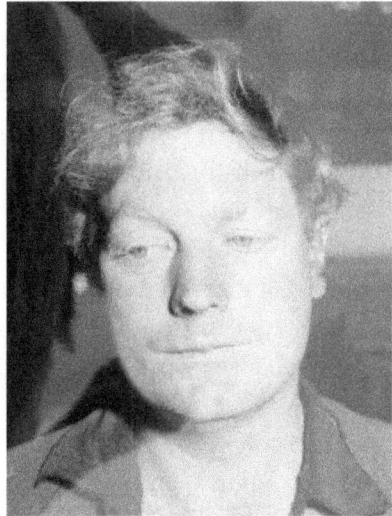

Fergus Cameron after his hospital visit.

immediately.' Forensic tests would later show that Fergus' blood was only found on the shirt he had been wearing, on a pink tissue in his bathroom and on a blue pullover belonging to Vivienne – but McFayden didn't know that yet.

Fergus said he agreed to go to the hospital and they rang Marnie and asked her to come back and mind the children. They left before she got there.

He said Vivienne was calm as she pulled up at the hospital, but, 'As she was turning off the ignition she turned to me and said, "I'm just going to get the little bitch".'

Fergus claimed he hadn't taken the threat against Beth seriously.

When they got back home, Marnie left them, and Fergus said Vivienne suggested: 'that we separate immediately, that she resign from her job and move to Melbourne [and] that I have custody of our children. I agreed to this and she said that I was an excellent father. She wasn't a very good mother and I disagreed and she gave me two warnings, one was not to be too stern with the children, and not to take it for granted that Beth was going to make an excellent mother.'

Fergus said that he and Vivienne had parted amicably when

she drove him up to stay at Marnie's house. He said that was the last time he'd seen her.

The next morning, he got a phone call from Pam Cameron who said that Vivienne had called a friend to come and get the children in the middle of the night.

'My anxiety was further increased when I was told that Vivienne had taken the Land Cruiser, which was parked in the shearing shed. On hearing the Land Cruiser, Beth would automatically think it was me and open the door. The two people who drove the Land Cruiser were either Beth or myself.'

The crime scene examiners did a search of Vivienne and Fergus' house. Brian Gamble sketched a floorplan, then examined every room. According to Fergus' statement, he and Vivienne had argued in the kitchen where she had attacked him with the wine glass.

Gamble found bloodstains in the hallway and spare bedroom, the bathroom and located the pink bloodstained tissue that Fergus said he had used to stem the flow of blood from his cut ear.

There was blood on the floor in the bathroom, and bloodstained clothing in the laundry. The front passenger seat of the Cameron's Holden Kingswood was also bloodstained.

Gamble also noted the blood splatters when he walked through the doorway of the spare bedroom.

His notes record: 'I then entered the front spare bedroom… scattered over the bed were a number of papers. I observed a number of blood stains in the room. On the floor between the western side of the bed and the western wall, were a number of blood droplets. On the bed spread and papers on the bed were a number of blood droplets. On the front of the chest of drawers was a blood smear'.

Gamble recorded no trace of the broken wine glass.

A backlog of cases meant that it was a month after the murder before Dr Bentley Atchison, a scientific officer with the Victoria Police State Forensic Science Laboratory, analysed material collected from the Barnard and Cameron homes.

At the crime scene and the Cameron home, the blood trail matched the stories. Beth had been attacked in bed and had bled in her room. The killer had washed up in the bathroom leaving blood around the taps. This blood would probably belong to Beth, but the drips on the path outside the backdoor might mean that the killer had bled at the scene.

At the Cameron home, Fergus said that he had been attacked by Vivienne and had walked into the spare room and then cleaned up in the bathroom. Accordingly, the blood found in these areas would be expected to be his.

In the analysis of the forensic evidence in pre-DNA days, scientist Dr Atchison used ABO blood groupings. There are four ABO blood groups – groups A, B, O and AB. Through analysing polymorphic enzymes present in blood, further sub-groups of the four main blood types can be identified. These further sub-groups of the four blood types are known as the PGM (Phosphoglucomutase) types.

Dr Atchison found, by analysing the containers of blood that he had received, that Beth's blood group was Type O, PGM 1 and Fergus' was Type O, PGM 2-1. He had no sample of Vivienne's blood to analyse, but according to hospital records from when Vivienne gave birth to her two sons, her blood group was Type A. Dr Atchison was unaware of her PGM sub-group.

But since the three people in this domestic tragedy had different blood types, it would be easy for Dr Atchison to determine who had bled where.

While the blood trail matched the stories, the analysis did not. Fergus' blood was found on his shirt and on a tissue in the bathroom. The blood in the spare room was Type A – Vivienne's type, and blood on the papers in the spare room was Type O, PGM 1 – Beth's blood type.

Blood examined to be Type A, which could have been Vivienne's blood, was found on a maroon towel from Beth's bathroom, the path outside Beth's house, a cigarette packet and the match box found in the Cameron's Land Cruiser and a face washer also found in the Land Cruiser.

Dr Atchison also found Type A blood in the scrapings taken from the spare bedroom at the Cameron's house and from their laundry. If the Type A blood belonged to Vivienne, it meant that she had bled enough to leave a trail through her house.

Dr Atchison made a sketch of the pink nightshirt that Beth had been wearing when she was killed. He coloured in the areas of blood-staining with a red pen, and indicated on his sketch where the knife had gone through the shirt when Beth had been stabbed. The sketch indicated seven cuts in the material of the shirt – six in the front and one in the back.

Dr Atchison later mused: 'I thought some of the cuts [on the front of the shirt] were unusual. There were two holes [close together], a longer one and then a shorter one, with a small gap in between. I asked the experts. They didn't really know. They thought it was a fishing knife. You had the double hole which you can start thinking of all sorts of knives... it penetrates making two holes. But other people who are much more experienced than I am said that you can get a hit with a knife and another sort of jab. It really didn't go anywhere. As far as I recall, I had problems saying that knife found near the body caused that sort of double hole.'

Homicide and local detectives interviewed as many people as they could find who might have information into Beth's murder and Vivienne's disappearance. Their enquiries turned up a couple of interesting facts. Beth had a young admirer who sent her flowers and apparently drove past her house a lot. In the days before stalking was a recognised phenomenon, the man was merely a nuisance that Beth had laughed about with friends. She even described his behaviour in a taped conversation she sent to an overseas pal.

'I've got this problem how he keeps mowing my lawns, and I don't want him to, coz I feel as if I owe him something when he does it. And, he mowed them again on Monday and I get home and yelled at him and he got really pissed off and, so anyway he just took off and comes back Monday night and I thought: *oh beauty, I've got rid of him now.* And he came back Monday night and got mad at me and, fair dinkum, I just feel like telling him where to go now, and then he came to work at the Camerons' house on Tuesday coz we were lamb marking, and all day I was in a real shit and I kept trying to find other jobs to do and he just comes and takes over my jobs and tells me what to do. Fergus thought I was being really good trying to do all these other things and I was just trying to get away and so I'm just sick of him. I wish they'd do something to stop him coming around. We gave him all these hints not to come around tonight, so if he comes, I think I'll just knock him out!'

At no time did his antics seem to do anything but annoy Beth. She never indicated that she was scared of him, but he was worth detectives talking to anyway. Although his statement never appeared in any formal briefs of evidence, detectives said that they spoke to him and he had an alibi for the night of Beth's murder.

It was one thing to look for people who might have had a grudge against Beth, but the solution to the murder and disappearance meant that both crimes were most likely connected. It would be too much of a coincidence to believe that Beth was killed in a random murder, and Vivienne disappeared on the same night in unrelated circumstances.

No, the detectives reasoned, as the story went, it looked very much like Vivienne had fought with Fergus who confirmed the affair. She dropped him off at his sister, Marnie's house – a fact that Marnie confirmed – and then organised to get the children looked after, and then drove out to kill Beth. She took the Land Cruiser on purpose so that Beth would think Fergus was visiting and open the door to him.

But a couple of things didn't add up. According to her friends, Beth was very security conscious and was attacked in her bed – that meant that she didn't open the door to anyone – or if she did, she then ended up back in bed for the attack to occur there. This was hardly something she'd do if Vivienne visited her in the middle of the night to confront her.

And then there was the phone call that Vivienne's friend Glenda got the morning after the murder. Glenda never wavered from her story – Vivienne sounded absolutely normal and there were voices in the background during their conversation.

And what of Vivienne? Was she the type of woman to give up everything in order to get revenge against a rival? Her friends say she wasn't. One friend claimed that in the days before she disappeared, Vivienne had spoken to her about leaving Fergus and taking her two sons to Melbourne. Friends also described her dedication to her children. They maintain that she never would have left them.

Vivienne had also said that if it hadn't been Beth, it would have been someone else. Would a woman direct murderous rage against the 'other woman' rather than a husband? If so, it was the only case on record in Victorian criminal history where this had happened.

When the investigation failed to turn up any concrete evidence or witnesses, the Homicide detectives were satisfied that Vivienne murdered Beth then took her own life.

An inquest for Vivienne Cameron was held less than two years after her disappearance. On 21 July 1988, Coroner Mr Maher, the same coroner who had conducted Beth Barnard's inquest 11 months earlier, made a very specific finding:

> I, Mr B J Maher, Coroner, having investigated the death of Vivienne Janice Cameron, find that the identity of the deceased was Vivienne Janice Cameron and that the death occurred on 23 September, 1986 near the bridge which separates Phillip Island from the mainland in the following circumstances. During the night of the 22 and 23 day of September, 1986 Elizabeth Barnard died from knife wounds in her chest and that Vivienne Janice Cameron has not been seen since 1.00am on the 23 day of September, 1986. On the night in question, it is believed that Vivienne Janice Cameron was driving [a] Toyota Land Cruiser... This vehicle was found abandoned near the said bridge on the Phillip

Island side of the bridge. Despite an intensive Police search, no trace has been found of the said Vivienne Janice Cameron with whom they wished to speak concerning the death of Elizabeth Barnard. Although her body has not been found, I am satisfied that she is dead and that she leapt from the bridge into the water. And I further find that the deceased contributed to the cause of death.

Interestingly, years later, a close relative of Vivienne Cameron spoke of briefing a Queen's Counsel to appear at Vivienne's Inquest to represent her interests. The relative said that the QC and several family members made the long drive from Melbourne and arrived at the Korumburra Court House before the scheduled Inquest time of 10am – only to find that the Inquest was already over. If the relative's story is accurate, one can only wonder how the Coroner had time to consider the vast amount of evidence and come to such a specific conclusion.

Another puzzle in this mysterious case was the lack of evidence to suggest Vivienne's guilt. Indeed, one wonders that if she surfaced, alive and well today, whether she would be found guilty of Beth's murder in a court of law.

Every devoted *CSI* viewer knows that every contact leaves a trace. The problem with this was that the items with Vivienne's A-type blood – except for the drops on the path – are all transportable. There was a hand-towel in Beth's bathroom and a face-washer found in the Land Cruiser.

Interestingly, when Marnie Cairns gave her statement to the police, she mentions a towel and a face-washer – she saw them at the Cameron's house when she went to mind the children after Fergus and Vivienne went to the hospital.

She said, 'I went into the toilet and noticed a pile of blood soaked clothing consisting of a singlet, T shirt, a pale blue shirt from the Penguin Parade, a face washer and a towel. There were also some tissues in the basin which had blood on them.

'Ian arrived shortly after and I showed him the clothing. He suggested that we leave it where it was and not touch it.'

One would assume Marnie mentioned the towel and face-washer along with other blood-stained items because they too had blood on them, but only the pink tissue and the blue shirt tested positive for Fergus' blood. The singlet is not mentioned in the list of items taken by police for examination. Nor is there a towel or a face washer mentioned as being taken from the Cameron house.

Another place where one would expect trace evidence is in the Land Cruiser. If Vivienne Cameron murdered Beth Barnard, she would have been covered in blood. She was last seen wearing a mohair jumper. When Beth's body was examined, it was found that the throat wound was probably caused by someone standing behind her holding her head to one side – one carotid artery was severed while the other wasn't – and cutting her throat with the other. This would mean the perpetrator's sleeve, at the very least, would be soaked in blood. And yet there is not a trace of Beth's blood in the Land Cruiser. Not even a single mohair fibre with blood on it. And not only that, there were no traces of mohair on the victim.

If every contact leaves a trace, why wasn't there more evidence to link Vivienne with the crime scene, and the crime scene with the Land Cruiser?

And as for the Land Cruiser – if Vivienne drove from Beth's to the bridge, how did her handbag get in the car?

And so the mystery endures. People still talk about it, behind closed doors. When no one is brought to justice, people look suspiciously at each other and rumours abound, so many in fact that three decades later, it is difficult to separate the fact from the fiction.

In 2005, an episode of the Australian television documentary *Sensing Murder* went to air. Three psychics were asked to look at the murder of Beth Barnard and try and make sense of it. If one believes in this type of investigation – and many don't – they would have been interested in the fact that none of the three psychics had any sense that Vivienne was the perpetrator.

One psychic, Scott Russell Hill, even claimed to have seen Vivienne's own murder.

More than 500 people emailed the producer of *Sensing Murder* after the episode went to air. Most of them called for the police to take another look at the case.

Homicide detectives in Victoria are willing to look at any solid evidence that comes to light, however, they don't put any stock in the word of psychics.

In 2018 the case, and my book, found a whole new audience of armchair detectives with the advent of the true crime podcast. But that's a story for later in this book.

Paul Daley and I at the launch of
The Phillip Island Murder.

3

A Book in the Hand

It took two years to write *The Phillip Island Murder* from start to finish. I remember when the book was hot off the presses, I stood at the letterbox with my advance copy. It was a small book for so much work but holding it in my hand made every moment worthwhile.

First came the book, then came the publicity. I was 27 years old and largely ignorant of the process of publishing. Until then, I thought it was a coincidence that when a new book came out, the author would appear on the radio or TV. (I know, right.)

My rude awakening came when I was asked to go on the Bert Newton morning show. Bert Newton was the TV legend of my childhood. I was so nervous, I hardly remembered my own name, let alone what I was there to talk about. It didn't help that I was left in the green room watching the show on a monitor with Bert's wife Pattie Newton who was there to surprise Bert at the end of the show because it was his birthday. When I was announced as 'coming up after the break...' she turned to me and said, 'You should be on set!'

They'd forgotten to come and get me!

In a flurry of hurrying up a flight of stairs and someone shoving a microphone pack into my belt and telling me not to be nervous because there were only five million people watching, I was plonked onto a couch opposite Bert, heart pounding, hoping not to have a heart attack. Luckily, I knew the case so well after living it for two years, I was able to answer questions on autopilot. I watched a tape of the interview later on and I didn't come across as nervous as I felt. Thank goodness.

Radio was the same. Before doing my first-ever radio interview, I nervously asked Melbourne radio interviewer Jon Faine (another legend of the airwaves) what he was going to ask me. He snapped back that I would find out when we were on air. He's lucky I didn't faint.

There was no training or advice for a publicity newbie. I just went where I was told and tried not to sound stupid. My family recorded each interview on cassette tapes, but I rarely listened to them afterwards. It avoided those *do-I-really-sound-that-annoying?* moments.

Not surprisingly, a young primary school teacher turned true-crime writer was a bit of a novelty and a couple of newspapers featured articles, not only about the book, but me as well. As fun as my 15 minutes of fame was, I always felt that I was just the storyteller; it was the stories I told that were important, not me. Maybe I needed to get a T-shirt with the slogan: 'Look away people. Nothing to see here.'

The Phillip Island Murder was released in the middle of 1993. I held a launch party at my house, and Paul Daley and I posed proudly with our little book. On 11 July 1993, *The Sunday Age* featured the book in a two-page spread. We later heard that *The Sunday Age* was not sold on Phillip Island that weekend. The book wasn't available on the Island either. Locals had to cross the bridge to get their copy. It didn't surprise me. While some people had been happy to be interviewed when we were writing the book, others had been most unwilling. Paul and I had both noticed a palpable fear among the locals. Being non-Islanders, it was hard to understand *what* they were afraid of.

The story was quickly picked up by a show called *Hard Copy* who wanted to film a segment on it. Before I could blink, there was a TV crew in my lounge room, and I began my learning curve about how things were done in TV land. When I told the crew that the Camerons were unlikely to be interviewed since they had refused our requests, one of the crew said, 'Oh that's okay. We'll get some footage of them slamming the door in our face.'

First illusion shattered.

I'd always thought door-slammings were genuine attempts to interview people, not contrived attempts to get people to slam doors. In the end, they didn't approach the Camerons.

The minute the story went to air, my home phone started ringing. That night, I learnt there were people in the world who watched TV with a telephone book by their side, ready to look up the numbers of random people they saw on TV and ring them. My address was also in the phone book and I realised that wasn't a good idea. The next day I organised a silent phone number.

While the publicity phase of a book is the only part most people see, for the writer, the opposite is true. Two years of interviewing people and sitting in front of a computer ends in a blaze of cameras, then the world rights itself again and a couple of weeks later, you're back where you started.

I had learnt so much from Paul Daley about writing, but on my next book, I would fly solo. I still felt I needed all the help I could get. I saw an advertisement at a community centre for a creative writing group run by Dr Katherine Phelps and enrolled, even though it meant more nights out in an already busy life. Writers will understand the compelling need to improve our craft that seemed more important than most other things.

And so, for a while, I taught kids during the day, and became a student myself in the evening. Dr Katherine Phelps was an amazing teacher who taught me how to add the senses to description, and how to make writing come alive.

The young true crime writer.

Katherine was a great storyteller. Every time we had to write a description of something, she would write too and share hers with the class. As a teacher, I found this kind of modelling wonderful and tried to do this with my students.

My daughter was nearly five years old when the book came out. At some point during my writing of the Phillip Island book, she had grown old enough to pick up on things without me realising. One day, someone asked her what her mummy was writing about. To my horror she said something like: 'Well, Vivienne killed Beth and jumped off a bridge.'

If there were hashtags back then, mine would have been #parentingfail. Note to self: stop talking about your book in front of your kid; she's listening!

Another clash of worlds happened when the famous Aussie actor Norman Yemm came to school to talk to the kids. He mentioned being on the Bert Newton show and my kids – Grade 3s from memory – excitedly said, 'Mrs Petraitis was on Bert Newton too!'

Norman Yemm turned to me and said in his wonderfully expressive voice: 'Fellow thespian?'

The kids gasped, thinking he'd just asked if their teacher was a lesbian.

As I grew more confident with my writing, I looked for a new project. Almost every cop I spoke to while researching the Phillip Island book, said the same thing: once this book is done, come back; we have plenty of stories.

I decided to do a compilation of short cases about the experiences of police officers. I contacted various departments of the Victoria Police and asked officers for their best story. It was a good tactic because their bar is pretty high. Stories that stood out to cops often had unusual elements that touched their hearts. And if it touched them, it would touch the reader.

I wrote a couple of stories and sent them to a publishing house called Victoria Press. They rang me the next day and said they were interested in the book – which eventually became *Victims, Crimes and Investigators* – so I kept writing.

And my eyes were opened to the world.

I learnt that some people didn't play by the rules. I learnt that cars can be deadly weapons, and I learnt that a lot happens after most of us are safely tucked in our beds at night. Each new story taught me something about life and something about the craft of writing.

One thing led to another, just as stories linked in unexpected ways. The observant reader of my books might have noticed some of these connections. CIB detective Jack McFayden, who searched the Phillip Island bridge after Vivienne went missing, gave me a story for the second book. So did crime scene examiner Sergeant Brian Gamble, who worked the crime scene at Phillip Island.

Gamble had a case he worked on where a body was found in a shallow grave on the Rye back beach, cut into pieces and wrapped in neat packages. Unlike CSI on TV, crime scene examiners don't do the investigation. So when he told me about the gruesome crime scene he encountered that cold day on the beach, I asked him for more details.

He shrugged. 'You'll have to talk to the detectives,' he said.

And so I did.

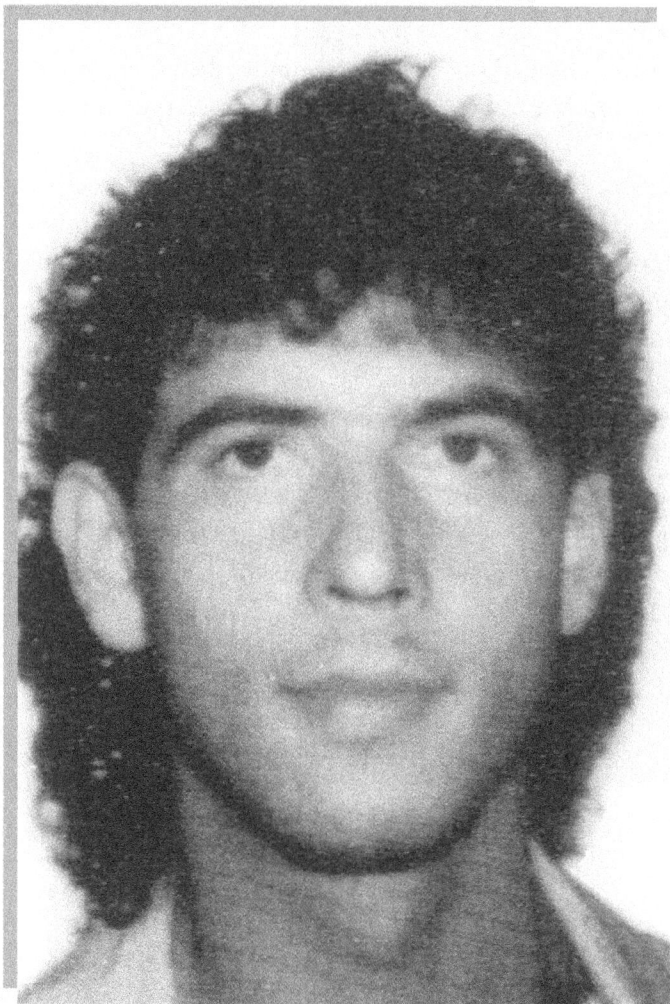

Dimitrios 'Jimmy' Pinakos

4

THE RYE CROSSBOW MURDER

Walking his dogs along Rye's back beach on a brisk afternoon on Tuesday 18 July 1989, a local man, John Miller, noticed a large package partly buried in a shallow hole near the beach car park. His dogs began sniffing and digging around the edges of the soft hole but Miller became concerned when he got close enough to smell the odour emanating from the bulky parcel. It smelt putrid, like something rotting.

Miller pulled his dogs away and returned home. But the more he thought about the package, its size and its smell, the more he wondered if it contained something sinister. He grew concerned enough to telephone the local police, offering to meet them in the car park and guide them to the find.

Rosebud police station logged Miller's call at 5.35pm, and two police officers were dispatched to investigate the package. Miller stood waiting in the Rye back beach car park as the police officers arrived.

As soon as the first cop looked down into the shallow hole and saw the protruding tarpaulin, he smelt the odour of decomposition.

Within an hour, two Frankston CIB detectives, Senior Detective Colin Clarke and Detective Sergeant Ray Air arrived on the scene to be assaulted by the smell of the partly buried object. Clarke gently dug some of the sand away and revealed the entire top surface of a large bundle wrapped in a tarpaulin and secured with masking tape. The smell was becoming unbearable. Gently prising the bundle open, Clarke saw the remains of a decomposing human torso.

The CIB detectives set the investigating machine in motion. Homicide, forensics, photographics and coronial services were all notified and duly converged on the car park to perform their respective tasks.

Unwilling to let darkness hamper their work, police called upon the State Emergency Service to provide lighting for what had now become a crime scene.

Melbourne homicide detectives, Senior Constable Mark Newlan, Senior Sergeant Sal Perna and Senior Constable Nigel Howard, made their way to the Rye back beach, half an hour ahead of crime scene examiner Sergeant Brian Gamble.

Gamble worked at the Victoria Police State Forensic Laboratory, in the aptly named Forensic Drive in the outer Melbourne suburb of Macleod. Having worked a day shift, Gamble was on call at home when the job came through.

Gamble's job was to collect any physical evidence that might help detectives solve their cases. He was required to make sketches of the crime scene, take detailed notes, prepare a written report, and examine the physical evidence – either personally, or by passing it on to the

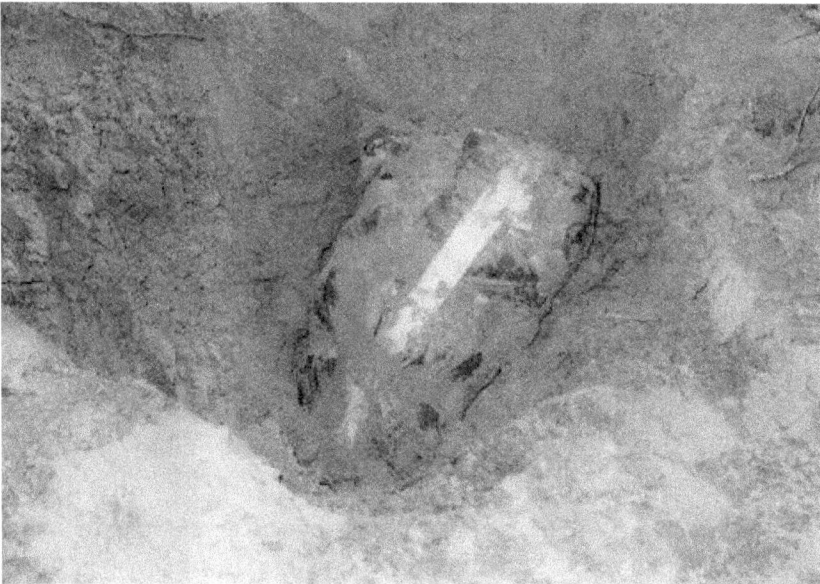

The wrapped torso found in the sand on the Rye back beach.

many experts who were employed or at the disposal of the Forensic Science Laboratory.

Gamble and his fellow officers – senior constables Gary Wheelan and Steve Batten, from the audio-visual section, and Chris Paulett from the photographic section – arrived at the crime scene around 10.30pm to begin a long night of work.

Paulett took photographs of the shallow grave site and the surrounding sand dunes while Wheelan and Batten videoed the scene before any further digging was attempted.

A little after midnight, the torso in its wrappings was transported by state-employed funeral directors to the Victorian Institute of Forensic Pathology mortuary.

Here, a post-mortem examination was performed by forensic pathologist Dr Shelley Robinson who had personally supervised the torso's removal from its sandy grave.

At the mortuary Dr Robinson made meticulous notes concerning the appearance of the package and noted the presence of maggots within the inner plastic wrapping.

The torso – clearly male from the genitalia – was then laid on the metal slab and visually examined by Dr Robinson while the investigators looked on and Senior Constable Chris Paulet took photographs.

The missing head, arms and legs had been cleanly severed, and despite the dirt and dried blood, a puncture mark was visible in the chest.

When Paulett had finished photographing and Dr Robinson had completed her visual inspection, the torso was washed and prepared for the internal examination.

Robinson cut around the small puncture wound in the chest and pulled open the flesh which devoid of dirt and smeared blood, was a ghostly white colour.

Inside the wound, the doctor found a broken arrow.

The triangular tip was intact but the bamboo shaft was broken in half. The arrow, Dr Robinson informed the police officers, had pierced the right ventricle of the heart and, from the downward angle of the wound, had been fired from above the victim.

A number of maggots inhabiting the remains were sealed in a

jar of formalin to be sent to the CSIRO in South Australia, where scientists would test them to find an approximate time of death.

After the post-mortem, Senior Constable Mark Newlan returned to his St Kilda Road office of the Homicide Squad to begin his paperwork – it would eventually fill several large folders. He worked through the night and at 7am received a telephone call from a friend of his who worked at the Prahran CIB, Sergeant Mick Hughes.

Hughes asked Newlan about the Rye case, which he'd heard about on the radio news on his way to work, and wondered if the body might be that of a missing person on his files. Jimmy Pinakos had been missing since April, and if the torso was his, it meant three months had elapsed since he disappeared.

Newlan told his friend that the torso at Rye didn't look decomposed enough to be three months old. Hughes told him to keep it in mind, nonetheless. Newlan drove back to Rye.

After catching a few hours' sleep, Sergeant Brian Gamble too returned to the Rye back beach to organise the sifting of sand around the burial site for evidence, and to complete diagrams and reports for the police and forensic files.

Homicide detectives had organised a line search of the beach and the surrounding scrub at first light.

Ironically, despite the number of police searching the dunes along the foreshore, it was another dog, sniffing and digging in an area of bushland near the beach that led police to the second grave site.

The familiar foul odour told searchers that they had found more of the body, and the process of photographing, digging and sifting began again. Another wrapped parcel was soon unearthed.

Mark Newlan spent his morning flying around the crime scene in the Southern Peninsula rescue helicopter so he and other officers could survey and photograph the crime scene from the air. The helicopter landed as soon as news was radioed through that another parcel had been found.

Contained in the new find were two severed hands, two feet, and some other pieces. Wrapped separately in a Safeway supermarket bag, was the head.

In addition to the body parts, police officers found a grey tie with blue stripes, a white and blue pin-striped shirt and a pair of underpants.

Newlan was given the unenviable task of flying back to Melbourne by helicopter clutching the re-wrapped body parts. They landed at the Yarra heliport and Newlan was picked up by police car and taken, with his parcel, to the city morgue.

Laying the parts on the slab, Dr Robinson completed a macabre human jigsaw puzzle. The head, the hands and feet had been cleanly severed. Other pieces were identified as portions of arms and legs.

When she examined the head, Dr Robinson noted the marked distortion of the facial features, but no apparent damage to the brain. The head was then sent to the Royal Dental Hospital in Melbourne for a forensic odontology examination – the teeth would be examined for later comparison with charts belonging to missing persons fitting the general description of the unidentified male.

Dr Robinson later concluded in her report:

1. Identification of the deceased was based on forensic odonatological examination of the head. The head was found separately packaged and situated from the torso, however there is no evidence to suggest that they are not from the same body, although the former was in a more advanced state of decomposition.

2. Decomposition changes obscured some pathological changes, however it is likely that the penetrating injury to the chest (involving the heart) by the arrow was the cause of death.

3. It is also likely that the decapitation and dismembering of the body took place after death, with a sharp instrument such as a band saw, however the exact time or course of events cannot be established on the basis of the pathological findings.

With the second find which included the hands, Senior Sergeant Jim Falloon from the Fingerprint Branch was called to the mortuary. After gaining clearance from State Coroner Hal Hallenstein, Falloon put the putrid pair of hands into a bucket and took them to the Fingerprint Branch offices so the fingertip skin could be removed and printed.

At his office, Falloon gently removed the skin from the fingertips and placed the ridged skin over his own fingertips and carefully rolled them in the ink and onto a fingerprint card.

Unfortunately for everyone working in the 19-storey St Kilda Road building, the smell entered the air conditioning system and wafted through the whole building. As a direct consequence, severed hands and fingers were henceforth banned from the fingerprint offices as a health risk.

Identification from fingerprint comparison and dental records showed the deceased to be Dimitrios Pinakos – known to his friends as Jimmy.

Mark Newlan was able to tell Mick Hughes that his hunch was correct. Pinakos, an insurance agent, had been missing since 20 April but, with the discovery of his body, the web of intrigue surrounding his disappearance began to unravel.

Dimitrios Pinakos was born in Greece in 1958 and immigrated to Australia with his family when he was still an infant. He anglicised his name to Jimmy, left school when he was 18 years old, and worked for a time as an electrician. He eventually bought his own small business.

Jimmy Pinakos began selling insurance in 1987, and it wasn't long before he created his own corporate agency, Limnos Insurance, operating under the umbrella of the Melbourne Mutual Group.

It was in the offices of the Melbourne Mutual Group in St Kilda Road, that Jimmy Pinakos met the man who would fire a crossbow arrow into his chest, carve his body into small pieces and bury him in the sands of the Rye back beach.

Ronald Lucas began working in the same St Kilda Road building in January 1989 with another corporate agency, also operating within the Melbourne Mutual Group.

Although Ron Lucas did not share office space with Jimmy Pinakos, many people would later tell police that the two knew each other well and had held private meetings in the week before Pinakos went missing.

Ronald Lucas was deeply in debt. He had a habit of borrowing money – to buy cars, a house, a swimming pool, among other things – and making only a few payments before abandoning his financial responsibilities.

Lucas was being pressed for money from a number of sources, particularly from his wife who had set up house in Perth. Lucas had joined her there for a couple of weeks and then moved back to Melbourne. He had instructed her to have a swimming pool put in the backyard with promises to deposit money into her bank account. The money never arrived.

Lucas owed Westpac Bank over $2,000, Diners Club $16,151, Statewide Building Society $80,000 for the mortgage on his Perth home (no payments had ever been made), $5,209 on an unpaid MasterCard debt, and $2,350 on a loan by Lucas and his wife that was still outstanding. He also owed American Express $1,462, and had recently borrowed $47,326 to buy a four-wheel-drive vehicle. True to habit he had only made one payment on the luxury vehicle.

In addition to his debts, Ron Lucas had a penchant for crossbows.

On Tuesday 18 April 1989, colleague Harry Triferis went to Jimmy Pinakos' office to collect his friend Ron Lucas to drive him home. In the office, Pinakos told Triferis and Lucas of a $60,000 development loan he had access to in a trust account. Access could only be gained if it were used for a mortgage.

Triferis would later say that he had come in on the end of the conversation and that Jimmy and Ron had been discussing the money before he had entered the office.

Jimmy Pinakos did not know that discussing being in possession of large sums of money to a man heavily in debt could be a fatal mistake. Pinakos also had no idea of the conversation that Lucas had with Triferis a few weeks earlier – about how easy it would be to chop up a body and bury pieces in different locations so it would never be found. Triferis himself did not see the significance of the conversation for many months to come.

On Wednesday 19 April, Jimmy Pinakos and his brother William, with whom he shared a house, went to the bank and received a cheque for $60,000 made out to Lucas' wife. Understandably, William questioned his brother about it and Jimmy told him that he was going to swap it for $80,000 cash that very night.

Later that evening, William phoned Jimmy to ask how the deal had gone. Jimmy told him that it had fallen through because the 'bloke had turned up dressed in a Rambo suit and armed with a crossbow'. The next morning Jimmy Pinakos took the cheque to work. It was the last time William Pinakos would ever see his brother.

That same morning Ron Lucas was visiting a friend boasting that he was about to collect money owing to him from years earlier. Lucas even promised the friend $13,000 from the windfall.

Jimmy's hours were numbered.

Lucas met Jimmy in his office in the early afternoon. Harry Triferis' brother, Peter, saw Lucas leave and expressed his concerns about Ron Lucas to Jimmy.

Peter Triferis would later tell police that at first Jimmy refused to tell him about the deal he was planning with Ron Lucas, but further prompting led him to reveal that Lucas had offered him '$80,000 black money for a $60,000 bank cheque'.

Peter Triferis said Pinakos told him how Lucas had turned up the night before armed with a crossbow and claiming his strange Rambo attire was because he had to be careful carrying that much money around.

Pinakos had shown Peter Triferis the cheque and told him that another meeting had been arranged at Lucas' home at 3 o'clock that afternoon. Although Triferis planned to meet Pinakos back in the office afterwards, he would never see his colleague again.

Jimmy Pinakos instructed his secretary to telephone his mobile phone at exactly 3.15pm and, for reasons he didn't explain, told her not to worry if he replied with the code word 'sweet'.

His secretary duly phoned him at 3.15pm, Pinakos answered, told her he had yet to arrive at his destination and instructed her to telephone again at 3.40pm.

At the appointed time, she telephoned again and heard Jimmy say, 'It was all sweet'. A third telephone call about another matter at 4.30pm, was answered by Jimmy. He said that he was in Springvale. The secretary later told police that he sounded as if he was in fact in his car.

This phone call was the last reported contact anyone admitted to having with Jimmy Pinakos – and he was obviously nervous. He knew what he was doing was illegal, and perhaps the thought of earning $20,000 in one afternoon made him act as if he were in a gangster movie, using code words and disguising his location.

Ronald Lucas was an hour late for a 7.30 meeting that evening, even though his business diary listed no prior arrangements. Lucas had excused his lateness by saying he was held up at another appointment.

It is likely that in those unaccounted-for hours, Ronald Lucas killed Jimmy Pinakos with a cross-bow and dismembered him.

The following day, Lucas didn't arrive at the office until after midday, and left two hours later for an unspecified appointment.

Concerned about his brother's uncharacteristic absence, William Pinakos phoned around. One of the first people he contacted was Ron Lucas who admitted that Jimmy had been at his home the day before, but had received an urgent phone call and left abruptly.

After telephoning his wife in Perth to cancel his imminent trip to visit her, Ron Lucas telephoned Harry Triferis and confessed that he was in 'a lot of shit at the moment'. Concerned, Harry Triferis immediately contacted his brother Peter and related the strange conversation.

Without delay, Peter Triferis went to visit Lucas who, as he would later tell police, appeared to have been crying. Peter Triferis asked about the cause of his worries, Lucas told him he was having money problems and that the bank in Perth was pressing his wife for money.

Triferis raised the subject of the financial deal that Pinakos had mentioned, but Lucas denied knowing anything about it; although he did admit inviting Jimmy over to his house to discuss a loan. Apparently the terms didn't suit Jimmy and he had left.

When Peter Triferis left Lucas at 7.30pm he bluntly told him there was talk he had killed Jimmy. On his guard, Lucas said that it was impossible because neighbours had seen Jimmy leave his house the previous afternoon. Neighbours later denied this.

That evening, relatives of Ron Lucas arrived at his home to stay. They later told police that Lucas wasn't home when they arrived at 10pm. It is likely that in the time between Peter Triferis' departure and the arrival of the relatives, Lucas drove the body to the Rye back beach and buried it in several locations.

If this was indeed the case, then Jimmy's dismembered body was in the garage when Peter Triferis visited.

Ron Lucas responded to the rumours that he had become a suspect by leaving home and staying with friends in Melbourne for two days. Using a false name, he then bought a bus ticket to Adelaide where he stayed with friends for three weeks.

Two days after Jimmy disappeared, William Pinakos found his brother's silver Porsche near a house in Prahran that he and his brother jointly owned; the same house where Jimmy had met Lucas dressed as Rambo. The Porsche contained Jimmy's briefcase which in turn contained the $60,000 cheque.

If Jimmy had been killed for the money, the murderer's plans had been thwarted. Perhaps he hadn't completely trusted Lucas and wasn't willing to hand over the cheque until he saw the cash.

Jimmy Pinakos had been killed for nothing.

A neighbour later told detectives he noticed the Porsche the previous evening around midnight.

Lucas had also abandoned his Holden ute which was found soon after the Porsche. Both vehicles were photographed and examined for fingerprints, blood and any trace evidence that might link Pinakos and Lucas. Nothing of incriminating value was found.

Detectives also searched Lucas' home in Reservoir and found no evidence that anything untoward had occurred there. The home was full of furniture and the garage was cluttered with tools.

Lucas next travelled to Queensland where he stayed with another friend for over a week before returning to Adelaide, where he began working as a builder. He asked a friend where he could get some jewellery valued, and produced a gold chain and a single diamond. He claimed he had received the jewellery as payment for mercenary work in Malaysia. Both items together were valued at $19,945, but the jeweller informed Lucas that he could only expect to receive $5,000 if he sold them. Lucas decided to keep the jewellery.

The friend became increasingly concerned about Lucas and his strange stories and expensive jewellery, and eventually contacted local police, who in turn contacted officers from the Adelaide Major Crime Squad. Melbourne detectives were notified and flew directly to Adelaide.

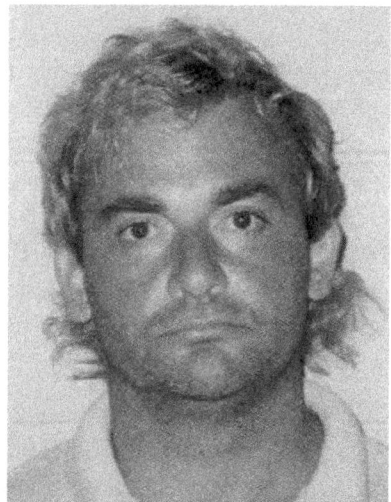

Ron Lucas

On 7 June 1989, Lucas arrived home from work to find detectives waiting for him. They had a search warrant and had already searched Lucas' room finding the gold chain and the diamond, which fitted the description of jewellery belonging to Jimmy Pinakos, who at that stage was still the missing; as well as the bus ticket that Lucas used to leave Melbourne.

Ronald Lucas was taken to the Adelaide Major Crime Squad office and questioned by detectives. Lucas had no satisfactory explanation for having the jewellery in his possession. This gave detectives a reason to extradite him back to Victoria to be charged with theft. Finally, back in his own state, Lucas was charged and bailed to report to the local police station every Monday and Friday.

Five weeks later, John Miller and his dogs discovered the remains of Jimmy Pinakos behind the Rye back beach car park.

The day following the discovery of the two burial sites, Ron Lucas telephoned the Melbourne police officer who had arrested him in Adelaide. He reported seeing a 'bloke hanging around' the night before and wanted police protection.

Lucas also casually asked the police officer, 'What's the go with the body on the beach at Rye?' When the police officer asked why he wanted to know, Lucas replied that he was 'just curious'.

That same morning, Lucas collected wages owing to him from a building site where he had been working and vanished again. He stayed in hiding with a number of friends until February 1990. He bleached his hair blonde, used an alias, told people he was a doctor of biochemistry from Sydney, and began a liaison with the 17-year-old stepdaughter of the friend he was staying with.

Three days after Jimmy Pinakos' body was discovered, police carried out an exhaustive search at the Reservoir home of Ron Lucas. When detectives had checked the property months earlier, the garage had been full of junk; now it was empty.

Crime scene examiners and a team of forensic science experts focused on the garage with its old carpet and its cement sheet walls. Biologists tested the dirty carpet and walls for the presence of blood. Using Hemastix – a preparation that changes colour when rubbed against a blood stain – marks on both the walls and the carpet tested positive. The experts scoured the garage for any other evidence linking Ron Lucas with the murder of Jimmy Pinakos.

The house in Reservoir had changed hands since Lucas had fled and the new owners had given police permission to examine it. However, even if permission hadn't been obtained, the Victoria Coroners Act gave investigators the right to "enter and inspect any place and anything in it" and "take possession of anything which the coroner reasonably believes is relevant to the investigation and keep it until the investigation is finished".

Accordingly, when Gamble and his team discovered splatters of blood on the garage wall, they simply cut out a huge section of the wall and took it with them back to their laboratories. Large sections of the garage carpet were also removed.

From the moment the body was identified as Jimmy Pinakos, Mark Newlan's investigation led clearly to the doorstep of Ronald Lucas. Suspicion and innuendo became fact.

On the day following the body's discovery and identification, Newlan went to the Reservoir home and was given the crossbow in its camouflage carry case by a neighbour who had been storing it for Lucas.

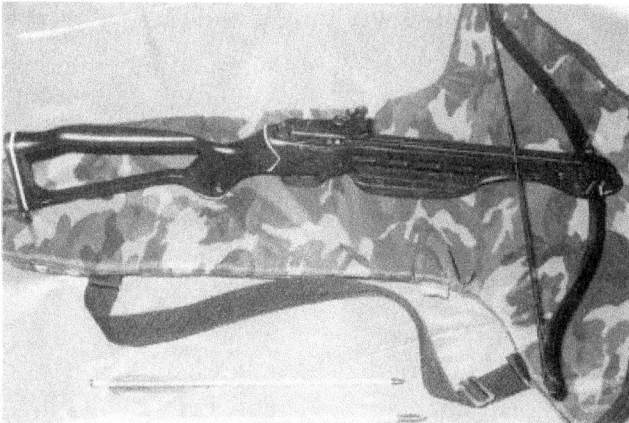

The crossbow Ron Lucas used to kill Jimmy Pinakos.

Newlan lodged it at the State Forensic Laboratory where a firearm and toolmark examiner tested the weapon. He found that the crossbow could only be fired after it had been loaded, cocked and with considerable pressure – 4.5kg – applied to the trigger. In simple terms, the crossbow couldn't be fired accidentally.

Another scientist at the forensic science lab was given documents belonging to Ronald Lucas. He analysed the handwriting on a Diners Club receipt from a Dandenong sporting goods store for the purchase of a Barnett Brand Crossbow and carry case. He identified the signature on the receipt as that of Lucas.

Ronald Lucas was eventually apprehended in Cairns on 19 March 1990 as a result of information given to police by the stepfather of Lucas' young girlfriend. When Lucas was picked up, he said resignedly, 'I suppose this is about Jimmy.'

Detective Mark Newlan flew to Cairns the following day. Within 24 hours, following a successful extradition hearing in the Cairns Magistrates Court, he made the nearly six-hour flight by light plane to Melbourne with Ron Lucas.

This was Newlan's first chance to chat with his suspect. He found Lucas to be an amiable fellow, but with a childish habit of boasting about everything. Looking out the aeroplane window, Newlan asked Ron Lucas if he had ever done any parachuting. Lucas told him that he had made hundreds of jumps. Later, when Newlan spoke of diving, Lucas told him that he was a diving expert. Newlan reflected wryly that it seemed that there was nothing Ron Lucas wouldn't brag about – except, of course, killing Jimmy Pinakos.

New legal and scientific grounds were broken in the realm of forensic evidence during the murder trial of Ronald Lucas, over the admissibility of DNA testing – specifically for the purpose of linking Jimmy Pinakos with the crime scene in Ron Lucas' garage.

When Leicester University geneticist Alec Jeffreys discovered the means to isolate the elusive genetic material in 1984, one of the first tests he performed was to see whether DNA patterns were inherited. His tests on family groups clearly showed that half the bands and stripes of DNA of offspring were from the mother and half were from the father.

The Melbourne courts argued this point at length because, owing to the advanced state of decomposition of the body of Jimmy Pinakos, DNA tests could not be conducted on his remains. The prosecution therefore conducted a series of DNA tests on blood samples from Pinakos' parents and compared the DNA profiles with blood samples taken from the garage. The results showed a 65 per cent probability that the blood in the garage belonged to Jimmy Pinakos – not certain enough for the court to accept as evidence.

It was vital for the conviction of Ron Lucas, to connect him to the body, or the body with his house. There was plenty of circumstantial evidence, but detectives were looking for solid forensic evidence.

Fingerprint expert Sergeant Sean Hickey provided that link by carefully examining the material in which the body had been wrapped. On a piece of masking tape used to bind the tarpaulin, Hickey discovered a clear latent fingerprint. It belonged to Ronald Lucas.

The masking tape, with its still clearly distinguishable fingerprint, held pride of place in a display cabinet at the St Kilda Road Fingerprint Branch offices.

Ronald Lucas was found guilty of killing Jimmy Pinakos. He was sentenced to 20 years in prison.

A decade into his 20-year sentence, Ron Lucas hit the headlines again when he and another prisoner escaped from the Ararat jail. At around 11.30am on Saturday 16 June 2001, the two scaled a wire fence but were recaptured after farmers reported them roaming through paddocks. They were back in custody before 5pm. Before the escape, Lucas was due for parole in 2006.

Book signing.

5

THE RIDE-ALONGS

In researching stories with different squads, some suggested I do a ride-along so I could get firsthand experience in police work. I had to apply for permission to police command, then sign a paper saying something to the effect that if they killed me, they bore no responsibility; and then off I went around the streets of Melbourne in a variety of police cars.

One place I wanted to visit to get a story was the police Air Wing. I ended up interviewing an Air Wing observer called John Williamson. John was a natural storyteller which was handy because I needed him to describe what it was like to work in a helicopter. While I got a general idea, I couldn't quite capture it in the story. Finally, he said, 'You really need to come up in the helicopter and experience a shift for yourself.'

'Well, if you insist,' I said casually. On the inside I was jumping up and down saying, *yippee*!

The first time I sat in the helicopter ready for the shift, one of the crew handed me a sick-bag and said there was no shame in being air-sick, as long as I did it in the bag and didn't mess up the helicopter. In a voice designed, I think, to make me feel nervous, he asked if I'd been in a helicopter before.

'No, but I've been in a really tall building. Does that count?' Coming from a family of five kids, I was no shrinking violet, even though I might sometimes look like one. The truth was I had never suffered from motion sickness and didn't imagine I'd start now. The only thing that did make me feel a little nervous was the crew made it very clear if they got a job outside the metropolitan area, they would deposit me onto the nearest sports field and I'd have to find my own way home.

I sat in the back, wearing headphones and a mic so I could hear the chat between the three crew members. Once the rotors were thumping at fever pitch, the helicopter lurched forward then rose straight up into the air.

Senior Constable Tim Morgan was the shift pilot. He was assisted by Senior Constable Roger Puehl, who was training to be a pilot, and the observer was Senior Constable Cameron Hardiman.

We flew over the Myer Music Bowl. There was a concert on and the pilot was careful not to go too low. 'We get complaints about the noise if we do,' he explained. The whine of the Dauphin engine was something every Melbournian recognised.

Who knew a true crime writer would have to do a photo shoot.
This was for the 27 August 1994 issue of the *Australasian Post*.

We flew down Swanston Street in the city. I stared in wonder at the buildings on either side – the helicopter has clearance to fly as low as 350ft during the day and 450ft at night. Then we swooped away from the city and headed out over the bay. At the time, I lived in Seaford. The drive to Essendon had taken over an hour, but flying back to my suburb only seemed to take about 15 minutes.

'Where's your house?' the pilot asked over the headphones.

I explained how to get there and the next thing there we were, high in the sky, looking down on my house. It felt surreal. We didn't stay long. Across Frankston Dandenong Road, near my place, there was a McDonald's. The golden arches were clearly visible from the air and the pilot explained they were good navigational aids.

The shift wasn't all sight-seeing. There are enormous costs to having the helicopter in the air, not least a significant fuel cost. We headed back towards the city. Our first call came through D24. An elderly man had reported noises on his roof and thought someone was trying to break in. We were close by and took a look. Roger Puehl shone the powerful Nitesun spotlight which really did turn night into day. The roof was clear.

'That's a negative,' Puehl said to D24. 'Probably a possum.'

The next job was a factory alarm, then a spot fire at a park in Keilor. Then came the car chase.

Having been on patrol with police the regular way – in a police car – it was a very different experience in a helicopter. A call came over the radio that police on the ground were in pursuit of a stolen late-model red Mazda in the Melbourne CBD.

'How do you find it from up here?' I asked.

But it quickly became obvious. From the air at night, the blue and red flashing lights of the pursuit cars were easy to spot. Not so easy was the Mazda they were chasing.

'Look for the brake lights,' said one of the crew.

Doing a sweep with the Nitesun, the crew scrutinised the surrounding network of dark back streets and alleyways and spotted a shadowy vehicle, headlights off; it was only visible when the brake lights flashed on and off as it turned corners.

'We've lost him,' came a voice from the ground over the radio.

'We got him!' Puehl radioed back.

He gave D24 the car's location and shone the chopper's powerful spotlight on the alley below. The Mazda slowed and suddenly, the passenger and driver's side doors of the stolen car opened simultaneously and, without stopping the vehicle, two men jumped out and ran off.

While officers on the ground pursued the thieves, I watched in horror from the air as the still-moving stolen car headed towards a main road – and into traffic.

'Oh God!' I said.

The driverless Mazda rolled onto the road, narrowly missed a bus and a couple of cars, continued across the lanes until it lost speed and crashed into a parked car on the opposite side.

The tyranny of distance in this case was vertical and, from the helicopter, there was nothing we could do but watch.

In the meantime, Puehl kept the Nitesun trained on one of the men as he ran into the driveway of a block of flats and disappeared under a tree. But you can't run from the helicopter. Puehl shone

Inviting the police helicopter to school gives
a primary school teacher some serious street cred.

the spotlight on the tree and the guy was trapped. He radioed the location and we watched as the blue and red flashing lights approached from several directions.

The guy was apprehended by ground police then we flew away.

I got home in the small hours of the morning, exhilarated. I was young enough to snatch a couple of hours' sleep, then get up and head off to school to my class of 30 kids.

A final moment, stuck forever in my memory, happened at the Air Wing. I visited the police hangar at Essendon quite a few times during the writing of my story. On one visit I was in the mess room, chatting to some cops who were eating dinner when a call came through. A little boy had fallen into the family swimming pool; he was not breathing and paramedics at the scene were performing CPR. The boy needed urgent transportation to hospital.

The pilot and two cops got up, left their dinners half-eaten on the table, and headed into the hangar. As a newbie to the immediacy of professions like this, I felt my own heart-rate increase and silently wished them luck as they raced to save the child.

The whine of the helicopter firing up outside added to the sense of urgency but as it reached fever pitch, ready to lift off, I heard a reduction in the speed of the rotor, and then it wound down to silent. A couple of minutes later, the three men came back into the mess room and sat back down at the table.

'Kid died,' one of them said.

They all resumed eating.

In 1993 I also rode along on a couple of shifts with the police accident squad whose job it was to attend fatal collisions. It was here that I first truly understood the black humour needed to balance the horror found at every job.

It seemed that these guys were impervious to what they had to deal with. They showed me photos of awful crazy things, like people who had suicided by train; there were pieces everywhere.

'We call them Sussan accidents,' one of the officers said. 'You know the clothing store jingle: *This goes with that at Sussan.*'

I understood the need for humour; to dehumanise the human tragedies. What else could they do? They had to create a safe distance from the carnage in order to do their job professionally.

But sometimes distance wasn't possible. I recall a story a cop told me about attending a decapitation on a train line. Someone had picked up the victim's head and was walking it back to the rest of the body when another officer pulled the dead man's ID out from his pocket. When he read out the man's name, the guy carrying the head blanched.

'Hey! I know him! I've been to his house for dinner.' He looked at the head with horror and recognition, his two worlds colliding.

I did a ride-along with the accident squad and attended a fatal collision at an inner-city intersection. At the scene, a young man lay dead on the footpath, a motorcycle on its side many metres up the road, a bewildered driver shaking his head, saying, 'They came out of nowhere…'

The dead man had been riding pillion on a motorcycle. He and his mate were flying through the intersection over a crest in the road, way too fast. A car turning right had hit them. The passenger on the bike was thrown across the intersection and hit a pole. He had a shocking injury to one leg where the car had connected, but the rest of him was deceptively unscathed.

'Are you sure he's dead?' I whispered to one of the crash investigators.

'Injuries are mostly internal,' said the seasoned cop, 'except for that.' He pointed to the leg.

'But there's no blood,' I said. There was a trickle that had found the crack between the concrete and wormed its way along.

'Once the heart stops, the bleeding stops too,' he said.

Some folks learn that in science class. I learnt it on the side of the road, looking down at a body.

Standing under a streetlight in the dead of night, next to a person who'd been alive an hour earlier is surreal to say the least. And what went through my mind was that while I knew he was dead, his family didn't yet. And that didn't seem fair. I knew their lives had just been irrevocably altered; and they didn't.

I felt so sorry for the young motorist. He looked dazed as the crash investigators inspected the front of his car, the corner that had clipped the leg of the pillion passenger. There was blood on it.

'You'll need to hose that off,' they told him. 'Otherwise, it will start to stink.'

With a world of stories of varying degrees of horror to choose from, I asked the crash investigators for a story that typified what they did.

In the story that follows, it seems like the biggest threats to driver safety in the early 1990s were drunk or speeding drivers.

While road safety campaigns may have improved driver behaviour when it comes to alcohol, speed is still a problem; and now drugs and other distractions like mobile phones have added a whole new dimension to the work of crash investigators.

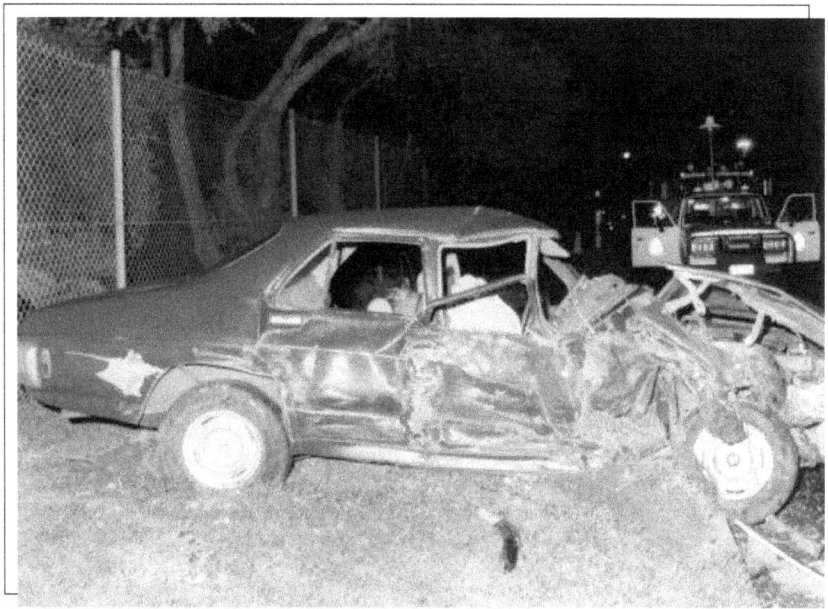

The wrecked red Holden and, in the background,
the police crash truck with its extendable roof light.

6

Four Car, Single Fatal, Double Hit-Run

Nick and Garry were driving their cars too fast – 100 kilometres an hour in a 60 zone – coming up on a white car some distance ahead of them. Garry moved onto the wrong side of the road to pass it, crossing double white lines in the process.

He didn't see the oncoming red Holden beyond the rise in the road until it was too late.

The crushing collision sent his car spinning back onto the left (correct) side of the road where it came to rest against the gutter, while the other car was slammed to its left and then hit again by another car travelling behind it.

The driver of the red Holden died instantly, leaving his heavily pregnant wife screaming by his side.

Nick pulled his green Holden Commodore up onto the nature strip next to his mate's gold Ford. Garry was injured, but not badly.

Nick walked back to the other two cars, surveyed the damage and noted that the driver of the red Holden looked dead. He returned to Garry, helped him out of the wreck of the gold Ford and drove him home.

They didn't call the police.

They didn't try to help the pregnant woman, nor the mother and son in the white Ford station wagon that had rammed into the red Holden as it spun across the road.

They merely surveyed the devastation they had caused and left the scene, no doubt concocting a story that cleared them of any blame on the way home.

Senior Constable Chris Field of the Accident Investigation Section was called to the scene along with Sergeant Tony Hill and Senior Constable Geoffrey Exton. Chris Field had been working an afternoon shift and had received the call at 8.30pm.

They drove the specially-equipped police Land Cruiser known as the 'crash truck'. One of this vehicle's most important features was the light on the roof which could be extended on a pole to a height of 4m to illuminate scenes at night.

The accident scene in the suburb of Heatherton was littered with debris from the mangled remains of three vehicles: a red Holden and a white station wagon on one side of the road; and a gold Ford further down on the other side.

Chris Field, having worked accident investigations for five years, was used to such scenes. His first duty was to speak with uniformed officers already on the scene.

Half an hour had elapsed since the collision and the only remaining victim at the scene was the dead man in the red Holden. His body would remain in the car until the on-site investigation was complete. In death he had, in a sense, become a piece of evidence.

The first officers to arrive at the scene had taped off the accident site with crime scene tape and they brought the crash investigators up to speed. A pregnant woman, from the red car, had been taken by ambulance to hospital for observation and sedation.

The woman and her young son from the white station wagon had been picked up by her husband after giving police a statement. She told them she'd seen the oncoming gold car speeding down the wrong side of the road and realised it was going to hit the car in front of her. She had heard a loud crash and then felt the impact of her car also hitting the red car in front.

The woman explained that she was temporarily dazed after the impact but then heard a woman screaming for help. She and her son got out of their badly-damaged vehicle, went over to the red Holden and helped the woman out of her car.

She told police they thought the expectant mother was the only occupant of the car – until she began screaming for someone to help her husband. In the darkness, they hadn't seen the woman's husband who had fallen back between the two front seats.

A man appeared, looked inside the red Holden, told her that the driver 'didn't look too good' and then left.

The woman remembered people coming and going, but delayed shock had set in and her memory of subsequent events was hazy. Her young son had run to call an ambulance from a nearby house.

Officers at the scene also informed the accident squad members that the third car – the gold Ford – was empty.

Chris Field immediately notified the police helicopter to begin a search of surrounding market gardens. He knew the driver could not have walked away from the twisted wreck uninjured. There was a possibility they'd suffered a head injury and had wandered off in a daze, so they had to be located as soon as possible. State Emergency Service officers, together with the police and sniffer dogs joined the search on the ground.

A second possibility was that the driver had deliberately left the scene of the accident to avoid the consequences.

Chris Field and his fellow officers began their investigation. The signs were easy for the trained crash investigators to read. Skid marks told them the direction in which all the vehicles had been travelling, the shape of dents told them the angle of impact and flakes of paint told them which vehicles had collided.

They started with the red Holden, which was a wreck. The front end on the driver's side was completely smashed in, as was the driver's side door. The dead man lay back against the seat – his face covered in blood. His feet had been jammed under the pedals on impact. Field concluded the deceased man was definitely the vehicle's driver.

Field noted that the red Holden had come to rest on the nature strip at right angles to the white station wagon, which he knew had been driven by the other woman. Scuff marks in the grass indicated the direction in which the car was spinning prior to coming to rest.

Field noted gold flecks of paint adhering to the red Holden at the point of first impact. The investigators checked the dash board in case the speedo had jammed on impact to give a clue as to how fast the Holden had been travelling but the needle sat on zero.

The dead man's seat belt hung slackly around his body. He'd been wearing it and on impact it had locked in position as he'd been thrown forward. But no seat belt could have saved him.

A cursory check of the inside of the red Holden revealed nothing to suggest that the dead man and his wife were anything but a normal, law-abiding couple. There were no beer cans or stolen property or drugs. It was the experience of the investigators that fatal accidents such as this often involve drunk drivers, drug addicts or burglars more concerned about absconding with their stolen goods than keeping their eyes on the road. Every possibility had to be considered.

Next, the crash investigators examined the white station wagon. It wasn't as badly damaged as the red Holden, but they could easily see the point of impact at the front where the collision had occurred. Chris Field photographed the car from a number of different angles, capturing all of the damage.

When this examination was complete, officers Field, Hill and Exton made their way to the third car further down and on the opposite side of the road. The gold Ford had come to rest against the gutter and it too, was very badly damaged.

Immediately the officers noticed tyre marks on the nature strip next to the car. The scuff marks were fresh and couldn't have been made by the gold Ford because it had not mounted the curb.

The gold Ford did, however, have flakes of red paint from the Holden lodged in its front grill.

Chris Field checked the nature strip closely and picked up a bit of plastic moulding, which he recognised as part of the bumper bar of a late model Holden – possibly a Commodore.

Something was amiss. Why were there pieces of a Commodore near the wrecked gold Ford — but no Holden Commodore in sight?

He then noticed a dent in the gold Ford that didn't seem to be associated with the damage caused by the collision with the red Holden. There were pieces of green paint lodged in the dent.

Senior Constable Field put two and two together. He figured that a green Holden Commodore had driven up onto the nature strip after the collision and then, in its haste to leave the scene, had tried to drive forward along the nature strip to get back onto the road. It appeared there hadn't been enough room to pass between the wrecked gold Ford and a power pole on the nature strip, so the green Commodore had clipped the Ford leaving behind part of its bumper bar and paint work.

Common sense told the officers that the driver of the green Holden Commodore had collected the driver of the gold Ford and driven him away. That made the collision a hit-and-run and the job became a four car, single fatal, double hit-run.

Field immediately put out a bulletin for a late model, green Holden Commodore with front end damage. He then radioed D24 for an officer from the state forensic science laboratory to attend the scene and gather evidence like soil samples and tyre casts.

Field and his team knew such samples may be needed later in court to link the missing vehicle with the accident scene.

The next step in the investigation was to find the owner of the abandoned gold Ford. Registration details were taken from the smashed window of the car and a police check was run on the owner; Garry's name was soon known to police.

Field sent uniformed officers to the address only to find that Garry hadn't lived there for some time. Field then ran an information bureau of records (IBR) check on Garry and wasn't really surprised to find he had a long list of prior convictions — most of which were for driving and drug offences. The IBR check also listed Garry's known associates.

Four addresses were checked before police officers located Garry's mother who gave them his current address – he was living with a mate called Nick.

Chris Field left Exton and Hill at the accident scene and went with uniformed officers to the house in Noble Park. Using their powerful police torches, Field and the other officers illuminated the green Holden Commodore in the driveway of the house. It had obvious, recent front-end damage.

It was now six hours since the collision. Examination of the exterior of the Commodore was interrupted by loud barking and the arrival of two dogs – one of them a bull terrier. Field recalls bluffing the dogs with his police baton before making his way to the front door of the house.

A woman came out onto the front porch when the dogs started to bark. Field asked to speak to the driver of the green Commodore.

The woman retreated for a moment, told someone to say nothing, and then returned to tell Field a story. Her boyfriend Nick, and his mate Garry, had been at the pub watching a strip show when they noticed Garry's car was being stolen from the car park. They'd pursued the thieves until Garry's car had been involved in an accident. Nick had driven them home and, according to the woman, was going to report the whole thing to the police the following day.

Understandably, Field was sceptical and asked to see Garry. He was led into the lounge room where a man in his mid-20s was lying on the couch covered with a blanket.

Field asked him to stand up, which he did reluctantly and with great difficulty. It was obvious Garry's legs were severely bruised and one of his wrists was swollen enough to suggest it was broken.

Ironically, as Garry repeated the story the woman had told, and denied any involvement in the accident, evidence to the contrary literally fell from his lap. As soon as he stood up bits of windscreen glass began dropping from his tracksuit.

Field cut him short. 'Don't insult our intelligence, mate. Tell us what really happened.'

Garry and Nick finally admitted to their part in the fatal collision but denied, when asked, that they'd been drag racing.

Garry and Nick showed no obvious signs of regret or remorse when told the driver of the red Holden had died.

Chris Field was used to such reactions. He cautioned the two men and took them to the Cheltenham police station to be interviewed. Worried about taking a statement from the injured Garry, he called in the police surgeon. The doctor recommended that Garry be taken to hospital for x-rays. Nick was later released pending further investigation.

In Heatherton, Tony Hill and Geoffrey Exton supervised the removal of the smashed cars – the gold Ford was sent by tow truck to the state forensic science laboratory while the other cars went to local police compounds to be sealed until examination by police mechanics attached to the accident squad. Using a geodometer, they measured the distance between the vehicles and the skid marks at the accident scene in order to prepare a scale map of the incident.

Police then began the painstaking examination of the evidence to put the puzzle together. From the witness statement of the driver of the white station wagon, they knew there'd been at least one other car on the road.

Chris Field appealed through the media for the driver of the car that Garry was trying to pass, before the collision, to come forward.

The man rang police the next day. He said he'd been driving along the road in Heatherton when he saw two cars in his rear-vision mirror speeding up behind. They were going so fast, he said, that he was sure they were going to crash into the back of his car. He had seen (Garry's) car swerve onto the wrong side of the road, to go around him, and hit the oncoming red Holden.

The man told police he had 'freaked' and was unable to stop – in fear of what he would see. He went home, had a stiff drink, and telephoned police the following day to offer his assistance. He was a valuable witness.

Garry was charged with: culpable driving causing death; recklessly causing injury to the wife of the deceased, negligently causing injury to the wife of the deceased, and recklessly placing the wife in danger of death; recklessly placing the woman and her son (in the other vehicle) in danger of death; failing to render assistance at the scene of the accident; failing to give name and address at the scene of the accident; as well as driving in a manner careless, driving in a manner dangerous, driving while disqualified, crossing double lines, and exceeding 60 km per hour.

Garry's alleged speed according to complicated calculations performed by accident investigators was 100 km per hour.

When his case finally came to court, Garry pleaded guilty to the charge of culpable driving – giving him an automatic one-third reduction of any possible sentence.

Senior Constable Chris Field said that Garry 'cried like a baby' when the judge gave him a 30-month jail sentence.

The full penalty for culpable driving was (then) 15 years in prison, but drivers never got the full term. Field explained he always tried to distance himself from the sentencing process because he felt the sentence was society's responsibility. He said he merely did his job, which finished when he gave evidence.

He did note his disappointment, however, that a man like Garry was given such a relatively-light sentence considering his list of prior convictions.

Garry had lost his driver's licence almost as soon as he got it. In 1987 he'd been convicted of unlicensed driving and exceeding .05; his blood alcohol reading was .170. He had also been convicted of dangerous driving and speeding. A year later he'd been convicted on a number of theft and drug trafficking charges. In addition to his considerable list of prior convictions, Garry continued to offend after the fatal collision.

It was the variety of the work in the accident squad that enabled

Chris Field to thrive in what was often a traumatic job. The squad was largely independent, which meant an investigation was followed from beginning to end. Field and his fellow investigators attended accidents, gathered evidence, took their own photographs, attended post-mortem examinations, collated evidence and appeared in court as expert witnesses.

Job satisfaction aside, they still had to maintain a safe psychological and emotional distance from the carnage. Often, throughout a shift, they'd catch sight of a speeding driver through the station window and say, 'There goes another customer'.

An altered TAC (Transport Accident Commission) campaign poster, on the office wall read:

If you drink and drive, you're a bloody ~~idiot~~ *customer.*

Seeing so much death on the road – mostly because of alcohol and speed – the officers felt that messages of road safety too often mean little to the public.

Accident investigator, Senior Constable Chris Field.

'People think it won't happen to them,' Field said. 'But my job proves it can and does happen to anybody.'

It's easy to see how the officers become hardened. Time after time, they are called to 'accidents' involving drunk young men with prior convictions who wrap their cars around power poles.

One incident that stood out in Field's memory was a triple fatality where one young man's body was found in a particularly stupid place. Investigators called to the scene found two dead young men in the front seats of the car. Empty beer cans had spilled out of the wreck onto the ground.

The vehicle's rear-end was jammed against a stone fence and it wasn't until the wreck was finally moved that police found a third body – in the boot of the car.

Investigations revealed that the men had gone on a beer run to the bottle shop, then loaded their purchases into the boot. The third victim had jumped in there 'to be with the beer'. For a lark, his friends had sped around the streets to throw him around inside the boot. They were all drunk and they all died.

Chris Field said that it was always the death of children that broke through the team's emotional barriers, because kids were always innocent victims.

One Christmas Eve Field was called to investigate a two-car collision near a small country town in Victoria. Five people had been killed. It transpired that a woman had been driving to New South Wales to visit her mother-in-law for Christmas. She was following her husband and father-in-law who were travelling in their own car. Her passengers were her two children, aged six and two.

Inexperience of country roads and possibly fatigue were blamed for the woman missing a bend and colliding head-on with a car containing two people – also on their way to visit relatives for Christmas. The scene was utter carnage.

Not only did Field have to investigate all aspects of the accident, he had to deal with the distraught husband who had pulled his car over when he noticed his wife was no longer following him.

The hardest part – and the thing that stayed with Field – was seeing the tiny bodies of the two children and then noticing the car full of Christmas presents with cards handwritten in a childish scrawl: *To Dear Granny.*

Field finished his lengthy investigation at 3am, returned home to catch a couple of hours sleep and was woken by his own small children opening their presents.

'All I could think about were those little kids who wouldn't be opening their presents that morning. It ruined Christmas.'

The tendency of some cars to burn following a collision, meant Field had many tragic cases stuck in his memory.

In one, a woman died on impact when her car hit a tree. The vehicle's roof had folded in, trapping her baby in its capsule in the back seat. Bystanders had rushed over to try to free the baby, but soon smoke began to billow from underneath the car. The would-be rescuers tried desperately to shield the trapped infant with blankets but were soon driven back by the flames.

Field shrugged sadly. 'There was nothing anyone could do.'

In another accident, a man lost control of his car on a corrugated country road, and careered into a small bridge where he was trapped. A private security officer saw the accident and stopped to help. He couldn't free the man's leg which was caught under the dashboard, so he began running to get help at a nearby farmhouse. He heard the man yelling and turned back to see smoke coming from the car's engine. The security man continued running to the farmhouse but help didn't arrive in time.

When Field attended the scene, the driver's charred body was found with his arms raised defensively in front to shield his face.

The security man told him, 'I would have given a million dollars for a fire extinguisher that day'.

Not all road fatalities are added to the state's annual road toll – some are suicides and some are murder – but any involving a car or a road may be investigated by the accident squad.

Field said investigators must have an open mind.

'It is easy for experts to tell the difference between someone who has been hit by a car, and someone who was run over to make it look like an accident.'

Pedestrians hit by cars typically suffer similar injuries, quite different to someone who is run over while already on the ground. Damage to the victim's legs at the height of the car's bumper bar is usual, as are head injuries where the victim is thrown up onto the bonnet and perhaps smash the windscreen.

Investigators get the occasional case of murder. Field says it is not unheard of for a husband to line up his car with the biggest power pole or truck he can find and, just before impact, unclasp his wife's seat belt, ramming only her side of the car. He kills her but walks away relatively unscathed.

These cases are difficult but not impossible to prove.

Chris Field says that the function of the accident squad is to investigate any road fatality with three or more victims; any case involving police – on or off-duty; and any case of criminal negligence. Field said police are just as accountable as everybody else and the accident squad is always called in as an independent investigator when police are involved in serious collisions.

Field occasionally lectured at the police academy and told new recruits bluntly of their responsibility on the roads. Field called it 'double jeopardy' if police are involved in a collision. He said not only are they investigated by the accident squad, but they are also investigated by the police internal investigation department. The case is then passed to the state Ombudsman for independent review.

Field said these exacting standards meant that the public could be assured that police neither receive nor expect special treatment.

The success rate of the accident squad is high. In fact 95 per cent of hit-and-run cases are solved with the examination of physical evidence and the help of witnesses.

Senior Constable Chris Field was understandably cynical about the general messages of road safety. He conceded that innovations such as speed cameras have slowed traffic down, but sadly concluded it was the 'hip pocket' effect rather than drivers behaving better because they should.

'Road safety is ultimately society's responsibility. If society believes that drink driving is wrong, then its members will actively encourage each other not to drink and drive.

'I remember when it was considered normal – even humorous – for a drunk to stagger to his car and drive home. This attitude has clearly changed. Death on the roads is no longer considered an inevitable part of driving.'

But one thing that Chris Field was certain of: as long as people continue to flout road rules, drink and drive, speed, and drive while tired, the accident squad will never be short of customers.

Australasian

POST

$2.40

$2

YOUR ALL-AUSTRALIAN
FAMILY MAGAZINE

FINE
COTTON!

TEN YEARS ON
AND MANY STILL
PAY THE PRICE

Urban sprawl
hits Birdsville

PEOPLE OF
POWER
TOWN

His Royal
Fredness
and Her
Highness
Noreen...

RUGBY'S
HORRIBLE
HIT MEN

Oh, mother!
*He's my
brother...*

Author
Vikki:

'MY
LIFE
OF VILE
CRIME'

And
other stories...

7

THE COVER GIRL
& THE SERIAL KILLER

My second book *Victims, Crimes and Investigators* came out in early 1994. I wanted to call the book *Cops* because essentially it was about policing and the personal experience of cops. The publisher, however, wanted a title to match a picture they'd found for the cover. It was a woman walking nervously down a dark alleyway.

Even though I didn't like the cover or the title, I wasn't about to argue with my new publishing house. My first publisher had told me what was on the inside of the book was mine and what was on the outside – cover image, title, tagline – was marketing.

I had my first ever author photograph taken for the back cover. I also met Shirley Hardy-Rix who was to be my publicist for the book. I visited Shirley at her home. In the room where we chatted, she had a bookshelf that contained multiple copies of her own books. She said it was important to keep a handful of copies for yourself because books went out of print and disappeared. My own library had hundreds of true crime books from overseas and on Shirley's advice, I added mine to the collection.

Shirley was a great publicist and got me a cover story on *The Australasian Post*.

A *Post* photographer and journalist came to my house. While the photographer was taking what would amount to nine rolls of film, my husband chatted away to the journalist. From my posing position, leaning at weird angles, I couldn't signal to him that he wasn't just 'having a chat' he was *being interviewed*. Sure enough, he was quoted in the article.

When the magazine came out, it was in every supermarket in multiple racks at the end of each checkout counter. Shopping with my seven-year-old daughter was embarrassing.

'There you are, Mummy!' she'd say loudly every time she saw a copy of *The Post*. 'There you are again! It's Mummy!'

Being on the cover of a magazine so widely available seemed to drive home to people close to me that writing wasn't just a quirky hobby that I worked around my real job. It was something important, something worthy of recognition. Something people around the country were interested in.

This realisation was a little jarring for me too. I hadn't been writing for fame. I had become a writer because there were stories I wanted to tell; worthy stories, important stories.

Such public exposure meant it was a little harder to keep my writing and teaching life separate. In the days before true-crime stories were popular in Australia, I could understand that a parent might not necessarily want their child taught by someone who spent their leisure hours writing true crime stories. I worked at a primary school – a land far, far away from the writing I did.

The world of public opinion was also something I had to learn to navigate. I had to learn to cope with comments about my books, or their subject matter, not all positive, from people I knew. One person made a point of saying to me, 'Oh I would never read *that* kind of book.' Never lost for words, I replied, 'Lucky for me and my book sales, thousands of people *do* read that kind of book.'

In an episode of *Dr Phil*, he performs an intervention on a woman and she calls him a quack. Dr Phil replies with words to the effect: 'Aren't I lucky that no part of my self-esteem is dependent on your opinion of me.' I loved this – he was saying exactly how I felt. A writer's self-worth has to come from within, not from how others see you or review your work.

Writers have to be self-motivated and self-driven and if lots of people love our books, we pretty much have to ignore those who don't. You can't please everyone. I'm reminded of this every time I go to Book Club. We are all reading the same book, yet reactions can run from 'best book ever' to 'I hated it'. The book didn't change; it is what it is. The variable is the heart and mind of each reader. And that is something the writer can't control.

In the autumn of 1993, while I was working on my second book, and doing ride-alongs with the Frankston police to get some life-on-the-beat cop stories, a serial killer began murdering young women in the area.

In my neighbourhood.

Newspaper headlines screamed *Corridor of Death!* and *Serial Killer!* and put the fear of God into everyone.

It's one thing to have an abiding interest in real crime, but quite another to have a serial killer operating in your own local streets.

For seven weeks from the first murder to the last, like other women in the area, I was very aware of the danger he posed. I had read every true crime book I could lay my hands on and, for a while, I thought the knowledge I'd gleaned gave me an advantage. There were reports of the wide-spread buying of guard dogs and security doors, but I'd read enough to suspect the so-called Frankston serial killer would not break into people's homes, because his victims had been snatched off the street. I figured that if I moved through my suburb only in well-lit spaces and didn't walk alone at night, I should be fine.

It turned out I was wrong on all counts because this killer *had* broken into someone's home, and he did attack in broad daylight. But I didn't know that then.

Living in Seaford during the seven-week killing spree, made me look at the world through a new lens – one of suspicion. I bet I wasn't the only woman waiting for my order in the fish and chip shop, casting suspicious glances at any man waiting near me. And

I bet I wasn't alone in checking out strangers in the video shop, or the newsagent, or the supermarket, wondering: *Could it be him? Or him? Is it you?*

In the middle of this seven-week killing spree I spent a shift with a police officer called Wendy O'Shea who worked in the Frankston Community Policing Squad. It was the evening after the second victim, Debbie Fream, went missing. Her disappearance was the talk of the squad but no connection had yet been made between this missing woman and the murder of Elizabeth Stevens in Langwarrin a month earlier. There was no reason to think the cases were linked.

In fact, when Debbie vanished after leaving her newborn baby with a friend to pop up to the shops to get milk, the only answer that made sense to the police I spoke to was that she must have been suffering from post-natal depression and decided to leave for a couple of days.

What else could it be?

Even so, that evening after she disappeared, when I arrived at the community policing squad for my ride-along. it was clear some officers were worried. Debbie's car had been found not far from where she was last seen, with the driver's seat pushed all the way back. Debbie was short, so the obvious conclusion was that someone else had driven the car.

I listened as the police officers around me discussed more sinister possibilities about what could have happened to the young mother.

When Debbie was found murdered four days later, the discussion at the community policing squad was fresh in my mind. The world seemed a much nicer place when Debbie might have just left to have a few days by herself.

But that night with Wendy O'Shea, after discussing Debbie's disappearance for a while, we moved on to a case of child sexual abuse that she had investigated. Wendy's case was about a girl called Gemma who was abused by her stepfather. The abuse began on Gemma's fifth birthday. I didn't know it then but writing about child sexual abuse for the first time with Wendy would point me in a direction I follow to this day. Wendy's Gemma has also played a role in fiction I've created which means her story got under my skin too.

There was one part of Wendy's story I'll never forget. When Gemma was asked in court if she still loved her stepfather after years of abuse, the girl held up her thumb and pointer finger and created a small space between them.

'This much,' she said. 'I still love him this much.'

This comment illustrated profoundly the complexities of child sexual abuse.

By coincidence, I did another ride-along, with a uniform sergeant called Mick – who was also my next-door neighbour – on the night the third of the serial killer's victims was found.

Despite an intense police presence patrolling the bayside suburbs, Year 12 student Natalie Russell had disappeared that day on the way home from school.

By the time I arrived with Mick to observe his night shift, there was a pall of disbelief over the Frankston police station.

One of the cops standing outside having a smoke, said what they were all thinking: 'Right under our noses.' There was a huge police presence and the killer had sailed through the net and taken a school girl. They had all done everything they could, but it wasn't enough.

Mick and I went inside just as a cop came downstairs and said, 'They've found her and she's dead.'

I was stuck by the lack of emotion in his voice. But I felt it too; it was like all the air had been sucked out of the place.

Mick and his partner were sent to the scene. Since I had permission to do the ride-along, he bustled me into the back of the police car and told me to keep in the shadows. The ride there was eerie. No lights and sirens. And a radio silence of sorts. All messages were cryptic. They didn't want to alert the media who used police scanners.

So there I was on a cold winter's night, sitting in the back of a police car in the carpark of the Monterey Secondary College looking at the track along which Natalie Russell had met her death. Mick and his partner left me there while they went off to join the other cops guarding the scene and keeping everyone away.

I didn't know anything about Natalie in that moment except her name.

But I would come to learn so much about her.

Alone with my thoughts for a couple of hours, I was filled with a deep sadness for the teenager who lay beyond the trees; and for her family who had lost her.

Until that night, the police stories I'd written had always been from at a distance. The cases, the investigations were always done and dusted by the time I got to them.

But this one was unfolding right in front of me. Just metres away. I was flooded with a nervous energy that sat alongside the disbelief that I was actually there, at the scene.

There were police everywhere: silent and searching and patrolling. The police helicopter hovered in the sky, shining its powerful Nitesun down on the horror below. Rain fell gently through its beam.

When Mick finally returned to the car, he told me to throw away my notes. Nothing could be written about this until after they caught the serial killer.

Of course, I wouldn't throw my notes away, because I wasn't a journalist. If I did write about it, it would not be for the media. I'd wait until it was all over and then write the story properly.

But a book about a serial killer would challenge me in ways I had not yet experienced. This was not a story that could be written from a distance, or just through the eyes of the police. I would have to approach the families and intrude on their grief. I felt sick at the thought, but I could already feel this case calling to me. I would have to talk to everyone I could find: the family of the killer when he was caught, police, SES, forensics, witnesses. The list was long.

I'd interviewed cops and people in law enforcement before,

but was I up to the challenge? And if I could approach all these people, would they want to talk to me? Was my writing up to scratch? Could I do the story justice?

The long solitary wait in the dark that night, convinced me there was no one better to do it than me. I was already a true crime writer. I was local, I was on the spot, I cared about the community, and the fear of this murderer had touched me too.

The police had acknowledged they were now hunting a serial killer. It's easy to fall for *The Silence of the Lambs* version of the serial killer – the genius psychopath taunting the police with his clues and signatures; a vicious killer who can disappear into the dark and escape detection. And that's what it felt like sitting in that police car, thinking about the unknown murderer – that silent figure, still out there, moving through Frankston, dodging police and killing women.

I wondered just how clever he was. I worried he'd never be caught.

It turned out he wouldn't be unknown for long.

Paul Charles Denyer was caught the very next day.

And he was no criminal mastermind.

I began writing the book properly after Denyer had been found guilty. In the meantime, I had collected newspaper articles and attended community meetings. At one of these, I saw Carmel and Brian Russell from a distance and felt anxious in the pit of my stomach. I knew I would have to approach them and ask for their story.

In the days before the internet swamped the world, I chose writing a letter as a way to contact all the families. The phone book provided addresses. I sent letters to everyone connected to the victims and to Denyer's family.

I got responses from everyone. Some chose to talk; others chose not to.

All up, I interviewed over 50 people for the book. They were relatives, cops, forensic people, witnesses, and people affected by what had occurred in Frankston in 1993.

This kind of work is not something you can let go of easily at the close of the day. Friendships form despite the circumstances. In hindsight, I had no professional distance at all. I had no training in writing or interviewing or keeping a distance. I was highly empathetic and wrote from the heart. Also in hindsight, that meant I constructed no protective barriers around myself. It didn't seem to matter at the time.

Natalie Russell's aunt, Bernadette Naughton, became the public spokesperson for the Russell family. She and I also became close friends. Melissa Denyer, Paul's sister-in-law, and I spent a lot of time together. And when Melissa wanted to meet Bernadette so she could apologise to the Russell family, on behalf of her family for what Paul had done, I was able to make that happen.

The two met around the time the film *Dead Man Walking* came out. We decided to go and see it together. I will never forget sitting in between Bernadette and Mel, one weeping in scenes where the victims' families were featured, and the other weeping when scenes showed the killer's family suffering.

It was all unchartered waters for me. I mean how many people do you know who have been to a film about capital punishment with the sister-in-law of a serial killer and the aunt of his victim? Nonetheless, these kinds of things felt like the right thing to do.

While I had been reluctant to intrude on the grief of those left behind, I came to understand that the simple act of giving them a place to tell their stories brings comfort. Airing sadness or anger or regret to someone prepared to listen can be cathartic. It helps relatives, friends and survivors process what has happened. The empathetic writer is not an intrusion at all.

One thing I've always done is show the story to the person I interviewed – before it went into the book. This gives them the opportunity to see that their story has been accurately told, and they can add or take away anything they want. This means no surprises in the end. People are always very grateful for that.

In the telling of these stories, it allayed my fear that in the years to come, the victims would become mere additions after the mention of their killer. We see it all the time: Serial killer

Paul Denyer murdered Elizabeth Stevens, 18, Debbie Fream, 22, and Natalie Russell, 17.

I wanted my book to *show* who they were, so that for the reader, Natalie, 17, became a girl who wanted to be a journalist and who loved making funny videos with her friends. And Elizabeth, 18, became the beloved niece who used to throw a ball down her home's long hallway and send the family dog skidding after it. And of course, Debbie, 22, was baby Jake's mum, lost when he was 12 days old. The girls had to come alive again in the pages of my book so that the focus was on their lives not just the hours of their death.

I felt honoured to hear these stories of grief and life. I'll never forget what Natalie's mum Carmel said to me.

'It sounds silly,' she said, 'but one of the hardest things was to remember to only set three places at the dinner table instead of four.'

'It doesn't sound silly at all,' I said in a quiet voice. 'Not at all.' And I realised this was what grief was: a big loss that fills the world, a daughter's empty bedroom, and only three places at the table.

If I could do this right, I thought, the reader would truly know what Denyer took.

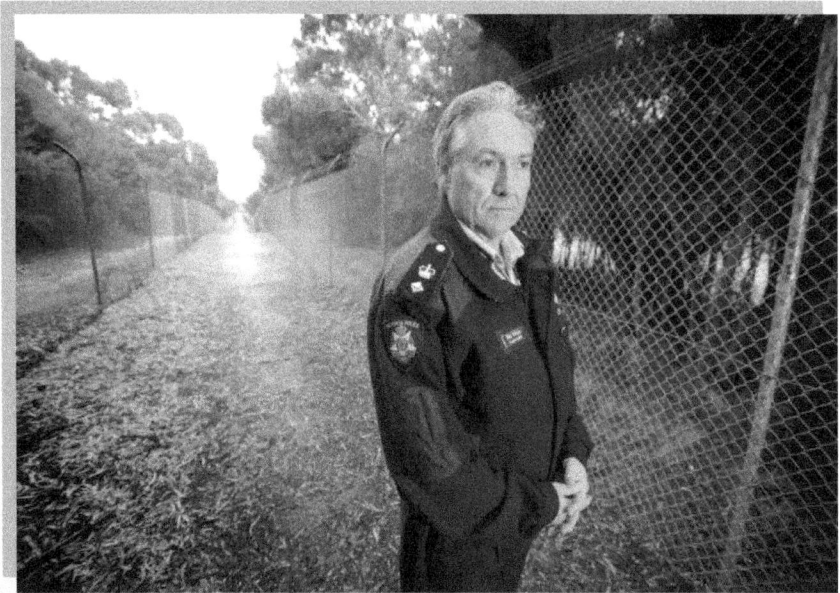

Now a superintendent, Rod Wilson was one of the homicide detectives who worked the Frankston serial killer case.

8

THE FRANKSTON MURDERS

Donna Vanes was uneasy. With her tiny baby nestled in a bassinet, she asked her boyfriend Les to take them on his pizza delivery run. She just didn't feel like being alone at the flat in Claude Street. It was a nice flat and they had only lived there for three weeks, but an anonymous telephone call a couple of days earlier had spooked her. The caller had telephoned, said nothing and then hung up.

When she returned home and walked into the darkened hallway of the flat around 11pm, Donna was hit by a foul odour; it was like nothing she had smelt before. She and Les were making their way through the lounge room towards the kitchen when Donna saw blood – it was smeared and splattered on walls through the flat. They quickly called the police.

On the white wall of the lounge room, next to the television, the intruder had written what looked like 'Dead Don' in blood. In the kitchen was the body of Donna's cat. It had been horribly slaughtered. Trailed across the floor about half a metre away from the dead cat was a string of intestines. One of the cat's eyeballs was bulging out of its socket, the other was missing. Adding to the bizarre scene was the picture of a naked woman placed on top of the cat's body, covering its abdominal wounds. Written in blood above the stove were the words 'DONNA YOURE DEAD' printed in block letters. Next to the words was a bloodied outline to suggest that the cat had been held or flung against the wall. In the bathroom, the cat's two kittens floated one at each end of a half-filled bath. Their throats had been cut and their blood had turned the water the colour of rust.

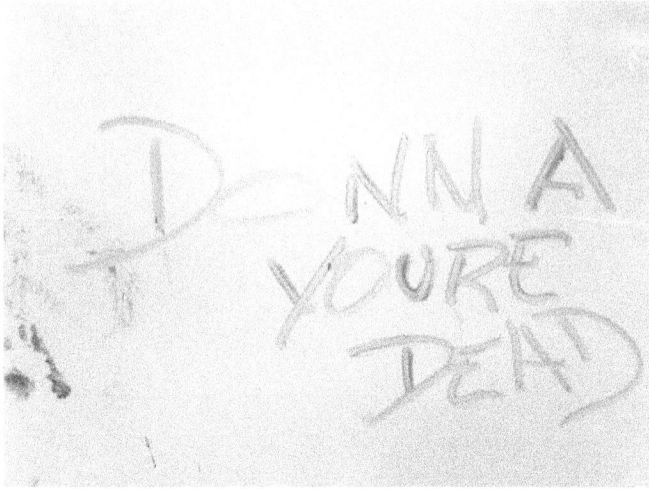

In the baby's room, the intruder had put a picture of a naked model into the baby's crib and stabbed through the picture into the bedding. Some of the baby's clothes had also been slashed.

So brutal and bizarre was the attack on the cats and the threat to Donna Vanes, that detectives called in crime scene examiners, photographics and fingerprint experts to examine the flat in Claude Street. It appeared the intruder knew Donna but she was at a loss to explain the vicious attack. Too scared to stay there, she moved out to stay with her sister Tricia.

One of Tricia's neighbours, who'd also known Donna for a while, reassured her and said she'd be safe there. Paul Denyer even told Donna that if they ever caught the person responsible, he would take care of him.

As 18-year-old Elizabeth Stevens jumped off the bus which had brought her from Frankston to Cranbourne Road, Langwarrin, she was unaware that she was being watched.

It was 7.15pm on Friday 11 June 1993, and heavy rain had soaked Elizabeth's wavy short hair so that it clung damply to her neck. She didn't usually come home this late, but she had been working at the Frankston Library for a bothersome English assignment that she had already completed but her teacher had asked her to conduct more research on the topic.

Elizabeth shivered in the cold June rain and hurried quickly down Paterson Avenue towards the home she shared with her aunt and uncle. The rain grew heavier and it was hard to see.

Out of the darkness, the man in the green army jacket and navy baseball cap lunged at her from behind, clasped a hand roughly around her mouth and pushed what felt like the barrel of a gun to her head. She screamed but the sound was drowned out by the wind and the rain. She struggled against him, thinking she could protect herself: she had taken karate lessons for four years, but he was a big man, strong, and he had a gun. There was nothing she could do.

'Shut up or I'll blow your head off,' he shouted at her, his voice chilling her into submission.

'Kiss the end of the gun!' he ordered but Elizabeth was too afraid to move. 'We're going to take a walk,' he told her, pushing her down the road. He forced Elizabeth down another street towards Lloyd Park. He knew exactly where he was going. He dragged Elizabeth into a clump of bushes.

'What's your name?' he asked.

'Elizabeth, but everyone calls me Liz,' she told him.

'How old are you?'

'Seventeen,' lied the 18-year-old. Perhaps she thought 17 sounded younger and he wouldn't hurt her. She was wrong.

'Do you want a fuck?' he asked bluntly.

The terrified young woman told him she didn't know how, and her abductor asked if she was a virgin. She nodded.

'Well, I won't rape you or anything,' he assured her.

Elizabeth's relief was very short-lived.

The man began walking her over towards the football oval goal posts and then he grabbed her around the throat and started choking her. When she collapsed onto the wet grass, he pulled a red-handled knife from his pocket and lunged at her throat, slashing until the blade bent.

When he finally let her go, Elizabeth fell heavily to the ground where he stamped his foot viciously on her neck. The frenzy was over. He could hear the blood and air gurgling from her neck. Impatient for her death, the man lifted his foot above her head and brought it crashing down on her face, shattering her nose and cutting her cheek and eyebrow with the sheer force.

The man dragged her by the legs the short distance to a creek bed flowing with shallow dirty drain water. Blackberry bushes clawed viciously at her skin but she was dead now. Her bra top ended up around her neck as she was dragged, exposing her chest.

Then the man took the blade of the broken knife and slowly and methodically made long cuts from her breasts right down to her stomach. When he had finished carving the vertical lines, he then carved four lines across at right angles. After the crisscross pattern was complete, the man stabbed the knife into her chest six times.

When he was finished, he put the broken pieces of the knife back into his pocket. Water lapped around the young woman's body washing away her blood. Grabbing a branch from a tree above the drain, he wrenched it free and partly covered the young woman's body. The rain and the water from the drain would wash away clues of footprints and blood.

The man discarded Elizabeth Stevens' bag 10m from where her body lay and began the long walk to his girlfriend's mother's house for dinner. He tossed the pieces of knife into nearby bushes. Less than an hour after the brutal murder, the man tucked into a hearty meal of soup and a roast and waited for his girlfriend to come home from work.

Elizabeth's body was discovered the following day.

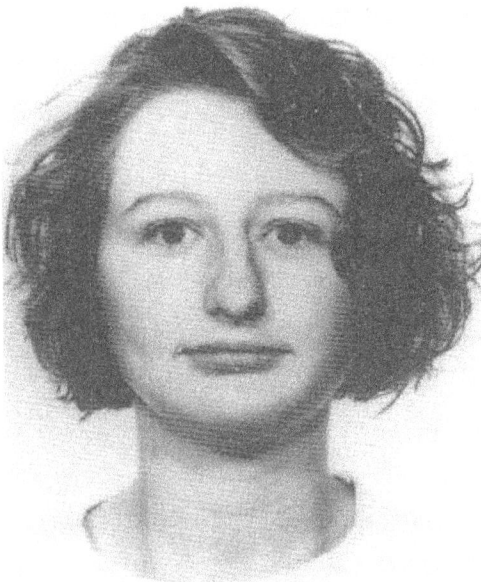

Elizabeth Stevens

On Thursday 8 July 1993, 41-year-old Roszsa Toth caught the 5.25pm train at Cheltenham alighting at Seaford at 5.50pm where she braced herself against the July chill for the short walk home. As she passed the sports reserve on Railway Parade, Roszsa saw a man about 20m away, near the toilet block. She took little notice of him and kept walking. As she passed, he began following her and before she knew it, he had caught up. He grabbed her by the hair and tried to force her off the footpath towards the toilet block. In the struggle, they both fell to the ground.

The man didn't say a word; he pushed her onto her back, struggling to get on top of her. Roszsa lay on the damp grass of the reserve near the busy road and couldn't believe what was happening to her. She screamed and he pushed something to her temple and told her he had a gun.

Roszsa caught sight of oncoming lights, which she thought might be a bike or car, and managed to push the man away, get up and run towards the road. But she'd barely taken three steps when the man grabbed her by the hair, pulling out a handful in the process, and dragged her down onto the ground again.

Now on her back, Roszsa continued to struggle and scream. She bit the man on the fingers, summoned all her energy and pushed him off her. She managed to grab her handbag and a shoe that had fallen off, and this time made it to the road where she ran out in front of the oncoming cars waving her hands desperately for them to stop. As she escaped, her attacker ran off into the reserve.

When the terrified Roszsa told the driver who'd stopped for her what had happened, the woman took her home to call the police.

In the meantime the attacker boarded the next Frankston-bound train and got off at Kananook station. Thwarted in his attempt to kill Roszsa Toth, the young man was still hunting. In no time his path crossed that of a young mother who had run out of milk while cooking dinner for a friend.

Debbie Fream had left her 12-day-old baby at home with her friend while she ducked out to the local milk bar, a short drive from her house.

When she hadn't returned half an hour later, the friend became concerned. And soon the disappearance of the young Seaford mother became front-page news.

Detectives quickly connected the attempted abduction of Roszsa Toth and the strange disappearance of 22-year-old Debbie Fream. The attacks occurred within an hour of each other near two railway stations on the Frankston line.

The situation became worse when the missing woman's car was found with the seat pushed right back, as if someone much taller than Debbie's 158cm had been the last person to drive it.

Four days later, a farmer in Carrum Downs discovered a body by the side of a road adjacent to one of his paddocks. At first, he thought it was a mannequin, but soon realised his mistake. He knew that the dead woman must be Debbie Fream. Like everyone else in Melbourne he'd seen the intense television and newspaper coverage of the missing young mother.

Post-mortem examinations on Elizabeth and Debbie found that both had suffered stab wounds and attempted strangulation. While the wounds were similar, the killer had scratched a strange pattern on Elizabeth's chest and stomach, there were no similar markings on Debbie.

Not wanting to assume

Debbie Fream

the worst – that there was a serial killer at large – the odds were obviously against there being two killers targeting woman in the same area at the same time. Nonetheless, detectives investigated all possibilities.

Three weeks later, the bayside community was still living in fear, despite the increased police presence in the area, as detectives and officers hunted the killer. Many parents were driving their daughters to and from school, authorities urged friends to walk together, and a public meeting was called to allay residents' fears and suggest ways to stay safe.

Students at John Paul College in Frankston, for instance, had stopped riding their bikes to school and some had bought hand-held alarms after teachers had warned them about personal safety.

But it was the weekend ahead, not a serial killer, that was on the minds of students as they left school on Friday 30 July.

Natalie Russell, dressed in her tartan school skirt and dark blue school jumper with its red crest, left the college grounds around 2.30pm. The 17-year-old walked down McMahons Road and across Skye Road to the bike track she regularly used as a short cut.

Two days earlier the principal had warned the school assembly it would be safer to avoid the track until the killer was caught. But local kids continued to use it, as the track was straight and you could see a fair distance ahead.

Natalie was heading straight home.

She walked the track alone. There was no one else in sight.

When her daughter failed to return home from school that Friday afternoon, Carmel Russell reported her missing.

Ordinarily, the police would calm anxious parents by saying a young girl only a couple of hours late home from school was nothing to worry about but these were not ordinary times. Hundreds of extra police had been rostered to patrol Frankston streets, and the entire district was on high alert.

Police took the disappearance of Natalie Russell very seriously, and imediately organised an intensive search for her. Officers and SES volunteers scoured the area.

At 10.54pm two SES volunteers climbed through a hole in the cyclone wire fence bordering the bike track. Moments later they retreated to get help and police soon verified that Natalie's body had been found. The worst fears of all the searchers were realised: there was some sort of maniac on the loose.

Crime scene examiners, Brian Gamble and Tony Kealy, dared not approach the body until daylight as they didn't want to risk missing any clues or contaminating the scene. Instead they concentrated their attention on the bike track, and on the fence which had been deliberately cut.

In the meantime Natalie's body remained in the bushes. It was cold and dark and there was a persistent drizzle of rain, but a canopy of trees overhead provided enough cover for the crime scene.

The forensic pathologist, Dr Tony Landgren, arrived at 9.30am to perform a preliminary examination of the body in situ; then Gamble and Kealy set to work photographing, documenting and collecting evidence.

At 11am, nearly 12 hours after she'd been found, Natalie was taken to the morgue for the post-mortem examination by Dr Landgren.

The killer had cut the teenager's throat. When the pathologist examined the wound, he found a small piece of skin that didn't belong to her. Landgren figured the killer had held her from behind with one hand and cut her throat with the other, and in doing so had nicked himself.

Natalie Russell

Detectives working the case were told to look out for anyone with a wound on his hand or finger.

Over the course of seven weeks a serial killer had murdered three young women in Frankston and struck terror into an entire city.

But, in the end, his capture was relatively simple.

Shortly after the murderer walked up the bike track to lie in wait for his third victim, his empty car was noted by two policemen. They'd been despatched because a postal worker had reported a suspicious man parked in a yellow Toyota Corona on Skye Road.

Early Saturday morning those two cops entered the makeshift Homicide Squad office at the Frankston police station to inform Detective Mark Woolfe about the yellow Toyota they'd checked at 3pm the previous day – 15 minutes after Natalie had entered the bike track and been dragged through the fence.

At that time, of course, no one knew Natalie was in danger.

Woolfe checked the details on their running sheet. The car had no number plates, so the officers had taken details from the registration sticker on the windscreen.

Mark Woolfe ran a check on the vehicle, and within seconds the the registered owner was revealed to be Paul Charles Denyer.

Officers went to the block of flats at 186 Frankston-Dandenong Road but had to leave a card – notifying the resident of a police doorknock – as there was no one at home. About 90 minutes later, an unsuspecting Sharon Johnson did what the card requested, and rang to let the police know she was home.

Detectives Mick Hughes, Rod Wilson and Darren O'Loughlin and other officers returned to the flat. Sharon happened to be out the front at the letter box, so it was Paul Denyer himself who opened the front door.

The tall, overweight young man with a round face happily let the detectives inside when they announced they were conducting investigations into the murders of young women in the area.

Once inside the sparsely-furnished but messy flat he shared

with his girlfriend Sharon Johnson, Denyer calmly answered the detectives' questions about all his movements the previous day.

He told them he'd taken Sharon to work, called by a couple of wreckers yards to get spare car parts, and had coffee with his mother's boyfriend, Jim, because she wasn't home. He said his car had overheated twice: once in the Langwarrin Flora and Fauna Reserve and then again in Skye Road. The second time he realised he needed a screwdriver and some extra work to fix the problem, so he'd walked home to get them. He said he'd returned to get his car around 4pm.

He collected Sharon from work and spent the evening at her mother's place.

Detective Wilson asked the young man about the cuts and scratches on his hands. Denyer showed both sides of his hands – revealing scratches and nicks on his fingers and thumbs and a larger cut on the middle finger of his left hand. He'd hurt himself working on his car, he said.

Right from the start, Denyer was a strong suspect. He knew all about the murders of Natalie and Debbie – from the news, he said – but also happened to know exactly what he was doing at the times of their deaths.

The detectives, knowing most people don't recall such detail, especially after three weeks, invited Denyer down to Frankston police station for futher questioning.

For hours, Denyer denied involvement in the murders. Detective Senior Sergeant Rod Wilson and Senior Constable Mark Wolfe questioned their suspect again about everything he'd done the previous day. After a couple of hours they worked to establish what he knew about the deaths of Debbie Fream and Elizabeth Stevens. He knew a lot – all gleaned from the newspapers and TV, he claimed. But he also knew precisely where he had been when the women were killed.

The interview was suspended for coffee and toilet breaks. In the early hours of Sunday morning, it was halted again to wait for a police doctor to attend and take the blood and hair samples that Denyer had agreed to give.

During that break Denyer was accompanied to the toilet and then the kitchen by Detective Senior Constable Darren O'Loughlin. Denyer asked him if they had 'something DNA because they've asked for my blood and stuff'.

O'Loughlin said he didn't know.

'When they get the blood, will the DNA match?' Denyer asked.

'Again, I don't know Paul,' O'Loughlin said. 'You really should be asking Detective Senior Sergeant Wilson about all this.'

Denyer said: 'Okay, I killed all three of them.'

The astonished detective hurried Denyer back to the interview room. At 3.45am – in the presence of Rod Wilson and Darren O'Loughlin – the Frankston serial killer, Paul Charles Denyer, began his official viedotaped confession.

Wilson asked him to describe the murder of Elizabeth Stevens in his own words. Denyer stared downwards, then up at the camera, hesitating a full 20 seconds before beginning.

'I saw her get off the bus. I was walking across the road. Just something hit me straight in the head, you know, go! So I ran across the road in front of all these cars and got to the other side, where I followed her around the corner.

'I walked up behind her and stuck my left hand around her head right here, and then I dragged her into the front lawn, told her to shut up, and she just agreed to my terms. And I said, "Well, we're gonna take a walk." So we walked down on the road. A couple of cars drove past us and I held her hand to make it look like, you know, a couple, I suppose... so it wouldn't arouse any suspicion. Walked

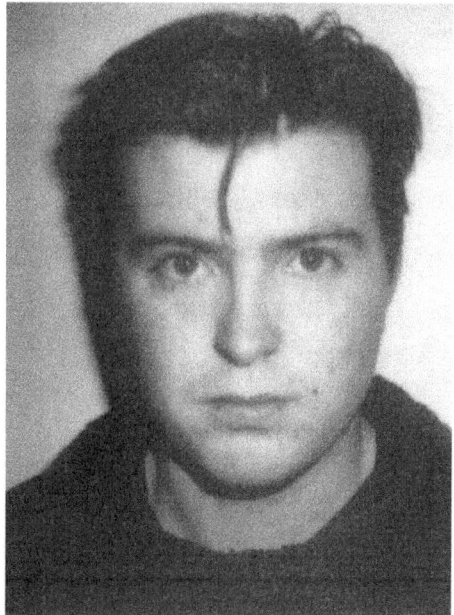

Paul Denyer

111

past two people on the footpath, a guy and a girl, and they just didn't take any notice.'

Wilson asked if Elizabeth had screamed or cried out.

'No, I told her I'd kill her if she did,' he said. Wilson nodded and Denyer added, a grin flashing across his face, 'With my fake gun.'

Using a street directory, Denyer showed the detectives where he had walked with Elizabeth Stevens and then he began describing her murder.

'Walked in a bit of bushland beside the main track in Lloyd Park. Sat there, you know, stood in the bushes for a while just – I can't remember, just standing there I suppose. Held the gun to the back of her neck, walked across the track over towards the other small sand hill or something. And on the other side of that hill, she asked me if she could, you know – could go to the toilet or – so to speak. So, I respected her privacy. So, I turned around and everything while she did it and everything.

'When she finished, we just walked down towards where the goal posts are, and we turned right and headed towards the area where she was found. Got to that area there and I started choking her with my hands and she passed out after a while. You know, the oxygen got cut off to her head and – and she just stopped. And then I pulled out the knife and stabbed her many times in the throat.

'And she was still alive. And then she stood up and then we walked around and all that, just walked around a few steps, and then I threw her on the ground and stuck my foot over her neck.'

Rod Wilson asked Denyer why he had stood on her neck and Denyer replied casually, as if it should have been obvious, 'Oh, to finish her off.'

His lack of emotion and casual manner was consistent throughout the entire confession.

He told the detectives that Elizabeth's body had begun shaking, then he demonstrated her final death shudders for the benefit of the video camera. He then described dragging the body to the creek bed where it was found.

Wilson knew that the injuries to Elizabeth Stevens were more extensive than those Denyer had admitted to and asked him about it. 'When the body of Elizabeth Stevens was found, it had a number of marks on the chest area and seven stab wounds around the breast. Do you know how they came to be there?'

Denyer said that he didn't remember.

'You don't remember? What do you mean by that? Could you have done this?'

'Possibly,' the young man conceded with a slight nod of his head.

Wilson wanted to establish the reason for the murder. So far Denyer seemed happy enough to talk about what he did, but the burning question was why.

'Can you tell me why you attacked her on that night? What led to it?'

Denyer considered. 'I just had... just the feeling, that's all.'

'What sort of feeling? Can you possibly describe it – where you had this feeling?'

'Just wanted... just wanted to kill.' Denyer looked down at the table in front of him.

Next, Denyer described his attack on Roszsa Toth and admitted that he would have killed her if she hadn't gotten away. After that, he had boarded a Frankston-bound train which took him from Seaford to Kananook – to search for another victim. Walking down McCulloch Avenue towards the milk bar on the corner, he had seen a woman pull up across the road in a grey Pulsar.

'What caused you to select her at the time?' asked Wilson.

'Just that *go* feeling. While she was in the milk bar, I walked up to the car and checked the driver's door and it was unlocked, so I opened the door and put my hand through and unlocked the back door. I hopped in the car and crouched down behind the seat and pulled out a gun that I had. Then I looked up out of the car window and I saw her in the milk bar. I crouched down and I could hear her footsteps coming closer to the car. And then she opened the door. The interior light went on and then she hopped in the car. She didn't see me in the back. And then she closed the door, you know, the light went out and everything and it was dark. And I waited for her to start up the car so no one could hear her scream or anything. And she put it into gear and she went to do a U-turn. And I startled her just as she was doing that turn and she kept going into the wall of the milk bar, which caused a dent on the bonnet. I told her to, you know, shut up or I'd blow her head off and all of that shit.'

Rod Wilson asked Denyer if he had noticed anything in the car when he had hopped in.

Denyer told him that he had seen the baby capsule in the back seat. Even if Debbie Fream hadn't told him, Paul Denyer would have had a pretty good idea that he was killing the mother of a young baby.

Denyer instructed Debbie Fream to drive towards Taylors Road. 'I told her when we got there that if she gave any signals to anyone, I'd blow her head off; I'd decorate the car with her brains.'

When they got to the remote location, Debbie had offered him her money and her car and that he had told her he didn't want either. He then told her to get out of the car. Denyer had tucked the fake gun down the front of his tracksuit pants and pulled a cord from his pocket.

'I popped it over her eyes real quickly so she didn't see it... 'cause I was gonna strangle her. But I didn't want her to see the cord first. I lifted the cord up and I said, "Can you see this?"'

'And she just put her hand up to grab it to feel it and when she did that I just yanked on it real quickly round her neck. And then I was struggling with her for about five minutes.'

'She was struggling?' asked Wilson.

'Yeah, until she started to faint a bit. And then when she was, you know, like weaker, I pulled my knife out of my sock then and started stabbing her around the neck and the chest several times.'

'You strangled her?' asked O'Loughlin. 'Is that the first thing that happened?'

'As she sort of weakened and fell onto the ground, that's when I stabbed her in the throat.'

'Once?'

'Many times and once in the stomach.'

'Where was she?' asked O'Loughlin.

'Lying on the ground.'

'Was she dead or alive when you stabbed her in the throat?'

'Almost dead.'

'So you stabbed her a number of times. And what happened then?' asked Rod Wilson

'She started breathing out of her neck, just like Elizabeth Stevens. I could just hear bubbling noises.'

'Did Debbie Fream put up any resistance?'

'Yeah, she put up quite a fight.'

'What happened after you stabbed her round the throat and chest area?'

'I lifted up her top and then ploughed the knife into her gut.'

The detectives knew that the top had a hole in it corresponding with the stab wound. Denyer hadn't lifted the top until the young mother was dead.

Wilson asked Denyer why and he replied that he wasn't sure.

'You lifted the top to do that?' asked O'Loughlin.

'Yeah,' Denyer affirmed.

'Do you know why you lifted her top?'

'I wanted to see how big her boobs were,' said Denyer.

'Beg your pardon?' asked O'Loughlin, taken aback.

'I wanted to see how big her boobs were,' he repeated.

'Was that part of the fantasy?' pressed O'Loughlin, trying to keep any hint of disgust from creeping into his voice.

'I don't know.'

'You actually recall thinking that way?'

'Sort of,' Denyer replied, 'and I saw her bare stomach so I just lunged at her with the knife.'

The rest of the confession detailed the most recent murder – that of Year 12 student Natalie Russell less than 48 hours earlier.

Denyer explained how he had cut three holes, that he could fit through, in the cyclone wire fence on the bike path earlier that day – in between shopping for car parts and having a coffee with Jim at his mum's place.

Just before 2.30pm he drove back to Skye Road to wait for a

victim. Twenty minutes later he spotted Natalie and, guessing which route she would take, he entered the track ahead of her and climbed through one of his holes.

Natalie didn't see him until she'd walked past his hiding place and he re-emerged onto the track. He stayed about 10 metres behind her until she drew near the second hole.

'I walked up behind her and stuck my left hand around her mouth and held the knife to her throat; and that's where that cut happened. I cut that on my own blade. Dragged her through the hole in the fence.'

'Was she struggling?'

'At first, but then she sort of stopped.'

'Why?'

'Because I told her I was gonna cut her throat. I said I was gonna, yeah, cut her throat... and I dragged her into the trees.

And 'like she offered, she said, "Oh, you can have sex with me if you want." She goes, "You can have all my money, have sex with me," and things – just said disgusting things like that really.'

It was the only time during the many hours of interviewing that Denyer showed any emotion. His anger and disgust at Natalie Russell was obvious.

It was equally obvious to the detectives that Denyer had no idea that Natalie had been begging for her life. She must have realised she was in the hands of the serial killer whose deeds had been splashed so extensively through the media.

She'd been willing to do anything to save her life.

But Denyer completely failed to see that.

'Did that upset you?' Wilson asked, surprised by Denyer's sudden outburst.

'In a way.' The killer's anger quickly subsided and his voice became even again. 'I got her to kneel down in front of me and I held the knife blade over her eye, really closely, and yeah, she had the same colour eyes as I have.'

'Why did you hold that knife so close to her eye for?'

'Just so she could see the blade.'

'And why was she kneeling?'

'No, she was lying on the ground at that stage and I was lying on top of her. I wasn't lying, I was kneeling on top of her. Just holding her by the throat and with the knife next to her eye. And she struggled and then the knife cut her on the face. And she was bleeding a bit then... yeah, and then when she got up, she started to scream a bit. And I just said, "Shut up. Shut up. Shut up. Shut up." And, "If you don't shut up, I'll kill you. If you don't do this I'll kill you, if you don't do that." And she said, "What do you want from me?" I said, "All I want you to do is shut up."'

'And so when she was kneeling on the ground, I put the strap around her neck to strangle her and it broke in half. And then she started violently struggling for about a minute until I pushed – got her onto her back again – and pushed her head back like this and cut her throat.'

Denyer mimicked Natalie Russell's last moments as he described his attack on her. But his description of what he did to the dying schoolgirl shocked the detectives.

'I cut a small cut at first and then she was bleeding. And then I stuck my fingers into her throat and grabbed her cords and I twisted them... my whole fingers – like, that much of my hand was inside her throat.' Denyer held up his own hand and indicated.

'Do you know why you did that?' asked Wilson.

'Stop her from breathing... and then she slowly stopped. She sort of started to faint and then when she was weak, a bit weaker, I grabbed the opportunity of throwing her head back and one big large cut which sort of cut almost her whole head off. And then she slowly died.'

'Why did you want to kill her?' asked Wilson rubbing his forehead.

'Just same reason as before, just everything came back through my mind again. I kicked her before I left.'

'Why's that?'

'While she was dead, just booted her.'

'Why did you kick her after? Like she was obviously dead at that stage.'

'Make sure she was dead.'

'Kicking her, would that make sure she was dead?'

'Well, if she had've moved, I would've known.'

Having satisfied his lust for blood, Denyer described how he had stuck his bloodied hands in his pockets and walked to the end of the track. Coming out onto Skye Road, he saw something that made him stop: two uniformed police officers were checking his car.

Denyer merely ducked his head, turned right and walked down Skye Road towards his home.

Wilson asked Denyer if there was anything else he would like to talk to them about.

'Yeah, I slashed her across the face.'

'Who's that?' asked Wilson.

'The last victim.'

'What do you mean you slashed her across the face?'

'After she was dead.'

'After she was dead?'

'Yeah, I just cut her straight down this side of her face.'

'Why was that?' asked Wilson.

He shrugged. 'Don't know.'

Paul Charles Denyer after his arrest for the murders of Elizabeth Stevens, Debbie Fream and Natalie Russell.

On Wednesday 15 December 1993, five months after his arrest, Paul Denyer fronted court, pleading guilty to all three murders as well as to the abduction of Roszsa Toth.

Denyer had initially been charged with the attempted murder of Roszsa Toth, but had refused to plead guilty.

A clinical psychologist, Ian Joblin examined Denyer for a number of hours in prison. In his view, Denyer appeared to be without remorse and even enjoyed talking about his crimes, seemingly getting a vicarious pleasure recounting his atrocities.

Joblin told the court that Paul Denyer was a rare breed of serial killer; one who committed his murders at random with no motive which made him the most dangerous type of criminal known to our society. The psychologist said Denyer had a cruel and demeaning nature and had exhibited aggressive behaviour since childhood; he seemed amused by the suffering that he had inflicted.

In his opinion, Denyer was a sadist whose pleasure and satisfaction after each murder dissipated quickly so that he would again feel the desire to kill. There was no effective treatment for such a sadistic personality.

When all the evidence had been heard, the prosecutor told Justice Frank Vincent that Paul Denyer should be given a life sentence with no minimum term for the despicable murders he had committed. He said that Denyer hated women and was a danger to the community.

'He is sadistic, he's a killer; he's not insane. He has a gross or severe personality disorder. The prognosis is poor,' he said.

Despite all the evidence, Sean Cash, appearing for Paul Denyer, urged Justice Vincent to impose a minimum sentence that wasn't inordinately long. Cash stressed how Denyer had pleaded guilty and saved the victims' families the ordeal of giving evidence. Denyer was a young man, he said, and should be given the chance to rehabilitate himself.

With most of the court room overtly hostile to the 21-year-old killer, many shook their head in disbelief when the lawyer said that not only was the case sad for the families, but it was sad for Denyer as well.

'It is fair to say,' said Cash, 'he'd give anything as he sits there now to be normal. He doesn't only deserve punishment, he needs understanding and compassion and a chance to rehabilitate.'

There was more than one person in the courtroom who thought the killer deserved nothing more than a hangman's rope.

At the end of the trial, Justice Vincent sentenced Denyer to life terms for each of the murders and an additional eight years for the abduction of Roszsa Toth. The sentences, he said, would run concurrently.

Emotion was evident in Justice Vincent's voice as he concluded, 'I do not consider that it would be appropriate to fix a non-parole period in your case. The apprehension you have caused to thousands of women in the community will be felt for a long time. For many, you are the fear that quickens their step as they walk home, or causes a parent to look anxiously at the clock when a child is late.'

After the sentencing, Paul Denyer's lawyer told the court that his client wished to make a statement. There was an immediate barrage of booing from the onlookers in the court. Natalie Russell's aunt, Bernadette Naughton stood up in the crowded courtroom and said, 'Let him speak if he chooses; it is his right.'

She looked at Justice Vincent who, after deliberating for a moment, nodded in agreement.

From the dock, Paul Denyer turned to the families of his victims and said, 'I'm truly sorry for what's happened. I'll do my sentence and I will become a better person and I will not re-offend. That's my promise to God and to the people of Melbourne.'

On New Year's Eve 1993, Denyer's solicitor lodged an appeal against the severity of Denyer's sentence. He was granted a hearing,

On Friday 29 July 1994 – one day before the anniversary of the day he killed Natalie Russell – Paul Charles Denyer was granted a 30-year non-parole period on a majority verdict.

In 2004, Denyer hit the headlines again. This time it was because he wanted to change his name to Paula and have a sex change operation. He was pictured in prison with his shoulder-length hair in pigtails.

His request was denied.

In April 2012, Denyer was investigated for four prison rapes, reportedly offering a massage to several prisoners before allegedly assaulting them. The inmates targeted were reported to have intellectual disabilities.

In 2013 he made the newspaper again, pictured flouting prison rules not to wear women's clothing.

Fast forward to this year, 2019, and Paul Denyer's 30-year non-parole period is nearly up.

This story continues, both out there in the real world and in the later pages of this book; as does the community's fight to keep the Frankston serial killer, Paul Charles Denyer, in jail.

My 30th birthday. My cake cutting assistant was Natalie Russell's aunt, Bernadette Naughton.

9

THE BESTSELLER

After having quick and easy publishing success with my first two books, I had no idea that getting a publisher was usually quite hard. For my first two books, I had sent off my proposals and within a couple of days a publisher had rung me and accepted my books. This did not happen with *The Frankston Murders*. Every publisher who responded said they weren't interested.

I didn't understand how they couldn't be! This was a huge story.

Being a writer means that life throws you learning opportunities all the time. Sometimes these moments are disguised as moments of anguish or despair, other times it's frustration and irritation, but once you get up and shake yourself off, you get on with things.

When the world says no, you have to find the pathway to yes.

I'd met crime journalist John Silvester a few times while visiting the Homicide Squad. We got chatting one night – at the squad's Cup Eve Ball – and I told him how I couldn't get a publisher for *Frankston*. He suggested I do it myself. He and Andrew Rule published their own books. It was easy, he said.

John told me to get in touch with Andrew, who was helpful and generous with his time. I followed all their suggestions, enlisted the help of the professionals who had worked on my previous book and paid the same editor and designer to do what they did best.

Then I set about bringing my third book to life. I took out a big bank loan, knowing I'd have to sell 2300 books just to break even. It was a calculated risk because my first two books had both sold about 3000, and I figured the Frankston story had a much higher profile.

The Frankston Murders was a runaway success. It sold 5000 copies in the first three weeks of its release. Shirley Hardy-Rix did the publicity again. The book launch was covered in the top stories on all of the major TV evening news shows. I'd never seen that before for a book launch. Reporters used the angle that families of the victims hoped the new book would keep Denyer in jail forever.

One of the best moments came when the book, which had only been out for a fortnight, made it into *The Age* newspaper's top five sellers for the week – in the same week I got a rejection letter from a major publishing company saying something like: 'we don't publish that kind of book, but we wish you all the best in finding a publisher who will'.

The huge sales figures of *The Frankston Murders* meant that publishers were wrong to think it wouldn't sell. How could they think that people would read about a case on the front page of every newspaper for months but not be interested in a book-length account of the story? It wasn't the first time that my ideas about what the public wanted to read would be at odds with the beliefs of publishing professionals.

I never doubted the book for a second. And I was right. It quickly became a bestseller. This meant I had written three books and my first bestseller before I turned 30.

After writing 95,000 words in six months, then setting up my own publishing company – all while working full time – I was exhausted. I retreated back into the comfort of my day job. It provided a haven from the brutality of writing in the genre I'd chosen. There's something very grounding about spending your days in a primary school. I kept in touch with Bernadette Naughton and she would often pop around for a cuppa or ring for a chat. I have photos of my 30th birthday where Bernadette is helping me cut my cake. She taught me that connections made during the telling of true crime stories didn't end once the book was published. We remained close for the rest of her life. When she was diagnosed with a cancer she knew would kill her, she rang me to ask if I would write her resignation letter for her since, she said, I had a way with words.

We sat together and composed the letter. While Bernadette loved life and her family, I think she was resigned to her fate and looked forward to being reunited with her twin brother, Mick, who'd died on their 50th birthday of a heart attack; and, of course, she would get to see her beloved Natalie again in the Great Beyond.

Months later, as I sat through her funeral, I imagined her with Mick and Nat strolling through Heaven. She was only 54.

The success of *The Frankston Murders* had an adverse flow-on effect. My own bestseller created a hurdle for me. The market was suddenly flooded with 'local' true crime books, many written by journalists who covered the cases for their newspapers then put a book out as soon as the jury said: *guilty*.

My full-time job meant I couldn't attend trials or be free to interview people, except when I was on school holidays. And no

The 1995 book launch of *The Frankston Murders*.
Chief Superintendent John Balloch and I talk to my daughter, Stacy.
On the right, Natalie Russell's aunt, Bernadette Naughton.

one was scheduling trials for a school teacher. My best recourse was to write stories about cases that hadn't made the headlines; to find the ones that slipped through the cracks. And conversely, by chasing cases that weren't well-known, I could make them better-known.

I thought about writing short stories for a collection again. They were easier and more finite than a book like Frankston had been. I started by ringing the head of the Victoria Police Child Exploitation Squad, Senior Sergeant Chris O'Connor. It took just one conversation to realise that this subject needed a whole book, not just a short story.

Even though I'd written about child sexual abuse, with the story of Wendy O'Shea's Gemma in my second book, there was so much I didn't know about the subject. I felt this was something I *should* have known because I worked full-time as a teacher. How much did my lack of knowledge hinder my ability to protect the children in my care?

When one of my primary school students did a modelling job, she proudly brought the catalogue to school for show and tell. I was horrified when Chris O'Connor told me some paedophiles used catalogue pictures of children wearing underwear as a form of pornography.

I also learnt that most child victims were abused by people who knew them – which challenged the Stranger Danger programs which were taught in primary schools in the 1990s. Most sexual assaults against children were by someone known to the family: relatives, friend of the family, teachers, community and sports group members, or neighbours. In fact, only 6% of children in the compiling of statistics from the Child Exploitation Squad were victims of strangers.

Over half the offences against child victims were committed in the home of the offender and 13% in the home of the victim. This meant parents were delivering their children to the homes of offenders or letting them in the front door. Parents were trusting the wrong people.

Luckily Chris O'Connor thought there needed to be a book on

this subject too. The result was *Rockspider* – perhaps one of the most important books I've written. It wasn't a huge seller, but I thought if it helped even one person, or alerted one adult, it would be worth it.

I became hyper-aware at school. I was teaching at a school that ran regular protective behaviours programs, in which we had children disclose abuse. I made sure I gave my students opportunities to share their stories through journal writing.

More than once, I sat opposite distraught mothers who thought I needed to know their child had been abused. I was never surprised when they told me it was an uncle or a father. Once you do the research I have, you can never again hide in blissful ignorance.

One mother told me that her ex-husband had sexually abused her three children. She left him the moment one of them disclosed the abuse. You'd think fleeing to safety would protect the children. But it didn't. The child in my class was 8 years old – an age the police had judged too young to be able to give credible evidence in court. The mother told me all of this with an attitude of hopelessness. Her latest fight was to deny him access to the children he was sexually abusing.

Maybe I overstepped my role as a teacher, but I knew too much to remain silent. 'Your child might be too young *now*,' I said, 'but you should know the police will still take a statement from them next year, or the year after.'

It was a point that both parents and offenders often overlooked. The kids might be young and vulnerable *now*, but every year that passes gives them maturity and a voice. Parent teacher interviews like this were defining moments. I had written *Rockspider* because I wanted the knowledge to help children. I had a voice.

A surprising side effect of writing *Rockspider* was that friends who had never spoken about being sexually abused, offered me their story. The #MeToo campaign of 2017 would later echo this phenomenon. When people knew they had a sympathetic listener, and most importantly, someone who believed them, they told me things they had told few others.

In the end, I concluded that the complexities of child sexual abuse – or any sexual abuse for that matter – are veiled in secrecy. And it seemed to me that the secrecy was almost as damaging as the abuse. I tested this theory with Derryn Hinch, then a well-known journalist with a huge following who went to jail because he revealed the name of a paedophile on his radio show.

Derryn had always been willing to discuss an incident that happened in his childhood when he was sexually assaulted. He saw sharing his story as a way to open the dialogue around sexual abuse. He was also candid about not suffering any long-term damage from what happened to him.

Derryn's sexual assault occurred when he was a child. His parents hosted a neighbourhood get-together. One of the neighbours brought her brother who was visiting from overseas. The man came into the bedroom Derryn shared with his brother and sexually assaulted him. As soon as the man left the room, Derryn's brother raised the alarm. Within minutes, the neighbourhood dads were out the front yard 'teaching the man a lesson' while Derryn sat in the kitchen with all the mothers of the neighbourhood drinking hot cocoa and being told it wasn't his fault.

I asked Derryn if his lack of damage afterwards might have been because within minutes of the assault, every significant adult in his life knew about it, offered him sympathy and told him it wasn't his fault. He had never thought of it like that, but agreed this might have been the reason.

Keeping silent about what happened, is damaging. Think about it this way: if your house was broken into, you would tell all your friends and receive immediate sympathy as you talk out your trauma. Others tell you their stories of burglary: *that happened to my mother-in-law too...* and you don't feel alone in your experience. If you are a victim of a sexual assault or one of your children is targeted, you don't tell all your friends. You don't receive sympathy. You don't receive support. Your damage remains hidden.

While writing *Rockspider*, I often wondered what made the topic off-limits. Why don't we openly share stories of sexual assault? Is it the 'sex' part of sexual assault that makes the subject taboo? Perhaps. When you think about it, sex crimes are the only crimes where the victim is routinely blamed or questioned about their role in the assault: *What were you wearing? Why were you out late at night? How much had you had to drink?*

Think about how silly these questions would be in the context of a house burglary: Did you leave your door unlocked? Did you expect to have fancy stuff and people not break in? Your house is nice; what did you expect?

And if your house is burgled, you don't feel guilty afterwards. But most parents of victims feel guilty because they didn't protect their children. They feel guilty because they were duped by an offender who probably groomed *them* as well as their children.

The complexities around this topic swirled in my mind, round and round, and have never really stopped.

From a serial killer to paedophiles. I'm not sure which book was the hardest to write, but for both of them, I had to find reserves of strength to process information that most people never have to deal with, and then tell a story that would do justice to those who had entrusted it to me.

Once again, the story was the master I served. And every time I had to sit in one of the interview rooms at the squad's headquarters in the old St Kilda Rd police complex, surrounded by sickening child pornography or witness statements that made me want to weep, I had to stay tough for the sake of the story.

Father Gerald Ridsdale pictured with a group
of First Communicants, circa 1963.

10

A Monstrous Betrayal of Trust

In 1976 a young boy, Matthew – not his real name – began his first year of high school at a Catholic college in a small Victorian country town. At the same time Matthew started at the school, a new priest joined the parish. His name was Gerald Ridsdale. In no time at all, Father Ridsdale had shortened the Gerald to Gerry and impressed those who met him with his easy-going style.

Between February and September 1976, Ridsdale would go out of his way to talk to Matthew and give him lollies – especially Pascall Chocolate Eclairs, which the boy loved. The priest took Matthew out on drives in his car. Occasionally, he even let the young boy steer.

Sometime in October, Ridsdale began getting overly affectionate towards Matthew. It started with hugging but then he would hug him from behind and rub himself against the young boy; stuff a priest shouldn't do. Nonetheless it took about five of these hugs before Matthew began to suspect they were inappropriate. Matthew could feel the priest's erect penis pressing against his back and when he tried to get away, Ridsdale enveloped him with his big arms and the boy couldn't move.

And then Ridsdale began asking Matthew to do odd jobs around the presbytery. Matthew's mum encouraged him. 'You should always help the priests,' she would say. But strangely, there never seemed to be any jobs. Matthew was led over to the presbytery, Ridsdale would lock the door, and the boy would simply play pool, watch television, or play on an old typewriter. The first couple of times that Ridsdale locked the door, Matthew thought nothing of it. He trusted his priest – why wouldn't he? But he became uneasy and frightened when Ridsdale started showing him magazines depicting men having sex with each other. He brought out the magazines every time Matthew came to the presbytery. Then the fondling began. And Matthew was trapped.

Detective: Do you recall if you ever had any pornographic magazines?

Ridsdale: No.

Detective: You never had any even mild magazines that could appear to a youth to be pornographic but maybe to an adult they might be–

Ridsdale: No, I don't. Unless there was a Pix or Post, but certainly no – nothing that I'd call pornographic.

Detective: He describes the magazines as being of homosexual men performing sexual acts together. Men were having either oral or anal sex.

Ridsdale: No.

Detective: Do you recall any magazines of that type?

Ridsdale: No, no I haven't had those. No.

One day in October, Ridsdale came into Matthew's classroom and asked Sister Francis, the nun teaching the class, if he could take a child to the presbytery to give him a hand with some odd jobs. Sister Francis told him to choose, and he chose Matthew.

Over in the presbytery, Ridsdale locked the door again and led Matthew into his bedroom. The priest undid Matthew's fly and began to masturbate the frightened little boy. Then he undid his own trousers and beckoned for Matthew to masturbate him. He refused.

Ridsdale reached for a jar of Vaseline on his bedside table and smeared the gel over both of them. The priest ejaculated. The young boy didn't. A quick wipe with a towel, and Ridsdale drove Matthew home. Nothing was said and Matthew didn't tell anyone. He barely understood what had happened.

Trips to the presbytery for 'odd jobs' happened on a weekly basis – sometimes more than once a week. Month after month, Sister Francis sent Matthew off with the paedophile priest. And

Matthew was molested on a regular basis. It usually began with a drink of Coke and Pascall Chocolate Eclairs on the couch. Ridsdale would sit beside Matthew, show him the magazines and then the molestation would begin.

Detective: In relation to Matthew?
Ridsdale: Yes, I remember Matthew.
Detective: What's your reaction to his name?
Ridsdale: Well, reaction to his name is I'm guilty. That's guilty with Matthew that I had some sexual contact with Matthew. From memory at the presbytery and at his home, and it would have been touchy. I'm not sure whether it had been mutual handling of the penis, but certainly a touching of the penis. It would have been on a few occasions, I'd say.

Just before Christmas, Ridsdale approached Matthew after Mass and asked him to come to the presbytery to help with some odd jobs. Matthew said he didn't want to but his mum said, 'You should always help the priests'.

At the presbytery, Ridsdale showed him the magazines and Matthew said it was sinful.

'Don't worry, it's all right,' the priest said. And he should know.

In Ridsdale's double bed, the boy and the priest lay naked together. The bed had been prepared earlier. The covers were pulled back and there was a towel covering the sheets. Ridsdale had turned on the heater before Mass to warm the room. Matthew said he didn't like being there. Ridsdale licked the boy and then opened the jar of Vaseline. When the priest penetrated him, the boy yelled in pain and begged him to stop. Ridsdale did stop – but only to position the child on his hands and knees. Ridsdale told Matthew to relax. The boy screamed with excruciating pain as he was raped.

'Did you enjoy that?' asked the priest.

'No!'

Consent meant nothing to the priest, and the feelings of his victims even less. Ridsdale got dressed and pretended nothing had happened. Matthew was in pain for days afterwards. He didn't tell his mum and dad because he was scared that he might get into trouble.

Detective: Did you have anal penetration with Matthew?

Ridsdale: No. I deny that I've ever done that... it's something I never thought possible for an adult, until I'd read about it, an adult to have anal intercourse with a child without doing a lot of physical damage and I wouldn't even attempt that. I know it sounds naive that I didn't know it but it's only recently – or in later years that I found out from cases that it was possible. So I can definitely say that is not true... rubbing – rubbing and physical – yes, yes. And the Vaseline and rubbing of a penis. But certainly not any penetration.

On Christmas day, the following week, Ridsdale was a guest at the table of Matthew's parents. After lunch he asked to take Matthew for a drive – ostensibly to a farm to check on some sheep. Even the priest's car was equipped with Vaseline and a clean-up towel. Afterwards he thought he could placate his victim with a packet of chocolate eclairs. Ridsdale dropped him home, said hi to his mum and dad and then left.

Detective: Tell me in your own words what happened.

Ridsdale: Well as far as I can remember, it sounds true that I would have pulled up and had a look to see if there was anybody around, and then got talking about penises or something or other...maybe it was like that, where I talked about or laughed about pubic hairs and mine being – what's he say – grey or something? And then remember him jokingly telling me he only had one testicle and I said, 'Give us a feel.'
And I felt his scrotum and his testicle and I think then I probably would have said, 'Well, look, I've

got two – you feel mine.' I probably joked about them because I think they're a bit over-sized. But I can't – I have no recollection of masturbation or ejaculation.

Two weeks later, Ridsdale invited Matthew to do odd jobs at the presbytery. Matthew couldn't refuse because the priest would simply ask his parents and he would have to go anyway. This time, Ridsdale ran the shower. Matthew told him he didn't need a shower but Ridsdale was a man and he was a boy and he was not strong enough or old enough to resist effectively. Matthew was petrified. He didn't want to shower with a naked priest and he knew what was going to happen – the same thing that always happened. And part of him thought, *the sooner I do it, the sooner it's over and I can go home*. And so he did.

A couple of weeks later, Ridsdale arrived at Matthew's house with another boy and asked Matthew to come over to the presbytery. Matthew thought he couldn't possibly do anything with the other boy there. Matthew was wrong again. The boys were both shown the magazines and Matthew realised that the other boy must have been abused too because he didn't look surprised or resist much. Ridsdale fondled them while they flicked mechanically through the magazines. Then he turned on the shower. The priest and the two young boys showered and Ridsdale fondled them and got them to touch him and said, 'Oh, that feels good.' The boys remained silent.

The abuse continued once or twice a week for over a year. Years later, in court, the charges against Gerald Ridsdale for the sexual abuse of Matthew totalled 14 indecent assaults. He got the hundreds of others for free.

On 19 August 1992, Victoria Police held their annual Operation Paradox – a phone-in encouraging victims of sexual abuse to come forward and report their abusers. Among the callers were a number of young men who made complaints about Father Gerald Ridsdale. Months of investigation followed. Ridsdale was arrested on 4 February 1993. He made frank – if not full – admissions about his abuse of young children in his parishes. There were 11 victims including two unknown boys. Ridsdale was released on bail to appear in the Melbourne Magistrates Court on 2 April 1993.

On 17 February, Ridsdale was again arrested. More victims had come forward. This time, Ridsdale was less forthcoming. He said that he required time to think about any further allegations, and he was released.

On 25 February, Ridsdale was arrested for the third time in as many weeks. Three more victims added to his already considerable number of charges.

Investigating officers added the following comment to the bulging police brief:

The Defendant stated that as these offences were committed so long ago, he had a lot of trouble remembering each specific offence. The defendant stated that at the time of these offences he had an ongoing problem. The defendant stated that he had no other reason for committing these offences other than the problem he had. The defendant gave the same explanation for each offence.

In May 1993 at the Melbourne Magistrates Court, Father Gerald Ridsdale was convicted of sexual assault on eight young victims. He got two years and three months – the two years was suspended and he served three months.

Three months.

Three months in prison for all the broken boys he left behind. After his sentencing and the ensuing publicity, other victims began surfacing.

Another victim of Gerald Ridsdale – let's call him Adam – made a statement. Adam was 12 years old when he was sexually molested on a weekly basis by the priest.

'Father Ridsdale's arrival [at the parish] opened communication channels making the presbytery more attractive to youths who would attend for frequent gaming activities and similar arrangement.' Adam later wrote in his statement.

'I felt overwhelmed by Father Ridsdale who was fairly

demanding in his own right. He knew how to put people in their own place and his position of authority placed me at a compromise psychologically. My parents encouraged me to assist him in any way possible in his capacity as the local priest because of their high regard for the church.'

Adam's brother was also molested by Gerald Ridsdale. He later told police: 'There was one other thing that I can remember about that priest. Whenever I saw him, he would make this face by screwing his face up like a pig face. He would squeeze his nose and eyes up. When the priest made this pig nose, I knew I had to keep quiet about "our secret".'

Then another boy named Morris made a statement. He was 15 years old and a member of the parish prayer group led by Ridsdale when the molestation occurred. Morris's parents had moved to another town mid-year and Morris stayed with a local family while he finished out the school year. With absent parents, Morris quickly became a target for the resident paedophile priest.

Ridsdale asked Morris to go away with him and some other boys for 10 days. Morris was keen – he had no reason not to be – and his parents gave permission. Ridsdale organised to pick him up on Sunday to begin the long drive. But then the priest rang to change the plans. One of his parishioners had died and he had to perform the funeral service in a nearby town on Monday. He arranged to pick Morris up on Sunday and he could stay at the presbytery that night, help with the funeral and then they could all set off Monday afternoon.

Morris slept in a spare bedroom at the presbytery. In the middle of the night, he was awakened. It was Ridsdale and he had his hands under the blankets fondling the teenager. When the priest sensed the boy was awake, he stopped and left the room. Morris cried all night and didn't know what to do. Nothing was said at breakfast. It was as if it never happened.

When the boys arrived at their camp, they were allocated beds in Ridsdale's dugout. There were two double beds and a single. The three other boys were allocated the single and double. Morris, said Ridsdale, could share the other double bed with him. After what happened the previous night, the boy was terrified.

Once again, Morris was woken in the middle of the night. The priest was almost lying on top of him pressing against the frightened boy. Morris pushed him away and Ridsdale rolled over and masturbated – but not for long. He grabbed Morris and performed oral sex on him. Morris struggled violently. The other boys were sleeping only metres away. The priest released him and masturbated himself to ejaculation.

In town the next day, Morris saw a public telephone. He desperately wanted to ring his mum but he didn't have any words to describe what had happened.

That night, Father Ridsdale again forced himself on Morris who repeated his successful struggle. This time, the priest masturbated and ejaculated on the sleeve of Morris's pyjama top. With the priest's semen on his sleeve all night, Morris was sickened beyond belief.

Towards the end of the trip, Father Ridsdale attempted to anally rape Morris who again struggled and made enough noise that he might wake the others. So the priest stopped.

In the car, on the long drive back, the priest said he was sorry.

Once away from Ridsdale, Morris started to receive love letters. 'I'm in love with you... I know I shouldn't be having these thoughts because I'm a priest... Sorry...' He also sent gifts – and a copy of his will – naming Morris as a beneficiary.

Morris didn't see Ridsdale for two years and then he arrived unannounced to apologise again. The priest had a small boy with him at the time.

During Ridsdale's trial on the new charges, Judge Dee heard the evidence, read the police statements, read the victim impact statements and then it was time for the sentencing. And he didn't pull any punches. He listed in clusters the charges against the 60-year-old priest and then read them aloud directing them towards the predatory paedophile.

'Gerald Francis Ridsdale, you have pleaded guilty to 30 counts of indecent sexual assault upon a male person under the age of 16 years, five counts of buggery, four counts of gross indecency, one count of attempted buggery, one count of indecent assault upon a girl under 16 years, and five counts of indecent assault. That was a total of 46 offences involving 21 victims – 20 boys and one girl all under the age of 16.

These offences spanned a period of 21 years between 1961 and 1982 upon children aged between nine and 15. During this entire period, you were a priest of the Roman Catholic Church and the offences were committed whilst you were positioned at churches throughout the Western District in Bendigo, and Swan Hill areas and later on in Melbourne.

In general the offences took the form of intimate fondling, mutual masturbation, anal penetration, and oral sex. At the present time, many of the offences would be described differently. You must of course be considered as committing the offences which existed at the time and with the penalties that were applicable. The victims of your crimes were members of your parish. Your usual method of operation was to press upon young boys many of whom were altar boys at the various churches where you were positioned. By reason of your respected status as priest you were trusted by the parents of many children and so under cover of that trust you were able to lure the children to places of privacy where you were able to perpetrate these crimes. You were also by virtue of that privileged position, able to enjoy the exercise of power over the children. Of the counts themselves, many of the offences occurred against a particular victim so frequently that certain of the counts are representative of crimes of an ongoing type rather than being a count involving a single criminal act.'

And then the judge listed the litany of abuse which had wreaked havoc on so many lives.

Counts 1 and 2 involved Morris. Ridsdale befriended his mother and with her permission, took him away for a week-long fishing trip. 'During the course of the holiday, you persuaded the boy to sleep in a double bed where mutual masturbation occurred.'

Count 3 involved an altar boy. Ridsdale was his parish priest and developed a good relationship with his family. The priest persuaded his parents to let him take the boy camping. 'You fondled the boy's penis. When he resisted, you became angry and took him to confession.'

Counts 4, 5 and 6 involved an 11-year-old boy. Once again, Ridsdale befriended the parents who were devout Catholics. Under the pretext of visiting other churches, Ridsdale took him driving in his car. 'The boy was allowed to steer the car during which time you masturbated him telling him to keep it secret.'

Counts 7, 10, 13 and 14 involved a 12-year-old altar boy. When Ridsdale moved parishes, he persuaded his parents to let him come and stay at the new presbytery. 'At the presbytery, you slept with the boy, performed oral sex upon him and penetrated his anus with your penis.'

Counts 8 and 9 involved another altar boy. 'You became known to his parents and were welcomed into their house.' The counts represented a range of offences including oral sex and masturbation.

Counts 11 and 12 involved a 12-year-old altar boy. Ridsdale gave him a lift home from church and fondled his penis. Ridsdale had repeated the offence. 'On the second occasion, you gave him a piece of sacramental bread as a reward.'

Counts 16 and 17 occurred when Ridsdale took two boys fishing and looking for gemstones. He targeted one of the boys. 'You organised for him to share your bed at the presbytery and on two nights, you masturbated yourself and the boy in bed.'

Count 18 involved a 10-year-old boy. Ridsdale befriended his parents and recruited him as an altar boy. 'On occasions you would take him driving around the area to celebrate Sunday Evening Mass during which journeys, you would touch him on the genitals.'

Counts 19, 20, 25, 26 and 27 involved a 12-year-old boy and his 10-year-old sister who had lost their father in a tragic accident: 'Following the boy's father's death, you took the boy and his sister aged 10 years to the presbytery for a few days. At the graveside, at the father's funeral, you persuaded the grieving widow to allow you to take the two children away so they might cope better with the tragedy of their father's death. You only did this so that you could perform oral sex and masturbate the boy on a number of occasions. You also indecently assaulted the girl at the presbytery the night of the funeral. The girl had seen her father die in an accident some four days earlier. She sat on your knee at your suggestion. You proceeded to touch the child's chest under her clothes and played on the outside of her vagina for about 30 minutes. Only that day you had presided at the grave side of the young girl's father.'

Counts 21 and 22 involved a 12-year-old altar boy. The boy's family befriended the priest and their son stayed overnight at the presbytery. 'There you performed oral sex upon him and masturbated him and attempted oral intercourse with your penis. You ceased the latter act when the boy yelled you were hurting. You insisted he not tell his mother of your activities.'

Counts 23 and 24 involved a 14-year-old boy Ridsdale met through the church. 'During a car trip, you masturbated him. Count 24 involved you taking the boy's pants down at the presbytery and penetrating his anus with your penis.'

Counts 28, 29 and 30 involved another altar boy. 'He was persuaded to go gold fossicking with you during which trip you touched him around the groin area and tried to kiss him.' On another occasion, Ridsdale took the boy to the presbytery after mass and molested him.

Counts 31 and 32 involved a 14-year-old boy. 'Offences of indecent assault and buggery occurred when you were parish priest at [the parish]. This boy came to see you about a personal sexual problem he was experiencing and troubling him. At that time the boy was confused and distressed about his own sexuality. He was extremely vulnerable at the time. He went to the presbytery and whilst explaining his difficulties, you took advantage and indecently assaulted him. The boy had buggery committed upon him by you in a toilet block...'

Counts 33 and 34 involved a 14-year-old boy who Ridsdale anally raped on a regular basis for over a year. When he first made statements to police, he was too embarrassed to speak of the acts of buggery you perpetrated on him.

Count 42 involved a 10-year-old boy who Ridsdale masturbated in a toilet block.

Counts 41 and 43 involved a 10-year-old boy who Ridsdale indecently assaulted. 'You grabbed him on the genitals outside his clothing.'

Counts 44 and 45 involved a 10-year-old altar boy. 'You masturbated him a number of times in the presbytery.'

Counts 37, 38, 39, 40 and 46 involved a boy who was 12 years old when the assaults began. They lasted for two and a half years.

And so Judge Dee came to the end of the charges. But his condemnation was by no means finished.

'The foregoing represents the briefest of summaries of sexual offences committed by you over a period of some 21 years against 21 young victims. You were at all times as a Catholic

Convicted pedophileand former Catholic priest Gerald Ridsdale leaves the Melbourne Magistrates Court, on June 4 2002.

Priest in a position of trust. Under the cover of your clergy you inveigled yourself into the trust of your victims and in a substantial number of cases the trust of their families. As a priest you held a privileged and trusted position and as such were able to use that position to lure your victims to secluded places in many cases to be with you overnight over significant periods of time. Nobody else comes to mind but a priest such as you were could achieve that trust. You abused that trust.

'You were able to exercise a power and domination over these children by abusing them in a reprehensible and abhorrent way you did. You preyed on children in a serious criminal way over a wide-ranging area of the Victorian countryside and finally in Melbourne. Certain of the counts are merely representative of a repeated similar conduct against the same victim. In seeking to satiate your perverted lust, it seems no victim was too frail or vulnerable or occasion so sacred that you would desist from perpetrating these outrageous crimes. The effect your depraved conduct might have on the minds of young victims never seemed to cross your mind or, if it did, it was quickly dismissed in your seeking satisfaction for your desires. You betrayed parental trust, abused your exercise of power and trust of vulnerable children and in a heartless way. Your acts of debauchery were wicked and appalling.

'These [victim impact] statements are an unhappy testament to the history of misery and pain you have caused them. You struck at them at a very early age in their lives. In each and every case you have caused significant emotional problems. Most have been living devastated lives as a result of your conduct. Many will continue to do.

'In general terms, common themes emerge. First was an inability to communicate your conduct to anybody, to discuss it with parents or friends. You instilled feelings of guilt in the victims which was so unwarranted. They were the innocent victims unable to speak up because you were the priest. You caused an inability to trust others or attain in later life, satisfactory relationships of their own. There were other traumas than those I have mentioned. For many the despair and misery of their lives through the years may be somewhat abated by them speaking out and seeing you brought before the courts to be dealt with.'

Judge Dee told the court that while the victims gave evidence, Ridsdale was 'only partially cooperative with police'. The judge acknowledged the three character witnesses who had told the court that Ridsdale was a hardworking and compassionate priest before expressing puzzlement as to how the priest could do what he did.

'It seems to me that how you could carry on the position and status of priest at the time of committing these offences is a mystery. The two aspects of your life were totally at odds. Your acting as a priest at those times can only be euphemistically described as hypocritical.'

And then came the sentence. Judge Dee said that he had taken into account Ridsdale's age, the guilty plea, the hardship of a prison term in protective custody, and that the priest hadn't offended since 1982 – but that the community and the victims must be considered. And considered, they were:

'The victims were not given in my view any priority by your superiors in the Catholic Church aware of your conduct. The image and reputation of the church was given first priority. You were given some perfunctory in-house counselling before being shifted off to continue your criminal conduct in other areas. That sort of prioritising I am assured has been changed by the Catholic Church and other churches and organisations who have amongst their midst a person like-minded as you.

'Children must be protected from predators like you and offences such as these are of increasing public concern. As well as deterring you, the sentence I impose must be such as to deter others also minded to molest children by indicating that their behaviour will be met by lengthy terms of imprisonment. Yours was a gross breach of trust that also involved the exercise of power and dominion over your child victims.'

Under the 1993 Amendment to the Sentencing Act (1991), Judge Dee labelled Ridsdale a serious sexual offender and proceeded to give him two years for each of the sexual assault charges, a year for each of the gross indecency charges, five years for the attempted buggery charge and eight years each for the buggery offences. Taking into account concurrent sentencing laws, Judge Dee concluded: 'The total effective sentence is therefore one of 18 years and I direct that you will serve a period of 15 years before being eligible for parole.'

It was a major sentencing coup. An 18-year sentence was one of the highest ever for a paedophile. At one point during his many police interviews, Ridsdale gave a hollow apology of sorts: 'I just – I deeply regret what's happened and I must say that, at the time, I do now but at the time, I never knew what kind of damage I was doing to that kid or any other kid. I just didn't know.'

Within months newspapers were reporting that four of the victims had sought and received compensation of up to $50,000. One of the conditions was that they sign a confidentiality agreement.

Despite his minimum sentence of 15 years, Ridsdale was destined never to see the light of day as a free man. In 2006, he was convicted of another 24 counts of indecent assault on a male under 16, seven counts of gross indecency and four counts of buggery. These were from historical cases. He was sentenced to 25 years with a non-parole period of 19 years. Further to that, in 2014, he was convicted of another 30 charges to make 28 years in prison. He pleaded guilty to all charges.

In 2017, Ridsdale, now dubbed 'Australia's worst paedophile priest' was back in court again. The litany of abuses he committed against children rang out in the court as victims spoke of their nightmares and damage and suicide attempts – each describing a life greatly diminished because of the acts of Gerald Ridsdale.

While he raped her, he told one young girl he was doing God's work. Another victim whose father was in hospital was told his dad could die if he told anyone. Before the latest victims, Ridsdale had already been convicted of abusing 53 children. The latest case brought the victim tally to 65. The true number will never be known.

Sensibly, the judge in 2017 ruled to keep Ridsdale in prison, concluding that despite his age and frailty he was still a risk to society. She added another 11 years to his sentence. Ridsdale will be eligible to apply for parole in 2022.

In May 2015 at the Royal Commission into Institutional Responses to Child Sexual Abuse, an aged Ridsdale gave evidence via video link. His precise and booming priest's voice was unbent by age.

Gerald Ridsdale gave evidence, via video link from his prison cell, at the Ballarat Magistrates Court during the Royal Commission into Institutional Respsones to Child Sexual Abuse.

The posters, with red backgrounds, were carried by protesters outside the court during the hearings into sexual abuse by Catholic priests.

The Royal Commission wanted to know who knew about his offending and what they did about it.

Other evidence heard suggested that Cardinal George Pell had been involved in the decision to move Ridsdale from parish to parish once his abuses became known. Pell was infamously photographed walking into court to support Ridsdale in his 1993 trial.

The Royal Commission findings were damning for the Catholic Church. Of the 8000 people who had private sessions with the Commission, 37 percent had stories about their abuse in the Catholic Church. Male victims made up 78% of the claims made against the church. The average age of victims of clergy abuse was 11 years of age. The average time between offence and disclosure was 33 years.

The number of offenders identified in claims of child sexual abuse was a staggering 1880. These offenders were priests, religious brothers and sisters, lay employees and volunteers.

In a media release from the Royal Commission about the Catholic Church authorities in Ballarat, it is worth noting the reference to Ridsdale:

The majority of survivors who gave evidence during the public hearing about sexual abuse by clergy in the Diocese gave evidence that they were sexually abused by Gerald Ridsdale. Ridsdale's conduct was the source of gossip among priests and in the community. He held 16 different appointments over a period of 29 years as a priest. His appointments were typically short, with an average of about 1.8 years per appointment, after which he was transferred to a new role or location. Commissioners were satisfied that by late 1975 Ridsdale had admitted to Bishop Mulkearns that he had offended against children and that Bishop Mulkearns knew that Ridsdale's conduct was known to the police in Bendigo and it is likely he knew of the general talk in the community about Ridsdale.

Commissioners heard that in 1981 Ridsdale was appointed to Mortlake in southern Victoria. Commissioners report that: 'During his time at Mortlake parish, Ridsdale sexually abused a large number of children, including Mr David Ridsdale, BPS, BPT, BPW, BPU, BPX, BPR and Mr Paul Levey'.

Bishop Mulkearns and other senior priests in the Diocese received numerous reports of Ridsdale sexually offending against children. These included reports that Ridsdale had a boy, 14-year-old Mr Levey, living with him at the presbytery. Mr Levey told the Royal Commission he was sexually abused 'all the time, just about every day' while he lived with Ridsdale 'it was common knowledge in Mortlake' that he lived at the presbytery and 'on one occasion Bishop Mulkearns visited the presbytery while he was there'.

Commissioners accepted Mr Levey's evidence and found that Bishop Mulkearns was aware that Mr Levey's mother was 'concerned about the situation and sought his assistance, but he ignored her'.

Commissioners concluded: 'This was an extraordinary and inexcusable failure by Bishop Mulkearns, and his failure to act subjected Mr Levey to ongoing sexual abuse by Ridsdale. Bishop Mulkearns' conduct was appalling.'

In late 1982 Ridsdale was transferred to the Catholic Enquiry Centre in Sydney. Commissioners found that Bishop Mulkearns wanted to remove Ridsdale from the Diocese and preferably from access to children 'to avoid further complaints and public scrutiny'. It had the effect of protecting Ridsdale. Commissioners also found that Bishop Mulkearns told the consultors that it was necessary to move Ridsdale from the Diocese and from parish work because of complaints that he had sexually abused children. 'Ridsdale continued to sexually abuse children while he was at the centre'.

Commissioners conclude 'Bishop Mulkearns again was derelict in his duty in failing to take any effective action to have Ridsdale referred to police and to restrict Ridsdale's contact with children'.

On no occasion during the public hearing did Commissioners hear evidence that Bishop Mulkearns or any other member of the clergy reported allegations or complaints of child sexual abuse to the police or other authority.

Commissioners found that the 'most likely explanation for the conduct of Bishop Mulkearns and other senior clergy in the Diocese was that they were trying to minimise the risk of scandal and protect the reputation of the Catholic Church'.

The welfare of children was not the primary concern of senior members of the Diocese when responding to complaints and allegations of child sexual abuse against their priests. Commissioners conclude, 'There is no doubt it should have been'.

Report into Catholic Church authorities in Ballarat released, 6 December 2017.

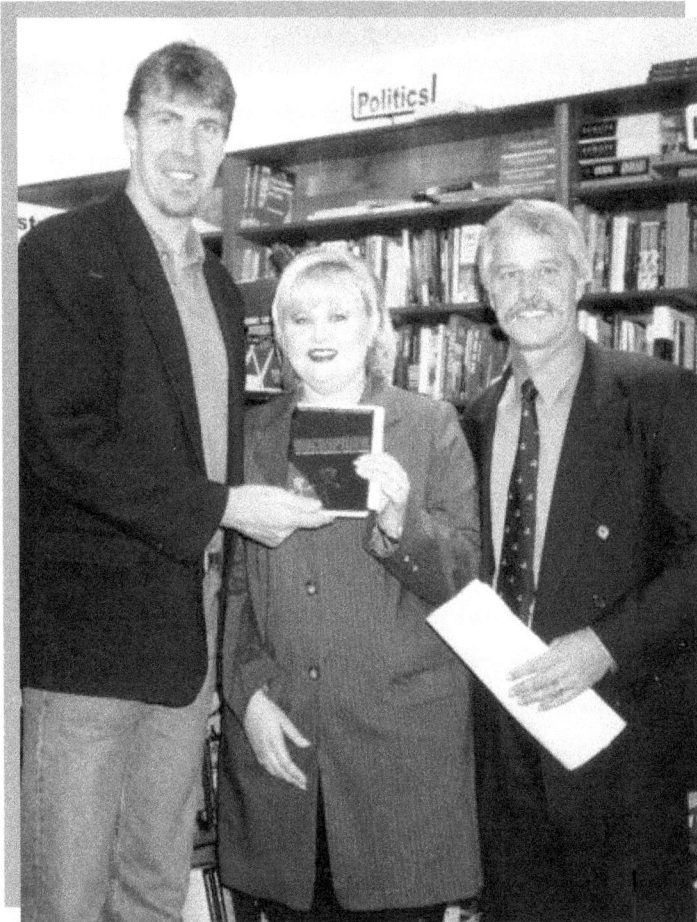

Photo: The late and beloved Australian rules football legend Jim Stynes launched Rockspider in 1999. Then one of the Melbourne footy club's top players, Jim was also a prominant youth worker in Victoria. In 1994 he founded, with film director Paul Currie, The Reach Foundation, to inspire young people to believe in themselves.

Jim towers over me and Senior Sergeant Chris O'Connor, of the Child Exploitation Squad.

11

Putting on my Smarty-Pants

After *Rockspider*, I had a hiatus from writing for a couple of years. It was time to focus on my career, the day job I loved. When I first studied, the requirement for teachers was a Diploma of Teaching. This had since been raised to a Bachelor and that meant that I was academically less qualified than new graduates. I didn't want to be disadvantaged when I went for other jobs.

In 2000, computers were becoming commonplace in schools and I wanted to embrace the technology which would serve me both in teaching and in writing. I enrolled at Melbourne University and did a Grad Dip then a Masters in IT education. I loved studying the second time around. The impatience of youth had gone and after teaching for ten years, new learning occurred within the context of my teaching experience. As the lecturers spoke, there were lots of: *Gee, that reminds me of that kid I had last year…* or *I could use that in class tomorrow.*

If I'm to be perfectly honest, I liked the thought of having a Masters degree. It's one thing to *feel* smart but by 2003, I had three sets of letters after my name to prove it. Being smart reminded me of all those years ago taking judo classes as a kid. I did it for 10 years and achieved recognition at state and national levels. But I looked like *just a girl*. I could see it in the eyes and the swagger of teenaged boys who donned a judo suit for the first time and tied their white belt incorrectly around their middles. They'd be paired with me. *Just a girl…* their smirks quickly replaced with a look of horror when they found themselves on the ground, on their back, wind knocked out of their sails, thinking: *What the hell just happened?*

I don't throw people any more, but that doesn't mean it's any safer to underestimate me. Without going into any details – because I don't think I'm allowed to – the defence barrister who chose me for jury duty made this mistake. A cursory glance at my appearance, and profession as a primary teacher, clearly marked me in his man-estimation as young, blonde and ditsy. The case was declared a mistrial (through no fault of mine!) but this one forceful primary teacher could've totally done an Atticus Finch or changed the opinion of 12 angry men.

Don't get me wrong. I'm normally very polite. I wield my power carefully.

The funny thing about studying is that the moment it's finished, it leaves the same gap as finishing writing a book. As soon as the mortar board was on and the scroll was in my hand, I was knocking on the door of the English department at Melbourne University to see if I could do another Masters degree – this one in creative writing. At the same time, I was approached by a Melbourne publisher, The Five Mile Press, who asked me to write a book for them. It gave me the opportunity to improve my craft, much like the Masters would have done, so I took the deal and ended up writing my next three books for them. Further study would have to wait.

The first book was *Cops* which was published in 2004. I wanted to repeat the formula of interviewing police about cases which made an impact on them. When looking for stories for *Cops*, I interviewed a woman who gave me an insight about what it was like to be an adult victim of a sexual assault. She had arranged for a man who worked for a removalist company to come to her house to give her a quote. During the tour of the house to list things that needed to be moved, he distracted her and slipped a pill into her coffee.

In the blink of an eye, the safety of her home was breached by a rapist.

Her story is horrifying on a number of levels, not least because women are always conscious of whether their surroundings are safe or not. We have an antenna for these things. Her home should have been safe.

I often think about what she went through and how it shook her to the core. Her damage stemmed from the fact that she got a weird vibe from the guy, but it wasn't one of danger. She just thought he was a bit of a big-noter. I've seen this over and over as a true-crime writer. When people discover they've been duped, they lose trust in others, but they also lose trust in *themselves*. They feel like their internal radar no longer works. They stop trusting their ability to protect themselves.

When I identified these patterns, my own expertise grew, and I moved from a storyteller to something more.

I'm often asked how these kinds of stories affect me. I've been pondering the answer for a long time. I am blessed with the ability to confront these horror stories without ill-effect. Perhaps writing about them *is* my way of processing. I take people at face value. I live a cheerful life. I see humour everywhere.

The flip-side is that if someone behaves in a way that reminds me of an offender I've written about, or if someone behaves dishonourably, a wall springs up between me and them – kind of like the ones in banks where if the bank is being robbed, a heavy shutter instantly slams down and separates the robber from the teller. Or the storyteller.

12

THE REMOVALIST

In Pascoe Vale, on a Tuesday in August 2002, 56-year-old Janis tried again to organise a removalist. She had bought a new house and the real estate agent had given her a fistful of brochures for everything she might need to move. The first removalist she contacted, made an appointment to give her a quote, but didn't show up. She was relieved when she contacted another removalist company and the phone was answered by a friendly man.

'And how many of you are moving?' he asked.

'Just me,' replied Janis. 'I'm on my own.'

'My name is Mark Sutherland,' said the removalist. 'I'll come and give you a quote this afternoon.' He had a nice voice and a very friendly manner.

'Thanks,' Janis replied, grateful that part of the moving process might be made easier by the man on the other end of the line.

Later that day, Mark Sutherland rang Janis back.

'I'm running late. Can I organise a different time?'

Janis was busy and organised for Sutherland to come around later in the week on Thursday evening.

The appointment was for 7pm but Sutherland rang three times with various reasons for getting there late. When Janice finally heard the car pull into her driveway, she went to the door and opened it. It was a cold winter's night and she stood in the doorway waiting for the removalist to get out of his car.

Come on, she thought impatiently as he sat in a vintage Mercedes coupe and seemed to be looking through some papers.

After several minutes, Mark Sutherland finally got out of his car and came to the door. He was slight of build, with a receding hairline and perhaps mid-40s. Janis noticed that his cheeks were a bit blotchy and she wondered idly if he was a drinker.

Sutherland introduced himself and came across a friendly, good-customer-service type. He gave Janis a business card with his name on it and Janis offered him a cup of coffee.

'I'll have one if you're having one,' he said.

Janis didn't really want one, but she made herself one as well – just to be hospitable.

She walked through her house pointing out items she was taking to the new house and Sutherland scanned his surroundings. Janis put her cup of coffee on a sideboard while they were talking and Sutherland commented on a plate hanging on the opposite wall, drawing her attention to the other side of the room. The decorative plate featured a 1940s picture of a beautiful young woman with Betty Grable hair and the writing next to the picture said, 'Gee, I wish I was a man – I'd join the Navy'. The model in the picture was dressed in a curvaceous Navy uniform.

'I used to be in the Navy,' Sutherland told Janis.

'Whereabouts?' Janis asked. 'My husband was in the Navy.'

'I joined in Western Australia.'

Janis, who'd been a Navy wife for 15 years, thought it likely he joined as a young recruit. 'What did you do?' she asked.

'I was an accountant in the Navy.'

Janis didn't say anything, but she felt that the removalist's story was a bit off; accountants in the Navy were referred to as 'writers' rather that 'accountants'. It was a small point, however, and she didn't give it a second thought. Sutherland told her that he went AWOL but got an honourable discharge.

Couldn't hack it, huh? Janis thought, but she didn't say anything. The two finished their coffee and Sutherland asked to take a look around the rest of the house. He looked in the bedrooms.

'Do you want us to pack your clothes?'

'No, I'll pack them myself,' Janis told him.

Despite it not being part of the job he was quoting, Sutherland checked inside of all the wardrobes anyway. They contained only women's clothing.

Sutherland then asked what was in the garage that had to be moved. Janis told him that the garage contained three boxes, a single bed and a ladder.

'I'll just take a look,' he said.

'Why?' asked Janis. 'I just told you what was in it.'

'I just want to take a look,' said Sutherland smoothly.

Janis took him out to the front of the house and, while she opened the garage door, Sutherland went to his car and retrieved a torch which he shone around the nearly-empty garage. Janis thought this was strange but again didn't say anything.

Back inside, Sutherland said he wanted a smoke and Janis, a smoker herself, told him to smoke inside, but he insisted on going out to her courtyard. He smoked cigars, he said, and they smelt.

'I don't mind,' she said. 'My dad smokes pipes, it doesn't worry me.'

Sutherland, however, insisted on going outside. Janis went too but got the distinct feeling he smoked the tiny cigar slowly as if she might go back inside rather than wait outside with him.

Janis did not want to leave him alone, and waited until he finished. Sutherland followed her back inside and pulled the sliding door closed behind him.

When the house inspection was over, Janis and Sutherland sat down in the kitchen. Sutherland got out his quote pad and began writing out the quote. As she watched him, Janis began to feel sort of swirly in the stomach and said as much to the removalist.

'I don't feel so good,' she said. He didn't make any comment in reply which Janis found vaguely rude.

It was about 45 minutes since she had finished her cup of coffee and by this time, she just wanted the removalist to go. There was a football show on television that she wanted to watch and it was after 10pm. When he handed her the written quote, Janis couldn't read it – partly because she wasn't wearing her glasses and partly because she was finding it hard to focus.

After the consultation was finished, Janis walked Sutherland to the door and watched him drive away in his Mercedes coupe.

By then she could hardly keep her eyes open and, as she climbed the stairs, felt unsteady on her feet. She got into her pyjamas, crawled into bed and turned on the bedroom TV to watch her footy show. But she was so tired, and after only a few minutes, she reluctantly turned off the TV and fell into a deep sleep.

She didn't hear the scraping sound of her garage door, or the smooth swish as her sliding door opened, or the footsteps on her stairs. And she didn't hear the man come into her bedroom and take off his clothes.

She didn't hear him climbing into bed beside her.

When Janis *did* become aware, she was lying on her side facing away from the bedroom door. She could sense someone lying beside her. Having slept on her own for many years, it was the feeling of someone else in her bed that jolted her into consciousness. Then she felt an arm slide over the sleeve of her satin pyjama top, reach around her. A hand took hold of her breast and then moved away. Her first reaction was to yell and scream, but a sense of self-preservation coursed through her.

Janis turned and saw the removalist lying beside her. She described the strange way he was looking at her as 'lovey-dovey'.

'No…' she said, 'What are you doing here?'

'You left the door unlocked, I thought you wanted me to come back,' Sutherland murmured soothingly.

Thinking as quickly as her befuddled mind would allow, Janis said, 'No, not tonight,' then added, 'maybe another time'.

Janis was desperate to sound like she thought nothing was wrong. Afraid of aggravating the naked man beside her, she hoped if he thought there was a chance, he might leave her unharmed.

Mark Sutherland said nothing as he slid out of her bed. Janis didn't turn but she could hear him getting dressed. She didn't say a word but her mind was screaming, 'Just go! Just go!'

Janis heard him walk out of her bedroom, waited several minutes all the while telling herself: *you have to get up, you have to get up!*

But, even though her mind told her she should get up and check the house to make sure the man had gone, her body was strangely uncooperative. She felt like she was in a dream.

Finally, she forced herself out of bed, and staggered through her house to check the front door and all the bedrooms to make sure Sutherland had really gone.

The following morning, Janis was woken by the phone ringing at 7.45am. It was her ex-husband ringing from interstate.

'Are you just getting up now?' he asked, surprised. 'You'll be late for work.'

Janis couldn't believe she'd slept so late. She was still tired, like she'd taken a handful of Valium; and she couldn't shake the feeling. She didn't tell her ex-husband what had happened. She knew he would overreact and she just wasn't in the mood for a scene.

Downstairs, she noticed the sliding door was unlocked.

As she drove to work an hour later, Janis felt oddly unsteady behind the wheel, almost as if she shouldn't be driving. And then it hit her – the removalist must have put something in her drink. The way she felt just wasn't natural.

Janis told her manager what had happened and then an appointment to see a doctor. Even though Janis felt like she was acting normally, her manager thought she looked spaced-out.

When Janis explained to the doctor what had happened, he agreed she may have been drugged but confessed he didn't know which drugs to test her for and suggested she visit her local police station and ask their advice. Janis drove to the Brunswick police station, where she was attended to by a young male constable. She quietly explained that she had been drugged and the doctor needed to know what to test her for.

As she leaned against the counter-top, Janis felt herself go weak at the knees and she knew that whatever the removalist had given her was still in her system.

The young constable disappeared behind the glass partition and Janis expected him to return with a police woman. Instead, the young man returned with a note. On it was a list of six drugs that might be used in a drug-facilitated sexual assault.

Realising the constable had little else to add, Janis, ever the take-charge person, told him she'd return to the doctor and then come back to the police and start proceedings against the man, once the results came back. She drove back to the doctor for the referral and then on to the local hospital for the blood tests.

Janis next explained things to two helpful nurses at the hospital who advised her to have a urine test as well as a blood test. The results would be quicker. They also advised Janis not to spend the night alone at her house, but to stay with a friend. One of Janis' friends offered her a bed for the night and both women went around to Janis' house to collect some overnight things.

As she walked into her dark empty house, Janis felt afraid – and then angry. How dare that man make her afraid to be alone! She lived alone and had done for some time. How dare he take that security away from her.

But mostly, she felt tired. It was early Friday evening and all she wanted to do was sleep. Before she left her house to go to her friend's place, Janis followed her doctor's advice and carefully placed the cups from the night before in the fridge to preserve any evidence. He'd also told her to gather up her bed sheets for the police. For good measure, Janis also located Sutherland's cigar butt from the night before and wrapped it in cling-wrap.

In among all the drama of the day, Janis had a thought. She wondered whether Mark Sutherland was expecting her to contact him since in order to get him out of her bed, she had led him to believe he might have a chance with her at a later date.

On Saturday morning, Janis rang the Brunswick police again and spoke to the same young constable from the day before. She told him that she had the tests done and that the results would be back early the following week.

On Sunday, she rang again. She was really worried that if too much time elapsed, she might not be able to get Mark Sutherland charged with what he did to her. The female police officer she spoke to assured her that it didn't matter how much time elapsed, the police could still charge him. It eased Janis' mind. A bit.

On Tuesday, the test results came back positive showing traces of the drug *Flunitrazepam* in her system. The results proved what Janis and her doctor feared – she had indeed been drugged.

But, now she had proof that Mark Sutherland had drugged her, another thought occurred to her. She rang her solicitor and explained what had happened. She had one major concern.

'If I go ahead with this,' she asked, 'will I be on the television?'

'Of course not,' her solicitor told her, explaining that the identity of sexual assault victims was always kept from the media.

It wasn't for her sake that Janis asked this. Both her parents were elderly and frail, and she didn't want them to find out what had happened to her.

Janis told the solicitor that the local uniformed police were going to handle it. The solicitor thought otherwise. It was a job for detectives at the Criminal Investigation Unit (CIU) – not uniform. This was serious. In fact, the solicitor knew one of the detectives there and he offered to ring for her.

Detective Senior Constable Justin Schulze from the Brunswick CIU took the call and drove immediately to Janis' house with a team to gather evidence. Often when detectives are called to investigate an offence several days after it happens, the evidence has been contaminated. To Schulze's amazement, Janis had collected every bit of evidence that she thought police might need. She'd placed the cups in the fridge, saved the cigar butt that Sutherland had smoked, and collected the sheets off her bed.

Schulze was impressed by Janis' presence of mind. Janis had vowed that no one would take advantage of her and she wanted the matter pursued with the full force of the law. To her, the arrival of Schulze and his team meant that the cavalry had arrived.

What struck Justin Schulze as he collected evidence from Janis' house, was how organised this offender seemed. It was as if he had refined the practice of gaining entry, drugging his victim, unlocking the doors, leaving, and then returning when the victim was incapacitated – in other words, Schulze suspected that Janis wouldn't have been the removalist's first victim.

Conversely though, the removalist had made no attempt to hide his identity; his name, Mark Sutherland, was written clearly on the removalist quote form, and he hadn't used any kind of disguise to alter his appearance.

Janis showed Schulze her statement. While she had been waiting around for the test results, she had made a careful written account of exactly what she remembered of the night the removalist came.

In her job, Janis often attended meetings and made notes on them afterwards. She employed the same technique to the assault.

Janis went with Schulze to the Brunswick CIU office and made a formal police statement. She was there so long that the detectives called out for pizza for dinner. At the end of her statement, Janis said clearly to Justin Schulze: 'Don't think I'm getting up in court to testify! I won't!' Schulze just nodded.

The thought of saying all this again in front of a court and Sutherland terrified her.

Given that the name Mark Sutherland could have been a pseudonym, the first thing Schulze did was check the offender's name with other details that Janis had given in her statement. She remembered him driving an older-model Mercedes coupe, so Schulze began there. He checked motor vehicle records and sure enough, there was a Mark Sutherland who owned the same model car. From the motor vehicle records, Schulze got an address for Sutherland in Tecoma which was a suburb not far from Belgrave.

With evidence of the drug used in the assault on Janis, as well as the butt of the small Café Crème cigar, Schulze was granted a search warrant on Mark Sutherland's home.

Together with Senior Detective Paul Tymms and Detective Sergeant Stuart Delbridge, Schulze drove to the Tecoma address. Once there, Schulze pulled the police car into the driveway of Sutherland's neat double-storey home nestled in a bushland setting. The detectives walked to the front door and knocked.

'Mark Sutherland?' Schulze asked when a man in his early 40s answered the door. He was slightly-built, gaunt, and had short-cropped grey hair and rotting teeth.

'Yes, I'm Mark Sutherland.'

'We have a warrant to search your house in relation to the assault in Pascoe Vale,' explained the detective, watching Sutherland for any sign of flight, denial, or potential violence. There was none.

'You're not obliged to say or do anything, but anything you say or do may be given in evidence.'

Sutherland nodded his head. He knew very well why the detectives were on his doorstep.

'Do you know which incident I'm referring to?' asked Schulze.

'Yes,' said Sutherland as Schulze, Tymms and Delbridge entered his neat, pleasantly decorated home.

'What happened?' asked Schulze, mildly surprised that Sutherland rolled over so easily.

'I put a drug in her drink.'

'Have you done this before?' Schulze had suspected right from the start that Janis wasn't the first victim. His hunch was right.

'Yep, two times. It's in my diary.'

Sutherland was quiet and cooperative. He showed detectives around his house while they bagged evidence: Café Crème cigars matching the butt found at Janis' house; his diary; and some *Hypnodorm* tablets – which contained the drug *Flunitrazepam* that the doctors had found in Janis' blood and urine samples.

Ironically, *Rohypnol*, the trade name for Flunitrazepam had been banned in Australian due to its misuse in drug-facilitated sexual assaults, yet products like Hypnodorm that contained Flunitrazepam were still prescribed.

Schulze took Mark Sutherland into custody, put him in the back of the unmarked police car, and took him to the Brunswick CIU. It took an hour to drive from Tecoma to Brunswick and the detectives used the time to establish a rapport with the offender.

It would help them later in the interview to know a bit of his history. Sutherland chatted about his house, the footy and, when the detectives drove past a certain road, Sutherland pointed to it and told the detectives that he'd had a car accident there in 1992.

Before the interview began, Schulze rang through to the Sexual Crimes Squad offices at the St Kilda Road police complex. He was put on to a member of Sergeant Tony Silva's crew. Silva was the overseer of all drug-facilitated sexual assaults and was fast becoming a veritable expert in this type of offence.

Schulze described what Sutherland had confessed to and said that it could get bigger. He was given the go-ahead to handle the case for the time being, but was told to keep the squad updated.

In the small interview room, at the Brunswick CIU, Justin Schulze and Paul Tymms sat on one side of the big timber veneer table and Sutherland sat on the other. Interviewing a sex offender is a tricky business. They *know* what they have done is legally wrong, but they don't *feel* it's wrong.

And detectives have to hide any feelings of revulsion they may have in order to let the offender think that they are offering a sympathetic ear. This is always difficult, but at the end of the day, detectives want a confession.

Schulze knew that because the Sexual Crimes Squad had given him permission to take on the investigation, he carried a huge responsibility. Things had to be done absolutely correctly, because in this kind of case – *especially* in this kind of case – no one wanted to see it lost in court on a minor technicality.

After the obligatory caution, Mark Sutherland was happy to talk, and explained how he'd gone to Janis' house and how he'd put a tablet in her drink.

'Why did you do it?' asked Schulze.

'So she would pass out and I could have sex with her,' he replied matter-of-factly.

Sutherland then told the detective how he'd noticed the sliding door was unlocked so he knew he would be able to get back into the house once Janis had gone to sleep. He said that if she didn't wake up when he came back, he would have had sex with her.

'Did you have permission to re-enter the property once you had been asked to leave?'

'No.'

Sutherland's admissions met the criteria for the Sexual Crimes Squad to be called in. If an offender enters a property illegally with the intent to assault, the offence is classified as an aggravated burglary and that, along with the drugging of the victim, meant that Schulze had to contact the squad as soon as the interview was finished.

'Tell me about the others,' Schulze said.

Sutherland described how he met a woman called Kimberly when she'd called for a removalist quote. He learnt that she was recently separated and moving up north. Sutherland called Kimberly back and, in the second conversation, she confided she was staying with a friend, but needed somewhere more permanent to live. Sutherland had offered her a room at his house.

Kimberly refused but over the following week, Sutherland called several times and repeated his offer. The young mother of two was desperate and finally agreed and moved into the bushland house in Tecoma.

The first night began well. After sitting around chatting, Sutherland produced a stash of marijuana which they both had smoked. But then Sutherland gave Kimberly a drink, which made her dizzy. She fell back onto the couch unconscious.

Sutherland waited half an hour before removing her clothes and then anally and vaginally raped her. After he was done, he fell asleep next to her on the couch.

Next morning, Kimberly awoke feeling groggy with Sutherland lying beside her. Sutherland got up, had a shower and left for work. Kimberly, however, was too groggy to leave the house. When he got home from work, he was surprised to see Kimberly still there. That night, she slept in his bed with him, but by the next day, she had taken her children and left.

The next victim Sutherland spoke about was Dana, a woman in her late 50s. Within days of his attack on Janis, Sutherland was at it again. Dana had rung for a quote at the same time he was organising to do the quote for Janis.

He attacked Janis on the Thursday and then went to Dana's house late Saturday evening to give her a quote. Sutherland inspected Dana's flat and then asked for a cup of coffee. Under the pretence of offering assistance in the kitchen, Sutherland slipped a *Hypnodorm* tablet into his client's coffee.

While they drank, they chatted and Sutherland smoked his trademark tiny cigars. Half an hour after drinking her drugged coffee, her phone rang and when Dana got up to answer it she bumped into the walls in the hallway and nearly lost her balance.

When she finished her phone call, she asked Sutherland point blank whether he'd put something in her drink. Sutherland said he hadn't but turned the lamp off and moved to sit next to Dana. He put his hand on her knee and asked for a kiss.

Dana refused and asked him to leave, which he did. She locked the doors behind him, and then passed out unconscious on her bed. He didn't return.

After explaining what he had done, Mark Sutherland tried to justify his actions. He said he couldn't meet women, or if he did, he couldn't hold on to them. He said pubs and loud music gave him sensory overload. He explained that in 1992, he'd had a serious car accident and it had left him with injuries for which he'd been paid a lot of money in compensation.

Since the accident, he had been seeing a psychiatrist for an anxiety disorder which made it difficult for him to form and maintain relationships. As part of Sutherland's treatment, he was prescribed *Flunitrazepam*, *Diazepam*, and *Clonazepam*.

When the interview was finished, Sutherland was allowed to leave. Schulze didn't lay charges yet because if he had, the committal hearing would have to take place within three months. Schulze suspected the investigation would take a lot longer than that and decided to wait until it was complete before charging him. They also needed time to identify further victims.

When Sutherland had gone, Justin Schulze rang the Sexual Crimes Squad and spoke to Tony Silva personally. Silva agreed that because of its serial nature, the case needed to be handled by his squad. He arranged to come straight out to the Brunswick CIU.

For the previous couple of years, Tony Silva had been assigned a special portfolio within the squad – that of investigating drug-facilitated sexual assaults.

Silva took on his new role with all the gusto of a keen young detective and applied for the Angela Taylor Memorial Scholarship to investigate overseas practices in this type of crime. Silva was confident he would get the scholarship because of the emphasis on policing violence against women – particularly in the area of drugging. Sure enough, the scholarship gave him $14,000 to use to attend conferences in Los Angeles, Orlando, San Diego and Las Vegas. Silva was part of the audience listening to FBI experts and scientists from around the world discussing this disturbing phenomenon.

In Las Vegas, the problem was two-fold. In the gambling mecca, not only were drugs used in sexual assaults, but they were also used to separate unsuspecting gamblers from their money.

During the lecture circuit, Tony Silva spoke to local cops, and he also met District Attorneys which was invaluable; in the American system, DAs are involved in the investigations and preparation of legal briefs – just like detectives do in Australia.

Silva learnt that people reacted differently to the kinds of drugs used in sexual assaults. In 2000, a study was done which monitored participants' reactions to drugs traditionally associated with sexual assaults. Some of the participants reported confusion, difficulty with speech, and during the test, they generally behaved in ways they wouldn't normally.

One subject said that she remembered going to sleep after the drug was administered and waking up when the effects had worn off, but supervising staff had witnessed her walking and talking and generally appearing quite alert. Most subjects were less inhibited, and one tried to remove her clothing before staff stopped her. Some victims of drug-facilitated sexual assault have reported losing consciousness and have no memory at all of what happened, while others describe regaining consciousness for short periods of time – usually in response to pain stimuli. Some victims have spoken of being paralysed, while other victims with complete memory loss acted like they were mildly drunk.

The effects of these drugs were amplified when used in conjunction with alcohol or cannabis – so if a woman was drinking at a bar and had her drink spiked, the effect would be worse than if she were completely sober when drugged.

As a result of his study tour, and several years' experience dealing solely with drug-facilitated sexual assaults, Tony Silva had become the expert. At the Brunswick CIU, he told Justin Schulze that his squad would take over the case against Mark Sutherland.

'You can take the case,' said the quietly-spoken Brunswick detective, 'but I'm not letting it go.' Something about it had convinced Schulze this might well be the biggest case of his career.

'Fine,' said Silva noting Schulze's white-knuckled grip on the case file. Silva sensed a tenaciousness about the young detective. His determination was obvious.

'How would you feel about coming into the squad? I'll assign a team to work on this with you.'

And with that, Detective Senior Constable Justin Schulze was seconded to Sex Crimes.

One of the first jobs was to investigate Mark Sutherland's diary. He had explained that because of his impaired memory from the car accident, he'd written down names and addresses of women he'd drugged. The diary contained many names, so Schulze began at the beginning and telephoned each woman in turn. He followed a set proforma so as not to bait or lead potential victims or witnesses.

One of the first phone calls was startling. Schulze identified himself as a detective and asked the woman if she knew a man called Mark Sutherland.

'Yes,' said the woman.

'What can you tell me about him?' Schulze asked.

'He drugged and raped me,' replied the woman bluntly.

Schulze was amazed. With each subsequent phone call, the story became eerily familiar. The women told Schulze how they had rung the removalist company for a quote and Sutherland had come personally. Many of the women agreed he had seemed really nice on the phone. One woman described him as 'having a woman's brain' meaning he could immediately identify with women and was a sympathetic listener.

In person, however, it was another matter. One woman said, 'If you look at him, you'd see there's something not quite right…'

This sentiment was echoed by many of the women. On the phone, he sounded great, but in person, he made women uneasy.

One woman told of a lucky escape. When she'd rung for a quote, Sutherland had asked her out to dinner. Wary of meeting a stranger for a meal, she agreed to meet him at a café. She let him describe himself and where he would be sitting so that she could observe him unnoticed before introducing herself. She told the detective that when she saw him in person, she walked straight past him. To her, he looked freaky.

Sutherland's *modus operandi* became obvious. He would speak to women on the phone, find out if they were either single or single mothers, or in a vulnerable situation. He would then organise to give them a quote after-hours; claiming it was normal company practice. This put the women at their ease.

He would ask for coffee or a drink shortly after arriving, whereon he would drug the woman's drink. Most of the victims felt disoriented and couldn't remember what had happened.

But, if they contacted him he would blatantly admit that sex had taken place. He did not try to hide his identity, and he made them feel that they had come on to him. The women then felt embarrassed, ashamed, or responsible; but if they became upset, Sutherland was immediately apologetic.

One of Sutherland's victims told the detectives something that Sutherland had shared with her: that he'd been married when he was younger, and his wife had contracted cancer. His sick wife's pain was so great that in order for Sutherland to have sex with her, she would have to be drugged to the point of unconsciousness. She had died in 1985.

Schulze knew that if Sutherland had drugged his wife back in the '80s, and had developed a penchant for drugging women, it was chilling to think that this might have been going on for 17 years.

Sutherland would later deny this ever happened.

Weeks after the attack on Janis, a friend phoned and told her to turn on the radio to 3AW. She was just in time to hear the end of the news item naming Mark Sutherland as an alleged rapist who had been charged with a number of offences. Janis was shocked.

She grabbed the phone directory and called 3AW and spoke to someone in the newsroom. She explained her situation and asked for the full bulletin. The obliging staffer read it out to her. She had been dumbfounded initially when she'd heard she wasn't Sutherland's only victim. She had thought of him as a weedy little man who didn't have the guts to go up to women in pubs and ask them out. She had even thought he might be gay when they'd met. But now to find out that he had done this to so many women really shook her.

It was around this time, Janis paid a visit to her local courthouse at Broadmeadows. She'd been adamant that she wouldn't get up in court and testify but Detective Schulze had suggested she go and have a look at a court in action. So she did.

The next time she was in the city, she told herself she'd just nip into the Magistrate's Court and have a look. And she did. And then the County Court… And then she received a letter calling her for jury duty. Janis wrote back and explained she was a victim of sexual assault and her attacker's case was going to court in the near future, but even that didn't get her out of jury duty.

For a woman who was scared of courts, Janis ended up spending a lot of time in them. The jury duty – even though she wasn't picked to go on a jury – helped demystify the process for her.

She realised that she could – would – testify in court, but by then she also knew she would do anything in her power to make Mark Sutherland pay for what he'd done to her and all the other women.

What surprised Janis was how many of the men in her circle of family and friends quietly offered to pay Sutherland – who was not in jail – a visit. They usually suggested the visit would include a baseball bat or a bikie. As tempting as the offer seemed, Janis had come to know Justin Schulze and his team of detectives and had complete faith that they would do the right thing and that justice would prevail.

It was chilling how easy payback could be, but decent law-abiding people had to believe in something stronger than violence. They had to put their faith in the system.

Another surprising thing for Janis was that she found herself crying a lot. She never normally cried. But at work or at odd times, she would notice her eyes watering and would find herself in tears. She thought she had a handle on what had happened, but it turned out, she didn't. She began to see a counsellor.

Two of Mark Sutherland's earliest victims were friends of his; no one was safe from his drink spiking. Donna and her teenaged daughter had been friends with him for a couple of years. Sutherland would occasionally spike Donna's drinks when they'd spend a Saturday evening together and she would wake up the next morning sweaty and sick to the stomach. He even offered to make Donna's teenager a chocolate drink and spiked that too. She walked into a door while trying to get to her bedroom to lie down.

Things became more serious when Donna had a drink with Sutherland one Friday evening in September 1991. He supplied cans of alcoholic drinks and the two were sitting watching the football on TV. Next thing Donna knew, she was in her bed and Sutherland was lying naked beside her, trying to pull her tracksuit pants down. In her dazed state, Donna punched out at Sutherland and told him to get out. He did, and Donna passed out, not waking until the next morning. She never heard from Sutherland again.

Sutherland flirted with his next victim, Genevieve, when she rang for a removalist quote. His skilled questions quickly revealed that she was single and lived with her daughter. Happy with his quote, Genevieve enlisted the services of the company he worked for. Ever helpful, Sutherland offered to deliver boxes for the move and arrived at her home at 9.30 the next evening.

Genevieve was in bed asleep, recovering from surgery and had taken pain medication. When her daughter went to wake her, Sutherland followed the girl into her mother's bedroom. He was carrying cans of bourbon and coke and offered her one. She drank it unaware that he had added a *Hypnodorm* tablet.

When she woke up the next morning, Genevieve found Sutherland asleep on top of her bed covers. She felt groggy and embarrassed. Sutherland woke up and apologised saying that he must have fallen asleep while they were talking. From then on, Sutherland visited her every day to help her pack to move. But there was a price.

On the day she moved, Genevieve welcomed Sutherland into her new house. Once again, he offered her a bourbon and coke and once again, he drugged it. But this time he didn't just fall asleep beside her – Mark Sutherland raped her. Waking the next morning with a headache that would last for days, Genevieve felt sore all over and physically worn out. Sutherland had left the night before, but he maintained regular contact with her.

On the third occasion Sutherland raped Genevieve, she awoke the next morning, stood up and knew she'd had sex. She was sore and had baby oil all around her genital area. There were oil stains all over the sheets as well. The last thing that she could remember was taking a bite out of a piece of pizza and drinking from a glass of wine the evening before – with Mark Sutherland.

Genevieve tried for days to contact her 'friend' and when he finally spoke to her, he admitted drugging her drink and having sexual intercourse with her. Genevieve screamed at him in anger. But for an offender like Mark Sutherland, it was like water off a duck's back.

Days after his third assault on Genevieve, Sutherland was at it again. Another friend of his, Hannah, lived with her young primary-school-aged daughter. Sutherland supplied Hannah with some of the cannabis that he grew. On Wednesday 13 February, Sutherland visited and offered Hannah a coffee and her young daughter a chocolate drink. This time, he drugged two victims at once. The little girl told her mother that she felt sleepy and was going to bed.

Seconds later, Sutherland and Hannah heard a crash from the girl's bedroom, but when Hannah tried to go to her daughter's aid, she felt dizzy and unsteady on her feet. The daughter appeared back in the kitchen and then bumped into the pantry door and fell backwards. As Hannah tried to assist her daughter, the young girl began to convulse and thrash around before being violently ill. The panic-stricken mother was herself feeling very strange; she couldn't see properly and had trouble thinking clearly.

Hannah begged Sutherland to take her and her daughter to hospital. Sutherland carried the girl to his silver Mercedes and placed her on the back seat. By this time, the girl was thrashing her arms and legs about and was incoherent.

With Hannah falling asleep beside him, Sutherland drove his victims around the streets. In one of her bouts of consciousness,

Hannah recalled that Sutherland became upset and emotional telling her that he had drugged her drink to make her 'feel good' and that he had accidentally drugged the girl as well.

Sutherland said that if they took the girl to hospital, then the mother could face custody repercussions since the girl had been drugged and the hospital might report her to the authorities. Hannah was terrified that she could lose her daughter and agreed not to take her to hospital. By this time, the girl had passed out completely.

Sutherland drove around for hours before taking his victims home. After carrying the unconscious girl to her room, Sutherland then sexually assaulted Hannah on her couch. She pushed him away and he left.

Early the next morning, Hannah woke on the couch wearing pyjamas that she didn't remember putting on. Sutherland phoned her at 7.30am to see how her daughter was. He was extremely apologetic and promised that he would never do anything like that again. Sutherland also gently reminded Hannah that she could lose her daughter if anyone found out what had happened.

Like Genevieve before her, Hannah would also be drugged by Sutherland on several occasions. The next time he drugged her, he was interrupted by visitors before he could assault her, and he was apologetic after the event. Hannah ignored his entreaties for several weeks. He kept ringing her telling her he only gave her the 'feel good' powder because he wanted her to feel good. Finally, she forgave him.

On the third occasion, Hannah was home alone and Sutherland came for a visit. He offered to make her a cup of coffee, but by this time, Hannah was wary. Sutherland insisted and Hannah followed him into the kitchen in time to see him holding a clear film canister containing white crushed powder. Hannah asked him what he was doing. Sutherland blushed and quickly put the canister away. Hannah refused to drink the coffee he'd made her. Sutherland kept nagging, she kept refusing, and then he became upset and left.

Two days after he had first drugged Hannah and her daughter, Sutherland gave a quote to another single mother, Sarah. They established a rapport on the phone and Sutherland told Sarah that she sounded nice and asked if she would like to have a drink with him. Since she had a friend staying with her, Sarah thought there was no harm in having a drink with the nice-sounding removalist. She was wrong.

Following his usual pattern, Sutherland drugged Sarah's drink while she was in the toilet. The next thing Sarah knew it was the next morning and she was wearing a pyjama top and nothing else. She was sore and knew that she'd had sexual intercourse. Later that afternoon, Sutherland phoned her to tell her what a great night he'd had.

Reluctantly, Sarah asked: 'Did we do it?'

Sutherland said: 'Oh Sarah! Don't you remember?' He went on to describe how she had come on to him and assured her that he had 'used protection'. Sarah declined a follow-up date, and instead went to see a doctor who told her that she could have been date-raped but he didn't take any samples or even examine her.

Sarah didn't go to the police because she blamed herself for what had occurred. She had no idea that Mark Sutherland was master of the art of making women blame themselves.

Sutherland's next victim had a lucky escape. While doing a quote for Shelley in May 2002, he arrived with some cans of alcoholic mixed drinks and the two chatted about their backgrounds. Shelley told Sutherland that she had had a difficult time since separating from her husband, and Sutherland opened up and told Shelley about the death of his wife and his car accident. As they spoke, Sutherland flirted with her.

When he finished writing out the quote, Shelley agreed to have a vodka and orange drink and left her open can on the table when she went to the toilet.

When Shelley returned, she could hear her drink fizzing which made her think that the removalist might have put something in it. She was suspicious enough not to drink any of it, and when Sutherland went outside for a smoke, she tipped the drink down the sink, then put the empty can back on the table as if she had drunk it.

By this time, Shelley wanted this man out of her house, but

she was reluctant to confront him. She feigned tiredness with a yawn and Sutherland said, 'Don't worry, you'll sleep well tonight.'

He kept talking and even invited Shelley to come and stay at his house for the night. She declined and told him to leave. Sutherland insisted she make him a coffee before he left, and then when he did leave, he sat in his car in the driveway. Shelley turned on all the lights in the house and rang a friend. After a quarter of an hour, Sutherland finally drove off.

As Justin Schulze pieced together a chronology of victims, he realised the next three were the women Sutherland had originally confessed to. While some women gave statements willingly to the police, others would not.

In all, Schulze identified 10 victims, but knew there were more out there. He was amazed to think that if Janis had not come forward, Sutherland may well have continued his pattern of drugging and raping women indefinitely. Only one of his other victims had contacted the police.

Now that he had as much detail from the victims as he could get, Schulze and a team of detectives had to back it up with expert testimony. Schulze contacted doctors who had examined some of the victims, and others who were experts on the effects of amnesia-type drugs such as the ones Sutherland used. Bit by bit, folders were filled with statements and documents building a strong case against Mark Sutherland.

On Friday 25 October, Mark Sutherland was brought back in for questioning in relation to three more victims. Unlike his original interview, this time he chose to make 'no comment' responses to all of the detectives' questions.

Schulze and Tony Silva decided to search the silver Mercedes coupe parked near the police station. Sutherland gave permission for the search. Inside the sports car, Silva and Schulze found cannabis, baby oil, a camera, and another diary.

Schulze applied for a second search warrant to look for earlier diaries as well as more cannabis. The search revealed 21.5g of cannabis, more *Hypnodorm* tablets, and an unregistered bolt-action .22 calibre Birmingham rifle.

The second search of Sutherland's Tecoma property failed to reveal any further diaries – either Sutherland didn't keep them, or they had been removed from the house.

Sutherland told the detectives that he cultivated the cannabis himself and that he sold it to others at $70 for 70g. When the interview was finished, Mark Sutherland was charged and remanded into police custody.

Sutherland had thought he was just coming for an interview, but at the end of it he was handcuffed and driven to the Melbourne Assessment Prison. Sutherland was not going home.

In the early stages, Sutherland had indicated that he wanted to plead guilty, but at the committal hearing, he contested the evidence. As a consequence, some of the victims had to recount their experience in court.

Giving evidence can be traumatic – especially for rape victims who have to stand before a court and relate in minute detail what they had been through.

Sutherland tried to introduce the fact that it was his car accident that caused him to commit the offences; that he wasn't responsible for his actions.

Justin Schulze, listening to the excuse from the public gallery, noted the 10-year gap between the accident and the subsequent sexual assaults. It was always a possibility that an accused might claim some sort of disorder or illness as part of his defence but the decade in this case would make it quite a stretch.

Sutherland was committed to stand trial and refused to make a plea offer. In other words, his victims might have to testify a second time. It wasn't until the day the trial started, two years later, that he finally offered to plead guilty.

In the meantime, Justin Schulze had to keep in regular contact with all the victims to reassure them. He knew if the trial took too long to eventuate, there was a chance some of the women could get anxious and decide it was easier to get on with their lives rather than face testifying again.

A lack of victim testimony, especially in rape cases, could lead to charges being withdrawn by the prosecution. So Schulze knew how important it was to keep the women informed and updated every step of the way. It was vital not only for his case, but also for their own healing processes.

For Schulze, the eventual court case was a culmination of many months of painstaking work. The accused appeared in court neatly groomed, an unimposing figure in a grey suit. He was 43-years-old with grey hair. He looked gaunt.

Mark Kimberley Sutherland, 44 of Tecoma, pleaded guilty to 12 charges, including three of rape and six of causing consumption of a drug for the purpose of sexual penetration. The charges related to incidents with seven women between March and August 2002.

In court, a whole row was taken up with Sutherland's victims. Janis was there – with bells on. This was her day in court too, even though Sutherland had pleaded guilty. As she walked into court, she hadn't realised that Sutherland was already there, sitting in the back.

Someone alerted her and she turned around and stared at him till their eyes met and locked together. Such was her anger towards the rapist, she mouthed what was clearly a string of swear words at him. His resilience was weaker than her anger, and he looked away first. Janis felt triumphant! It was a victory – a small victory, but a victory nonetheless.

Judge John Smallwood sentenced Sutherland to 14 years in prison; with a nine-year minimum. He cited the victim impact statements which showed the women suffered ongoing consequences such as panic attacks, feeling ashamed, being suspicious of men, and having relationship difficulties.

Janis couldn't help herself; she clapped quietly. A court officer gave her a stern look and she told him through gritted teeth, 'Don't you tell me not to clap! I was one of his victims!' She was denied her opportunity to testify, and her victim impact statement was read privately by the judge, prosecution and defence, but not out loud in court. So a small round of applause was the only voice Janis had.

That evening, Janis and another of Sutherland's victims were interviewed for the nightly news. In the time between the sexual assault and the court hearing, both Janis' mum and dad had passed away without ever knowing what had happened to their daughter; so Janis agreed to be interviewed on television. The two women told the reporter they felt the sentence was too short.

Detective Schulze and his colleagues had sighed with relief at the sentence. They knew an average sentence for a sex offender was around six years with release in just over four.

Mark Sutherland's sentence was relatively high showing the judge's condemnation for the nature of his crimes – even murderers serve, on average, less than 12 years.

After the sentencing, Justin Schulze stopped by the Sex Crimes office in St Kilda Road to visit the detectives he'd spent months working alongside. They were genuinely pleased with the sentence and Schulze was patted on the back and congratulated by a number of colleagues.

'Good on ya, mate! Great result!' they all said. In this business, a victory for one is a victory for all. After hundreds of hours of painstaking detective work, it was rewarding to finalise the case with a conviction.

Schulze is at a bit of a loss to explain the actions of an offender like Mark Sutherland. While Sutherland could seem very kind and thoughtful, his actions were always calculated to put women in his debt. Schulze says, 'He'll do anything for you, but at the end of the day, you owe him something.'

In hindsight, Janis is glad she reported Sutherland and stood up for herself. She knows that she coped better with what happeened to her because she had a hand in bringing a rapist to justice. She is proud of herself and knows that if she hadn't reported him, she would have spent forever wondering how many other women were suffering because of her silence.

Women were made vulnerable by Mark Sutherland and many didn't report him because they felt embarrassed – or simply because they couldn't remember what had happened. When questioned by some of his victims, Sutherland was apologetic and vowed that this was the first time he'd ever drugged anyone and begged them not to tell the police.

Sutherland described the drugs that he gave to women without their consent, as 'feel good' drugs and said that he just wanted women to feel more comfortable so that his chance of having sex with them was better.

Whether he comprehends the terror of a woman who wakes in the morning feeling disoriented and sore from sex she doesn't remember having, lying on sheets stained with baby oil, and having no memory of anything at all, is debatable. Mark Sutherland drugged women he'd just met, and friends alike. No woman was safe from his 'feel good' remedies – until, of course, the judge locked him away for his crimes.

Through Sisters in Crime Australia I get to meet, and socialise with, all kinds of real-life crime professionals, like forensic pathologist, Dr Shelley Robertson. I wrote about Dr Robertson's work in The Strange Death of Lindsay Jellett.

13

THE CSI EFFECT

When the TV show CSI started in 2000, the public thirst for forensics was awakened. Almost every cop show on TV featured beautiful people in white overalls collecting evidence from crime scenes. The evidence was then entered into huge computers that magically gave them the names of the guilty.

Years earlier, I had read a book called *The Blooding* by Joseph Wambaugh. On 22 November 1983, a schoolgirl was found raped and murdered in the small town of Narborough, Leicestershire in England. The body of 15-year-old Lynda Mann was discovered in the grounds of the Carlton Hayes psychiatric hospital. She had been attacked while walking down a path alongside the hospital.

Police investigations led nowhere, but a forensic pathologist was able to get a semen sample left by her attacker. The sample was analysed and found to belong to a person with A-type blood. About 10 per cent of the population have A-type blood so the evidence had the potential to narrow down any suspect lists. This was the only lead police had.

Three years later, on 31 July 1987, the body of Dawn Ashforth was discovered in the same area. She too was 15 years old and had been raped and strangled. Police suspected the same man was responsible for both murders.

During the investigation, 17-year-old Richard Buckland was taken into custody. In his often-garbled account when interviewed by police, he finally admitted to killing Dawn but not Linda.

Because police thought that the same person had killed both girls, they got the idea to use a new forensic technique known as DNA fingerprinting. The technique had nothing to do with fingerprints, but rather used advanced technology to record a person's unique genetic code which then could be compared and matched to other samples from the same person.

Leicestershire police contacted Dr Alec Jeffreys at Leicester University, who had developed the technique. Jeffreys compared semen samples from both murders, against a blood sample from Richard Buckland.

The test proved conclusively that semen from crime scenes came from the same man – but that man was not Richard Buckland. His confession had been false. As a result of the negative test, Richard Buckland became the first person in the world to be exonerated by DNA.

When Buckland's innocence was proven, police decided on a bold move – they would take DNA from all adult males in three surrounding villages. Five thousand men were asked to volunteer a blood or saliva sample. All the samples didn't have to be DNA tested because police already knew the killer had A-type blood, and so only A-type blood samples needed to be tested. Even so, the testing took six months and failed to produce a match.

And then, while drinking in a pub with some co-workers, a woman overheard a man named Ian Kelly admit that he had given a blood sample for another man. The woman passed the information on to police and Kelly was interviewed. He told the investigators that a man named Colin Pitchfork had asked him to take the test in his place. Pitchfork had told Kelly that he in turn had already taken the test for a friend who had a police record for indecent exposure.

According to Kelly, Pitchfork was worried that if he took the test twice, he could be caught out in his deception.

When police visited Colin Pitchfork, he admitted that he had killed both girls. His DNA was later compared, and matched, to the semen samples taken from the victims.

Colin Pitchfork was sentenced to life in prison for the two murders and had the dubious honour of being the first person in the world to be convicted with the help of DNA evidence.

In those days, DNA was extracted mostly from blood samples, and because around 5000 men gave a blood sample to police during the mass screening, the Pitchfork case became known as 'the blooding'.

Advances in forensic science were exciting to true crime fans. DNA led to more certainty in convictions. But alongside this was a phenomenon called the CSI effect. Jurors (and the true-crime loving public) expected a forensic element in each crime, and sometimes there just wasn't.

Cops around the traps were also torn. A lot of them told me that investigations needed good investigators who pounded the pavements and put in the hard yards. Forensics didn't replace good old-fashioned investigating, it simply added to it.

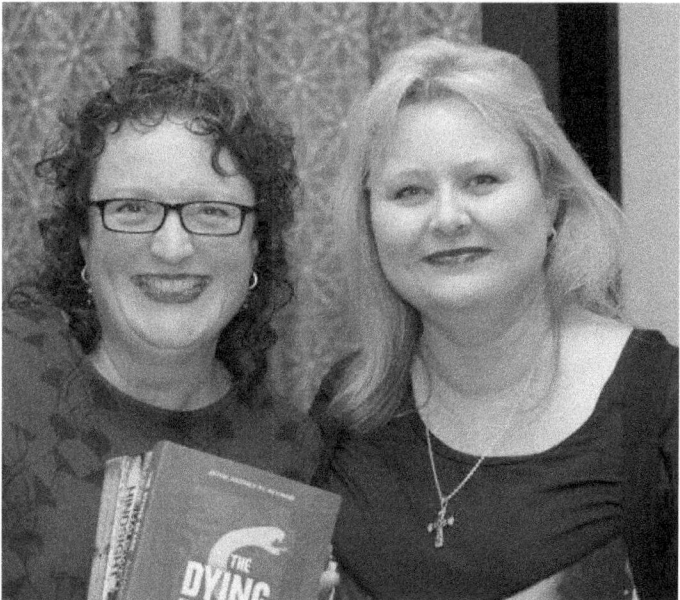

Hanging out with another writer friend, Dr Angela Savage. Angela was one of my first writer friends to work towards her PhD. I suspect it was so we'd have to call her (#popcultureref) Doc Savage.

And there were cases like the Phillip Island murder where DNA testing years after the event didn't tell investigators anything they didn't already know. Three people bled during the events of 23 September 1986 and they all had different blood types. DNA testing later confirmed this, but it brought investigators no closer to knowing what happened in the early hours of that morning.

With the prevalence of CSI-type shows police worried that criminals might figure out ways to outsmart science. While that may have happened, crime writers and cops alike are still privy to cases where the offenders proved just as stupid as they've always been.

One case I wrote about involved two hapless bank robbers. They'd made off with their loot, but the teller had included a dye-bomb in the haul. The dye-bomb had activated and stained them, the money, the car, their house, the gutter where they'd tried to stuff the blue money down the drain, and their shower where they'd tried unsuccessfully to wash the dye off. And when the detectives followed the blue trail from the bank to their house, the guys they interviewed were the colour of Smurfs.

Around 2007, I started going to events organised by Sisters in Crime Australia, the organisation dedicated to celebrating and promoting crime fiction and fact written by women.

Several panel events in the years since – always featuring women forensics professionals and police officers – have focused on the still relevant topic of 'the CSI effect', how it works in reality and how it differs from crime fiction.

For my next book, *Forensics*, published in 2006, I went on the hunt for cases that were solved with a combination of good police work and forensic evidence. My hunch about the public interest in the field was proven correct when the book went into reprint before it was even released. It was an immediate best-seller.

The case from this book that reminds me of the ground-breaking Pitchfork case, happened in the small Australian town of Wee Waa. A 91-year-old woman was attacked and raped, and all the adult men in the town were asked to give a DNA sample. The difference between the English case, where DNA testing had been in its infancy, and the Australian case, just over a decade later, was that the science had been refined and it was no longer necessary to take actual blood.

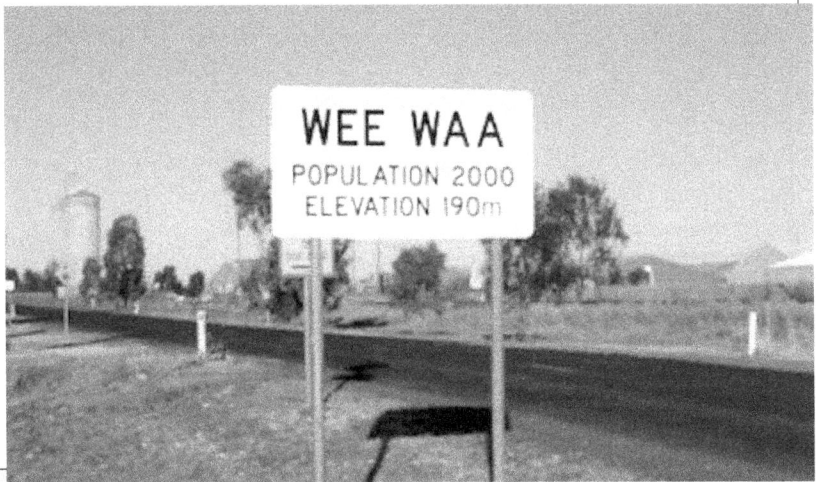

WEE WAA
POPULATION 2000
ELEVATION 190m

14

THE BLOODING

Crime scene examiner Detective Senior Constable Greg Carnell of the NSW Police Service had a Diploma of Applied Science in Forensic Investigation and had been investigating crime scenes since 1993. His cases numbered over a 1000.

In the early hours of New Year's Day 1999, Carnell was called to a job in a small town two-and-a-half hours drive inland from his base in the country town of Tamworth, itself 570 km north-west of Sydney.

An elderly woman in the quiet town of Wee Waa – Cotton Capital of Australia, 'gateway' to the Lighting Ridge opal fields, population around 2000 – was the victim of an unthinkable crime. She had been bashed and raped in her own home; a house she'd lived in for 90 years.

Detective Carnell called into the Tamworth station to collect a crime scene kit. This included a small square machine called a Polilight which could produce light of different colours like infra-red, ultra-violet, and white-light that could detect blood, semen, hair, and fibres not visible to the naked eye.

He teamed up with fingerprint expert, Detective Senior Constable John Stanford, and the two men drove the 214km to the Wee Waa police station for a briefing.

The victim, Miss Rita Knight, was 91 years old. She had been asleep in bed in her Cowper Street home when a man attacked and raped her. When the assailant left, Miss Knight had staggered out to her front porch, bleeding from her many injuries, and sat in a garden chair calling for help. Luckily, some New Year's Eve revellers walking past had heard her and come to her aid.

Rita Knight's
house in
Wee Waa

The lead investigator into the attack on Rita Knight was Detective Senior Constable Greig Stier, who'd been on duty on New Year's Eve when he got the call from the Wee Waa police station.

Detective Stier went to the local Wee Waa hospital where he met with Rita Knight's niece, Nola. Miss Knight was still being attended to and was in no condition to speak to the detective.

When Nola spoke about her aunt, it was obvious she was the most innocent and vulnerable of victims. A pillar of the community, the elderly woman had never married, and lived alone in the Cowper Street house which had been her childhood home.

Early reports from doctors suggested that because of her age, Rita Knight might not survive the attack.

After their briefing, crime scene detectives Carnell and Stanford headed to the victim's house. On the way, they drove past a down-and-out looking man walking down the street, minutes from their destination. They gave him nothing but a cursory glance.

The house was a well-kept old weatherboard surrounded on all sides by a veranda, and situated on a double block of land. Across the road was a large park, and there were only a few houses spaced out along the street. There was no front fence, but tall trees on either side afforded some privacy. Unfortunately, the trees had also given Miss Knight's attacker privacy.

The crime scene examination started outside the house.

Carnell and Stanford first spoke to a uniformed officer guarding the property out front. He had kept a log of who had entered the scene since the attack, and had kept unnecessary people away.

The detectives checked the power box on the front left-hand side wall of the house. There was no cover, so anyone could have gained access to it, and it was clear the offender had flicked the main switch to turn off the power to the house.

This would ensure his victim would be unable to turn on a light.

Carnell and Stanford then photographed and followed a trail of dusty foot prints – most likely left by someone wearing thongs – along the wooden veranda to the French doors near the back of the house.

A jagged pane of glass had been broken from the right-hand door. It seemed the offender had removed the glass, reached through and slid back a bolt to gain entry.

Stanford dusted the doors for prints but could only find a fabric impression which, if made by the offender, meant he was probably wearing gloves or had pulled his sleeves down to cover his hands before he broke the glass.

On the kitchen floor inside, there was not enough broken glass to account for the size of the piece missing from the door; and no sign of it in the immediate area.

Stanford, on the search for fingerprints, examined any items that might have been touched by the offender on his route from the back door to the front bedroom.

Carnell, meanwhile, examined the rest of the house. He took photographs of each room from different angles, and then videoed each room.

Furniture from another era, wicker chairs, a piano, overstuffed arm chairs and antique wooden dressers decorated the house. Pastel-coloured frocks hung from hangers on wall hooks in the second bedroom, and an old wrought-iron bed was laid out with clothes and bags and items of jewellery. None of it had been disturbed. Robbery didn't appear to be the motive here.

Religious icons were prominently displayed throughout the house. Miss Knight apparently attended church every day.

The detectives noted that apart from the point of entry and the victim's bedroom, the house was undisturbed. There was nothing out of place.

It seemed the attacker had come into the house with only one thing on his mind – raping the defenceless old woman. He hadn't searched around or opened drawers looking for money or valuables in other rooms.

It was time for Detective Carnell to process the crime scene in Rita Knight's bedroom which overlooked the front veranda.

While the rest of the house was neat and tidy, Rita Knight's bed told a violent story. Not her bedroom – just her bed. Nothing else in her room, except the place she'd been peacefully sleeping, was distrurbed.

Her bed was splashed with blood.

Carnell photographed the disturbed blankets and blood-stained pillows as he found them. Then he pulled back the blankets and sheets. He found a pair of blood-stained dentures – another reminder of the age of the victim; and, stuffed under the pillows, a pair of blood-stained underpants.

The scene of the crime: Rita Knight's bedoom

Carnell photographed each item and made notes about what and where he found things.

Aside from the blood and the messed-up bed, nothing else in the room had been disturbed. The victim's handbag was sitting on a table; no money had been taken. China ornaments on the old dressing table were still standing; drawers were all closed.

There was nothing to suggest the offender had anything else but sexual assault on his mind. He had broken into the house and walked straight into Rita Knight's room to rape her.

Carnell set up the Polilight, pulled the bedroom curtains shut to make the room as dark as possible, then donned a pair of protective goggles. He swept the metal arm of the torch around the dark-burgundy Axminster carpet to search for semen, which fluoresces under the light. There were no traces of it.

The detectives knew that, after the attack, Rita Knight had somehow managed to get from her bedroom, out through the nearby front door and onto the veranda. She had sat down in her nightgown on a white plastic garden chair to call out for help.

Carnell and Stanford examined and photographed the chair and its surrounds. It told a sorry tale: the seat where she had rested was smeared with the victim's blood; and so were both arms.

Halfway through his examination of the house, Greg Carnell was called to the Wee Waa hospital. Rita Knight had been treated and was judged well enough for Carnell to visit her to collect evidence and photograph her injuries. The doctor had also finished his forensic examination, using a Sexual Assault Investigation Kit (SAIK).

When Carnell entered the room and saw the battered elderly woman lying in the hospital bed, he was reminded of just how important his job was. If he and his colleagues could find the evidence to catch the offender who had so brutally attacked Miss Knight, they could also prevent him doing this to anyone else.

The first thing 91-year-old Rita Knight said to the crime scene examiner was: 'I want you to get him, and I want you to whip him.'

Rita Knight had a huge bruise on the right-side of her face.

She told Detective Carnell she remembered screaming when she woke to find the man in her bedroom.

He punched her and then pushed a pillow over her face to silence her. Miss Knight had lost consciousness around that time.

She said she hadn't seen his face, and had little to offer to help identify her attacker. Her hearing impairment meant either the man hadn't said anything or she hadn't heard him.

She had told the local police earlier that the rapist had smelt like he had been drinking alcohol.

Rita Knight's injuries were appalling. Because of her age, her skin was tissue-paper-thin and wherever the rapist had touched her roughly, it had torn. Her arms and her legs were red raw from bleeding; and a laceration in her hand had proved difficult to suture because her skin was so frail.

The doctor explained the policeman's role to her: he needed to photograph her injuries in order to have a record of what had been done to her.

Miss Knight readily agreed. She seemed as angry as she was upset. And justifiably so, detective Carnell thought. Her home had been violated and she had been attacked.

Newspapers would later report she never returned to the house she'd lived in her whole life. After she was released from hospital she moved straight into a nursing home.

Carnell took photos of her battered face, legs and arms in the presence of a doctor and a nurse. The doctor then handed over the SAIK evidence in a sealed bag. He had taken swabs from the victim that police hoped would yield evidence that would help catch whoever had done this to her.

Carnell passed the evidence on to Michele Franco who worked at the Division of Analytic Laboratories. If Franco was able to get DNA evidence from the swabs, it could be matched to the rapist – once the police caught him.

Back at the house, Greg Carnell and John Stanford finished their examination of the crime scene. Carnell bagged the bed sheets and pillow cases to examine later back at the office.

And, outside the house, in the garden near the back door,

Carnell found the missing pieces of broken glass from the kitchen door. It looked like the offender had thrown it there after breaking the pane.

Minutes after Carnell and Stanford had seen the down-and-out man when they'd first driven to Cowper Street that morning, a Toyota Hi-Lux ute was reported stolen from that very area. The theft was to provide the first red herring of the investigation.

Cotton farming is the biggest industry in Wee Waa, and there are a lot of wealthy farmers. One farmer offered to utilise his private aeroplane in the search for the missing ute driven by the suspicious man. He spotted the ute in a remote area, and the man, who had been seen so close to Rita Knight's home the morning after her rape, was caught and brought in for questioning.

When asked if he had been near Cowper Street the night before, he told police he had spent some time in the park across the road from Miss Knight's house.

When asked if he'd had sexual intercourse the night before, he

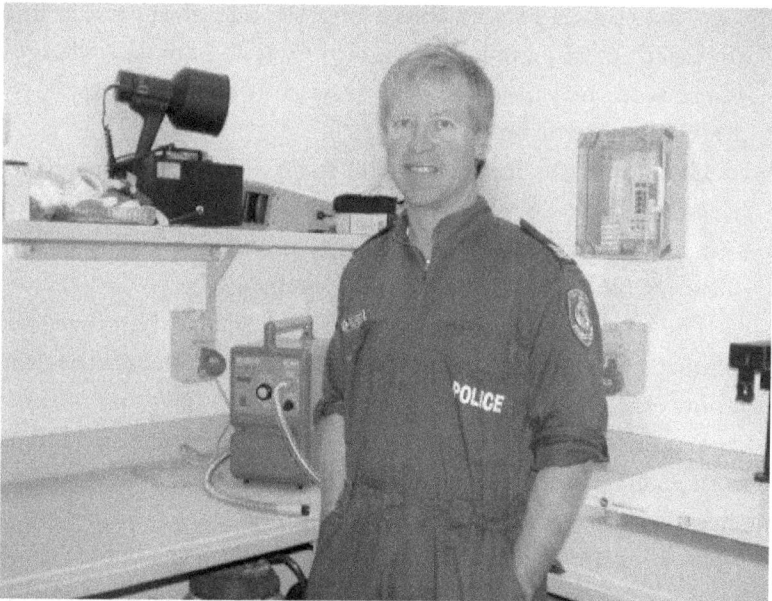

Crime scene examiner Detective Senior Constable Greg Carnell.

replied that he had, but when asked who he had sex with, he told the investigators an odd story.

He said that he had been making a phone call from a phone box in the park when a woman had approached him and asked him for sex. He said that they had sex in the phone box. Even considering it was New Year's Eve when many people drink too much, police thought his story unlikely – until they located a woman who admitted she had indeed asked the man for sex in the phone box.

In the end, the suspect had done nothing worse than steal a car.

On New Year's Day, it was all hands on deck. Senior Constable Ken Anderson, a well-respected local cop, had worked in Wee Waa for around 15 years. He knew his area well and spent the day making enquiries to see if any locals had returned home the night before with blood on them; or if any locals hadn't returned home at all.

Anderson met with Detective Senior Constable Greig Stier and the two discussed the case. Because Anderson knew the place so well, he said there was something strange about the immediate aftermath of the rape – no one in town had any knowledge of it. There were no rumours, no gossip, not even guesses as to who the culprit might be.

He had always joked that the townsfolk knew everything that happened in Wee Waa – sometimes before it even happened – and the fact that no one had any knowledge of it, meant that whoever had done it, hadn't told anybody.

The immediate assumption from the public therefore, was that it must have been an outsider or perhaps one of the itinerant labourers.

But, after having a look at Rita Knight's house, Anderson was convinced it was someone who knew she lived alone and knew the power box was on the front veranda.

There were seven police stationed at Wee Waa before the influx of detectives and crime scene examiners. Wee Waa was the kind of small community where most people knew each other and there was a good community feel. The population of Wee Waa was about 70 per cent Caucasian and 30 per cent Aboriginal, and the relationship between the police and citizens was a positive one.

Wee Waa cops practiced the type of country policing where if they were out patrolling in the van with no pressing duties, and they saw a bunch of kids playing a game of handball, they would pull up and join the game and have a chat. Over the years, Wee Waa police had been involved in charity fundraising that raised over $300,000 for local organisations. And, when they came calling, the cops would take their boots off at your front door. That was the way things were done in Wee Waa.

In the early days of the investigation, Ken Anderson talked to many people. An Aboriginal woman told him that a man she knew, Stephen Boney, had a conviction for rape and had served time in prison.

Anderson knew Boney, who was an Aboriginal man in his early 40s. Boney was a loner who people didn't really notice. He didn't really drink, and didn't say much, rarely drawing attention to himself. Boney had separated from his partner recently and had been living alone a couple of streets down from Rita Knight. Boney hadn't been seen around the town since New Year's Eve.

Ken Anderson made a mental list of people to speak to and put Stephen Boney at the top of it.

Following up the many leads that came in from people trying to be helpful, Ken Anderson checked Boney's prior convictions. While there was no rape conviction on Boney's record, there was a conviction against a relative of his with the same name; perhaps the woman who had spoken to Anderson had her facts confused. Boney slipped down the list.

In the days immediately after the attack on Rita Knight, doctors became more optimistic that she would survive her injuries, and eventually recover. Detective Greig Stier met with her a number of times and took her statement.

Miss Knight still couldn't remember much except that she had gone to bed around 10pm – she had looked at a little clock that she kept beside her bed. She remembered she hadn't fallen asleep straight away, but was then woken by a man in her room. He had hit her and then put the pillow over her face. She didn't remember much after that.

Stier hoped that as she regained her strength and recovered, she might recall something else that could help police.

What impressed the detective about Rita Knight was that she was so alert, and had a calmness about her. She told him she had been praying to God that her attacker would be brought to justice and was confident that the police would catch him. Indeed, every conversation between the elderly victim and the detective ended with her saying, 'I *know* you'll get him'.

Perhaps it was her age, or her wisdom, but she never wavered in her complete faith in the investigators, which in turn boosted the faith they had in themselves.

Stier also noted that Rita Knight was held in such high esteem that it seemed the whole town turned out in support. They wanted the rapist caught as much as the police did.

Wee Waa was predominantly a well-established farming community and many of the farms were now being run by second-generation farmers. That meant that many members of the first-generation were now elderly and had moved into town. With the callous attack on one elderly citizen, the community was nervous that the offender would strike again.

And despite Rita Knight's confidence and prayers, and the hard work of the investigators, the rapist proved elusive. Police had set up a taskforce, Operation Ramat, to catch the offender. The crime was considered so heinous that Greig Stier had any resources he needed placed at his disposal.

Local politician, Ian Slacksmith, provided every assistance he could right from the start, and often met with police to stay up-to-date.

One day, Slacksmith even suggested DNA testing every man in town, but the detectives knew that such a thing was unheard of in Australia.

And, although swabs had been taken from Rita Knight after the rape, there was no certainty that the long process of DNA extraction would yield any results. They would just have to wait.

In the meantime, Greig Stier relied heavily on the homegrown police knowledge of the men of Wee Waa. Suspects were brought in and their alibis were checked out.

The community tended to blame the region's many itinerant workers, but Stier had a feeling that this violent perpetrator had not simply passed through town. Who else but a local would know that Rita Knight, a defenceless old lady, lived alone in that house on Cowper Street?

Many of the early suspects could be eliminated by establishing alibis, but some couldn't. Stier and his colleagues spent over five weeks in Wee Waa checking alibis, tracking down leads, talking to locals, and leaving no stone unturned. But it all led nowhere. When the leads petered out, the detectives returned to their own hometowns but still visited Wee Waa at every opportunity.

Then on 12 May, over five months after the rape on New Year's Eve, the detectives received the best possible news. The rape swab had tested positive to semen, and DNA had been extracted.

At the time of the attack on Rita Knight, the population of Wee Waa was around 1900 people. Calculating half of them as male, and discounting children, it meant the possible suspect pool – if the perpetrator was even part of the community – was around 600 men.

The most significant evidence the police had was the assailant's DNA – which was only useful if the offender was caught.

Some of the possible suspects, who couldn't be eliminated with alibis, were located and each volunteered swabs for DNA testing.

On no occasion did Detective Greig Stier encounter a man unwilling to give a DNA sample. About a dozen were taken, but none proved a match and all the suspects were eliminated.

Wee Waa residents still clung to their theory that the rapist had to be one of the many itinerant workers who flooded into the area to work in the labour-intensive cotton-picking industry.

Almost everybody in town knew old Miss Knight. Nobody could believe that someone they knew, one of their own, could have attacked her so viciously.

Time passed and police were no closer to catching the rapist. And then several things happened that injected a new energy into the investigation.

First, in May 1999 nearly five months after the attack, the case was featured on *Australia's Most Wanted*. The popular TV show highlighted unsolved cases from around the country and called for members of the public to come forward with any information they might have to help solve it.

Then, crime scene examiner Greg Carnell attended a seminar where Detective Sergeant Kris Illingsworth was a guest speaker. Illingsworth had been trained as a Criminal Investigative Analyst, through an FBI program she'd done in the US. Her expertise was to prepare psychological profiles of unknown offenders, based on the known facts of the case. She was one of only a few such experts in Australia.

Carnell was so impressed with the profiler's skills he talked to Greig Stier about requesting her assistance with the Wee Waa investigation. Carnell told him that Illingsworth would need a comprehensive report, as well as Rita Knight's statement, all investigation notes, all crime scene photographs, forensic analysis, a Wee Waa town map, and local demographics.

Detective Senior Constable Stier, who was just about to take annual leave, felt the report needed his undivided attention.

Since the New Year's Eve rape, he had become friendly with both Rita Knight and her extended family. He'd even taken his wife and kids to visit Miss Knight in the aged care facility into which she'd moved. The more he got to know her, the more he was driven to catch the man who had hurt her.

The dedicated cop worked on his report for a couple of hours every day of his two week's leave. He handed it, and a copy of the story on *Australia's Most Wanted,* to Detective Sergeant Illingsworth.

Illingsworth took the case material with her to Adelaide where she and some colleagues undertook a month of field training with their profiling sponsor, South Australian police officer, Bronwyn

Killmier. As part of their training in criminal investigative analysis, they all looked at a number of unsolved cases, including Wee Waa. In group consultation, they developed the crime scene analysis and offender profile.

Illingsworth then wrote-up the Wee Waa case analysis when she returned to Sydney, and delivered the profile to Greig Stier.

Not every cop believes in methods that don't burn shoe leather, but if Stier faced any criticism over the use of a criminal profiler, he always had the same response: 'There are many tools to do our job and this is one of them. We've got to try everything we can.'

The bottom line of Detective Sergeant Illingsworth's report was that the pool of possible suspects was small. The behaviour analysis indicated the offender was not only a local man, but he knew Rita Knight and had probably been to or in her house before the attack. This narrowed the number of suspects considerably.

The detective's report served the vital purpose of drawing attention to a range of people who were *more likely* to be the offender.

She described the crime as being in the low-risk category – as far as the offender was concerned. There was little chance of him being caught inside the elderly woman's home; and, because it was New Year's Eve, any sound of breaking glass or an old woman's screams could be mistaken for revelry.

The offender knew the victim was elderly and, possibly, that she was deaf. But to make doubly sure he could not be identified, he turned off the mains power to the house preventing her from turning on a light and seeing him. The fact he was worried she *could* identify him also pointed to him being local.

Because there were no weapons used, and no evidence of the offender wearing a disguise, Illingsworth concluded the crime was spontaneous rather than planned.

Despite the injuries to the victim, the only time the offender struck Rita Knight was once to the face.

Illingsworth suggested the injuries suffered by Miss Knight were control injuries – meaning the offender had only done what was necessary to control her. He had ample opportunity to beat her further, or strangle her, but he didn't. His intention was to rape her without causing any other unnecessary harm.

Kris Illingsworth concluded, therefore, that the offender probably had a history of break and enter offences that were unlikely to have involved violence. As he hadn't used a condom, to prevent leaving his DNA behind, he also probably had no priors for sexual assault.

Looking at the assault from a lateral perspective, Illingsworth concluded the offender was someone who lacked power in his life, both at work and socially. It was likely that someone or something had triggered a negative response in him, making him feel more powerless, and that he had sought to gain power and control over someone weaker than himself.

The fact that he chose a 91-year-old woman meant that he was pretty low on the power scale.

Finally, using statistical data and all the information in Detective Stier's report, Illingsworth listed the traits she thought the offender would possess.

She believed that the offender would be Caucasian, 20-35 years old, live within the township or surrounding area but most likely close to the victim, and would be unemployed or have only intermittent work. He was probably in a relationship, or married, but it would be unsatisfying and the offender would be the least

Profiler, Detective Sergeant Kris Illingsworth

powerful in the relationship. Sex with a consenting partner would have been unavailable that night; perhaps due to an argument, or the partner might have been unavailable for other reasons.

The offender would not be popular; be a loner, with introverted or selfish tendencies; be weak in character; and perhaps have a minor criminal history involving breaking and entering. He was probably left-handed since the injuries were to the right side of the victim's face.

Detective Sergeant Illingsworth concluded the pre-offence behaviour leading to the crime was likely to be a triggering event, probably involving his partner, which stressed the offender, and led him to act out while intoxicated. She believed this event probably occurred shortly prior to the attack, and in close proximity to the victim's residence.

While the investigation in Wee Waa was taking place, an interesting development was unfolding in Federal Parliament. Politicians were attempting to introduce the Crimes Amendment Forensic Procedures Bill.

The purpose of the amendment was: to give authorities the power to conduct forensic procedures on certain convicted offenders and on volunteers, to create a national DNA database.

Both the politicians and senior police officers involved were looking for a test case to sway public sympathy towards the new legislation.

Superintendent Robin Napper was a British police officer who had worked in the National Crime Faculty at Bramshill near London. He and another British police officer had been invited to join the NSW police force by Commissioner Peter Ryan, who had also come from Britain.

Superintendent Napper had been involved in DNA screening operations in Britain, and one of his new portfolios was to help develop support for the introduction of DNA legislation in New South Wales. He did a lot of work to achieve this and was instrumental in the eventual introduction of DNA legislation in Australia.

It was Robin Napper's idea to use Wee Waa as a test case. He consulted with Kris Illingsworth to verify her expert opinion that she thought the Wee Waa offender was a local man.

The two police officers discussed the case and agreed that the geographic isolation and the size of the town would provide a good opportunity to demonstrate how a voluntary mass DNA screen could solve an otherwise unsolvable case.

Greig Stier believed a mass screening could catch or flush out Rita Knight's rapist. Hard-pressed to think of a community more pro-police than Wee Waa, he knew the locals badly wanted the rapist caught. They'd already willingly assisted police every step of the way. Stier also knew that, with the eyes of the nation directly on Wee Waa, every resource available would be put towards catching the offender.

Stier had been impressed right from the start with how generous the police hierarchy had been with resources. This case, after all, was a rape, not a murder or multiple murder. And, sadly, the truth was that thousands of women were raped every year without generating the media attention and the police manpower assigned to the investigation.

On another level Stier understood why the case got so big. Rita Knight's standing in the community had a lot to do with it. People had admired her before the attack, and they certainly admired her stoicism afterwards.

Many people her age simply wouldn't have survived it, but she did. And of course, her age was a factor, as was the fact that she had never married. It was difficult to imagine a more innocent and vulnerable victim.

Perhaps what happened to Rita Knight was everyone's worst nightmare for their parents or grandparents.

The wheels of bureaucracy slowly turned and by the time the mass DNA screening was given the green light for the township of Wee Waa, over a year had passed since the rape.

When the news became public, the little town became the centre of international attention. Representatives from the worldwide media began phoning the Wee Waa police station for comment.

For the country cops, the attention was a bit daunting. For many weeks, they didn't know, when they answered the station phone, whether it would be a resident in need of assistance or a journalist from London's BBC. They referred all media to the senior officers.

When the actual logistics of the country's first mass screening were considered, the authorities realised it was one thing to okay and organise the voluntary collection of mouth swabs from up to 600 men, but another thing altogether to get any results from the saliva samples in a timely manner.

This was not CSI TV. In the real world, in the year 2000, the most efficent lab analysis capacity was for around 500 samples every six months. If the lab concentrated just on the Wee Waa case to the exclusion of all others, it could still take up to six months to test all the samples against the DNA left at the scene to identify the perpetrator.

Rita Knight at the Weeronga Aged Hostel on April 9, 2000, the week police and DNA specialists descended on Wee Waa to find the man who'd assaulted her over 12 months before.

To counter this problem, police profiler Kris Illingsworth suggested the men of Wee Waa who were prepared to volunteer their saliva should also fill out a questionnaire. She would devise questions to elicit a certain emotional response in the offender and, after analysing the answers, would prioritise the more likely suspects to have their collected DNA tested first.

Hundreds of screening kits were put together. Each paper bag contained: swabs and sealed containers; barcodes, so evidence could be labelled; forms to check for identification; the questionnaire and a consent form.

Volunteers were asked to provide two types of identification, give a thumb print, and have a Polaroid photo taken.

The comprehensive ID and the barcodes in the Wee Waa case was the direct result of Superintendent Robin Napper's previous experience with screenings in Britain. He wanted to avoid the UK situation where killer Colin Pitchfork had avoided taking the DNA test by getting a friend to take it in his place.

On Friday 7 April 2000, a team of experts – in their own NSW Police Forensic Services bus – arrived in the country town from Sydney. It was just over 15 months since the attack on Rita Knight, when the Wee Waa police met with 30 extra officers, including seven detectives from the Sydney-based Homicide and Violent Serial Offenders Agency, for a briefing and training session.

Crime scene examiner Greg Carnell, who'd been a part of the investigation from the beginning, also returned to Wee Waa to help with the screening.

Among the speakers was profiler Kris Illingsworth, who instructed police on how to use the questionnaire. She planned to stay in the town over the week of testing to personally go over each response as soon as it was passed to her.

When she'd first arrived in town, Illingsworth had been shown around by the local police, and noticed the population makeup. The proportion of Aboriginal residents to white was more significant than the demographics had suggested, particularly in the built-up areas. Although she had profiled the offender as Caucasian, she began to wonder if, in fact, he might be Aboriginal.

Superintendent Robin Napper was also part of the police contingent at Wee Waa. Greig Stier took Napper and Kris Illingsworth to meet Rita Knight at the Weeronga nursing home. They were both impressed with her strong and spirited character and her determination that the offender would be caught. They all hoped the mass screening would be the answer to her daily prayers.

Local police officers who were in Wee Waa on the evening of 31 December 1998 – the night of the attack – offered to be the first to volunteer a DNA sample. The media was there to photograph them doing so and their smiling faces appeared in the next day's newspapers.

Also appearing in response to media interest was Rita Knight herself. Police had suggested one interview by one journalist which could be shared among the media. They didn't want to tax the elderly lady who by then had celebrated her ninety-third birthday.

At 7am on Saturday 8 April, the mass screening began of every male aged between 18 and 45 who had been present in town on the night of the rape.

There were two ways local men could participate. A police caravan with a large awning was set up outside the Wee Waa police station, and teams of police were systematically making their way around town knocking on doors.

Parliamentarian Ian Slacksmith organised for the local footy team, the Wee Waa Panthers, to attend the screening in their football jerseys and pose for the media. They did so willingly.

In the first three days, 330 men volunteered their DNA at the police station caravan, and the rest were being tested in their homes.

Illingsworth, meanwhile, was using her expertise on the answers to her questionnaire. Some questions – name, age, address – were to establish if the volunteer fitted into the demographic she was seeking. The question about being right or left-handed was important because Rita Knight had been punched on the right side of her face, which meant the attacker was likely left-handed. Other questions were things like what kind of person they thought the offender might be, and whether he deserved a second chance.

8 April 2000: Members of the Wee Waa Panthers football team queue outside the mobile New South Wales Police Forensic Services van to submit to voluntary DNA testing.

Given, even if he was a local resident, the offender might leave town over the screening weekend, Kris Illingsworth knew it was vital to check that all males in the demographic had been approached by police for their DNA samples. If anyone was out of town, they needed to be tracked down.

In all, only eight men – including a local lawyer – objected and refused to give a sample. In the lead-up to Australia's first-ever mass voluntary DNA screening, the media made much of the event. Civil libertarians had raged against the idea but, by and large, the men of Wee Waa itself just wanted to help catch the man who had assaulted one of its innocent citizens.

Detective Illingsworth informed her colleagues, with confidence, that the offender was not among the first 330 men who'd been tested. This wasn't surprising because it was unlikely that the offender would be among the first volunteers.

And while her profile might fit a number of men, Illingsworth knew that the post-offending behaviour would affect only one of them. It was likely that the offender would be extremely anxious over the mass screening. He alone would have something to fear.

Wee Waa's Senior Constable Ken Anderson worked with Greig

Stier to compile a list of men who had yet to give DNA samples. Thirty men made this need-to-be-tested list; with the name on top being Stephen Boney, who he'd considered early on in the investigation.

Anderson had bumped into Boney a couple of months earlier, in a town a couple of hours away, and had greeted him and asked him if he'd been into Wee Waa lately. Boney said he hadn't. Anderson had told him that detectives would like to speak to him about the rape – just like they were speaking to all the men around town. The week before the screening, Anderson had seen Boney at the local post office, so he knew he was back in Wee Waa.

Officers began working through Anderson's list of 30 men, one by one. On a closer look at their backgrounds, they discovered Stephen Boney had in fact been convicted of rape and served time in prison, but his conviction had been incorrectly attributed to the relative with the same name. This mistake explained why there was no record of priors for sexual assault for Ken Anderson to find in the early days of the investigation.

Profiler Kris Illingsworth was also shown the list of suspects generated by local police which included Stephen Boney's name. She was told of Boney's history of break and enter convictions, and also of his history of committing sexual offences. She thought it suspicious that he had left Wee Waa immediately after the offence and again when the screening operation began. Illingsworth agreed that Boney's DNA be sought as a matter of priority. Ken Anderson was tasked by the officers in charge of the screening to find Boney and request he provide his sample.

On Tuesday 11 April, Senior Constable Anderson went looking for Stephen Boney. He started with a call to local police in a town called Brewarrina, where Boney's sister lived. The officers checked his sister's house and confirmed he was there.

Anderson drove the two-and-a-half hours to Brewarrina to get Boney's DNA. It wasn't just that the man had left town before the screening that worried Anderson, it was the new information he'd been given by another local Aboriginal woman. She had told him that when Boney had raped two young women, he had cut the power to their house and removed light bulbs.

Anderson had also interviewed a local contractor when he was mowing a lawn across the street from his own house. The contractor admitted employing Stephen Boney on several occasions and remembered they had last mowed Miss Knight's lawns on Christmas Eve – a week before the rape.

'Did you collect the money, or did he?' Anderson asked.

'Boney did,' the contractor replied, explaining how he would have gone around to the side doors to get it.

The same doors through which the rapist had entered.

By the time Anderson met with Stephen Boney in Brewarrina, the police officer knew the man was shaping up as a most-likely suspect.

Boney was a mild man, quietly spoken and neatly dressed but Anderson could see he was very nervous.

Boney was obviously reluctant to give a DNA sample, but with his family members around, it would have been awkward for him to refuse. So he filled out the questionnaire, swiped the inside of his cheek with the swab stick and handed over his sample to Anderson who put it straight into a cooler.

Anderson drove the 240km straight back to Wee Waa.

When Kris Illingsworth read Stephen Boney's questionnaire, she could see his answers were totally unique from the hundreds she'd already read. The questions were designed to elicit an emotional response in the offender, and Boney had responded emotionally. He went to the top of the list of suspects.

On Monday 17 April 2000 – six days after he'd given his DNA sample and filled out his questionnaire – 44-year-old Stephen Boney walked into the Wee Waa police station and asked to speak to Ken Anderson. He was holding a Bible.

'I'd like to give myself up,' he told Anderson. 'I've put my trust in the Lord and I was baptised before I came here today. The reason why I done it is because a lot of people have evil in them and I wanted to get the evil out of me. That's why I turned Christian…when I was baptised that washed away all my sins.'

Ken Anderson advised Stephen Boney of his rights and then the Wee Waa rapist told his story.

Boney explained that on New Year's Eve, he had gone looking for his partner and mother of his children. They had been arguing and she had moved out of the house they had shared. He couldn't find her because she'd gone to another town to spend New Year's Eve. Boney had gone to a friend's place to watch a video.

'As I was walking back downtown, it was raining… and at the time, I was going home but I don't know why I went to the old lady's house. I went to her place and she was awake. I could see her through the window. She was having a cup of tea.

'Then I could see her walking into another room and she sat down and watched TV. All the doors on the side of the kitchen were locked but one of the doors had a cracked glass on it, and I pulled it out because it was loose. I then put my hand through it and unlocked the door.

'I got inside the house and I waited for a couple of minutes, but this had happened after the old lady had finished watching TV. I then walked to the door where she slept…the door was open and she was laying on the bed. I walked up to the bed and just put my hand on her leg…sort of grabbed her leg and sort of…she sort of sat up.'

It was here that Ken Anderson stopped the interview. If this was to be done, it needed to be done properly. Stephen Boney had a chance to call and organise a lawyer to represent him.

Three hours later, a formal taped interview began. Ken Anderson sat in on the proceedings with Detective Senior Constable Paul Jones, who ran the interview with Stephen Boney and his legal representative.

For the purpose of the taped interview, Stephen Boney repeated his name and address and went over the confession he had made earlier to Ken Anderson.

Paul Jones began with Boney's responses to the questionnaire that he filled out when he'd given his DNA swab the previous week.

Boney admitted that his responses to questions like 'do you know who sexually assaulted Rita Knight?' were incorrect and that he was in fact the culprit.

When Jones asked if Boney had been to Miss Knight's house before, he said that he had mowed her lawns a couple of times.

'Did you ever speak to Miss Knight while you were mowing the lawn?'

'No,' replied Boney quietly.

'Did she ever come out to the yard while you were mowing?'

'No, she just was sittin' down on the veranda.'

The detective established that Boney had never entered the house before the night of the rape.

'Did you know how old Miss Knight was?'

'No,' replied Boney. 'I didn't know.'

'Do you agree that she's an elderly woman?'

'Elderly woman, yeah.'

Jones established that Boney had gone to a friend's place on New Year's Eve and watched a video. And then he had left to go home but made a detour.

'What happened?' asked Jones.

'I don't know...I just started...I don't know what sort of...what made me change my mind, and I started walkin' across the park... I dunno what sort of made me go to that old woman's place.'

'You don't know what made you go there?'

'No.'

'Okay, but you did go there?'

'Yeah.'

'And what did you do when you got there?'

'I didn't do anything. I was just standing outside...on the veranda.'

'What did you do when you were standing on the veranda?'

'I wasn't doing anything. I just was looking in.'

'And what did you see when you looked inside the house?'

'The old lady.'

'And what was the old lady, Miss Knight, doing?'

'She was havin' a cup of tea.'

Boney described how he had stood on the veranda and watched Rita Knight have a cup of tea in the kitchen and then she went into another room to watch television. Boney said he had watched her for over half an hour. After that, she had gone to bed. He said that she had turned all the lights off in the house.

He had then cracked the glass in the door, pulled some of the pieces out and threw it out into the garden. He knew that Rita Knight wouldn't be able to turn on a light and see him because he had turned off the power at the main switch.

Stephen Boney described walking into the kitchen and down the hallway towards her bedroom. Once again, Boney described grabbing Rita Knight's leg and her waking up screaming. He said that he put his hand over her mouth to stop her screams.

'Did you do anything else to stop her from screaming?'

'Yeah, I grabbed a pillow.'

'And what did you do with the pillow?'

'I put it over her face.'

'Did you at any stage strike Miss Knight to the head?'

'No, no, I did not.'

'Okay. When you put your hand over her mouth, how much force were you applying to her?'

'Oh, just enough to stop her screaming.'

'Okay. When you put the pillow on top of her head, how much force were you applying on top of the pillow?'

'I just pressed with one hand.'

'Once you placed the pillow over the top of Miss Knight's head, did she stop screaming?'

'Yeah. I didn't have the pillow on her face too long.'

'Did you remove the pillow from her face?'

'Yeah.'

'Did Miss Knight scream then?'

'Yeah, she was still screaming, yeah.'

Boney described how he raped her while she screamed. He denied hitting her or causing her any injuries even though she clearly suffered severe physical trauma during the attack.

'When did you decide that you were going to have sex with Miss Knight?'

'Probably when I got inside the house,' replied Boney.

'Can you recall if you made the decision to sexually assault Miss Knight before you went into the house?'

This was the logical assumption. Boney had stood on the veranda at least half an hour and waited for Rita Knight to go to bed. But Boney denied this was his motive for entering the house.

'What was your motive for going inside the house then?'

'To see if she had any money.'

'Did you look in any of the rooms for money?' asked the detective, knowing there was no evidence the intruder had done anything but rape Rita Knight.

'No,' admitted Boney.

'So, it was obviously shortly after entering the house you changed your mind about the money. Is that right?'

'Yeah.'

'Do you agree it would have been difficult to look for money when you turned the power off...considering you didn't have a torch?'

'It was, yeah.'

'After you had sex with Miss Knight, what did you do then?'

'I left the place.'

'How did you leave the place?'

'The same door what I got in.'

'Once you left the place and out that door, where did you go?'

'Well, I walked out the front and I walked down Cowper Street.'

'Did you hear or see Miss Knight after you left the house?'

'Oh, I could still hear her screaming.'

Again in the interview Stephen Boney denied hitting Rita Knight. He suggested that she might have got the injuries to her cheek by falling over. He said he'd seen her interviewed on television soon after the attack.

'Do you agree,' asked Paul Jones, 'that those injuries...you've seen on TV were quite serious?'

'Looked serious.'

'Did you feel anything in relation to seeing those injuries?'

'Oh, I feel...feel ashamed.'

Boney then told the police officers how he had left town the following day ostensibly because of a death in his family. He explained how he had thrown out the clothes he'd been wearing on the night of the attack because had bought new ones. He said that he hadn't noticed any blood on his clothes before he threw them out.

Jones then asked if Boney would complete a video reconstruction the following day at Miss Knight's house.

Boney's solicitor explained to him what that would entail. He would walk through the house and show the police what had happened. The solicitor explained that Miss Knight no longer lived at the house and assured Boney that he wouldn't be seeing her at the house.

At the end of the interview, Jones asked Stephen Boney if he had anything to say.

'Yeah, all I can…I'd like to say that, yeah, I'm sorry…I'm sorry for what happened…it shouldn't happen, and I'd just like to say that I am not a violent person, and I did not hit Miss Knight that night…and that's all I'd like to say. I'm sorry.'

After the six-hour interview, Boney was charged with aggravated sexual assault, aggravated break and enter to commit a felony involving violence, and break and enter to commit a felony.

Crime scene examiner Greg Carnell was again called back to Wee Waa – this time to video Stephen Boney's re-enactment of his crime. What struck Carnell most about the rapist who had proved so elusive for 16 months was that he was so softly spoken and so meek and mild. Perhaps with the brutality of the attack, investigators were expecting someone more forceful. Boney was small in stature, portly around the middle, and neatly dressed.

Because the media had started to gather at the Cowper Street house, police accompanying the video re-enactment team held up a large white screen to protect Boney's privacy. Boney also had a pink towel which had been given to him at the Wee Waa police station to cover his face from the media.

Stephen Boney was escorted out of the police car in handcuffs. He was asked if he had any connection to the house and he said that he had twice been employed there to mow the lawns.

The old house, which in the intervening time had been sold, looked essentially the same. Boney walked up the front steps with his police entourage and spoke so quietly when questioned that he had to be asked several times to speak louder so that the video's microphone could pick up what he was saying. Boney walked to the power box while the two officers holding the white screen shuffled along between him and the front of the street.

He stood in front of the power box and was asked to indicate the switch he had turned off on the night he attacked Rita Knight. Raising both handcuffed hands, Boney pointed to a switch on the left-hand side of the box.

The group then made their way down the left-hand side of the veranda and stopped at the door where Boney had entered. In a quiet murmur, Boney described watching Rita Knight for about half an hour on the night of the attack. He had watched her make a cup of tea in the kitchen and then waited while she drank her tea and watched television for a while. He stood on the veranda for around half an hour before he entered the house.

He said he could hear a loud party going on in the house behind Miss Knight's. Boney again claimed that his original thought was to rob the old lady and he'd only decided to rape her when he stood outside her bedroom door.

Boney was no different from the many rapists who minimise their crimes. It wasn't the last time in the re-enactment he would do this.

For the camera, Boney explained how he broke the pane of glass in the French door and then slid back the bolt to gain entry. When he stepped inside the house, he told the investigators that he had seen the broken glass on the floor and had picked it up and thrown it out the door. He made a movement with his cuffed hands to indicate an area in the side garden.

He described making his way through the kitchen and down the hallway to Rita Knight's bedroom. It was standing at this door, he said, that he had decided to rape the old lady. He had entered her room in the dark and saw her lying in her bed asleep.

The police and Boney crowded into the front bedroom. Boney described how he had grabbed Rita Knight on the leg and how she had woken up.

'She sat straight up and started screaming,' Boney explained.

'What did you do when she screamed?'

'Put my hand over her mouth.'

Again, Boney didn't mention hitting the elderly woman, but did describe how he had put the pillow over her head to stop her from screaming.

When the questioning began to cover details of the sexual assault, Boney hung his head, whether out of shame or embarrassment, it was hard to tell.

There were long pauses between the investigator's questions and his responses. He struggled to explain what he had done to expose his penis before the attack. He mumbled that he had pulled down his trousers and when questioned further, he said that his trousers remained around his ankles during the attack.

'I removed her pants and started to…have sex with her.'

For the record, Boney was asked: 'In all the circumstances that were going on here with Miss Knight screaming, did you know that she didn't consent to having sexual intercourse with you?'

'Yes.'

'And that was before you started having sex with her?'

'Yes.'

'And it was whilst you were having sex with her?'

'Yes.'

'And it was after you'd finished having sex with her?'

'Yes.'

'Okay.'

And then for a brief moment, Stephen Boney turned petulant: 'I mean it only happened for…it wouldn't even have been 10 minutes.'

As if that made it okay.

After Stephen Boney's confession, profiler Kris Illingsworth had time to look over the investigation and evaluate its effectiveness.

Boney was nine years older than her upper profile age limit, but age was the most difficult aspect to profile as offenders can often be less emotionally mature than their chronological age.

Boney was Aboriginal and not Caucasian but Illingsworth felt that if she had gone to Wee Waa when she was compiling the profile, she would've made different conclusions considering the demographics.

But, aside from that, Boney was everything she thought he would be. He was in a relationship, but lacked power in his life. He lived within a couple of streets of Rita Knight, and knew her because he had mowed her lawns while working for the local contractor.

Illingsworth was also correct in anticipating that something triggered the offence on the night of the rape. Boney had been trying to contact his wife ready to confront her about their domestic difficulties and had been unable to find her.

Detective Illingsworth felt the value of her work was evident in the fact that she knew the man police were seeking was not among the first 330 respondents.

Stephen Boney was not caught with DNA evidence – his confession came before his DNA could even be tested. But he, like Colin Pitchfork before him, saw the writing on the wall and confessed. This perhaps illustrates the power of DNA and other forensic evidence – sometimes it catches offenders, and other times, it simply flushes them out.

Stephen Boney was sent to trial and received a 12-year sentence; with a minimum of eight years before he could apply for parole.

Judge Robert Bellear, of the Moree District Court, gave a reduction in the sentence (from the maximum of 16 years) because Boney had volunteered his DNA and confessed to the crime.

Bellear said he hoped the sentence would act as a powerful deterrent to Boney and others from committing 'depraved and despicable acts' on 'such vulnerable women'.

The judge noted that the attack on Miss Knight bore a striking resemblance to Boney's previous rape of a 22-year-old woman in Brewarrina on 8 February 1984. Boney served three years of a six-year sentence for that crime. Bellear ordered that Boney undertake psychiatric treatment while in prison and after his release.

It was ironic that Boney found God and was baptised before he came in to confess. Perhaps he had found the same God that Rita Knight had been praying to every day since the rape, praying that her rapist would be caught.

In a victim statement read to the court Miss Knight said: 'I really thought I was going to die. It will always be with me, that man putting a pillow over my head...pulling my pants down, that's when I passed out.

'My independence has been taken away from me as I am no longer able to live on my own.'

When Greig Stier visited Rita Knight after the long investigation was over and Boney had been arrested, her response was typical. She looked keenly at Stier and said, 'I *knew* you'd find him.'

Even though Boney said he had mowed her lawn a couple of times, Rita Knight had little more than a vague recollection him.

Greig Stier knows Rita Knight's case gave the community a reason to support and embrace the new use of DNA in the fight against crime. The result was good for her, but it was also good for the entire community to know for sure who had committed the terrible crime against her.

In the early months of 2005, Rita Knight passed away in her nursing home. She was a couple of years shy of a century.

Greig Stier attended her funeral and paid his final respects to the old lady of whom he'd grown so fond. He thought of her spirit and her plucky nature. She had never been defeated by what had happened, even though it had taken a terrible physical toll on her. Stier remembered what she'd told him over and over again, 'I'll get over this.'

And in many ways, she had.

A found-family of crime writers:
Anne Buist, Megan Norris,
me and Emily Webb

15

FAMILIES

As hard as it is for families to cope with the loss of a loved one, on occasion, I've spent time with families who have had to come to terms with having a killer among them. Sometimes, denial is the easier road. It can't be him! Why aren't you out catching the real killer?

To accept that you have a killer in the family comes with so much else: guilt, sorrow, ostracism, blame, and in a real sense, the loss forever of the person you thought you knew.

When I wrote the Frankston book, members of the Denyer family I spoke to were no-less traumatised than the families of the victims. On the day Paul was arrested, they not only lost their brother, but they lost the good memories they had of him which would be forever tainted by what he'd done. They never imagined the serial killer terrorising their own community would be someone they loved. The shattering of their family was compounded by the guilt that somehow they should've known.

But honestly, who among us would think to look at our own family? We don't discuss an odd friend or relative and conclude *serial killer* or *murderer*. (Disclaimer: crime writers might!)

The sad truth is that more people are murdered by someone they know, than by a random stranger or a killer on a mission, like Paul Denyer.

Either way, too many families have to deal with this reality. And whether the murderer in *their* family killed members of their own family or strangers, the pain, confusion, and horror of the family living with the fallout is immense.

Around 2004, I went on the road for stories. This is not something I could do too often because of my full-time job. Even though teachers get generous holidays compared to other professions, holidays for me up, until then, involved juggling parenting around my writing. By 2004, my daughter was 17 and well and truly able to look after herself; even though my absence at that time would almost certainly guarantee most of her clothes would end up tie-dyed and my house would be filled with teenagers who were disproportionately named Jess.

Aside from escaping my tie-dying teenager and the Jesses, there was another reason for hitting the road. Publishers wanted national stories. Cases that occurred in Melbourne were too parochial, they said. It was easier to sell a book interstate if it had stories from other Australian states.

So, for my school holidays, I organised a road trip interstate to New South Wales to interview some police officers. I'd put out a call through the *Australian Police Journal*. Over the years, I had contributed stories to the APJ which was good for recognition and now served me well as I had a good track record with cops. From memory, the quarterly journal had about 60,000 readers – and they were all in my author demographic.

Through the journal, I proposed that if any officers needed help telling a story or had one they were interested in sharing, I would be happy to write it. I gained quite a few contacts.

A lot of cops have a story to tell or a whole book to fill, but almost never get around to sitting at a computer to write it themselves. Hint: writing is much harder than it looks.

Going on the road was fun. I'm someone who is happy in my own company. I drove away from home feeling quite the writing stereotype, hitting the road in search of a story. One of my stops was the police complex in the seaside city of Wollongong, about 70km south of Sydney. The cops there told me they had so many incredible cases, they thought there should be a TV show called *CSI Wollongong*.

I had to agree. Half a dozen years earlier, the city had been rocked by the gruesome murder of Wollongong's former mayor,

Frank Arkell. After three decades as a lord mayor, Arkell was charged with 27 counts of sexual abuse but was tortured and murdered before he came to trial. His murder came hot on the heels of the beheading murder of another Wollongong man. An unemployed 19-year-old, Mark Valera, was eventually charged and found guilty of both murders.

But by far the most horrific case the Wollongong crime scene cops told me about was the De Gruchy murders. Jenny De Gruchy and two of her children, Adrian and Sarah, had been murdered by her eldest child, Matthew. The case had a devastating impact on the community, the family, and on some of the police who investigated it. The injuries to the victims were so severe, it looked in the early stages, like they'd been shot at point blank range with a shotgun.

I'll never forget being told how one of the investigators walked out of the De Gruchy house and never worked again. The crime scene was so awful that, when they went to check the garage, he suffered a moment of terror because he was convinced they would find the gunman responsible lying in wait. In that split second, he thought he was about to die. For some, there's no going back from the moment. I've seen it before and no doubt I'll see it again.

Some people believed that those who work in traumatic careers, like police and paramedics, have a finite number of jobs inside them. And when that number is exceeded, they break. I don't know if this is right, but I've seen so many break over the years.

When fear slips through cracks in the armour, the armour is forever compromised.

For a seasoned investigator to walk away from the De Gruchy house spoke volumes about the horror they all saw that day in 1996.

Fast forward to my visit in 2004. When one of the lead investigators working a nightshift offered to take me to the scene of the crime, we drove slowly through the streets of Wollongong to Albion Park Rail where the murders took place. There's something about a dark police car on a dark night. Voices soften, become reflective. On the way, he described the hopeless situation everyone faced. Three members of a family had been murdered. The son was charged. The extended family's disbelief that the teenager could kill. When it was all over, the father came to visit the detective. The two men sat down and the detective took him through the evidence, piece by piece, until the father knew the awful truth.

There were no winners in the guilty verdict.

Perhaps that was my biggest thing I learnt on my road trip. I was approaching my 40th birthday, and I finally understood the huge canyon between the law and justice. Maybe there was no such thing as justice. There was incarceration, sure. But balance could never be restored, the dead could never be returned.

What was taken could never be given back.

Rather than turn cynical, I made myself try and make sense of this world I was writing about. I realised that while lives were invariably changed when tragedy struck, that very change forms

When I began writing there weren't many Australians writing true crime, and I was the only woman doing it.

Now I'm often surrounded by them. I'm here with Rachael Brown, Kate Wilde and Maryrose Cuskelly

the next version of those left behind. Moving through grief, we are all transformed into something different. We don't leave grief behind; we tuck it inside our hearts and it comes with us and becomes part of our transformation. The hidden gift inherent in this transformation is that we are strengthened. We are wiser. We are more compassionate. We are more human.

As I left my 30s behind, these lessons were largely esoteric. The only loss I had faced in my life were my elderly nanas who'd had the proverbial 'good innings'. Until we lose a loved one, we don't know who we are as grievers. Will I be stoic? Will I crumble? Am I a crier?

At this stage of my life, I had no answers to these questions. But I soon would.

16

THE HOUSE OF HORROR

It was early in the morning of Wednesday 13 March 1996. Steve Bailey was out the front of his house in Shearwater Boulevard in Albion Park Rail, talking to a neighbour, when another neighbour, 18-year-old Matthew De Gruchy, came running out of his house, shouting in distress.

'Something's happened to Mum and Sarah!' Matthew yelled.

Steve Bailey rushed over and followed the young man into a horrifying scene in the master bedroom at the front of the residence. It took only a few seconds – before he ran out again to call police – to see that Jenny De Gruchy, Matthew's mother, was battered and bloody and obviously dead.

Detective Sergeant Danny Sharkey – head of a crew of eight detectives covering the New South Wales suburb of Shellharbour, which included the Albion Park Rail area – was working that day. He and a colleague Ron Smith and two other detectives drove to Shearwater Boulevard.

When they pulled up near the De Gruchy house, Sharkey saw an ambulance parked on the road outside, and a young man doubled up on the lawn with an older man attending him.

The fewer people who enter a crime scene the better, but Danny Sharkey had to verify there was in fact a body inside the house.

First he spoke to Steve Bailey, who told him he'd entered the house and then called 000 after the son, Matthew, had said something had happened to his mother and his sister, Sarah.

Detective Sharkey entered the front bedroom, where a woman was lying in bed under the covers. Her head was such a bloodied mess he thought she'd most likely been killed by a shotgun blast.

When he checked the other bedrooms, he found 13-year-old Sarah also dead on her bed. She too had received severe head injuries.

Oddly, considering the damage done to them, there wasn't much blood splatter around the beds of either victim.

Sharkey and his detectives did a quick walk through the house, without touching anything, to ensure there weren't any further victims, or an offender, then called in the crime scene examiners.

Matthew De Gruchy, in the meantime, was so distressed at finding the bodies of his mother and little sister, after coming home from spending the night at his girlfriend's place, the ambulance had taken him to hospital.

Detective Senior Constable Barry Doherty was the first crime scene examiner to enter the house. His job was to record the two specific crime scenes, and the rest of the house, and collect any evidence that might indicate who killed Jenny and Sarah De Gruchy.

A cursory inspection of the tiles in the hallway showed that someone had tried to clean up what looked like blood on the floor. In other rooms, cupboards were open, disconnected cords in a cabinet under the television suggested a video recorder might have been removed. There was no sign of forced entry, but not every window in the house was locked, and the rear sliding door was closed but not locked.

Barry Doherty called his boss, Detective Sergeant Steve Hodder, at the Wollongong Forensic Division and explained the situation. In cases like this, it was all hands on deck. Hodder, and a fingerprint expert and video operator, made their way to Shearwater Boulevard.

With Matthew De Gruchy in hospital, and his mother and sister dead, there were two members of the family unaccounted for. There was no sign of husband, Wayne De Gruchy, or the other son that neighbours had mentioned, 15-year-old Adrian.

But it was Wednesday, so Detective Sharkey figured Adrian might be at school. He sent officers there.

When they reported back that the boy hadn't turned up for classes, Sharkey began to wonder if perhaps Adrian had killed his mother and sister and then run away; or had witnessed the crime and was hiding.

Because the whole house was considered the crime scene, it was some time before anyone got around to looking in the garage.

Detectives Danny Sharkey and Ron Smith, and crime scene examiner Barry Doherty, walked through a neighbouring property and out its back gate to access the De Gruchy house from the rear. All the yards on that side of Shearwater Boulevard backed on to a large nature reserve, which meant it was important to organise a line-search for any evidence that might have been left by the killer in the parkland. If that was the way he had left the scene.

At the back of the De Gruchy house was a pergola, under which was a spa and a door into the double garage. When Sharkey and his team opened that door, they made another shocking discovery.

The garage was awash with blood – from the body of the missing teenager. Adrian De Gruchy's body was visible, but his head had been covered by a doona cover; a red-and-white one with a pattern of Motocross trail-bike riders. There was a glue gun oozing glue on Adrian's right side, and a small wooden chair underneath his right hand. It looked like he had been fixing the chair when he was attacked.

Photographs were taken before the investigators pulled back the doona. Adrian's injuries were as brutal as those of his mother and sister. He had been so severely beaten around the head, that a number of his teeth were on the ground next to him.

'Cast-off blood' is a term used to describe the blood spattering that occurs when a victim is hit. It's not just the splatter from the connecting blow itself, but also from the blood that adheres to the weapon and gets flicked off as that weapon is drawn back before further strikes.

The blood evidence in the De Gruchy garage told the story of a brutal, prolonged attack. The cast-off was evident on the ceiling of the garage, indicating that many blows had struck the defenceless teenaged boy. Unlike his mother and sister, nothing had been used to cover his head during the attack. There was blood everywhere.

At some point of the chaotic morning at the Shearwater Boulevard house, the telephone rang. Danny Sharkey answered it. On the other end of the line was Wayne De Gruchy. Over the course of the morning, detectives had tried to locate the missing husband but the company where he worked told the detectives he was on the road. Now, he was obviously back at the office and ringing in to check on his family.

Given the tragic nature of the news he had to break to the father, Sharkey asked Wayne De Gruchy if he could put his secretary on the phone. De Gruchy obliged and a woman came on the line. Sharkey introduced himself and said, 'Stay with him because I've got some very, *very* bad news for him.' The secretary agreed and put Wayne De Gruchy back on the line. The detective gently broke the news to the shocked husband that his wife, daughter and younger son were all dead.

Immediately after the phone call, Sharkey contacted police at Parramatta, close to De Gruchy's workplace, and organised for officers to collect him and take him to the Warilla police station.

The sight of Jenny, Sarah and Adrian lying dead in their home with terrible head wounds was distressing, even for the seasoned investigators. But the idea of it, as the news spread, was horrifying and incomprehensible for those in Shearwater Boulevarde who knew the family. Indeed, emotions were running high all around. Danny Sharkey organised for a mobile command post to be set up in a police van outside the house and, as distressed neighbours gathered outside the De Gruchy house, he also organised for grief counsellors to talk to anyone who needed it.

The detective also organised for a large contingent of State Emergency Services volunteers to search the nature reserve behind the De Gruchy house. Nothing of any evidentiary value was found.

One of Sharkey's detectives was sent to interview the distressed

Matthew De Gruchy in hospital. Unfortunately, that officer was diverted to interview a young woman who'd been sexually assaulted, and by the time Sharkey could spare another cop, Matthew had been collected by an aunt.

Crime scene examiners Barry Doherty and Steve Hodder began to process the house. The master bedroom was furnished with a double bed, a dressing table and an exercise treadmill. Holland blinds covered the windows which were closed and locked. Two other doorways leading from the room went into a walk-in wardrobe and an ensuite.

The bed, against the northern wall, had a wooden bed-head and bedside tables. The ceiling fan was fitted with a light, which was turned off.

Jennifer De Gruchy's head, neck, right shoulder and arm were visible above the blanket which covered everything else. The head and facial injuries inflicted on her were so severe that she was unrecognisable.

Her head was on the pillow leaning against the bedside table, and there was a lot of blood soaked into that pillow and down into the mattress. On the floor next to the body was a broken denture plate.

Strangely, a large piece of the grey carpet near the side of the bed was cut out and missing. Doherty noted that two other smaller sections of carpet had also been removed.

Given the severe nature of Jenny's injuries, and the lack of

Crime scene photo of the area of missing carpet in Jenny De Gruchy's bedroom.

blood in anywhere but the immediate scene, Doherty formed the opinion that something had been held over her head during the attack. His boss, Steve Hodder, agreed. There was only a spray of fine blood spatter on the wall above the body, which Doherty swabbed for further analysis.

In the adjoining ensuite, Barry Doherty found a small reddish stain at the bottom of the wash basin near the plug hole. He took a swab of it.

Next to be examined was Sarah's room. A big white teddy bear sat on the floor by the door. Sarah's body lay on pink sheets on a single bed. Posters of her favourite bands were stuck to the wall above where she lay. A Walkman was on the floor by the bed. Resting on Sarah's head was a blue and white coloured seat cushion from a chair in the dining room. The cushion was heavily blood-stained. The teenager had sustained the same severe head and facial injuries as her mother.

In addition to the head injuries, Barry Doherty noticed what he described as a 'tram track' bruise on Sarah's right forearm. The bruise was about 15cm long and 5mm wide consisting of two parallel lines that seemed to close off at the end. This kind of bruise, which was obviously the shape of whatever weapon had been used to make it, could help investigators narrow their search for the weapon.

In the hallway connecting the bedrooms, Barry Doherty examined the faint reddish-coloured stains on the white tiles. He placed numbered markers beside the stains and photographed them. Preliminary tests proved positive for blood. He then swabbed the areas and put the evidence in sealed containers.

While Barry Doherty continued the examination of the interior of the house, Steve Hodder instructed members of the Police Rescue Squad to search the backyard, which included a fish pond and fountains. He also had members of the squad get up into the roof space of the house to see if anything had been hidden up there. Nothing of evidentiary value was found.

Well-respected forensic pathologist Dr Allan Cala from the

Institute of Forensic Medicine was called to the scene. It was his job to examine the deceased in situ and try to determine when the three victims died. Dr Cala checked each of the bodies for signs of rigor mortis, lividity, and took body temperature readings. His best estimate for the time of death was somewhere between 8pm and 1am.

Dr Cala also noted the tram track mark on Sarah's arm which looked like it had been caused by a long thin weapon with a squared-off end. When the doctor examined Adrian and lifted the dead boy's T-shirt, he saw the exact same parallel marks on Adrian's chest, but in addition to the tram track bruises, there was also a circular mark on Adrian's chest.

It was Dr Cala who concluded that the three victims had not been shot at all, but had been beaten to death with the weapon that had left marks on both Adrian and Sarah. It dawned on the doctor and the investigators that the circular wound and the long parallel bruises could have been caused by a wheel brace – the device used to loosen and remove the nuts on a car wheel before changing the tyre.

Steve Hodder and Barry Doherty immediately went to inspect the boot of Jenny De Gruchy's white, late model Toyota Seca which was in the driveway. Police on watch outside the house verified the vehicle hadn't been touched by anyone since they arrived.

Steve Hodder discovered the small hatch to the space that contained the jack was closed but not clicked shut. He opened it, saw the jack was where it should be, but there was no sign of the wheel brace. Hodder lifted the boot carpet. The spare tyre in the storage cavity was obviously brand new as it still had the flashing – tiny rubber pieces – around the edge.

If the tyre had never been changed, why was the jack hatch of Mrs De Gruchy's car open, and where was the wheel brace? And if the wheel brace from the Toyota was the murder weapon, then who had access to the car?

According to early reports, Matthew De Gruchy had driven the Toyota to his girlfriend's house the previous night, and back again that morning when he found the bodies of his mother and sister. If this was so, then when was the murder weapon taken from the car?

Examining the vehicle more closely, Steve Hodder noticed a tuft of carpet fibres on the floor near the back seat. To the naked eye, the tuft was a similar colour to the carpet in Jenny De Gruchy's bedroom and included a tiny reddish-stain, which both crime scene examiners thought might be blood. They bagged the sample and organised for the car to be towed to the Wollongong Crime Scene Unit for further examination.

When he learned that Wayne De Gruchy had arrived at the Warilla police station, Detective Danny Sharkey took one of the grief counsellors from the crime scene command van outside the house and drove to the station.

By this time, Sharkey had also located Matthew De Gruchy and had him brought to the police station. After Wayne spent some time with the grief counsellor, he was reunited with his only surviving offspring.

Matthew was questioned by detectives and confirmed that he was at his girlfriend's house the previous night when his mother and Sarah and Adrian were killed.

When his girlfriend was questioned, however, she told police that Matthew had telephoned her around 8pm and said he would be at her house shortly but he didn't show up until much later. She told detectives she had rung the De Gruchy house at 10pm but there was no answer.

When Matthew finally arrived at her house at 11pm, he told her his family had received some crank calls implying that three members of his family would die that night, so they'd all decided not to answer the phone.

This information, provided by the girlfriend, was curious because, in his interview, Matthew hadn't mentioned anything about crank calls and death threats.

Back at the house, Barry Doherty continued his work. In the laundry he found a number of blood smears on the floor which he processed. The washing machine contained two towels and a pair of green-and-yellow rubber gloves. Although they had all been washed, there was faint staining on the towels that might be have been blood. All in all, it looked like someone had tried to clean up the scene – at the scene – which was not the likely action of a random attacker.

Doherty found more reddish stains when he examined the family bathroom, this time in the bottom of the wash basin and on the mirror above the vanity unit. Again photographs and swabs were taken. In a faint red smear on one of the vanity unit doors, Doherty found what appeared to be a partial fingerprint. This was closely photographed, and then, in consultation with the fingerprint expert, the whole cupboard door was removed as evidence.

There was little evidence to be gathered in Adrian's bedroom – not surprisingly as he was killed in the garage – but there were a couple of smears of what appeared to be blood near the light switch.

In Matthew De Gruchy's bedroom, some drawers in a wall unit were open as were the doors to the wardrobe; and there were a number of items, including a metal money box, on the floor.

In the lounge room, Barry Doherty examined the area around the television for clues. While a video recorder had apparently been taken, the video cord was still attached to the back of the television. On the floor in front of the TV cabinet, were a few video cassettes and an empty box from a Sega video game system.

Aside from where the apparent ransacking had taken place, the house in Shearwater Boulevard was extremely neat, tidy, and clean. This was good for crime scene examiners because most of the things that were out of place in the house looked like they were connected with the crime.

After many hours of crime scene work, it was finally time for the bodies to be moved. Barry Doherty organised with Dr Cala for the three family members to be transported to the Institute of Forensic Medicine in Glebe for examination the following morning.

When it was time to move Adrian De Gruchy, both Doherty

and Dr Cala noticed large areas of skin peeling off his left arm in sections that had been in contact with the concrete floor. As soon as the body was moved, they were hit with a strong smell of petrol. A closer examination of Adrian's clothing revealed that both his shorts and shirt appeared to be soaked in the stuff. A red jerry can nearby was examined and a number of prints were found on its handle.

It was horrible to think that after beating the boy to death, the killer had poured petrol on him, perhaps intending to set him alight.

Right from the start, the investigators knew there was something about the De Gruchy murder scene that wasn't quite right. Jenny De Gruchy had been killed in her bed. She was under the covers and wearing a nightie, indicating she may even have been asleep when she was murdered. Sarah De Gruchy was also attacked in her bed possibly while listening to music on her Walkman.

Adrian had probably been fixing the little chair when he was murdered. As the garage was accessed via the back patio or through the external double tilt-doors, it meant the killer had sought him out.

And was it odd that the 15-year-old was still up when his mother and sister were in bed, or did that give an indication of the timeline of the murders?

In the collective experience of the investigators a burglary gone horribly wrong was unlikely – mostly because of where the bodies were found. And, while a housebreaker disturbed in the act, might assault a homeowner in order to get out of the house quickly, committing a triple murder – of such violence – seemed an extreme way to cover up the theft of a video recorder.

Indeed, the alleged robbery looked staged. The most likely scenario was that someone wanted members of the De Gruchy family dead and tried to throw police off the track by throwing a few things around and taking the VCR.

Also curious, and telling, were the pieces of carpet removed from the bedroom, and the fact that someone had tried to clean up after the murders.

The blood on the hallway floor was diluted with water which meant someone had tried to wash it away, not simply wipe it up. The investigators wondered if the killer had been injured and was worried about leaving blood at the scene. What other reason could explain the trouble taken to cut out a section of carpet, and wash a tiled floor?

What the killer clearly didn't realise was that crime scene examiners had equipment that could detect even the minutest traces of blood. The floor, bedrooms and garage had been examined with a Polilight machine, that assisted with the detection of blood, semen, hairs and fibres not visible to the naked eye.

Barry Doherty worked the crime scene at the De Gruchy house from 8am until 1.30am and then, after snatching a couple of hours sleep, was back on duty at 7am to attend the post mortem examinations of the deceased. He had to be on hand to collect forensic samples from Dr Cala, who would examine the bodies. The intense working hours immediately following a murder were crucial for all investigators.

The sight of the three bodies lined up on adjoining steel tables in the autopsy room brought home to Doherty the enormity of the loss to the De Gruchy family. Mother, daughter and son were all examined and found to have massive head injuries from repeated assaults, probably with the wheel brace, which had yet to be located.

A wheel brace from the same model Toyota Seca owned by Jenny De Gruchy, had been obtained from a local Toyota dealer. The handle matched the tram-track bruises on Sarah and Adrian, and the round head corresponded to the bruise on Adrian's chest.

Dr Cala found that Jenny De Gruchy suffered severe and multiple fractures to her skull and facial bones, causing severe and extensive underlying brain trauma. He said the cause of death was the due to severe blunt force head trauma, and the resultant blood aspiration and loss, most likely from a wheel brace or sledge hammer and quite probably, at least initially, while she slept. He found defence injuries on Jenny's hands indicating that early in the attack, she may have tried to defend herself.

Chillingly, he wrote towards the end of his report: 'The injuries sustained would have been caused by a large amount of force. The facial bones in particular, were grossly fragmented. I believe that numerous blows were delivered to the face and head of the deceased. Death was not instantaneous given the amount of blood aspirated into the lungs. This could only have occurred whilst the deceased was alive.' This meant that Jenny De Gruchy had survived long enough during the attack to breathe in a large amount of her own blood.

Dr Cala found that 15-year-old Adrian had 21 injuries to his neck and head and six injuries to the trunk, including some tram track or linear bruises to the chest. He had a grossly fractured face and base of the skull, lacerations to the back of his head, right forehead, and mouth, as well as fractures to the cheekbones and jawbone. Blood had haemorrhaged into his brain, and many of Adrian's teeth were either broken or missing. The head injuries were similar to his mother's, and Dr Cala concluded that they could have been caused by the same weapon.

Dr Cala noted that the skin peeling on Adrian's left arm and left hip region was consistent with petrol being poured on him after he had died. Aside from the peeling skin, there was no other physical reaction to the petrol.

He described Adrian's injuries as coming from a 'blitz-type' attack. 'It would appear that Adrian De Gruchy was working in the garage at the time of the attack and may have been struck from behind initially. There were no defence-type injuries to his arms or elsewhere.'

Dr Cala listed Adrian's cause of death as: 'complications of severe blunt force head and facial trauma'.

Next, the pathologist examined Sarah's body and concluded the 13-year-old had also died as a result of severe blunt force head trauma. He noted, however, 'there were some aspects of the scene in conjunction with the post-mortem findings which were suggestive of smothering... frothy clear fluid was present around the nose and mouth, and in conjunction with the finding of the flat pillow adjacent to the deceased's head at the crime scene, was suggestive of smothering.'

Dr Cala noted the defence-type injuries on Sarah's right arm, suggesting it was probably raised to fend off the attack. The pillow therefore may have been used to muffle her cries.

The pathologist wrote: 'the injuries on the deceased's head were similar to those on her mother's and brother's heads and were probably caused by a heavy, possibly metal object such as a crowbar or wheel brace'.

In many murder cases, especially in a domestic situation, suspicion always falls first on members of the immediate family. Since three members of the De Gruchy family were now dead, that left husband or son, Wayne or Matthew, as possible suspects. It is more usual for a husband to be the perpetrator in this type of killing, so it was vital for police to ascerain Wayne De Gruchy's whereabouts for the time of the murders.

It was quickly established that the father of the family had stayed with his parents in Sydney the previous night. An early red herring was that a neighbour reported seeing a car similar to Wayne De Gruchy's – and driven by someone fitting his description – in Shearwater Boulevard in the early hours of the morning before the murders were discovered.

Police considered the possibility that Wayne had driven back to his house in the middle of the night to kill his family, but soon found out that his car was in for repairs, and he'd driven a different make and colour to his parents the night before.

Wayne De Gruchy had a cast-iron alibi.

Matthew De Gruchy, on the other hand, did not.

Matthew's whereabouts on the night of the murders was less certain. He told his girlfriend he'd be at her place soon, after his 8pm phone call, but didn't get there until 11pm. And no one had answered the De Gruchy phone at 10pm when she rang to find out where he was.

On Friday 15 March, two mornings after the murders, Detective Sergeant Danny Sharkey arranged for members of the De Gruchy extended family to attend the police station. It was obvious to the detective that the family thought he and his fellow officers were suspicious of Matthew and they were not happy about it. Wayne De Gruchy's brother Paul had even advised Matthew not to cooperate with the police.

Undeterred, Sharkey took Matthew into an interview room.

'Matthew, I want you to understand very clearly what I am now about to say to you,' he said to the young man. 'I want to ask you questions about the death of your mother, sister and brother. Do you understand me?'

'Yes,' Matthew said in a quiet voice.

'Matthew, you have been given some advice by your Uncle Paul. I understand that his advice to you was that you do not have to speak to me or any of the other police or answer my questions. What you have been told by your uncle is true; you do not have to answer any of my questions. I want you to clearly understand what I have just said to you.'

Again Matthew said, 'Yes.'

Sharkey pushed a little harder. 'Matthew, I believe that you know a lot more about what happened to your mother, brother and sister the other night. More than what you said in the statement you made. Is there anything you want to say to me about what happened the other night?'

Matthew sat with his arms across his stomach, rocking back and forward with his head bowed. He said nothing. One of the other detectives asked if Matthew had anything to say about the night of the murders. Again he said nothing.

'Matthew, this is not going to go away,' said Sharkey. 'We will be investigating this for as long as it takes. Do you understand what I'm saying?'

After a long silence, finally Matthew spoke. 'I told the policeman the other night what I know.'

'Matthew, I believe that you had something to do with the deaths of your mother, brother and sister. Do you understand what I have just said to you?'

Matthew repeated himself. 'I told the policeman the other night what happened.

Another detective said, 'We think you know a lot more about

this than what you told the policeman. Firstly can you tell us why you didn't come home until after 8 o'clock in the morning?'

Matthew said nothing.

'We have been told that you have to be home earlier than this so that your mum can use the car to take your brother and sister to school. What can you tell us about that?'

Matthew didn't answer.

'The wheel brace and jack handle are missing from the car that you had possession of on that night. Do you know where they are?'

Matthew remained silent and sat with his arm hugging his stomach rocking back and forward in his chair.

'Are you feeling all right?' asked the detective.

'No, I feel sick,' replied Matthew.

Sharkey continued. 'We found a lot of blood through the house and also some hair. We will need to get some blood and hair samples from you for elimination purposes. You better speak to your uncle about this.'

When Sharkey opened the door to the interview room, Matthew's uncle Paul was right outside the door. Matthew was taken back to the rest of his family while Paul De Gruchy made his displeasure at the questioning of his nephew known to the detectives. As far as the family were concerned, the loss of Jenny, Sarah and Adrian was being compounded by the suspicion against Matthew. Sharkey could understand how they felt. The family had been through so much in the past few days, but he had a job to do, and everything so far indicated that Matthew knew more than he was letting on.

Arrangements were made for Matthew and his father to attend the local hospital where both men would give samples of blood and hair.

Detective Sharkey wanted a record of Matthew's exact movements in the house when he discovered the bodies because then his account could be matched against the evidence that was turning up under analysis. Under questioning which was video-recorded, Matthew leaned his chin on his hand and showed little emotion.

His answers were often monosyllabic. His father and uncle were present during the interview.

Matthew said that he had arrived home at 8.30 in the morning of Wednesday 13 March and walked inside to get his wallet. He then left straight away to go to the shop to buy cigarettes. He hadn't seen any members of his family at the time. When he returned, he said the house seemed quiet so he had gone past Sarah's door and then into his mother's room. It was then, he said, that he had discovered his mum's body and had immediately run outside.

Sharkey asked Matthew whether he had gone into Sarah's bedroom. Matthew said that he hadn't. This was one of the first anomalies in Matthew's account. Neighbour Steve Bailey was certain that when Matthew had come running out of the house on the morning of the murders, he had said, 'There's something wrong with Mum and Sarah'. But according to his police statement, Matthew hadn't gone into Sarah's room at all, so how could he have known there was anything 'wrong' with her?

The detectives asked Matthew to make a list of stolen property. By then, Matthew and his father had been allowed back into the house. Matthew listed CDs, the VCR, and a number of other items including two calculators belonging to him and his brother.

Danny Sharkey wondered how a young man who had just lost three members of his family would notice that his brother's pocket calculator was missing.

The detectives had heard stories, while talking to neighbours and taking other statements, that Matthew had sometimes been violent towards his mother, and apparently fought with her about driving the Toyota. When asked if he had argued with his mother about using her car, Matthew replied: 'I wouldn't call them arguments'.

He would often borrow his father's vehicle but, as that was in for repairs, Mathew had driven Jenny's car on the night of the killings. The detectives wondered if that had been with her permission, or whether the whole terrible incident had been over something as trivial as: 'Mum can I borrow the car?'

The case was starting to build up against Matthew De Gruchy.

Blood on the floor in the hallway had by now been analysed and was found to be his. He was the last to use the Toyota, and carpet fibre had been found in the car with blood on it. The partial fingerprint in blood on the door handle in the family bathroom belonged to Matthew, and his prints were on the jerry can of petrol. While he did use the jerry can to put petrol in both the family cars – investigators knew the last person to use the can would have been the person who poured petrol on Adrian's body.

According to Matthew's girlfriend, and a police examination, Matthew had no wounds on his body that could account for his blood in various places around the house, but experts agreed that when under intense pressure people can suffer from spontaneous nose bleeds.

Detectives working on the case checked the phone company for incoming and outgoing calls from the De Gruchy house around the time of the murder. Matthew's calls to his girlfriend were listed, but there was no record of any calls coming in at the time he claimed the crank caller had threatened the deaths of three members of his family. More holes in the story of Matthew De Gruchy.

While some detectives never get to investigate a murder, Danny Sharkey had had more than his fair share, including other cases that turned out to be 'domestic' homicides or family murder-suicides. Those cases had been fairly cut and dried and in many ways the De Gruchy case was too.

But even with the evidence pointing to Matthew De Gruchy, the detectives still had to build a strong case before any arrest could be made. This careful process couldn't be rushed. But, while the detectives had to conduct thorough interviews and wait for evidence analysis results, the community and the media were crying out for a quick arrest.

As evidence began to mount up against the remaining De Gruchy child, Danny Sharkey brought him in for further questioning. He wanted to put certain allegations to the young man to see how he responded. Matthew again arrived at the police station with his father and a number of other relatives in tow.

Luckily for police, however, Matthew was 18-years-old and could be interviewed without another adult present.

Wayne De Gruchy and the other relatives were shown into an office down the corridor. They were angry with the police because they felt that while the detectives were focusing on Matthew as a suspect, they weren't out there 'catching the real killer'.

Cases like this are fraught with difficulty for police. Trying to explain to a family dealing with the loss of three loved ones, in horrific circumstances, that one of their own could be responsible, was almost impossible; especially when that suspect was only a teenager.

In the interview room, Matthew was starting to feel the pressure. Just as Detective Sharkey thought the young man was weakening and on the verge of making admission, one of his uncles burst into the room. Even though the detectives escorted the uncle out again explaining that Matthew was an adult and the police had every right to question him alone, the moment was lost forever.

With nothing even approaching a confession, it was up to the forensic evidence to prove Matthew De Gruchy was a killer. Over a hundred samples, specimens and exhibits had to be examined. The carpet tuft found in Jenny's car, that Matthew had driven on the night of the murders, was analysed and an expert concluded it was 'highly probable that the carpet tuft had its origin in the bedroom carpet'. Even more damning was Matthew's DNA found on the carpet tuft, on the hallway tiles, and on the wall above his mother's bed.

With Matthew De Gruchy fairly and squarely in the cross-hairs, Danny Sharkey looked at his suspect's known movements on the night of the murders. He had spoken to his girlfriend from the Shearwater Boulevard house at 8pm and then arrived at her place around 11pm so the only places detectives knew Matthew had definitely driven that night was the route between his house and hers.

Sharkey discovered there were 15 creeks and waterholes between the two houses – including the one directly behind the De Gruchy house. He organised for Police Rescue Squad officers to search each watercourse to a distance of 500m from the banks. If Matthew had ditched evidence on the way to his girlfriend's house, Sharkey hoped the police divers would find it.

Nine days after losing his mother, sister and brother, Matthew De Gruchy attended their triple funeral. He wore a white shirt, dark trousers, and dark sunglasses. His long hair was tied back in a pony-tail.

It took police exactly two months from the day Jenny, Sarah and Adrian were killed to find the evidence that would lead to Matthew's arrest.

Although the item was first found by some kids a couple of days after the triple murder, it was some time before the information came to the attention of police

A group of boys had been riding their BMX bikes alongside a dam at the old Boral Brickworks on the western side of the Princes Highway in Woonona, when they spotted a bag in the shallow water. They fished it out and went through its contents. Among other things, the bag contained a hammer and a big piece of carpet. The boys took a couple of items from the bag then tossed it back into the dam.

While they thought nothing of it, one of the boys mentioned the find to his father, and a few weeks later it occurred to that man the bag might hold some significance to the investigation.

On Monday 13 May 1996, police went to the area indicated by

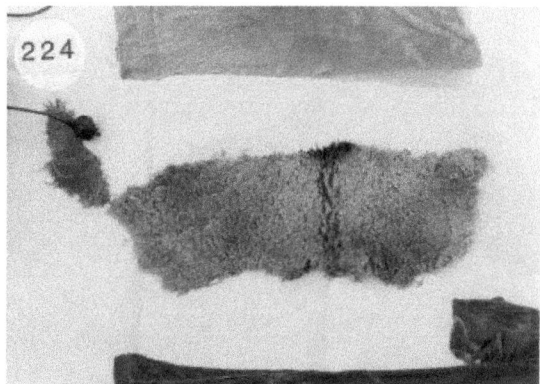

Crime scene photo of the carpet piece found in the bag in the Boral Brickworks dam.

Crime scene photo of the plastic zip-lock bag.

the BMX riders. Police divers were called in and Detective Danny Sharkey supervised the search. The divers located two bags: a red-and-white sports bag, and a black backpack.

Crime scene examiners Steve Hodder and Barry Doherty supervised the removal of items from the bag onto sheets of plastic, where they photographed and documented along with other things found loose in the mud.

The items including a video recorder, a calculator labelled *A De Gruchy*, various CDs and videotapes, and Jenny De Gruchy's purse – all the things Matthew De Gruchy had said were stolen from his house when the murders were committed.

The sports bag also contained a piece of carpet similar in size to the piece missing from Jenny De Gruchy's room, and a small zip-lock bag containing a number of Band-Aids in their wrappers and pieces of a torn-up note.

One of the police officers joked, 'Wouldn't it be funny if that note was a How To list!'

That's exactly what it was.

Danny Sharkey drove the distance between the De Gruchy's Shearwater Boulevard home, the old Boral Brickworks dam and the house of Matthew's girlfriend. The 31km drive could be comfortably completed in 26 minutes travelling 5km below the speed limit. Matthew certainly had time between his phone call to his girlfriend at 8pm and his arriving at her house at 11pm to drive via the dam and ditch the evidence.

When the items from the sports bag in the dam were taken back to Forensics to be examined, Barry Doherty carefully dried out the torn note and put the pieces together like a jigsaw puzzle. The letterhead on the flip-side of the paper read: *Noah's on the Beach.*

Pieced together, the note revealed a chilling list. It read:

    * Open gate
    * throw bottle down the track
    * throw things down wall in roof
    track suit pants 1
    Knife 2
    T Shirts 2
    Shoe's 2
    hanky
    pole
    towel
    * open blinds to see
    through   Sarah   mum
                   Adrian
    head but ~~mirror~~ bench
    Have shower
    * throw hi fi down back
    * hit arm with pole
    * hit leg with pole
    * cut somewhere with knife

While, obviously, it was possible that the items in the bag could have been stolen and discarded by a burglar who had, for some unfathomable reason, also decided to murder three people in cold blood it was the note that put paid to that notion.

The note tied Matthew De Gruchy to the murders of his own

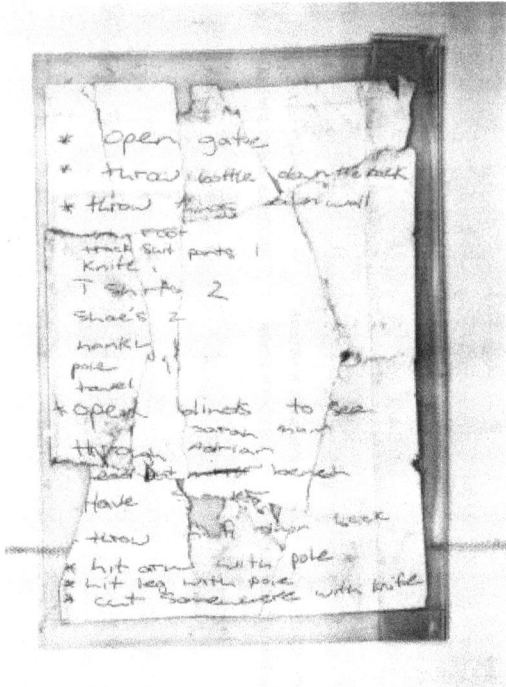

The reconstructed list found in the zip-lock bag
inside the sports bag in the dam at the Boral Brickworks.

family, for who else but one of her own children would refer to Jenny as 'mum' and would know the names of the siblings?

A handwriting expert later found 12 points of comparison between the writing on the 'how to' list and Matthew De Gruchy's handwriting. His report said: 'there were many significant similarities between the note and samples of Matthew's writing and no significant differences. It is my opinion that the person who wrote the specimen writings also wrote the questioned writings on item 1...'

Police made arrangements to drain the dam to search for anything else that might have been thrown into it. The draining process began on 27 May and, again, Steve Hodder was on hand to examine any items they might find, and also to photograph the search. A Sega case was located in mud on the western side of the dam, a video tape and a handkerchief were found on the western bank.

Matthew De Gruchy was taken into custody at 7.30am on Saturday 22 June. Detective Danny Sharkey found him at his girlfriend's house and told him that he wanted to speak to him again about the murders.

'When?' asked Matthew.

'I want you to come back to the Warilla police station with me now,' replied Sharkey.

'I need to speak to my dad.'

'That's fine. Get dressed and you can ring him before we leave.'

Matthew got dressed and then went into the lounge room of his girlfriend's house and rang his dad. He turned to the detectives and told them that his dad wasn't home and the answering machine was on. Sharkey left a message for Wayne De Gruchy and then Matthew was taken to the Warilla police station.

Wayne got there soon after his son and called his brother Paul to come to the station as well. He also used the phone at the police station to arrange legal representation for his son.

After video-taping another police interview during which Matthew made no admissions of guilt, Sharkey charged the 18-year-old with the murder of his mother, brother and sister.

Later that day, Steve Hodder and Barry Doherty went back to the house in Shearwater Boulevard, accompanied by detectives investigating the case, to search Matthew's bedroom. They found a single sheet of a note pad bearing the words *Noah's on the Beach* – the same letterhead that was on the back of the 'how to' list.

Just to make sure, they checked the roof space again. The note had indicated that evidence was to have been discarded down the walls through the roof. The roof space was accessed through a manhole in the garage. A search of the area revealed that the internal wall cavities could not be accessed because of timber capping nailed over the top of the wall frames.

In the immediate aftermath of the arrest, headlines in the *Illawarra Mercury* screamed: 'Father vows to stand by his son'. In the court appearance after his arrest, Wayne De Gruchy was quoted in the

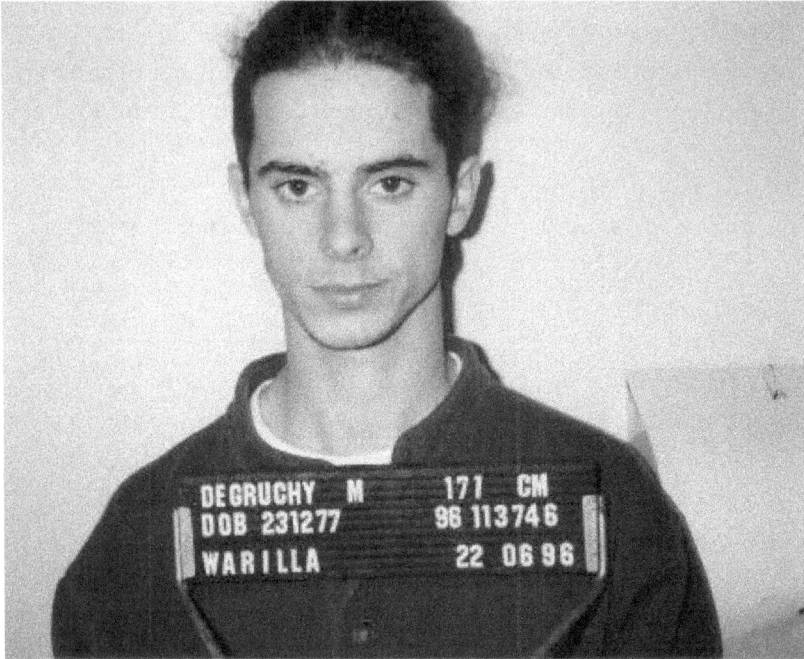

Matthew De Gruchy on the day of his arrest, 22 June 1996.

media as 'offering to put up $100,000 surety for his bail, to open his home to him and to drive him to and from work each day in an effort to acquire his freedom'.

Matthew De Gruchy's Legal Aid solicitor Justin Hutchinson applied for bail, telling the court the accused youth had the full support of his father and the remaining members of the family. Hutchinson said that the family had found the allegations against Matthew 'unbelievable' and that Matthew had continued to live with his father in the Shearwater Boulevard home where the murders had happened.

Despite his father's unwavering loyalty, Matthew De Gruchy was denied bail and remanded into custody.

By the following day, the family had appointed a QC, Malcolm Ramage, to represent Matthew in court in another bail hearing. Ramage came in guns blazing and was quoted in the media as having 'angry outbursts' about the 'disgraceful' long delays in the

DNA testing relevant to the De Gruchy murders. Ramage was also critical of the police case, saying that it was 'dangerous stuff' when people were convicted on forensic evidence alone. Ramage claimed 'numerous convictions' in England based on only forensic evidence had to be 'sorted out' by the appeals courts. He didn't elaborate on what these cases were.

Despite Ramage's appeals, the magistrate said: 'I am also not satisfied he's not a danger to the community or that he would not commit further offences.' Matthew was again denied bail.

Two and half years later, Matthew De Gruchy stood trial for the murder of his mother, brother and sister. Although he never confessed, the murder weapon was never located, and no clear motive for the murders was ever established, it took the jury just six hours, on 14 October 1998, to find him guilty. He received a maximum sentence of 28 years and a minimum non-parole period of 21 years.

In November 1999 Matthew appealed against these convictions. His Counsel also included an application for leave to appeal against the sentences. The Appeal Court judge, Justice James Wood, denied the appeal and said the sentences imposed were manifestly appropriate for the offences of which De Gruchy was convicted.

Matthew and his defence team did not give up – but to no avail. In 2000 his appeal against conviction was again unanimously dismissed in the NSW Court of Criminal Appeal by chief judge James Wood and his colleagues Caroline Simpson and Brian Sully. The murders were said to involve 'brutality beyond description'.

In 2002, when Matthew was 24-years-old, the High Court rejected his last chance for appeal and his conviction was again upheld. The five judges of the High Court's full bench, again unanimously, agreed that the arguments offered against his guilt were 'too improbable'.

On that occasion Justice Ian Callinan said the circumstances of the murders which rocked the Illawarra region in 1996 were horrific.

'The mind recoils from the idea that an apparently quiet, gentle young man of good character and with no known animus against his family should brutally slay his mother and young sister and brother.'

Seven years after the murders, Wayne De Gruchy contacted Detective Danny Sharkey. There had been a lot of bad feeling between the De Gruchy family and the police. Many members of the extended family felt Matthew had been unfairly 'stitched up' by the investigators. It is sometimes impossible for families to come to terms with the fact that one of their own is guilty of murder. Wayne De Gruchy was no exception.

At the trial, Wayne De Gruchy was a witness, and because of court rules barring witnesses from being in court until after they've given evidence themselves, Wayne had never heard the full case against his son. Enough time had elapsed for the bereaved husband and father to want to know the truth.

When he contacted Detective Sharkey, the experienced investigator knew that Wayne had reached the point where he

Matthew De Gruchy during his murder trial in 1998.

just wanted to know. The two men arranged a time to meet and Sharkey promised to give him as much time as it took; it ended up taking nearly a whole day.

Sharkey showed Wayne statements, photographs and evidence lists, and patiently explained why the detectives had targeted his son in the investigation. Right from the start, everything had pointed to Matthew. Sharkey detailed the holes in Matthew's story until it became obvious to the father that his son was a killer. Danny Sharkey knew that it was a lot for Wayne De Gruchy to take in all in one go.

He told Wayne to get in touch with him if he needed any further information. Sharkey didn't hear from Wayne again.

2019 UPDATE

The infamous Circle at Goulburn Main Prison houses some of Australia's worst murderers, violent armed robbers, and rapists. Among the inmates in 2009 were the four notorious 'K' brothers, convicted in 2002 of the gang rapes of eight Sydney girls aged 13 to 18; the Murphy brothers who abducted, raped and killed Anita Cobby; the backpacker serial killer, Ivan Milat; and family killer, Matthew De Gruchy.

In March of that year, Matthew, then 31 years old, fronted Goulburn Court via videolink, charged over a 2007 jail-yard gang-bashing that almost killed one of the infamous 'K' brother pack rapists in jail. Matthew was one of six inmates, including three other convicted killers and two violent sex offenders, charged over the brutal attack on the two eldest of the four 'K' brothers – so-called because their identities cannot be revealed for legal reasons. The prison attack resulted in the second-eldest of the brothers requiring brain surgery.

De Gruchy's legal representative entered not guilty pleas to four assault charges, including two charges of maliciously inflicting grievous bodily harm.

Matthew De Gruchy's full sentence ends in June 2024. His earliest possible release date was 21 June 2017 – the day he was first eligible to apply for parole. In that year, as an inmate of the Junee Correctional Facility, Matthew was approved for day release and had been working in an abattoir at Junee. A Corrective Services spokeswoman said, 'De Gruchy had been working in the chill room and had no access to knives.'

Despite being granted day release, Matthew was refused parole in May 2017. The State Parole Authority (SPA) found he presented an 'unacceptable risk to the community and had not participated in the required external leave programs'.

Two years later, however, on April 21, 2019, a spokeswoman

Matthew De Gruchy in prison circa 2001

said the SPA had 'formed an intention to grant parole' to De Gruchy.

'A public review hearing will be scheduled to hear submissions from the State of NSW and registered victims,' she said.

Shellharbour MP Anna Watson said while the parole determination was outside her jurisdiction, her concern was for the community.

'There's people who still live in that street, who were there when this terrible crime occurred,' she said.

'I understand that while he's probably going to get parole, [it's] in his best interests and in the best interests of the community that he should look at maybe not coming back into this particular area.'

The MP said the parole conditions needed to be known. 'He was a kid when this happened ... he's never lived outside of jail as an adult.'

The state government hasn't ruled out opposing De Gruchy's release.

At the time of going to print, in June 2019, Matthew De Gruchy still waiting to hear theresult of parole hearing, after serving 23 years of his 28-year sentence.

Ironically, at 41, he is now the age his mother was when he murdered her. As the parole board considered his release, De Gruchy watched on via a video link from jail. While his father and an aunt promised to support Matthew on his release, neither of them attended the hearing.

Former detective sergeant, Barry Doherty who'd examined the crime scene, was quoted in the media expressing his concerns. He figured if Matthew De Gruchy could snap once with such catastrophic results, what would stop him from doing it again?

Another clutch of true crime writers. This time I'm with:
Helen McGrath, Robin Bowles and Cheryl Critchley.
I wonder if I can claim to have started something.

17

YOUR BEST STORY

Once, I went on a nightshift with police working out of the old Oakleigh police station. The shift included: licence checks and house alarms, seeing a couple indulge in a sex act on the Clayton railway station platform, dealing with a drunk couple arguing outside a party then getting arrested for drunk driving, and playing referee when a violent young man who wanted to collect his PlayStation from his ex-fiancé then threatened to cut her kitten in half and leave her the arse-end.

At the end of the shift, the cops I rode with apologised that it was such a quiet shift.

'Are you kidding me?' I said.

It might have been quiet by their standards, but not at all by mine.

This is why when I interview police, I ask for their 'best story'. Because in their world of big stories, the ones that stand out are bigger, more dramatic, more intriguing than most people's stories. I've found that in a cop's career, there is always one or two that gets under their skin, that they can't forget — for the best or worst reasons.

Cops and writers have something in common. They become the keepers of stories — big and small.

I've written many stories of cases that should have hit the headlines but didn't; that were not high profile because the people involved were not high profile.

And more often than not, the 'best stories' that police gave me were similar; they were the ones that most affected them, the cases that touched their hearts.

All of this also begs the question: What makes one victim 'worthy' of headlines and another, ignored?

After 25 years of writing, I still don't know the answer to this.

I found one such story in the murder of Lyndsay Jellett. While his story did not make the headlines, it did get a few column inches in the newspapers.

When I interviewed the detectives who investigated Lyndsay's death, it was his vulnerability that made a huge impact on them. Lyndsay had received a brain injury when he was a baby and lived his life in care.

I had worked in residential care houses in between finishing uni, having a baby, before I started full-time teaching. I had an insight into the place Lyndsay live in, and I also knew the horror of what he might have faced in institutionalised care.

In the late 1980s, I worked in homes where you had to use the word 'casserole' because you could never say the word 'stew'. This was because some of the residents were triggered with awful memories of the 'stew' served in the asylums they'd come from.

These days when I'm asked to do a crime-writing presentation, I will often tell Lindsay's story. For the same reasons he touched the heart of the detectives, he touched mine too.

He was a man with a disability who deserved to live a long life, doing what the loved best: taking long walks, buying Coke, chocolate, and cigarettes, and collecting lost golf balls to sell.

He didn't ask much of life.

But Lyndsay Jellett was murdered by someone he trusted.

When there was no one left to fight for him, a bunch of dedicated detectives vowed to bring his killer to justice.

After being told his story, I took a road trip to Ararat. The cops explained to me how they'd searched for hours into the night when, at first, Lyndsay was simply missing.

I sensed the rising panic they'd all felt when he disappeared; more so after one of the officers revealed what all the searchers knew: Lyndsay might get scared and hide when he heard them calling his name.

I pictured him as they must have, hiding in a shed or a barn, shivering, scared and alone.

I stood on the road where he died

I saw the asylum where he grew up – which gave me chills even from the safety of my car – and I saw the unit where he lived when the asylum was closed. I interviewed crash investigators, homicide detectives, and crime scene investigators – all dedicated cops who would not let Lyndsay's death go unpunished.

Writing about Lyndsay gave him the space he deserved and it meant that he – and what happened to him – would not be forgotten.

They say: 'it's not what you know but who you know'.

I've no idea who 'they' are, but it seems I know Liane Moriarty (yes, author of *Big Little Lies*) (l); and Melbourne crime writer Kathryn Ledson (b).

Aradale still looms large in the landscape of Ararat.

18

THE STRANGE DEATH
OF LINDSAY JELLETT

Before anyone even knows he is missing, Lindsay Jellett lies dead on the side of a dirt road in Ararat. In death, he is a pitiable figure. Even though his time on earth spanned only 41 years, Lindsay looks a lot older. Lying in grass and gravel, he wears a pale-blue fleecy top which is pulled up exposing his thin white torso. While his belt is still buckled, it has been ripped apart on the left-hand side and his trousers are pulled down a bit so you can see his brightly-coloured underpants. His blue eyes are half-open and so is his mouth.

Three packets of smokes and a cigarette tin lie next to his body; a five-dollar note is discarded at his right elbow. He wears white runners; the right shoe is crushed and its sole is bursting from the torn stitching.

Lindsay Jellett's body reads like a road map of assault. His torso is stained with a liver-coloured patch of congealed blood under his skin. His left cheek is grazed and his nose has an unnatural bend.

At first, it looks simple. An intellectually child-like man with a history of walking the neighbourhood is found dead on the side of the road. Probably hit by a car. End of story.

Lindsay Jellett lived in a residential home for the disabled in the small Victorian town of Ararat. He had suffered brain damage when he was around two years old when a car collided with his pram as his mother was crossing the road. She had edged the pram out between two parked cars and the van had hit the front of it. While Lindsay was injured, his twin sister Judith, who was sitting behind him, was unhurt.

Lindsay had lived most of his life in the Aradale Mental Hospital which had been built in the 1860s. It had its roots in a time when such facilities had 'modernised' from being insane asylums to mental hospitals. Wards were locked, and inmates learned to live their lives around clocks and schedules.

Lindsay Jellett was freed from Aradale which closed in 1993. Many of its residents were given the opportunity to set up house in one of the community housing units in Ararat, where they were watched over by staff who helped them to manage the outside world.

After his accident, Lindsay was awarded £15,000, which had grown into over $120,000. It was administered by the Supreme Court and used to purchase items for Lindsay's welfare and to pay for his medical needs. When Aradale closed, nearly $20,000 was taken from Lindsay's trust fund to buy into a shared residential unit for the disabled in Grano Street, Ararat.

In adulthood, Lindsay spent his days working in a sheltered workshop. After work, he loved walking the streets of Ararat. He was a cheerful chap, always ready with a wave and a smile that made him well-known to locals. One of his favourite pastimes was walking to the golf course down the road from where he lived to hunt for lost golf balls. He would take them back to his neat room, clean them up, then sell them. He lived with four others under the watchful eye and guidance of 24-hour rotating staff. Lindsay was a favourite among the carers.

When Lindsay Jellett failed to return from his afternoon walk on Tuesday 10 May 1994, Tania, a staff member at the unit, was worried. Lindsay wore a watch and could tell the time; it wasn't like him to be late back. He knew the evening meal was served at 6pm and he was rarely late for dinner. Once or twice before, Lindsay *had* lost track of time on his nightly rambles around Ararat, but he was never more than half an hour late. In light of these previous transgressions, Tania gave it until just before 7pm before she telephoned the police.

The May weather had turned cold and it had begun to rain on and off. When Lindsay left the house, he had been wearing a blue fleecy top with a shirt underneath, and a pair of dark trousers. He hadn't taken a coat and had nothing to protect himself from the rain. Another concern was that Lindsay was epileptic and needed to take the drug *Tegretol* at 8am and 8pm. A missed dose might put him at risk of a seizure.

The police at Ararat took Lindsay's disappearance seriously and coordinated a search with the local SES. At midnight, when no trace was found of Lindsay Jellett, the search was called off until first light the following morning. Bulletins were read over local radio stations.

Hearing the reports of Lindsay's disappearance, a farmer called Kerry kept an eye out on the way to his farm. Around 500m along Down Road – which was hardly more than a dirt track – Kerry spotted a white sand-shoe on the grassy verge at the side of the road. He kept driving but further up the road, the image of the shoe worried him. He did a U-turn and drove slowly back. As he got closer, he saw a cigarette packet near the shoe and realised the shoe was on the foot of a figure lying on the grassy verge. The man was wearing the same clothes as the description on the radio. Kerry used his CB radio to all for help.

A couple of minutes later, a police divisional van turned into Down Road. The police officers took one look at the body and knew that the search for Lindsay Jellett had ended. And it hadn't ended well.

To the local coppers, it looked like a hit-run.

Police and detectives converged on the area. Given that it was obvious a car was involved, they all thought it best to call in the Accident Investigation Section.

Senior Constable Denise Mears, Sergeant Steve Wilson and Senior Constable Jacquie Donald from the Accident Investigation Section made the 200 km drive north-west of

Melbourne. They were given an overview of the case by local cops and drove out to the scene.

In the case of Lindsay Jellett, the accident investigators were lucky. As soon as the body had been reported, the immediate scene had been taped off and the road had been closed to all traffic. At the scene, the local cops pointed out tyre marks both from their police vehicle and the tyre marks from the farmer who had found the body for elimination purposes. Any other recent marks on the dirt road could have been made by whoever had hit Lindsay Jellett.

As soon as the AIS investigators saw the body of Lindsay Jellett, they knew something wasn't right. For starters, Lindsay Jellett's body was arranged too neatly by the side of the road. If he had been hit by a car while walking along the road, his body would have been flung and landed awkwardly. His top was pulled up as if someone had gripped him under his arms and dragged him off the road; lines in the dirt looked like they had been made by the heels of his shoes as he was moved.

With this clear evidence of human intervention, the AIS investigators knew that the case wasn't what it had first looked like to the local cops.

There are six elements that invariably go with a hit-run. The first three are injuries to the shin area where the bumper strikes the victim, then injuries to the hip where the person hits the bonnet, then injuries to the head when the victim hits the windscreen or the top of the car. The next two things to expect at the scene of a hit-run are lots of blood, and some trace of the car involved – broken glass or plastic or paint flakes.

And the last element is that the victim is usually shoeless: it was a little-known phenomenon, but people hit by cars are almost always knocked out of their shoes. Even a cursory examination of the scene showed that none of these six elements were present. Lindsay was wearing shoes, there was little blood around his body, and there were no broken car pieces. In addition to this, his injuries were not consistent with being *hit* by a car but rather, they suggested he'd been *run over* by one. He had abdominal bruising consistent in width with a car tyre, and the lower parts of his legs had severe crush injuries. All over his body were signs that a car had gone over the top of him. There were smears of grease on him and his clothing, and there were burn marks on his body where he had come into contact with the hot exhaust section underneath a vehicle.

But it was the drag marks in the dirt adjacent to where he lay that told the story of Lindsay Jellett's last moments. It looked like he had been dumped on the road – most likely from a vehicle – then dragged to the side of the road before he was run over on the verge.

Fibres consistent with Jellett's trousers were found near the drag marks.

In the tyre impressions imprinted in the dirt, the car that had run over Lindsay Jellett had left behind its exact movements. Alongside the body, were acceleration tyre scuff marks and the resulting spray of gravel told the investigators which direction the car had been travelling – a vehicle had reversed to where the body lay and then backed right over him. Twice.

The investigators could see that the car had turned around after running over the body and then headed back in the direction of Ararat.

The person who did this might have thought they would get away with it, but the investigators knew that these tyre impressions could be matched to a suspect's vehicle. They also knew that if there were traces of grease from underneath the car on Lindsay's body, then there would be traces from Lindsay – his blood or fibres from his clothes – underneath the car. Evidence of this transference would be found easily if the car responsible was identified.

While the AIS investigators measured out the scene and took photographs, they knew the case wouldn't be theirs for long. It was clearly a case of homicide, not a hit-run.

Senior Sergeant Gavan Ryan and Senior Constable Charlie Allen from the Homicide Squad picked up forensic pathologist Dr Shelley Robertson and drove to Ararat. They were closely followed by crime scene examiners to process the scene.

Arriving at the scene at 4.40pm, neither Ryan nor Allen had seen a case of murder by car before, and they listened as the accident investigators outlined their findings.

The Homicide detectives were well-versed in the most common of homicide motives: love, lust, loathing or money. Early reports painted Lindsay Jellett as a harmless simple man who was well-known and well-liked by Ararat locals. It was hard to imagine motives of love, lust or loathing. It was easier to imagine the reputed $100,000 in his trust fund might be the motive for his death.

Dr Robertson was struck by the lack of blood on and around the victim. Her early impression was that it was likely the victim had in fact been dead when he was run over. That would account for him not bleeding much from his severe leg wounds.

Gavan Ryan asked AIS investigator Steve Wilson about the type of damage one might expect to find on the car that did this. Wilson speculated that there might be some damage to the spoiler, but the evidence would largely be underneath the car – especially if Lindsay was in fact lying dead on the ground when the car went over him.

A couple of Homicide detectives were sent to visit Lindsay Jellett's twin sister, Judith Cengiz. Judith had visited him just before he had gone missing so she would be able to help them piece together his movements on the day he died. While Judith would be treated with all the sympathy due to a woman who had just lost her brother in tragic circumstances, the detectives had to keep in mind that she was Lindsay's next-of-kin and would inherit a considerable amount of money.

In Melton, Detective Senior Constable Murray Gregor and Detective Senior Constable Paul O'Halloran arrived at Judith's house at 3.40pm. She had already been notified by local police that Lindsay's body had been found.

Before they knocked on her door, they looked over her car which was a 1982 Ford Fairmont Ghia sedan. There were no obvious fresh dents on it, nor signs of recent damage.

Judith invited the detectives into her home. She was clearly upset by her brother's death. One of the first things the detectives noticed about Judith's house was there were medicine bottles everywhere. Murray Gregor numbered them in their hundreds. He had never seen such a collection of pills. It wasn't long into the visit before they knew of Judith's litany of health problems. Detective Gregor wondered how anyone, even with bad health, could possibly take so many pills. Nonetheless, Judith was able to tell them exactly what each bottle of medication was for. She spoke like a chemist.

It was important to get Judith's statement as soon as possible. They took her to the nearest police station to record what she had to say.

It was nearly dark when three police officers from State Forensic Science Laboratory arrived at Down Road at 6.10pm. The crime scene examiners travelled together in a van loaded with equipment. When the initial call had come through, they had been given as much information as was available about the suspicious hit-run and then they were briefed further at the scene.

The Accident Investigation Section had examined the scene from a collision point of view and would be able to reconstruct the collision. The crime scene examiners had a different job. They had to examine the scene for evidence and find links between the scene, the victim, and later, hopefully, the car that ran over him.

The State Emergency Service had been called out to provide lighting and the crime scene examiners began their work.

One of the first things crime scene examiner Trevor Evans noticed about Lindsay's body was that his grey-coloured belt had snapped right above an obvious burn in his trousers where the polyester-type material had melted.

Evans was fairly certain that it would have melted on the exhaust pipe. And knew that if this was the case, then the exhaust pipe – when the car was located – would have traces of the melted material on it.

The next thing that Evans noticed was the smears of red fluid on Lindsay's white runners. From his extensive knowledge of cars, he guessed that the red fluid was automatic transmission

Crime scene examiner Trevor Evans

fluid (ATF), and if he was right, then that told him two things. First, the offending vehicle was an automatic; and second it was probably an older car which was more likely to leak. And leaking ATF didn't drip, it formed a film over the transmission pan underneath the car. The transference in this case, would have been when Lindsay's shoes had come into direct contact with the underneath of the car that ran over him. This contact would also leave marks on the ATF pan. Lindsay's body was smeared with grease also suggested an older car.

Accident investigators Denise Mears and Jacquie Donald found a local tyre store and a man who worked there identified the tyre impressions as Bridgestone Eager S340 tyres.

Near the body were some acceleration marks that were deeper than the others. Conferring with the AIS investigators, the crime scene examiners theorised that the body had at one point become stuck under the front of the car and the driver had hit the accelerator to dislodge him and to make sure the car went over the top of him.

Any way you looked at it, the crime against Lindsay Jellett was callous in the extreme.

At the Melton police station, Judith Cengiz gave a formal written statement. She stated her full name and date of birth which, being twins, was the same as Lindsay's. The detectives began by asking her about her brother.

She told them how Lindsay had been injured as a toddler. He'd been in a coma for nine weeks and suffered severe brain damage. She explained that in 1958 Lindsay had been awarded £15,000 by the Supreme Court which managed the money.

Judith said that Lindsay had lived in institutions since he was seven before finally buying into the house in Grano Street, Ararat. The purchase had been arranged through the Supreme Court funds.

Judith had been appointed as Lindsay's official guardian in 1989; but in 1992, that guardianship was revoked and she instead became the administrator of Lindsay's estate with control over his personal and financial affairs. She said his capital then was $129,000 and that she wasn't comfortable being in control of such a large sum of money. According to Judith, she asked for the Supreme Court to manage his affairs.

She said that she visited him every month or so and when she did, she always took him clothes, cigarettes, lollies and drinks. The cost of the gifts, she said, was reimbursed by the Supreme Court fund, along with the petrol she used – and now the gas since she had her car converted to LPG – to visit him.

The detectives asked Judith what medicines Lindsay might have been taking. Information had filtered back from the scene that even though he had been run over, it was thought that Lindsay was dead before that happened. Something must have killed him, and drugs or poison were possible contenders.

Judith said that Lindsay suffered from epilepsy and took Tegretol to help prevent seizures. Aside from that, as far as she knew, Lindsay didn't drink or take any other medications.

Judith then related a curious incident. If Lindsay's carers had to bring other clients to Melbourne, they would ring Judith and arrange to drop Lindsay off with her for a couple of hours. She said that just after Christmas 1993, Lindsay had been brought to her house for a visit. They'd eaten lunch then, Lindsay had stepped outside for a cigarette.

Judith said she had gone to a house across the road to hang out washing for a neighbour called Denise. She said she had only been gone around 10 minutes and when she got back, Lindsay said that he was tired and didn't feel well. Eventually, she called an ambulance which took her brother away. Judith noticed a drawer had been opened in her bedroom and she'd wondered if Lindsay had taken some of her medication. She rang the hospital and told the doctor Lindsay might have taken Valium or pain killers. Judith said the doctors had given Lindsay an antidote for Valium and he was okay. When he was released from hospital, she drove him back to Ararat.

Judith said that the previous day – the day Lindsay died – she had arrived at McGregor House where Lindsay worked just after 11am. She attended regular meetings with staff to monitor his progress. She had driven her XD Ford Fairmont Ghia sedan, spoke to a woman at McGregor House, and then drove Lindsay back to his home in Grano Street around lunchtime. Judith took Lindsay out to lunch. Her description of the day included pokies and eating pies at a BP Roadhouse. At Grano Street, Judith met with two of the regular house staff, Rod and Tania, and discussed Lindsay's on-going care. After a trip to the chemist for some supplies for Lindsay and some ice-cream, the visit was over.

Judith told detectives that she had spoken to one of the house staff for a couple of minutes after Lindsay set off for his walk, and then around 4pm left Grano Street to head home to Melton. She took the Western Highway, then stopped at McDonalds in Ballarat for a Coke. Outside of Ballarat, Judith said that her car had overheated.

'I stopped on the side of the highway and waited for about half an hour until it cooled somewhat. I have previously had my car checked by Bill's Auto in High Street, Melton for the same problem and he showed me what to do if it overheated. I released the radiator cap lightly and shut it until the pressure was released. I was there for about 30 to 40 minutes then continued to drive to Melton without stopping and drove straight to Maureen's arriving around 7.20pm and collected the children. I stayed about 15 minutes talking.'

Judith told the detectives she had driven to the Shell Service Station near her house, 'filled the tank with LPG gas and opened the radiator to reduce the pressure… I then washed my car in the service station carwash as I normally do after visiting Lindsay. I then bought milk and Coke and paid for the gas, car wash and what I bought and went directly home arriving around 8pm.'

By the time she got to her house in Melton, there was a message from Tania telling her Lindsay hadn't come home. She rang Tania and told her Lindsay had been late home before. Judith told the detectives she had rung the house several times during the night but Lindsay hadn't come back.

This morning, a staff member had called 8.00am and told her that Lindsay still hadn't returned. Judith said she had been so worried that she had hardly slept a wink all night. Nonetheless, she told the staff member that she had some errands to run and to leave a message on her answering machine if there was any news about her brother.

Judith had visited Peter Herbert, a mechanic in Melton, to get her car looked at. She then drove to Sunshine at 9.50am and went to the Housing Commission to fill in some forms. Then she went to Sunshine and drew $200 out of the bank. She stopped at the Deer Park Hotel Tabaret and played the pokies until a neighbour finally tracked her down there with news the police were looking for her.

Judith left the hotel for home and once there, rang the Ararat police. She was told that Lindsay had been killed in a hit and run accident. By the time she had spoken to a couple of neighbours about what had happened, detectives Murray Gregor and Paul O'Halloran from the Homicide Squad were on her doorstep.

Judith signed her statement at 9.30pm at the Melton police station and then the detectives drove her home.

When Gregor and O'Halloran talked about it afterwards, there was nothing in Judith's statement to suggest she wasn't being honest with them. The only thing that didn't add up was that according to Judith's statement, she had left Ararat around 4pm and arrived in Melton at 7.20pm. The less than two-hour trip took three-and-a-half hours. Even with Judith's half-hour radiator stop, there was still an hour unaccounted for.

The next morning, Homicide detectives Gavan Ryan and Charlie Allen began their investigation. In light of the physical evidence pointing to the fact that Lindsay was dead before he was run over, the two Homicide detectives discussed other possible causes of death that would leave no obvious trace. The post-mortem examination later that morning would hopefully give them a bigger picture, but in the meantime, Ryan and Allen discussed possible poisons or drugs that might have been used to incapacitate or kill Lindsay. They knew that he took Tegretol for his epilepsy – was it possible that he could have either taken or been given something else that could have reacted with that medication? They put Lindsay's doctor's name on the long list of people they would need to speak to.

Detectives Murray Gregor and Paul O'Halloran attended Lindsay's post-mortem examination. After their interview the previous evening with Judith Cengiz, they were working the case from the Melbourne end.

Dr Robertson concluded, from the lack of blood on either Lindsay's body or his clothes, that most of his injuries occurred after he was dead. She found that the major trauma to both Lindsay's legs and his lower back area was consistent with him being run over by a motor vehicle.

Swabs were taken of the blackened areas around the body to see whether they were grease or perhaps rubber from a vehicle's tyres.

With the post-mortem examination, it was what *wasn't* found that was of most interest. Dr Robertson found no head injury that could have caused death, nor was there evidence of any disease that might have killed him. An internal examination showed the massive damage caused by the tyres. Lindsay's ribs were staved in and his pelvis was badly damaged.

Dr Robertson had Lindsay's full medical history which detailed his epilepsy. There is a little-known syndrome called Sudden Unexpected Death in Epilepsy (SUDEP) which opposing studies had either put at being responsible for one death in every 1,000 people with epilepsy at the optimistic end of the scale, or one death in every 10 at the pessimistic end. In a typical case of SUDEP, the person dies in his or her sleep, more often when they are sleeping on their stomach. What the experts generally agreed upon, was that in cases of SUDEP, a post-mortem examination would show no cause of death.

Dr Robertson considered SUDEP during the post-mortem examination, but there was one thing that didn't add up. An examination showed Lindsay's bladder was full. Dr Robertson told the detectives that when a person has a seizure, they usually discharge their bladder. Usually, but not always.

The contents of Lindsay's stomach showed that he was killed within 60-90 minutes of eating a substantial meal. Due to digestion, it wasn't possible to tell what he had eaten. And this fact was interesting.

According to Judith's story, she had taken him to lunch around midday. He was last seen leaving his home at 3.45pm. The detectives remembered Judith saying that they had gone for ice-cream around 2pm, but an ice-cream couldn't be called a 'substantial meal'. Had whoever killed him, given him food an hour beforehand?

At the conclusion of the post-mortem examination, Shelley Robertson was able to say that Lindsay's injuries were consistent with being run over by a car after he was dead, that he had rotated underneath the car, and that he had eaten about an hour to an hour and a half before he died. Aside from that, she was unable to say for certain what killed Lindsay Jellett.

Dr Robertson removed samples from the body to send to the toxicology lab. The detectives discussed with her the theory that Lindsay could have been drugged or poisoned prior to being run over. They would have to look at his access to medicines or poisons. The toxicology results wouldn't be available for several days.

At this early stage, Judith Cengiz was definitely a person of interest in the investigation. She was the only one who would benefit financially from his death and she was one of the last people to see him alive. And there was the missing hour and a half in her account of her journey home. After interviewing her the night before, Murray Gregor wondered if perhaps Judith could have poisoned Lindsay when she had taken him out to lunch. The detectives hoped for something definite from toxicology because the lack of a firm result at the post-mortem would cause problems down the track.

Gregor and O'Halloran telephoned the results through to Gavan Ryan and Charlie Allen who were still in Ararat. The post-mortem examination findings only added to the mystery. Ryan and Allen considered the possibility that Lindsay had died during a seizure but the question always remained – if he died during a seizure, why would someone deliberately position his body by the side of the road and run over it?

Who would want a natural seizure death to look like a hit and run?

Ryan and Allen interviewed Tania, the worker at Lindsay's house who had originally reported him missing. Like the rest of the staff, she was most upset at Lindsay's death. They couldn't believe that their simple friendly charge could have been so brutally killed and agreed to help in any way they could.

Tania explained Lindsay's daily routine varied little. Each weekday morning, he would be collected by taxi at 9am and taken to McGregor House which ran a day program for the intellectually disabled. There was a woodwork program at McGregor House which Lindsay particularly enjoyed. At 3.40pm, he would return to Grano Street, greet the house staff and then ask if he could go for his walk before dinner. On weekends, Lindsay would walk two or three times.

Another house worker devastated by Lindsay's death was Rod who told detectives that went Lindsay stayed with Judith on holidays and at Christmas and Easter, things were not rosy.

Rod spoke about the unusual incidents that had happened when Lindsay stayed with his sister. She usually returned him earlier than planned. Rod also mentioned the time Lindsay ended up in hospital. 'Lindsay was very happy on this day,' he said, 'and was glad to see his sister… I only planned to leave him at Judy's for about five or so hours.'

When Rod had returned to pick Lindsay up, there had been a

note on Judith's front door to say she was at her neighbour Denise's house. Rod went there and Judith explained there had been a problem and that Lindsay was in hospital.

'She told me that he must have got the medication from one of her drawers while she was in the shower. She told me that he often when through her drawers when she wasn't looking.'

It was interesting for the detectives to note that in Judith's statement, she said that Lindsay had taken the overdose while she was hanging out washing for her neighbour, Denise. When she was telling Rod about the incident in front of Denise, Judith said that Lindsay had taken the medication while she was in the shower. The devil was in the detail.

Tests found Lindsay had overdosed on Valium and Panadeine Forte. Consumer Information on Panadeine Forte tablets specifically states that it could affect epilepsy medication, making it especially dangerous for Lindsay.

Police set up a roadblock on Grano Street, stopping all cars at the time Lindsay was last seen the previous day. A man called William was stopped at the roadblock. He knew Lindsay Jellett by sight and told the detectives he had seen Lindsay the previous day around 4pm climbing into a car. The car was an older model dark-coloured Ford and it had a red LPG sticker on its numberplate. William said the driver was a middle-aged woman with dark hair who he didn't recognise.

Investigators went straight to Judith's house. Not only did her car match William's description, it also had the red LPG symbol *and* Bridgestone Eager S340 tyres matching the tyre impressions found at the scene.

The car was impounded for further examination. Even though Judith had put the car through a car wash as soon as she had arrived back in Melton, crime scene examiner Trevor Evans was confident that if this was the car that had run Lindsay over, he would still find evidence underneath it to prove it.

When Judith's 1982 Ford Fairmont Ghia was hoisted over a pit, Evans climbed down beneath it. The undercarriage was covered in dirt, grease and oil expected of a car that age. The sump was leaking and covered in a coat of oil as was the lower side of the bell housing. There were certainly enough sources of grease and oil to have caused the smears on Lindsay's body. The automatic pan was also leaking and covered in a film of automatic transmission fluid – just like Evans predicted at the crime scene.

Spots of blood were clearly visible on the caster rod near the front driver's side wheel and further down the undercarriage towards the rear driver's side wheel on the handbrake cable guide. Close to the blood on the handbrake cable were fibres caught in a screw head.

As well as blood and fibre evidence, there was a burn mark on the engine pipe that was consistent with the melting of Lindsay's belt that Evans had documented at the scene. There were also several fabric impressions in the grease and dirt underneath the vehicle from the front end to the rear to suggest that Lindsay's body had been in contact with all sections of the undercarriage, rolling, bumping and scraping, leaving tell-tale signs.

Trevor Evans had no doubt that this was the car used to run over Lindsay. Despite this, a case had to be built before any arrest could be made.

When the toxicology results came back, they were a surprise to the detectives. Because they had found out that Judith had filled a prescription at the Ararat chemist for Rohypnol on the day Lindsay was murdered, they had half-expected to find it in his system. Although with the hundreds of medicines at her fingertips, Judith could have chosen something else.

While there was no Rohypnol, another drug was found in Lindsay's system – it was called Noctec which is the commercial name given to chloral hydrate – otherwise known as the knock-out drug, 'Mickey Finn'. It was prescribed by doctors as a treatment for insomnia and could be dangerous because the treatment dose was close to the toxic dose. Chloral hydrate became infamous in 2007 as the drug that killed celebrity Anna Nicole Smith.

The problem with the toxicology report was that the amount found in Lindsay's system was listed as a 'therapeutic' dose – in other words, there was not enough in his system to kill him. But

Lindsay was also taking Tegretol for his epilepsy and the detectives wondered if the Noctec could have reacted with the Tegretol. Medical advice certainly suggested that these two drugs not be taken together. Small traces of alcohol were also found in Lindsay's system. Tegretol and alcohol shouldn't be taken together. Could the combination of Tegretol, alcohol and chloral hydrate have been toxic? A beer can had been found near Lindsay's body.

If Judith was responsible, did she give him beer on purpose only hours after being told by Tania, in the meeting, that alcohol could be particularly harmful to Lindsay?

Tests on the empty beer can found near Lindsay's body found no traces of Noctec or any other drugs. An examination of Lindsay's stomach contents could not confirm nor deny he had consumed alcohol before he died; a body produces alcohol as part of the decomposition process and so small alcohol readings are far from conclusive in proving the deceased had consumed it.

Nothing in the toxicology results pointed to a direct cause of death and the detectives were left to surmise ways in which Lindsay could have met his end. One idea was that Judith gave her brother Noctec in a drink – perhaps Coke as an empty bottle top was found near the body but there was no bottle – and waited until he passed out. She could have then smothered him with something soft like a pillow, which would have left no trace. Then, either to make it look like an accident, or to make sure she'd finished the job, she ran over him twice. Investigators contacted an eminent forensic pathologist who said that the Noctec combined with Lindsay's Tegretol could have stopped him breathing.

Everyone from the Grano Street house and anyone who Lindsay had contact with was re-interviewed to see if they had ever been prescribed Noctec – none had. Detectives even asked local chemists to go back through their records, but there had been no prescription written for Noctec in the last two years. There was little chance that Lindsay could have come upon the drug by accident.

When Lindsay's financial records were examined, the detectives found something interesting. On 20 April, three weeks before

Lindsay died, a clerk had written to Judith. Since Aradale had shut down, Lindsay's fund balance had dropped from $128,333 to $107,178. This depletion was due to the fact that Lindsay had moved out of government care and had bought into the Grano Street unit. The clerk wrote: 'I have recently reviewed Lindsay's file and have noted a rapid depletion of his funds, particularly in the past six months. This rate of depletion is such that the capital is eroding and will continue to do so even if his funds only make payment of the service charge and household expenses for Grano Street. I have enclosed a financial statement which shows the expenditure for the previous seven months. Could you please contact me at your earliest convenience to discuss this matter.'

The clerk told the detectives that Judith had replied and told her that she was visiting Lindsay every five to six weeks and on those visits, she was forced to buy him everything he wanted and if she didn't, Lindsay became very aggressive and would steal instead. Judith told the clerk that Lindsay's demands had become worse since he'd moved to Grano Street and that was why her requests for reimbursements had drastically increased.

Three weeks later, Lindsay was dead.

In their quest to see if Judith had ever had access to Noctec, the detectives finally got a lucky break. They visited a medical clinic in Springvale near where she used to live and spoke to a doctor who had seen Judith five years earlier. She checked back through her records and gave a statement to the police saying that she had prescribed Noctec three times to one of Judith's children who was having trouble sleeping. From the doctor's Springvale surgery, the police visited local chemists and found the chemist who had dispensed the Noctec prescription to Judith.

For Gavan Ryan and Charlie Allen, it was the break that they were looking for. Now they had the proof that Judith had once Noctec in her possession. Although it wasn't found in her house, anyone who'd been in Judith's house could see that she didn't throw out medicine – the hundreds of bottles of medicine bore witness to this. In their minds, it was highly likely that when it had been prescribed five years earlier, Judith would have kept what she hadn't used on the children. Could Judith have dosed Lindsay with a fatal dose, but the Noctec itself had lost some of its potency? That would account for the 'therapeutic' dose in his system. They had found out that medications of this nature have a use-by date, but this theory, like many others, was hard to prove without finding the Noctec in question.

When the first search warrant was executed, Murray Gregor and Paul O'Halloran were looking for *any* drugs that could have been used to kill Lindsay. Now that they knew Noctec had been used, they needed to go back to Judith's house and search for it specifically. Gregor and O'Halloran arrived just after 9am along with Charlie Allen and Gavan Ryan who were meeting Judith for the first time. By this stage, they knew she was involved in Lindsay's death – she was the only one who had access to her car and even if someone else could have broken into her car, her oldest son, Greg, had recently installed an alarm which would have sounded if anyone else tried to drive it.

Being the senior police officer, Gavan Ryan took charge. When Judith answered the door, he introduced himself and Charlie Allen and all four detectives entered Judith's house. Ryan told her they had another search warrant.

'What for?' Judith asked.

'Noctec,' replied Ryan.

'Never had it!' replied Judith.

'I've had experts look at the car,' explained Ryan calmly, 'and they are convinced it was used to run Lindsay over. Do you have any comment?'

'It can't be! I didn't run over him.' Judith said, with a touch of anger in her voice, but in Charlie Allen's opinion, the anger wasn't because of the accusation, but rather that the police were questioning her story.

'They are positive about it,' persisted Ryan.

'I didn't do it.'

Judith Cengiz was taken to the Homicide Squad for questioning. She rang a lawyer who obviously told her to say 'no comment' to anything the detectives asked her. Judith did as she was told. Gavan

Ryan read out her previous statement that Gregor and O'Halloran had taken on the night Lindsay's body was found. When Ryan asked her if she agreed with what she had said, Judith replied, 'No comment' to that question and every question after that.

It was a game of cat and mouse. The detectives knew that Judith was involved, and she knew they knew. After the interview, Gavan Ryan and Charlie Allen drove her back to her house. As they dropped her off, Gavan Ryan made her a promise.

'I'll be back,' he said. And he meant it.

Judithl looked coldly at the detective, then walked inside.

The wheels of justice may not always move quickly, and so it was that on the morning of 21 September, four months after Lindsay was run over, Charlie Allen and Gavan Ryan stood in front of Judith Cengiz's Melton home ready to charge her with the murder of her twin brother. As soon as Judith opened the door, she knew.

'Are you here to charge me?' she asked.

'Yes,' replied Ryan, savouring the moment.

The detectives let Judith shower and get dressed. She made arrangements for her children to be cared for and called her lawyer. At the Homicide Squad, Judith once again said she had nothing to do with Lindsay's death. She was taken to the Melbourne Magistrates' Court and remanded into custody.

While Judith was on remand, Detective Charlie Allen took a statement from her eldest son, 24-year-old Greg. He described his mother's three marriages and listed the children that came from each union. Greg recalled that his grandparents would often have Lindsay to stay but when they became ill and died, his mother had taken over visiting Lindsay and attending meetings for him. Greg remembered visiting Lindsay and described the visits as happy. 'He was always happy and enjoyed himself when we visited him. He would laugh a lot and make jokes.'

Charlie Allen asked Greg if he knew about Lindsay's money. Greg knew a lot about it from conversations with his mother.

'I am aware that Lindsay had a sum of money. I was told by my mother that this sum was $103,000. I don't know how Lindsay came by this money. I don't know who looked after Lindsay's money. I know when my mum went to visit Lindsay, she would get a couple of hundred dollars to buy food and clothing for Lindsay and for maintenance on her car.

After the car had been impounded, Judith rang Greg to tell him. She said that the police had taken all her medication and prescriptions and the tapes from her answering machine.

'During this conversation,' said Greg, 'we talked about her washing the car. She said the police asked her why she had washed the car. She said to me, "You know that I always wash the car and under the car after I have been to see Lindsay". It was as though she was asking me to confirm this over the phone. I thought this was unusual. I know that she washes her car but I have never seen her wash under her car. I don't recall her specifically washing the car when she returned from seeing Lindsay.'

Greg said Judith told him she'd had been 'set up'. 'She said she thinks someone may have stolen the car out of the driveway, driven the car to Ararat, run over Lindsay, then returned the car to the driveway. I thought this was ridiculous and impossible. Mum's car has an alarm fitted. I fitted the alarm myself.'

Greg said his mother was very keen to get her car back. 'She put in an application to get Lindsay's money. She was told by someone in authority that she was able to apply for it. She was supposed to receive the money on the Thursday or Friday after her arrest. I asked her what she was going to do with the money and she told me she wanted to buy another car. I started to look for another car for her so that when Lindsay's money came through, I could organise another car for her. I asked her if she would buy me a car also. I said I would like a Hilux four-wheel-drive and that it would cost about $10,000. I recall she said, "No, it's my money".' When Greg told her that she inherited it and should share it around, Judith repeated that it was *her* money.

When Greg finally spoke to his mother in Fairlea Prison, he asked whether her application to receive Lindsay's money had been successful. 'She became very angry and said she was doing time for a crime she didn't commit and if I touched her money, then she would commit a crime.'

With the evidence under her car and the doctor's statement that she had prescribed the very drug found in Lindsay's system to Judith's son, the detectives presented what they had to the Department of Public Prosecutions. The case was always going to be hard because of the lack of a cause of death. As bizarre as it may seem to the lay person, it is legally difficult to convict someone of murder when the Crown can't prove how the victim died.

Indeed, when the committal hearing went ahead in Ararat, the magistrate threw it out. His decision was a disappointment to the detectives who'd worked for months on the case. And it didn't help that Judith walked smugly from court, a free woman.

But Judith hadn't realised there is more than one way to skin a cat. Another option to get a suspect to trial is for the Crown to present them directly to trial without testing the evidence at a committal hearing. After much discussion, this is what the Office of Public Prosecutions decided to do. Judith was re-charged with murder and summoned to trial. Charlie Allen delivered the summons and remembers that day as a very good day.

Again, everyone involved expected the lack of a cause of death to present difficulties. And they weren't wrong.

Judith had been seeing a counsellor so Charlie Allen interviewed the counsellor to try and gain further insight into the accused woman. Luckily for Allen and his team, the counsellor told him Judith blamed her ex-husband, Ilie Chifiriuc, for the murder. Her story was that he must have waited until she got home from Ararat, disarmed the car alarm, stolen her car, driven to Ararat, located Lindsay (who at that stage had been missing for hours despite an extensive police search), run him over, and then returned the car to her driveway in Melton.

Despite it being such a bizarre tale, Allen located Ilie Chifiriuc, who'd moved to Queensland, and flew north to take his statement.

Ilie Chifiriuc had apparently suffered at the hands of Judith Cengiz. He wasn't surprised at the allegations; he saw it as simply another way of Judith getting to him. His interview with Chifiriuc gave Charlie Allen the best insight into Judith Cengiz yet. Chifiriuc explained his short history with her. He had come from Romania in 1987 as a refugee and had been granted residency two years later. He still spoke in heavily-accented broken English.

'I met Judy Cengiz when I was living at Deer Park. I met her in the Railway Hotel in Fitzroy. I first met her one year before I married her. I think 1988… I saw her every Saturday and Sunday, she come to my place in St Albans… when I met her she separated from her husband but I know she still see him cause I go to her house one day and he there.'

Chifiriuc said the marriage was rocky from the start. He had moved in with Judy after the wedding, but Judy told him to leave three days later, after she realised her pension had been cut off. Weeks later, she persuaded him to come back, but Chifiriuc found out Judy was still sleeping where her ex-husband and moved out.

'After I got married, Judy tell me she three month's pregnant. She say I the father. I was annoyed she not tell me she pregnant. She gave birth to a boy… we were separated when he was born. I did not know if I was the father… but I accepted responsibility… I still pay maintenance. I pay $183.23 per week.'

Maintenance money wasn't all Judy got from her ex.

'After we were separated, I still ring Judy and I still see her. After we were separated for one year, we got divorce. Judy fix up the divorce. It might have been less than 12 months. She fix the papers and she asked me to sign… there was no property settlement when we divorce. I just pay maintenance… I also pay for the nappy for [the child]. This was $30 a week. I also buy the vacuum cleaner for Judy. This $3,000. I pay $200 a month for the Avco finance for the cleaner. Also, when I visit [the child], she say she no have money so I give her money.'

Not being familiar with Australian courts, Ilie Chifiriuc left everything to Judith and gave her anything she asked for.

'Judy want me to go to her house because when I go there, the fridge is always empty, so I go buy food for all the children. She very nice to me at Christmas and Easter and public holiday because I go to her house and I buy all the children the presents. She ring me at home all the time.

'If I go out with another woman, she come and talk nasty to

this woman. She use [the child] to keep getting money from me. She ring me and say [the child] wants to see daddy or [the child] in hospital and use [the child] to get me. I want my son and I want him to be with me but I have to leave Melbourne because of what she do to me. She just use me from start to finish.'

It was then that Ilie Chifiriuc dropped a bombshell.

'On the 28th day of February 1993, I think Judy, she poison me. Judy ask me to dinner. I go and I eat at Judy's place. The next day, I got sick. I could not go to work. Judy take me to Doctor Ken in Melton. The doctor sent me straight to hospital. I was admitted in the Footscray Hospital. I stay in hospital for nine days. Doctors say I have poison in my blood and pneumonia. Doctors no say what type of poison. Judy with me when I was in hospital and she talk to doctor for me. After hospital, Judy took me to Melton and I stay at her place for one and a half months while I was off work with pneumonia. I feel Judy gave me something in that meal because I was well before I had that meal.'

When Charlie Allen asked about Lindsay, Chifiriuc said he'd seen Lindsay half a dozen times in the year he and Judith were together. He had a different perception of Judith's relationship with her twin brother.

'Before we go to Lindsay, we go shopping for Lindsay and spend $30-$40 on drinks, lollies and biscuits for Lindsay. All the time pick up the receipts from the supermarket and say the things for Lindsay, but it's not. She would claim for money from Lindsay's money every month. She claim $500, sometimes $1,000. She claim for things for her car like tyres, petrol and pretend she have to fix up car. But she no do this. She just say to make the claim from Lindsay's money. Judy tell me if Lindsay die then all of Lindsay's money go to Judy. It's my opinion that Judy just go to check up on Lindsay, how healthy he is, cause of the money. She no care for Lindsay. She just interested in the money.'

According to Chifiriuc, Judith wasn't happy when Aradale shut and Lindsay had to use $17,000 of his money to pay to live in the residential accommodation. 'Judy was very angry because the other people no pay cause they don't have their own money.'

Charlie Allen asked about the children. He was most interested in the medication she gave them to help them sleep. He asked Chifiriuc if he had seen her do this. Chifiriuc said on New Year's Eve just passed, he had gone around to Judith's so he wasn't alone. He got there around 10pm. The lights were on, but her car was not in the driveway. When he went inside, Judith's younger children were asleep and alone in the house. He rang several places to try and find her. It was around 1am when he finally found her.

'She said that she had just left to go and play the pokies. I knew she lie because I been there from 10pm. Judy gave the children syrup to make them sleep. I don't know what this syrup is called but I saw her give it to them. I don't know where she got it from. She said it's for sleep. She keep this syrup on the fridge. She give it to them when she want them quiet and in bed at 6 or 7 o'clock.'

Chifiriuc told Charlie Allen that Judith had a blank prescription pad for $100 and could write herself any prescription she wanted.

Allen asked Chifiriuc if it was Judith's custom to wash her car after each trip to Ararat.

'For the six times I went, we never washed the car when we came back.'

Detective Allen asked Ilie Chifiriuc outright if he had anything to do with the death of Lindsay Jellett.

Chifiriuc's logic made sense. 'I did not kill Lindsay. If I killed Lindsay then I would go to jail and Judy would get his money and Judith would be happy.' When put that way, it did sound like strange behaviour from an ex. Chifiriuc's alibi checked out.

The trial finally began, the prosecution received a blow to their case. While Judith had purchased Noctec three times, the presiding judge ruled that there was no evidence to suggest she still had that medication five years later. The judge ruled that if the jury knew that Lindsay had therapeutic doses of Noctec in his system, then they would assume that it was part of the plan to kill him. This too, according to the judge, could not be established.

The Crown argued that the Noctec must have been administered to Lindsay because no one else in his shared house was taking it and therefore, he couldn't have accessed it inadvertently. The judge said that since Lindsay had shoplifted before, that presented another way for him to potentially access the drug. As such, he did not allow the Noctec evidence to be put before the jury.

It is always frustrating for investigators when the facts of a case cannot come out in open court. It was indisputable that Noctec had been found in Lindsay's system. It had been administered between one and three hours before he died and Lindsay had been with Judith most of the day.

When the Crown had finished its case, the second blow came when the judge ruled on the murder charge. He concluded that even though Lindsay was dead when he was run over, there was enough evidence that the jury could find that Judith believed he was alive when she ran over him and could therefore be guilty of attempted murder. He threw out the murder charge and left the jury only to decide on the attempted murder charge.

The case was diminishing before the eyes of the detectives. In the end, the jury only had one option – to convict Judith of the attempted murder of a dead man. And they did.

The judge gave Judith a 10-year sentence with a six-year non-parole period.

The lonely road where Lindsay Jellett died.

Judith appealed against both conviction and sentence. Her lawyer argued that if the judge threw out the murder charge, then he also should have thrown out the attempted murder charge since the only thing the Crown could prove was that Judith did was run Lindsay over, but he was clearly dead when this happened. On 23 June 1997, three Supreme Court judges in the Court of Appeal denied her appeal.

On 28 March 2000, Coroner Iain West dismissed Judith's efforts to have new evidence introduced to an inquest into Lindsay's death. By this time, Judith had served four years of her 10-year sentence. Judith told journalists outside the court that she was angry that her 'new' evidence had not been accepted.

She was quoted as saying, 'I don't believe it. I've been accused of abusing the system but it's the system that's abusing me. I think it's wrong. It's so unfair.'

Her lawyers were trying to raise doubts about the DNA evidence used to link her car to her brother's body. The coroner argued, quite rightly, that the role of an inquest was to discover Lindsay's cause of death, and even if the DNA evidence *was* discredited, that wouldn't help solve the mystery of *how* Lindsay died.

Judith's lawyer also spoke to journalists. He was quoted as saying that he wanted to present evidence that could implicate Judith's former husband, Ilie Chifiriuc, in Lindsay's death. Through her lawyer, Judith was singing the same old tune.

She vowed to continue to fight for freedom.

On 1 February 2002, Judith Cengiz was released from jail. She had served her minimum sentence and was free to return to the community.

On 19 March 2004, an application was made to the Masters Office that held Lindsay's money. According to the Masters Office, surviving relatives of Lindsay Jellett agreed among themselves as to how his money would be divided. Who got what, is sealed in confidential court records.

Meetings heroes: one was a true crime professional; the other is an internationally-famous writer of fiction.
Here I am with UK crime writer Val McDermid (L) and now-retired Assistant Police Commissioner Sandra Nicholson.

19

Meeting Heroes

One of the most impressive people I've interviewed is an ex-cop called Carl Donadio. He was 19 years old when he was seriously injured in the infamous Russell Street bombing in 1986. After a morning on guard duty in the Melbourne Magistrate's Court on the corner of Russell Street and La Trobe Street, the newly-minted constable headed back to police headquarters for lunch. While waiting at the traffic lights with his colleague, Angela Taylor, he realised he didn't know how to get to the police canteen via the south door of the Russell Street complex. There was barely any traffic, so he doubled back and crossed Russell Street diagonally to head towards the north door. The pedestrian lights went green and Angela Taylor crossed at the lights.

That's when the bomb went off.

I was writing a story for the *Australian Police Journal* – to mark the 20th anniversary of the bombing – and arranged to interview Carl Donadio at my house.

When he walked in the door, he opened with: 'It's been 20 years. I'm not sure I've got a lot to say about what happened.'

He talked for four hours.

He told me about his boyhood in Ballarat, about how he had joined the police force, and then about that fateful day when simply not knowing how to get to the canteen saved his life.

He told me about bomb technologies where a fireball explodes out one side, and shrapnel out the other. So while his shrapnel injuries were brutal, Angela Taylor's burns were catastrophic. For

24 days, she lay in another guarded hospital room down the hall from him, with injuries she couldn't survive.

Carl felt lucky to be alive. He felt lucky to understand profoundly how important family and friends were. He felt lucky that his injured body would repair from the effects of the bombing. And he felt lucky to discover so young that every day was precious because any day could be your last. He felt lucky to be alive to seize each day and take opportunities that put him outside his comfort zone.

Carl Donadio's life philosophy is incredible to listen to. While it would be perfectly understandable for him to see himself as a victim, he is the exact opposite. He took the terrible experience of being injured in the Russell Street bombing and learnt some profound lessons from it. And it changed his life and the way he looked at the world for the better.

Having a naturally resilient nature, Carl figured he was simply in the wrong place at the wrong time and was unlucky.

And what does Carl think of the men responsible for his injuries? The truth is, he doesn't think of them at all. 'The bombing wasn't directed at me,' he told me, as we sat at my kitchen table. 'It was directed at the Victoria Police. I never took it personally.'

And, he explained, if he spent time and energy hating the bombers then that would mean they win. And Carl won't let that happen. He said he still tries to make every day count.

Over the years, my work as a crime writer has allowed me access to people who have been through extraordinarily bad things. At the heart of all stories – fiction or non-fiction – is how the things that happen affect someone and how that person changes as a result. In fiction, the hero is challenged and knocked down and the reader rejoices every time they pick themselves back up again. It's the same with non-fiction and has become a major focus in my work – how do people get through it? How do they process what has happened? Where does resilience come from?

Dealing with grief and loss and the resilience people develop is something I write about a lot.

I have developed a theory on what makes the most difference in the aftermath of a challenging event. I have met people who have been crushed and defined by what they have suffered. The people who survive and thrive in the wake of suffering seem to be the ones who ask: *what can this teach me?* rather than *why me?*

I make no judgement here. In the midst of loss and grief, the *why me?* question is a natural response. But in the longer term, when grief loses its raw edge, those who wonder what they can learn and how they can share their knowledge to help others, turn their grief into action. They give it an outlet.

Because my worlds ebb and flow between being a writer and being a teacher, I try to incorporate lessons of resilience I learn from the people I meet into lessons with the students I teach.

And the students teach me all the time. What you *think* about something alters the effect of it. This is true in the classroom as it is in life. If two students walk into a maths class with the same ability, but one thinks: *I hate maths and I never understand what the teacher says,* while the other thinks: *I'm not a fan of maths, but today might be the day something sticks* – which student will do better?

Here I am with my everyday hero: my mum, Helen Burke.

The wreckage of the car bomb detonated outside the
Russell Street headquarters of Victoria Police in Melbourne.

20

THE RUSSELL STREET BOMBING

On Thursday 27 March 1986, Constable Carl Donadio was 19 years old and had been in the police force for five months. After graduating from the police academy, new recruits rotated through different areas of the police force to gain wider experience. For the young lad from Ballarat, every aspect of policing was fascinating. He'd joined up on a bit of a whim because a good mate had applied. Ironically, the mate didn't get accepted and he did.

And because he'd joined the Force without much thought or research, Carl Donadio found the rotating exposures to different aspects of policing enlightening. His first stint was the St Albans police station, in the heartland of the Melbourne's western suburbs. In the first couple of weeks, he and another police officer had been called to a domestic dispute at a St Albans house. The door was opened by a boy of about four or five years old and to Donadio's horror, the small child said, 'What the fuck do you want?'

The young cop started to tell the child that he shouldn't use language like that, but realised he was wasting his breath when the kid ran up the front passage way, yelling to his feuding parents, 'Mum! Dad! The pigs are here!' This was Donadio's first glimpse of the hatred of police that could be passed on, via the umbilical cord, from one generation to the next.

It was during his time at St Albans, that Carl Donadio decided where his future direction lay as a cop. He was waiting at red traffic lights riding shotgun with a more senior police officer.

'Don't look left,' his partner said to him.

'Why not?' Donadio asked, resisting the natural urge to look to the left at the car pulled up next to them at the lights.

'They're dogs,' said his partner, using the police slang for undercover surveillance operatives. Sure enough, Donadio could see out of his peripheral vision, an undercover hold up a police badge surreptitiously at the window before they roared off after another vehicle.

Donadio was full of questions: how did his partner know they were dogs? What did dogs do? And when his partner, who had worked in surveillance, told him about life as an undercover operative, Donadio knew he would pursue it as a career path. He reckoned that surveillance work would fit with his policing philosophy – he was there to catch crooks.

At 19, things were simple. There were good guys and bad guys. And cops caught the bad guys.

After a couple of months at St Albans, Donadio rotated through city traffic, the traffic operations group, and then the records department. From there, he landed a stretch doing court security.

At the start of a shift he would first go to the Russell Street police headquarters where his duty sergeant would allocate him a court to guard. It was his job to sit at the back of the courtroom and provide protection for the magistrate should any angry family members disagree with a sentence, or if a prisoner got violent.

On 27 March – Easter Thursday – Donadio was allocated a courtroom across the road from the Russell Street police headquarters at the Melbourne Magistrates' Court. It would be his last shift before Easter, and he was looking forward to a couple of days off to spend the long weekend at home in Ballarat. Aunts, uncles and cousins would all descend on the Donadio family home for one of his mum's roast dinners. He was the only cop in the extended family and he was looking foward to entertaining them with his policing stories.

Working court security wasn't quite as interesting as St Albans. It was only Donadio's third shift at the court – the first two had involved boring fraud cases which had made the young cop look at his watch every couple of minutes – mostly in disbelief at how slowly the time was going. But this case was a criminal case and more interesting than the others.

Around 12.30pm, one witness finished his testimony, and rather than start the next witness so soon before the lunch break, the magistrate adjourned early. Donadio stayed behind to ask the Clerk of Courts a question about court procedures. He was keen to learn as much as he could in his rotation period. He chatted to the clerk for a while and then made his way out the front door. He would head over to police headquarters to get some lunch at the canteen.

As Donadio was leaving the courthouse, another police officer, 21-year-old Constable Angela Taylor flipped a coin with a colleague; the loser had to go buy the lunches at the police canteen. Taylor lost the coin toss and waited at the lights on the corner of Russell Street and Latrobe Street. Donadio waited near her until he realised that he didn't know how to get to the police canteen via the south door, which was the closest door to Latrobe Street. He only knew the route to the canteen through the north door a bit further up Russell Street.

Rather than wait for the lights to change, Donadio walked back up Russell Street past the Magistrates' Court and began to cross the road diagonally towards the north door entrance to the police building.

A sudden impact sent him flying 15m up the road. He landed on his backside and, momentarily stunned, thought that he must have been hit by a car. But then he saw plumes of smoke. He knew it wasn't a car that hit him.

At the same moment, but on the opposite side of the road, Angela Taylor was caught in a fireball.

Inspector Bruce Knight of the police special operations group (SOG) had been looking out his office window. He noticed a bus had picked up a group of passengers outside the entrance to the Russell Street police headquarters and traffic lights at both ends of the block went red, momentarily emptying the street of traffic. It was 1pm and the day had been slow. Knight wondered what he was going to do to fill in a couple of quiet hours and was just about to say as much to a colleague when he heard the explosion.

Before his eyes, he saw what looked like a car bonnet come flying up past the window. At the same moment, an explosion shook the building raining debris in the usually quiet city street.

The SOG was normally called out to such events; this time the action had come to them.

Hundreds of other occupants of the Russell Street police headquarters were rocked by the explosion as well. Windows all over the building shattered, and fine black dust shook free from the wooden roof and covered desks and equipment inside the building. Shocked police officers looked out their broken windows and saw thick black smoke funnelling furiously from the source of the explosion – a car parked right outside their front door.

The first indication to the wider policing community that a

The wreckage of the car bomb at the front door
of Russell Street Police Headquarters.

major incident had occurred at Russell Street came over the police radio:

Russell Street 750:	...I presume you heard that loud explosion
D-24:	Russell Street 750, it's totally shattered our windows.
Russell Street 750:	Copy that 306...a loud explosion's took place outside the front of the complex. There's mess everywhere.
D-24:	Copy that Russell Street 306. All units approach with caution just in case there's a second... Russell Street 150, we just had a large explosion occur outside the building – a car bomb, it seems. Shattered all the windows of this office. Received.

Members of the highly-trained SOG launched into their precision response. Dressed in their customary dark overalls, everyone on duty in the SOG offices raced down three flights to the street below. The scene looked more like a street in war-torn Beirut than down-town Melbourne.

The epicentre of the blast was a car parked outside the south entrance to the building. From the outset, it looked like the results of a bomb rather than an accidental explosion. Injured people lay moaning on the ground and fires from the blast were sending palls of thick smoke over the city. Many people had been hit by pieces of shrapnel forced outwards by the explosion with the velocity of bullets. Nobody was prepared for something like this to happen, but, for the special operations group, scenes like this were exactly what they had trained for.

The first priority for the SOG was to clear and contain the area. Inspector Knight and his men removed the wounded as quickly as possible because a second bomb was a real possibility, indeed a series of small explosions continued to emanate from the bomb car.

Civilians – ordinary people enjoying a lunch break – also helped drag the wounded away from the blast site. Fire engines screamed to the scene, and chaos reigned. Fierce flames radiating out from the explosion site had ignited an unmarked police car parked directly behind it. It too burnt furiously.

Having been caught in the full force of the blast, Angela Taylor staggered across the street into the Magistrates' Court where she was helped by lawyer Bernie Balmer.

It was a sight Balmer would never forget. One of her shoes was on fire, her shirt was nearly torn from her body, and with each breath she took, blood pumped out of her. He smothered the flames and gently sat her down on the ground and asked for her name. She said it was Angela. The lawyer telephoned for medical assistance and did the best he could to comfort the badly injured policewoman.

Meanwhile, Carl Donadio tried to stand up, but his right leg had gone numb. He felt for a wound and was shocked when his fingers disappeared inside a deep gash in his thigh.

He realised immediately that a car had exploded outside the south door and that it was the force of the blast that had thrown him down the road. The first explosion was quickly followed by several smaller ones.

He knew he needed to find cover quickly, so he dragged himself towards the gutter. Two female police officers, Selena and Vanessa, helped him to the relative safety of the wall of the Russell Street police building. A couple of civilian women were there also but Donadio shouted at them to get as far away as they could.

Vanessa removed her shirt and wrapped it around the gaping wound in Donadio's leg, while Selena fashioned a tourniquet to keep it in place. Selena sat on the footpath and rested her downed colleague's head on her lap, speaking gently to sooth him. But, as soon as Donadio lay flat, he started gasping for breath.

In that moment, when his breathing became laboured, he realised his injuries might be more serious than a leg wound. The more he tried to breathe, the more it hurt. He started to panic.

Vanessa and Selena urged him to keep calm, and Selena told him there was blood on the back of his shirt, so he might have punctured a lung.

Donadio considered this. The sensation was similar to the time he'd punctured a lung playing footy after a knock to the ribs; but this felt much worse. His previous experience told him it was vital to calm down because panicking only made breathing more difficult.

When he stabilised his breathing, the policewomen tried to take his mind off things. Referring to his face, which had only sustained a small cut above his right eye, Selena said, 'You still got your good looks though.'

And despite his injuries, he managed to joke. 'Yeah,' he gasped, 'my Mona Lisa face'.'

Within what seemed like minutes, he was collected by an ambulance and was on his way to the Royal Melbourne Hospital.

When the car bomb exploded, flames and heat shot out one side of the vehicle, and the bulk of the shrapnel blasted out the other.

This was the reason Angela Taylor was so severely burnt, while Carl Donadio was barely burnt but struck by flying shrapnel instead.

Magistrate Iain West, who was also on the shrapnel-side of the explosion, suffered serious injuries, as did nine other police officers and 10 civilians.

Once the area was cleared of the injured, members of the SOG went into action. Their immediate priority was to extinguish the burning cars. Fire had already spread to the unmarked police car behind the bomb car and, if not extinguished, would lead to a domino effect engulfing the line of cars parked up Russell Street.

It seemed like the whole top end of Melbourne had turned black. Sirens screamed as police, fire trucks and ambulances converged on Russell Street. Media flocked to the scene and helicopters flew overhead to film the damage sometimes barely visible through the thick black smoke.

Because small explosions continued at the centre of the blast, fire fighters were unwilling to get too close. The job of extinguishing the flames fell to the SOG. Dressed in a bomb suit, SOG member Senior Constable Dennis Tipping cautiously approached the burning cars.

Tipping had been trained that the first bomb is not necessarily the only one. Sometimes terrorists use a first explosion to lure police and civilians to the site, and then set off a second explosion to kill them. There were grave fears that a second device could go off at any time.

Nonetheless, Tipping, with a line tied to his waist so that he could be pulled out if anything went wrong, approached the blazing epicentre. He was fed a long line of fire hose by firemen keeping a safe distance from the blaze. As he got closer, Tipping could see detonators scattered across the ground – he knew these were the source of the smaller explosions after the initial bomb. Tipping was careful not to tread on any of the detonators. If he did and one exploded, he could lose a foot.

Once he was close enough, Tipping blasted the fierce flames with the fire hose until they sizzled into smoke and steam, and the immediate danger was lessened. As soon as the fire was extinguished, the SOG examined the surrounding areas for any other explosives. There was always another likelihood that part of the bomb had failed to detonate so the danger was very real.

Members of the SOG are specially trained in explosives – they knew what they were looking for. They combed the area for a second device, but found only more live detonators as well as sticks of gelignite that hadn't exploded.

They proved the explosion was deliberate. Someone had planted a car bomb right outside the Russell Street police headquarters.

Within an hour, the area was evacuated, all the injured had been taken to hospital, and the surrounding streets had been sealed off. As the news footage flashed onto televisions all over the country, Carl Donadio's parents, Bev and Vic, watched the unfolding drama from their Ballarat home. Bev turned to her husband and told him that she knew Carl had been injured in the explosion. She could feel it in her bones.

Not long after, their phone rang.

Suddenly, every car parked in the city seemed suspicious and members of the SOG had to check out one report – among many – of an old car parked in nearby McKenzie Street with no registration plates and the keys in the ignition. Many people fled the city while others stayed to watch the drama unfold.

After the initial scene containment by the SOG, the first people called to the bomb site were the crime scene examiners. The initial call-out went to the new Victoria Police state forensic science laboratory in the north-eastern suburb of Macleod. Police crime scene examiners had operated from Macleod since 1983 and the rest of the lab workers were slated to move into the new buildings in a couple of months' time – for the present, they were still in the old lab in Spring Street in the city.

The first indication that a major incident had occurred at Russell Street came over the police radio and was quickly followed by a call from Spring Street requiring the crime scene examiners to attend. At the time, protocols dictated that crime scene examiners worked in pairs, but it was obvious from early reports, that this was an all-hands-on-deck job. Every examiner on duty piled into the unmarked forensics van loaded with equipment and headed towards the city.

Sergeant John Moushall was the senior officer on duty; the rest

Victoria Police and crime scene examiners at the site
of the Russell Street bombing.

of the crime scene examiners were senior constables: Wayne Ashley, Allan Nilon, Steve Spargo, Peter Guerin and Dave Royal. On the trip to the bomb-site, the officers could only speculate as to what they would find.

They knew a number of people had been injured; they knew the police headquarters building had been damaged; and they knew that communications had been affected, because D24's visual display units had broken down from the force of the blast and subsequent power failure. The lines of communications had been disabled until the emergency generator kicked in, and even now, were not running at full strength.

Windows at D24 had been shattered and the only things that saved the operators inside from flying shards of glass were the heavy drapes that covered those windows.

On the way to Russell Street, the crime scene team listened to frantic calls over the police radios. Breathless officers shouted communications back and forth. While panicked communications can sometimes be exagerrated and unreliable, the officers could see, from as far away as Fitzroy, the thick black smoke hanging over the city. They were in no doubt they'd have their work cut out for them.

When they finally made it through the snarl of traffic, the crime scene van headed straight for the command post, which had been set up on the corner of Latrobe Street and Exhibition. It was far enough away from the bomb site to be considered safe. Even so, that area of Latrobe Street was strewn with bits of rubber, metal, bricks and glass.

At every crime scene, one officer assumes responsibility for overseeing the operation. Sergeant John Moushall nominated Senior Constable Wayne Ashley to take charge of the scene. Ashley had six years' experience as a crime scene examiner under his belt and had worked the 1983 Ash Wednesday bushfires; he therefore had ample experience with wide-spread devastation.

At the command post, the crime scene examiners were introduced to Bob Barnes and Peter Kiernan from the Materials Research Laboratories in the Department of Defence. Barnes and Kiernan were post-blast experts and had been called in by the

SOG in the immediate aftermath of the explosion. The two experts had done a sweep of the site and officially confirmed that the explosion was caused by a bomb. As the various teams swapped notes and organised plans of action, the odour of burning rubber hung thick in the air hours after the explosion.

In consultation with the Department of Defence experts, crime scene examiner Wayne Ashley agreed that Barnes and Kiernan could work the immediate area around the bomb site, and he and his men would do everything else.

Debris had spread over several city blocks and the crime scene examiners, with the assistance of the SOG, would be responsible for its systematic collection and examination.

With debris crunching underfoot, the post-blast team moved in. They could feel the aftermath before they saw it. The streets of Melbourne looked like a war zone.

The first thing that Wayne Ashley saw as he turned into Russell Street was the mangled wreck of the bomb car. Stripped of everything but its frame, it looked like a giant black spider. The second thing Ashley took in was the blackening of the entrance to the Russell Street police headquarters. Up until this moment, the concept of the attack on the police had been abstract. Now, seeing the shattered windows of the art deco monolith and her blackened façade, the reality and the affront was palpable.

Initially, Wayne Ashley had been surprised that the scene had been so quickly out-sourced to the Department of Defence experts, especially since all crime scene examiners were trained in post-blast examination, but when he and his team made their way into Russell Street, the breadth of the devastation became obvious. He was glad of any assistance they could get.

Ashley and his colleagues could see that the force of the blast had moved the car several metres to the east leaving behind a shallow crater of sorts, measuring 15cm by 1.5m, which had formed with the impact of the explosion.

Because the back of the car was more mangled than the front, investigators concluded the bomb had been in the vehicle's boot. The high number of live detonators and unexploded gelignite strewn around the bomb car told another story: the bomb had not exploded to its full capacity. A second explosive device had been placed either on the front seats or in the centre console.

Investigators theorised it had been dislodged in the first explosion. They also estimated that if the bomb had exploded to its full capacity, the structure of the Russell Street building itself might have been compromised.

Senior Constable Dennis Tipping, who had earlier extinguished the flames, examined the immediate area for clues. He noticed a block of wood near the steps of the south entrance. Nailed to the wood were the remains of an alarm clock. It was only metres from the bomb car and remarkably still intact.

The experts concurred that the block of wood looked like it had been sawn from a fence post. The clock had been nailed into place by a strip of metal fixed with 2-inch nails. There were wires attached to the block of wood and also a green and white Chux Superwipe dishcloth.

It looked like the bomb maker had used the dishcloth to keep the wires from connecting on the drive to Russell Street.

In the immediate vicinity were bunches of wires tied together in bundles. Scattered around were automotive sockets and other

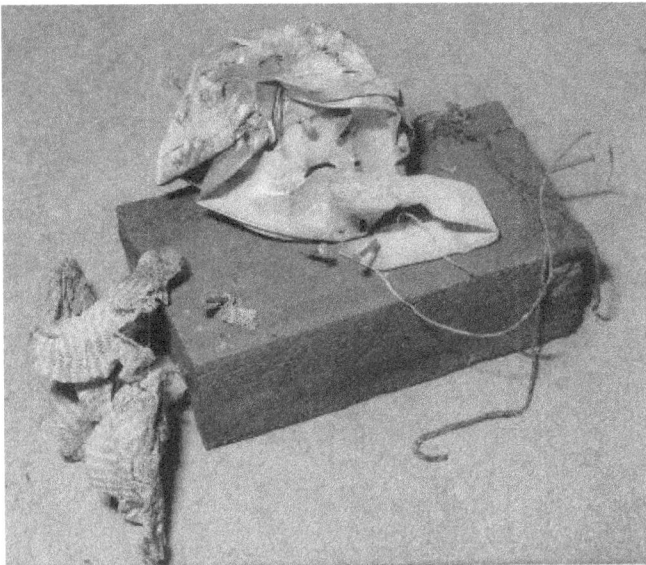

The remains of the car bomb's timing device nailed to a block of wood.

metal tools that had been packed around the bomb to act as shrapnel in the explosion.

This was another sign that the people who built the bomb had intended to do maximum damage to anyone nearby. It was a deliberate and vicious attempt to maim and kill.

At this early stage, it was by no means certain the attack was directed against the police. Early media reports speculated the bombing target could be the Melbourne Magistrates' Court across the road. Perhaps it was a disgruntled person who held a grudge against a court ruling. It could even have been a terrorist attack.

Whatever the reason for the bomb, the crime scene examiners had to take a clinical rather than an emotional approach. Even though police may have been targeted, and police officers had been seriously wounded in the attack, this scene had to be treated methodically.

Wayne Ashley also knew they had no time to waste – a shower of rain or strong winds could interfere with potential evidence. Somewhere in this chaos may be clues that could eventually identify the perpetrators and help bring them to justice.

The first priority for the Department of Defence team was to examine the bomb car; it could link back to the offenders, so its history was vital.

Despite the damage to the vehicle, the make and model were still ascertainable. The car was a 1980 two-tone VB Holden Commodore with gold mag wheels, a V8 engine and a twin exhaust system.

Luckily one of its numberplates was found nearby and police were immediately able to trace the car's owner who had reported the Commodore stolen from the Brandon Park shopping centre in Mulgrave two days before the bombing.

Incredibly, they found a red and cream chequered blanket inside the twisted wreck that had survived the blast relatively intact. The rug was removed and placed in an evidence bag.

When Bob Barnes and Peter Kiernan were checking the car for identification marks, they noticed among the blackened remains of the engine, that the chassis number on the radiator support panel, had been drilled out. The drill was circular and whoever had removed the number, had drilled through the panel at the beginning of the number, removed the drill bit, then placed it on the next part of the number, and drilled through again. This had been repeated until the number had been obliterated leaving a line of joined holes that looked like a caterpillar.

This was not the way car thieves usually removed identification numbers. If they were removed at all, they were more usually ground down with an angle grinder. When stolen cars were made to look legitimate, it was more usual for the numbers to be altered. Numbers that were removed altogether meant that the person responsible hadn't being trying to legitimise the car at all.

While Barnes and Kiernan busied themselves with the car, Wayne Ashley began the wider examination. The first thing to do was to grid off sections as far as the debris had flown – which in this case included parts of Victoria Parade, Exhibition Street, Little Lonsdale, to as far away as sections of Swanson Street. In the immediate bomb vicinity, the grid squares were 5m by 5m. Further away, they were 10 by 10. Every grid was numbered so that evidence collected in each square could be labelled and referenced.

All the bags of evidence would be taken to the Russell Street police auditorium and stored, waiting for examination. Wayne Ashley knew that while Russell Street would be closed to traffic indefinitely, the other city streets would need to be cleared as quickly as possible to allow traffic through.

Inspector Bruce Knight from the SOG offered his team for whatever tasks needed their expertise. Members were called in from rest days and it was all hands on deck. It was vital to collect as much debris as was recoverable so that the investigators could piece together what had occurred. The evidence could also contain clues to link the bomb with its makers. A wheel from the bomb car was found in the carpark behind the multi-storey Russell Street building. This meant it must have been blown right up and over the roof, then over the building behind the police headquarters and into the carpark. A live detonator was found in the women's gym on the fourth floor of the police building.

Police combed the surrounding streets for clues until late into the evening. The search for evidence would start again at first light the following day, Good Friday.

That evening, television news reported that terrorism had hit Melbourne as 'bomb after bomb' exploded in Russell Street. Journalists also reported that police were checking lists of people who were to appear in the Melbourne Magistrates' Court that day.

It was a wonder more people hadn't been killed. Around 1pm, the Magistrates' Court usually began emptying of people for the lunch break, and there were often buses of school children – visiting either the Courts or the police communication centre at D-24. When children visited D-24, they lined up along the wall between the north and the south door of the headquarters. It was sheer luck that a class of kids weren't caught in the fireball. And because the bomb had gone off at 1.01pm, it hadn't given the Court time to empty.

When Bev Donadio was first informed that Carl had been injured in the blast, she was told it was just a broken leg. She rang the Royal Melbourne Hospital while her son was having tests but the nurse promised to ring back as soon as she heard anything. When that call came, the nurse said Carl's injuries were more serious than a broken leg and that the family should get to the hospital as soon as possible.

It was then that Bev panicked.

Victoria Police had sent a Traffic Operations Group car and driver to the Donadios' Ballarat home. As soon as the younger two Donadio children were collected from school, the family sped, lights and sirens all the way, to Melbourne.

For the injured young police officer, drugs were taking the edge off his pain and he was not really aware of what was going on. His parents got the full story when they arrived at the hospital.

The gash in his leg was caused by a piece of shrapnel that had cut him through to the bone. It was a miracle, the doctors said, that his femur hadn't been broken. The shrapnel had, however, completely sliced through his muscle. It would not be an easy fix because the gap was too wide and too swollen to be stitched up. The injury would need a skin graft.

X-rays had revealed shrapnel had also punctured one of Donardio's lungs, and sliced one of his kidneys almost in half. Miraculously the piece of metal had pushed through his ribcage without breaking any bones. Surgeons told the anxious family that they would have to operate to assess the full damage.

The saving grace was that Donardio was young, and fit from playing sports three nights a week and keeping up a full training schedule. He was in the best physical condition he could be to survive what had happened to him.

As his police colleagues finished a day's evidence gathering and investigation, surgeons operated on the 19-year-old police officer, inflating his punctured lung, and sewing his kidney back together. They stitched up a gash behind one of his knees and removed a painful piece of shrapnel from his right ankle. It had lodged there after penetrating the leather of his boot.

His other boot, blown off in the blast, was later found on the roof of the Russell Street police headquarters.

A taskforce was set up to find those responsible. Heading it was veteran investigator, Detective Inspector Daryl Clarke, who quickly put together a team of a dozen detectives.

One of the first things for the Taskforce was to speak to the owner of the bomb car. A numberplate, AVQ 508, was found near the wreck, and it matched the engine number. Even though the car thieves had drilled down the chassis number, they had left the stolen car with its original numberplates.

The owner was understandably upset that his stolen car had been used in the bombing. He told detectives that he had left two tracksuit tops, a red-handled screw driver, a Stanley screwdriver set, a rope, and a chamois in the car when it was stolen. None of those items were recovered at the bomb scene.

The chequered blanket found in the car wasn't his.

On Saturday 29 March at first light, the search continued for evidence at the bomb site and surrounding Melbourne streets.

Members of the SOG abseiled down the façade of the Russell Street police headquarters and neighbouring city buildings in the hunt for evidence lodged on window ledges and roofs.

Crime scene examiner Wayne Ashley had been put at the disposal of the newly-formed Russell Taskforce. He spent much of his time in the police auditorium cataloguing and organising the bags of evidence into areas.

He sectioned off a part of the spacce to store material gathered from the safe zone – the immediate bomb area that was under the control of the bomb experts Bob Barnes and Peter Kiernan. All evidence from the safe zone was collected either by them or under their direct supervision.

Even though the crime scene examiners were trained in post-blast analysis, their practical experience was limited to pipe bombs and exploding letter boxes. Barnes and Kiernan could call upon a wider expertise and the resources of the Department of Defence Materials Research Laboratories.

As each bag of debris was brought into the auditorium, it was given a letter denoting the street or building where it had been located. Ashley devised a grid map so that at a glance, investigators could see where each piece of evidence had come from. Some of the items came via the Fingerprint Bureau, including the dented registration plate, AVQ 508, from the bomb car.

Even in the relative order of the auditorium, Wayne Ashley got regular stark reminders of how the attack had directly affected Victoria Police – like when a detective handed him two plastic bags each containing a small jar.

The jars were labelled:

Hos. 27/3/86 Donadio, Carl, specimen removed, L kidney

Hos. 27/3/86 Donadio, Carl, R leg, near knee.

Inside the jar were the pieces of shrapnel surgically removed from Carl Donadio after the bombing.

On Easter Sunday, Ashley received a similar jar from the hospital containing another metal fragment. This one had been taken from Angela Taylor who remained critically injured in hospital.

On Easter Monday, items of police clothing were sorted out from among the bags of debris. Wayne Ashley put aside two police hats – one belonging to Angela Taylor and the other to Carl Donadio.

He also received, via the hospital, Angela Taylor's charred and bloodied police uniform. The right pocket of her slacks still contained the money she was going to use to buy lunch. He took a moment of respite from his clinical approach to think of his injured comrades. But only a moment.

On Tuesday 1 April, materials from the safe zone were removed from the auditorium and transported to the Materials Research Laboratories. On the same day, the bomb car was finally removed from outside the Russell Street police headquarters where it had sat, covered by a tarpaulin for five days. It was taken to the stolen motor vehicle squad in Port Melbourne on the back of a flat top truck.

Over those five days, the grids had each been examined four times. During the first examination in the post-blast search, SOG members and crime scene examiners were instructed to gather, bag and label every obvious bomb component. The next time, police were looking for any items of interest which may or may not have been connected with the bomb. Thirdly, miscellaneous items were collected, and then all other debris was bagged and labelled. Bags of twisted metal and bomb components slowly filled the auditorium.

After the safe zone debris had been removed, and the bomb car taken away, the police auditorium was locked and put under police guard. The hundreds of other bags of debris would need to wait their turn.

Around the fifth day after the bombing, Carl Donadio began to regain his senses. He didn't remember much of the first four days, but the fifth day, he felt more aware of his surroundings, although he would begin a conversation with someone and then fade out. When the doctors told him that he might be in hospital for up to six months, the young man told himself he'd be out much sooner than that.

It was a few days before Donadio became aware that the explosion which injured him was in fact a bomb, deliberately set against the police. When two detectives from the Russell Taskforce came in to take his statement, he tried his best to include everything that had happened, but he hadn't seen anyone suspicious and had little to add to their investigation.

At the end of the visit, one of the detectives said, 'Don't worry, we'll catch these pricks!'

Donadio could understand their vehemence. He would've felt the same in their position, wanting justice for the injured cops. But it was all he could do to focus on getting well; he just didn't have the energy for revenge as well.

Instead, Donadio's most immediate concern was food; he had come to loathe the bland hospital food of grey meats and boiled vegetables that all seemed to smell like cabbage. The strapping country lad refused to eat anything except the fruit and sometimes the soup. It got to the point where he could smell it coming down the corridor and it would make him feel ill.

His mother, Bev, did her best to smuggle in food, but her son's dramatic weight loss soon became a concern to his surgeons. One doctor told Bev to bring him in anything as long as he would eat it.

Fellow cops lined up to visit the wounded officer. Even cops Donadio had never met wanted to pay their respects. In the end, the hospital and the police force sent out a message that only close friends could visit.

One police officer who *was* admitted was Chief Commissioner Mick Miller. Respect for the chain of command had been drummed into recruits at the Academy; and as a constable, Donadio was supposed to salute any senior officer. When the Chief came in, Donadio nervously saluted from his hospital bed and called him Sir. To his surprise, Miller said to forget the 'sir' and call him Mick.

Donadio was grateful for the Chief's support and genuine interest in his recovery. Miller spoke to Bev and Vic Donadio, and when one of the doctors came into the ward, he also got a medical update. He told Donadio that the Force needed enthusiastic young chaps like him and to get well soon. He visited on several further occasions.

Another bright spot on Donadio's horizon were the constant visits from his squad mates who he'd gone through the Academy with. Both he and Angela Taylor had police guards while they were in the Royal Melbourne Hospital, and it was Donadio's squad mates who were assigned this duty. Whether he needed protection or not, Donadio enjoyed their visits. Unlike the adults around him who saw the severity of his injuries and put on the kid gloves, his young mates ribbed him and joked around.

While Donadio slowly recovered, the investigation continued. The bombed Holden Commodore had been fitted with a V8 engine which still had its original engine number. As noticed at the scene, the chassis number had been drilled leaving holes 8mm in diameter. Casts were made of the drilled holes to be compared – should the investigators locate it – with the drill responsible. Both the vehicle identification number (VIN) plate and the identification plate had been removed from the radiator support panel leaving behind only one rivet and a piece of alloy from each plate. It looked like one rivet from each plate had been removed, and the plates had been torn off leaving the other rivet behind.

In addition, the bomb car was examined for fingerprints in a way that had never been done before. Latent prints that can't be seen with the naked eye or with fingerprint dust, can become visible after fuming with superglue. Normally, this procedure is done on small items placed in a tank at the fingerprint branch, but in the case of the bomb car, something bigger was needed.

Under the direction of the fingerprint experts, the car was placed in a freight container along with tubes of superglue. Heaters were used to evaporate the glue. The resultant fumes solidify on objects that contain water and since fingerprints are made up primarily of water and fats, investigators hoped some prints would show up on the car. Unfortunately, none were found.

When the bomb car was finished with, it was returned to the stolen motor vehicle squad's compound in Port Melbourne.

The red and white chequered blanket from the bomb car was examined by Bob Barnes at the Materials Research Laboratory. As it didn't belong to the vehicle's owner it must have been put there by the bombers. The rug was in remarkably good condition given Barnes concluded it had been used to cover the bomb's timing device.

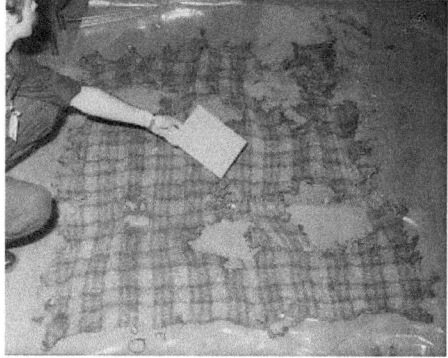

The bomb blanket

Barnes examined the blanket for explosives residue and in the process found some short hairs from a terrier-type dog. He passed his findings on to detectives from the Taskforce.

Detective Sergeant Bernie Rankin was in Adelaide on vacation when he heard a radio newsflash that a bomb had exploded outside Melbourne's police headquarters. Like many detectives, he'd come across a couple of crooks in his day who might hate the police enough to do this. One such criminal had recently lost a friend in a shoot-out with the SOG and had openly discussed revenge.

Rankin theorised the pool of suspects was limited because, firstly they would need to hate the police enough to plan the such destructive payback; and secondly, they'd need to know how to build a bomb. Bomb making skills were not common on the curriculum vitae of the everyday criminal.

When the Russell Taskforce was set up on the day of the bombing, Rankin contacted the detective in charge, Daryl Clarke. Clarke asked Rankin if he wanted to come on board when he returned to Melbourne. Like every cop in the state, Rankin wanted the bombers caught and within a week he was back home and a part of the team.

A room at the Russell Street police headquarters had been set aside for the Taskforce. Initially consisting of a dozen detectives, the number had increased to 30 in the week following the bombing. The brass wanted a couple of detectives from each of the northern, eastern, south-eastern and the western suburbs so that they could draw on local knowledge from all points of the compass. Also seconded to the Taskforce were members of the Arson Squad, Major Crime Squad, and Homicide.

A week after the attack, the analysis of the bomb exposed the intentions of the bombers. The explosives – about 50 sticks of gelignite – had been packed into the boot of the two-tone 1980 Holden Commodore. Among the debris found in Russell Street, the remains of a plastic bread crate had been identified. It was in this, according to the experts, that the main part of the bomb had been packed. It was then covered with the assorted sockets, tools and leftover detonators that became deadly shrapnel, making the bomb design and its intention callous beyond belief.

The bread crate was identified as similar in make and colour to some stolen in a milk bar robbery in Braeside six weeks before the bombing. Cigarettes and confectionary were also stolen.

The timing device was an alarm clock nailed to the block of wood, possibly a fence post, that Dennis Tipping had found next to the exploded car. When the alarm sounded, the metal piece at the back of the clock clicked over and connected the wires, which completed the circuit and set off the bomb. This first explosion had detached a mechanism from the second explosive device which then failed to detonate.

The fact that the bomb makers had used a Chux Superwipe to keep the wires from connecting indicated the bomb was probably built by amateurs. The police experts were amazed it hadn't exploded on the drive to Russell Street. It would have only taken a small jolt to dislodge the Superwipe and set off the bomb.

The type of bomb also gave investigators an insight into the offenders they were looking for. They were clearly not experts or experienced in handling explosives. In other words, they were lucky rather than criminal masterminds. They had some knowledge though, as they'd wrapped the gelignite in newspaper in a crude attempt to stop it from sweating and exploding prematurely. So the bomb was homemade yet powerful enough to kill anyone standing nearby; and amateurish, in that it failed to complete its full mission.

No group had claimed responsibility for the bomb which meant it probably wasn't a politically-motivated attack. But, as no solid suspects had emerged, it was acknowledged the bombers could be anyone – with a grudge against the police or the judiciary.

Regardless of who did it or why, the cops took the attack personally. It was on their turf, and one of their officers was fighting for her life in hospital. Detectives were usually on the outside of a crime looking in. This time, they were the likely target and the victims, and they badly wanted to find those responsible. At the same time, they had to put personal feelings aside, and gather strong admissible evidence to present at a trial for when they caught the perpetrators.

The police used a time-honoured method of investigation. They made their presence known in other areas of criminal activity. The gaming industry, for instance, was as good as shut down during the investigation, which meant the police weren't the only ones interested in having the case solved. And if the cops could exert enough pressure in the right directions, then information could come from unlikely sources.

A link was soon made with the gelignite.

The previous October, a large quantity of gelignite had been stolen from the Triconnel Mine at Blackwood. The bomb gelignite was identical to that stolen in the robbery, which suggested the bombers had planned this for at least six months.

A week on from the bombing, Constable Angela Taylor still hadn't regained consciousness. With burns to 70 per cent of her body, doctors said if she lived, it would be nothing short of a miracle.

An anonymous caller telephoned Chief Commissioner Mick Miller five times in response to media appeals for information. He said not only did he know who the bombers were, but he had photographs of them. If what he said was true, he could hold the key. The only catch was the man wanted a significant reward for his information.

The calls were traced to several public phone boxes around the St Kilda area. Police were unsure whether the caller had genuine information or whether it was a hoax. In any case, they begin to stake out telephone boxes and detectives soon became familiar with the location of every St Kilda public phone box.

On Friday 4 April, eight days after the bombing, state Premier John Cain and Chief Commissioner Mick Miller offered a reward of $500,000 for information leading to the capture and conviction of the bombers.

Police hoped that if the anonymous caller was genuine, the promise of such a large reward would flush him out. As soon as the reward was announced, additional police were used to watch phone boxes around the St Kilda area.

The anonymous caller wasn't the only member of the public phoning police with potential information. Regular re-enactments and reminders in the media brought forth hundreds of phone calls. One woman said she had seen a man parking a two-tone Commodore in front of the Russell Street police headquarters at 12.30pm on the day of the bombing. With her help, police compiled an identikit photo of the suspect and circulated it among detectives.

Several cops thought the photo bore a strong resemblance to a known small-time crook called Claudio Crupi.

When Taskforce detectives went looking for Crupi, further witnesses came forward to say they'd seen him wrapping up what appeared to be sticks of gelignite on the day of the bombing. Crupi was also known to have a grudge against a detective at the Major Crime Squad.

A number of search warrants were issue on Crupi's house and places he was known to frequent. Nothing, including Crupi, was found. Neighbours said he'd left his home a few hours before the bombing and returned a few hours later. It was rumoured he'd left town soon after. With the evidence stacking up against him, Crupi quickly became one of the main suspects.

When Inspector Bruce Knight had initially mobilised his Special Operations Group colleagues to respond to the explosion in Russell Street, most members assisted.

That same afternoon, however, he also had to deploy a team from the Armed Robbery Squad to respond to a bank robbery in Donvale. The getaway vehicle used in the robbery was a silver Holden Brock Commodore Special. Detectives liaised with officers of the Stolen Motor Vehicle Squad on a list of stolen Commodores and less than two weeks later, on 7 April, one was fished out of the Yarra River near Wonga Park.

On Monday 14 April, Detective Sergeant Arthur Adams from the Stolen Motor Vehicle Squad arrived at the Port Melbourne compound to examine the Brock Commodore. The car used in the Donvale robbery was still en route to the compound, which also housed the Russell Street bomb car.

While he waited for his evidence to arrive, Detective Adams and his colleagues took a look over the bomb car. They noticed the caterpillar of holes where the chassis number had been drilled out and, like the investigators before them, they too thought the drilling was unusual.

In fact Adams had only seen it once – a decade earlier. And then, when the stolen Brock Commodore was delivered, they discovered it too had the serial numbers drilled out in exactly the same way. Arthur Adams immediately alerted the taskforce and met with Bernie Rankin and Daryl Clarke.

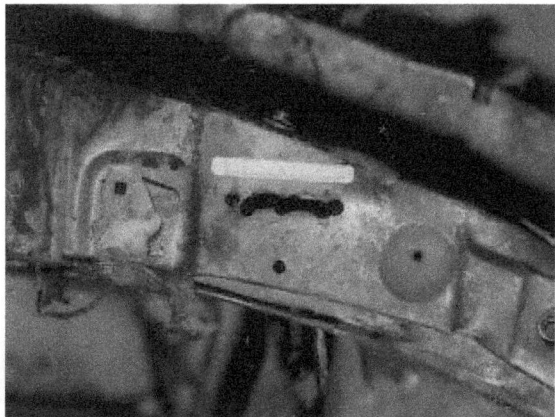

The drill holes in the support panel of the bomb car.

'If I were a betting man,' Adams said, 'I would say these two cars were connected'.

This couldn't be a coincidence. A Commodore explodes in Russell Street at 1.01pm. Three hours later, another Commodore with the same drill markings is involved in a bank robbery in Donvale – at the exact time when all available police resources were tied up in the city.

The three Stolen Motor Vehicle Squad detectives were able to provide another connection. Three weeks before the bombing, a red Daimler was pursued by police along the Calder Highway in East Keilor. The car crashed and the driver escaped, though shortly after he stole another car at gunpoint. The man was dangerous, and the police were anxious to catch him.

As the Daimler had already been reported as stolen, detectives from the Stolen Motor Vehicle Squad were called in. In the boot of the crashed vehicle, officers found a bag containing cut up pieces of car number plates, including plates from a stolen Brock Commodore Special – CCH 997. Detective John Bradbury made a note in the police data base that if the the car was found, he wanted to be notified immediately.

When forensically examined, the holes drilled into the chassis number in the Brock Commodore were 8mm in diameter – the same size as those drilled in the bomb car. The VIN plates as well as the compliance plates had also been removed using the same method; and, while some of the pop rivets were still in place, the plates had been torn off. As with the bomb car, the engine number hadn't been touched.

Clarke and Rankin discussed this new development. They couldn't ignore Crupi as their strongest suspect, but at the same time, they needed to explore this new lead. Clarke put a small team of detectives to follow up the Brock Commodore link.

On Tuesday 15 April, 19 days after the bombing, police finally caught up with Claudio Crupi. News footage captured him being led out of the Russell Street police headquarters over to the

Magistrates' Court. The irony of the proximity to the bomb site didn't escape the news commentators.

Two Taskforce detectives interviewed Crupi, after which they told waiting colleagues that a lot of work would have to be done to prove he was involved. Crupi was charged with an aggravated burglary he'd committed before the bombing. Apparently, according to Crupi, the bomb he'd been 'seen' making was a fake he intended to throw through a window of the Flemington police station. If Crupi was innocent, then he had certainly picked the wrong day to make a fake bomb.

On Wednesday 16 April, the anonymous caller rang the Chief Commissioner again. This time, the police were ready. As soon as the man was on the line, D-24 informed St Kilda police who spotted a man using a public phone. They took the receiver from his hand and spoke to the Chief Commissioner on the other end of the line. It was beyond frustrating when it became obvious that the caller, despite being an industrial chemist, didn't have any real information at all. He was charged with hindering a police investigation. While detectives couldn't ignore his phone calls, many hours had been lost chasing him that could have been more productively used hunting the real bombers.

The Taskforce soon had another strong contender in the frame. With the spotlight on the connection between the stolen red Daimler and the Brock Commodore, it was imperative police locate the driver who had crashed the Daimler and later hijacked another car at gunpoint.

Detectives spoke to the traffic cop who'd originally chased the Daimler, and had caught enough of a glimpse of the driver to pick him out of a group of mugshots. He recognised the driver as Peter Reed who had priors as a car thief. Police began a massive manhunt to locate Reed who was also wanted for questioning in connection with a number of bank robberies.

Taskforce head, Daryl Clarke, left the Brock Commodore crew of detectives to follow up the Reed connection, while other crews stayed on the investigation of Crupi and other suspects.

Detectives from the Armed Robbery Squad told the Taskforce they were also interested in Reed for some particularly violent armed robberies on banks, including the bank job in Donvale on the day of the bombing. Covert surveillance teams began watching Peter Reed very closely.

Constable Angela Taylor, died on 20 April. For 24 days, her family sat by her hospital bed as she slowly lost her battle for life.

Carl Donadio had wanted to visit Angela. He was still in the same hospital himself, but he contracted a golden staph infection and decided to hold off. He didn't get another chance.

His parents had met Angela's parents in the hospital canteen, and become friendly. They were united in their anxiety and bedside vigils for their children. Bev Donadio had visited Angela. The dying policewoman was a sight she would never forget, but Bev had her own anxieties. There was a time that the doctors wondered whether her son would keep his badly injured leg, and the golden staph infection on top of his injuries was serious.

Against the advice of his doctors, Donadio was determined to attend her funeral. He had received so much support and encouragement from the police force, and wanted to give something back. He also wanted to go for Angela. He had only known her to nod to when they passed each other at work, but now they'd be forever united as the two police victims of the Russell Street bombing – the one who survived and the one who didn't.

It wasn't until Donadio put on his police uniform that he realised just how much weight he had lost in the four weeks since the attack. The young sports fanatic had lost most of his muscle tone and his ribs stuck out.

Angela Taylor's funeral was held at the Victoria Police Academy and was attended by over 1200 people including Victorian Premier John Cain, Governor Davis McCaughey and Chief Commissioner Mick Miller. Five hundred cops lined the route leaving the chapel on the way to the cemetery.

For Taskforce detectives, Angela's death strengthened their resolve to find the bombers and charge them with her murder.

On 25 April, Anzac Day, Taskforce detectives raided Peter Reed's house in Kallista, 50km east of Melbourne. It was one of several simultaneous raids on different properties.

Wayne Ashley and his crime scene crew waited outside in their van while the initial raid took place. It would be their job to check the premises for any evidence that matched the bomb scene: drills that drilled the 8mm holes in the chassis of the bomb car; terrier dog hairs – or the dog – matching those found on the blanket in the bomb car; small bunches of wire, socket sets with tools missing, gelignite from the same batch as that stolen during the burglary at the Triconnel Mine; or even the fence post that the block of wood had been sawn from that held the bomb clock in place.

Detectives John Bradbury and Steve Quinsee from the Stolen Motor Vehicle Squad accompanied Taskforce detectives for the joint raid.

As police stormed the house, guns drawn, shouting, 'Police! Don't move!' over and over again, Steve Quinsee entered with Taskforce detective, Sergeant Mark Wylie. While some of the detectives headed into a bedroom on the right of the central passageway, Quinsee approached a bedroom on the left. The house was in darkness, illuminated only by torches carried by the police raiders.

When Quinsee got to the open doorway of the bedroom, he reached around, found the light switch and flicked it on. In the sudden light, a figure from the room was reflected in the bedroom window. Out of sight from the doorway Peter Reed, wearing pyjamas, was kneeling on the bed pointing a gun towards the door.

The seconds between the shouting of 'Police! Don't move!' and going through a doorway is known as the 'tunnel of death'. In a raid, it is the moment of extreme vulnerability – the crooks know where you are from your shouting, but you don't know where they are.

The sight that greeted Sergeant Mark Wylie was the same one Quinsee could see in reflection: Peter Reed pointing a gun straight at him.

As Wylie pulled back from the door, Detective John Bradbury yelled out, 'Peter, I'm John Bradbury from the Stolen Motor Vehicles Squad. Put the gun down!'

But it was too late, the madness had started and Reed responded by firing two shots at Mark Wylie's retreating figure. They swooshed past Wylie's nose and thudded into a plaster wall.

Using Reed's reflection in the window, Wylie returned fire. He pointed his pump-action shotgun at the door and fired twice through it to where he thought Reed was. Momentarily distracted by a jam in the shotgun as he reloaded, Wylie looked up to find that Reed was no longer on the bed. Wylie edged forward to take another shot at Reed.

From behind the door, however, Reed could see the barrel of Wylie's shotgun coming around so he fired twice through the door shooting the police officer. Bradbury dragged Wylie back down the passageway and Quinsee took his place.

By this time, Reed had moved from behind the door and was standing on the window side of the bed from where he fired two shots at Quinsee. He missed.

Quinsee returned fire, aiming for the central body mass, and hit Reed twice in the stomach. When the injured man fell to the floor, Quinsee ran to him, kicked the gun out of his hand and handcuffed him.

Bleeding from the stomach, Mark Wylie staggered into the lounge room with the help of his fellow officers. He was wearing a parka with an elasticised band. When he unzipped the parka, the bullet, which had passed right through him, dropped from the band and landed at his feet. He was aware enough of what was happening to tell his men to mark it as evidence.

Raids were always tense. Police at every entrance, bursting into premises shouting. And for those waiting outside, the worst thing was to hear guns go off followed quickly by urgent voices over the police radio: 'Member shot, ambulance required.'

Something had gone terribly wrong. And the crime scene examiners in the van outside could do nothing but look on helplessly. By the time Wayne Ashley and his team made their way up the steep driveway to the country property, they were walking past ambulances with their lights flashing as paramedics inside tended to the wounded, including one of their own.

Bomb expert Bob Barnes joined Wayne Ashley and the other crime scene examiners at the house. Because he and Kiernan had spent the last month examining the bomb car and the evidence directly connected with the bomb itself, his knowledge was needed to spot things others might miss. When the crime scene crew entered the house in Kallista, ambulance officers were still attending to Mark Wylie in the lounge room and Peter Reed in the bedroom. When the injured men had been taken to hospital, and the house cleared, they began their examination. The shooting had turned the house into two different crime scenes – one for potential bomb links and the other for the shooting. Each had to be processed separately.

The Kallista house was the equivalent of a crime scene examiner's gold mine. Ashley collected a Smith and Wesson .45 calibre Magnum revolver from Reed's bedroom. Its serial number had been drilled out in the exact same manner as the bomb car and the Brock Commodore. Under a pillow in the laundry, Ashley found a sawn-off Winchester 1500 shotgun. The serial number had been drilled out too.

Several items of interest were scattered around the lounge room floor: old and new pairs of overalls, car registration plates, VIN and compliance plate numbers.

Near the fireplace, Ashley collected Mark Wylie's blood-stained parka and bagged it for evidence. Learning against the northern wall of the lounge room were two Remington shotguns. On the floor near the weapons, were items of clothing, and a canvas bag. On top of the canvas bag were two detonators with very short white and blue wires. There were two sawn-off Browning shotguns; three of the shotguns had their serial numbers drilled out in the now familiar caterpillar of joined holes.

Also in the lounge room were four sticks of gelignite individually wrapped in sheets of newspaper. Bob Barnes carefully removed the gelignite from the newspaper and gave the wrappings to a sergeant from the Fingerprint Branch.

In the end, police collected an arsenal from the home of Peter Reed: shotguns, pistols, ammunition, gun holsters, detonators, a hand grenade, and gelignite.

In one of the bedrooms, they found automotive parts: white and silver moulded panels similar to those of the Holden Commodore then residing in the Stolen Motor Vehicles compound. They also found scanners capable of monitoring police radio frequencies.

The day after the search and shooting, Wayne Ashley returned to the Kallista house and supervised the removal of several cars parked at the rear of the property. One, a Holden HQ sedan was taken to the crime scene section at Macleod, while others were taken to the Stolen Motor Vehicles compound.

It was Ashley's job to make sure all the collected evidence went to the appropriate sections of the police and that all possible bomb-related evidence went to Bob Barnes and the post-blast team from MRL. All firearms and associated ammunition went to the Firearms division, and anything else of value was handed over to the Taskforce.

Taskforce officers not present at the Kallista raid, were shocked at the Wylie shooting. Luckily, his prognosis was for a good recovery, but it was a reminder that police were dealing with people who were prepared to shoot it out with them.

Until Peter Reed fired on police, he had been viewed mainly as a petty car thief. His actions at Kallista put him in a whole different category. Why would a petty car thief fire on police? Had he supplied the bomb car? And did the fact that Reed was seen driving the red Daimler with the Brock Commodore numberplates in its boot, connect him to the bank robbery in Donvale?

The fingerprint search hit pay-dirt. Prints found on the newspaper that had been wrapped around the gelignite, belonged to Rodney Joseph Minogue. Others lifted from the toilet door of Reed's house belonged to Rodney's brother, Craig Minogue.

The other police raids – carried out at the same time as the one at Peter Reed's house – targeted people he'd been seen consorting with during the police surveillance of him.

The raid on the Boronia house of Reed's brother, Steven Komiazyk, went much more smoothly. Among the items police collected there were: a PVC chamois, two tracksuit tops, a red-handled screwdriver, a Stanley screwdriver set and a rope. These were identified by the owner of the bomb car as being in his vehicle when it was stolen.

Searchers also found a drill-bit with paint fragments identical to the bomb car, and a rivet which investigators believed came from the removal of the identification plates on the bomb car. Like his brother, Steven Komiazyk had his own guns. Their serial numbers had been drilled out too.

Another address raided was one Peter Reed had visited a number of times during the surveillance period. The house in Haros Avenue, Nunawading belonged to a friend of Reed's called Karl Zelinka who lived there with his girlfriend, Karen.

Zelinka was taken in for questioning by members of the Taskforce. He denied knowing Peter Reed. As the investigators knew this wasn't true, they wondered what Zelinka had to hide. He had no prior convictions, and his connection to the bombing investigation did not sit easily with him. The only items found in the initial sweep of his house were cigarettes and confectionery consistent with that taken in the Braeside milk bar robbery. Zelinka also had a sawn-off shotgun.

At each of the raids, police checked fences and fence posts for a match to the block of wood that the bomb clock had been nailed to. They didn't find anything.

Carl Donadio, who felt like he had cabin fever, really wanted to prove the doctors wrong. They had predicted a six-month hospital stay, but he started his rehabilitation three weeks after the bombing. On the first day of rehab, the physiotherapist came into his room, got him up to walk three or four steps, then she put him back to bed. The minute she left the room, Donadio begged his family to help him out of bed again.

Behind the physio's back, he repeated the exercise and walked five steps. He did this every day until his muscle condition slowly started to return.

Constable Carl Donardio in hospital after the Russell Street bombing.

Much to the surprise of his doctors, Donadio recovered enough to return to light duties five weeks after the bombing.

He wasn't able to put on his uniform because doctors had decided to repair the gaping wound in his leg by inserting a surgical balloon under his skin. This was inflated daily so the skin could stretch around it. When there was enough skin, it would be used to close the wound in his thigh once and for all. Until this procedure, surgeons had to leave the wound open. It wasn't a pretty sight for visitors and some of his more squeamish squad mates had fainted during their visits.

Donadio started working at the Carlton North District office, happy for at least his mind to be active, even if his body wasn't quite there yet. Loose casual pants hid the balloon in his leg.

On 3 May, Peter Reed had recovered sufficiently from his gunshot wound to be brought in for questioning. He was dragged by detectives from Russell Street police headquarters to the Magistrates' Court, doubled over, screaming his innocence in a high-pitched voice.

Reed denied all involvement in the bombing. He was charged, for the time being, with the attempted murder of Sergeant Mark Wylie and remanded into custody.

Meanwhile, Taskforce detectives were investigating the link

between Reed and the Minogue brothers, whose fingerprints had been found at his house.

It turned out that Peter Reed and Rodney Minogue had served time in prison together. Rodney and his brother Craig were small time crooks so the question was: were they involved in the bombing. Craig's fingerprint on the toilet door was not in itself incriminating; it simply indicated he'd been in Reed's house.

It would be more difficult, however, for his younger brother to explain how his fingerprints came to be on newspaper wrapped around gelignite that came from the same batch used in the bombing. The brothers had left town right after the bombing.

In Craig Minogue's police file, there was a notation about a car that had once picked him up after a court appearance. The car belonged to Karl Zelinka. The connections were forming, but Zelinka now denied knowing the Minogue brothers.

Taskforce investigators canvassed Zelinka's neighbours in Haros Avenue, several of whom identified pictures of the Minogue brothers and Peter Reed as being regular visitors to the house.

While the investigators hunted for the bombers, the forensics staff processed the evidence from the Reed search, and began to see connections between Reed and the bombing. The khaki canvas bag containing the detonators found in Reed's lounge room had identical buckles to that found at the bomb scene which meant a similar bag could have been used in the bomb car. Wires on the detonators found at Reed's house had been cut with the same instrument that had been used to cut the bomb detonators. If the cutting instrument could be found with one of the suspects, that would further link them to the crime.

Both the gelignite and detonators were the same as those found unexploded at the bomb site. Plastic bread crates identified as being stolen from a Braeside milk bar, and identical to the ones that the bomb had been packed in, were found at Reed's house. The silver Commodore accessories found in the spare room were identified by the owner as coming from the stolen Brock Commodore.

Bob Barnes made another break-through. One night as he lay in bed, he had a Eureka moment when he realised that the strip of metal connecting the clock to the block of wood making up the circuit, was in fact the handle from a metal rubbish bin. The following day, he told the Taskforce detectives to be on the look-out for a metal bin missing a lid or a handle.

In light of Karl Zelinka's denials about knowing Reed and the Minogues, Taskforce detectives decided to go back to his house for another look on 14 May. The Minogue brothers had still not been located, and none of the other key players were talking.

Zelinka's metal rubbish bin had no lid. One of the handles on the bin itself, looked like someone had made an attempt to cut it off. Could someone have tried to cut this handle off, and then settled for the handle on the missing lid? Zelinka was vague about the whereabouts of his bin lid.

And then came the discovery that many of the Taskforce investigators still consider their finest investigative moment. In the course of each of the raids, all fences had been checked to see if they were missing the block of wood that the bomb clock had been mounted on.

There were no obvious anomalies in Zelinka's fence, but on this second search, bomb expert Bob Barnes had an idea. He climbed up on the fence and jumped over into the next-door neighbour's yard. Behind a large camellia tree was a sawn-off fence post on the neighbour's side of the fence. Holding the bomb block of wood in his hands, Barnes placed it on top of the fence post. Even to the untrained eye, there was no doubt they were a perfect match – faults that ran through the bomb block continued through the fence post.

From that moment on, Taskforce detectives regarded the house in Haros Avenue as being the bomb headquarters. All evidence pointed to the bomb being assembled at Karl Zelinka's house. Up until the match with the fence post, Zelinka had been unwilling to cooperate with police. Now, with evidence connecting his house with the bombing, he quickly changed his mind.

Bernie Rankin took Karl Zelinka back to the office for a serious chat. He laid out all the information that detectives had so far:

how he'd lied about knowing the Minogues and Peter Reed, his missing rubbish bin lid, and the bomb block of wood matching his fence post.

'Imagine you were in our shoes,' said Rankin, 'How do you think it looks?'

Zelinka knew the game was up. He asked for police protection for his girlfriend and his family and agreed to tell police everything he knew. Interviews took place over the next couple of days.

According to Zelinka, Craig and Rodney Minogue had lived with him at Haros Avenue, where Peter Reed would often visit. Two days before the bombing, Zelinka had seen a two-toned Commodore, later used as the bomb car, being driven into the garage. He had also seen the stolen Brock Commodore at his house. Earlier, he'd seen a case of explosives in the garage but when he asked about them, Craig Minogue told him to forget he'd seen them.

Zelinka admitted to committing a burglary with Craig Minogue and Peter Reed on the milk bar in Braeside. It was during this burglary that the milk crates had been stolen. He also said that Craig had a bull terrier puppy who slept on a blanket similar to the one found in the bomb car.

As well as Reed, the Minogues had another regular visitor, an older man they referred to as 'Stan the Man'. Zelinka didn't know his full name.

Craig Minogue had bought Zelinka and his girlfriend tickets to Sydney for Easter; they had left on Wednesday, the day before the bombing. When they returned, the Minogue brothers were moving out of the Haros Avenue house. It was at this point, they told Zelinka to get rid of his rubbish bin lid. He tossed it onto a pile of rubbish bound for the tip.

Using police intelligence sources, and checking known aliases against the description Zelinka gave of Stan the Man, Taskforce detectives soon identified him as 50-year-old Stanley Brian Taylor whose prior convictions dated back to 1949. He had first been arrested and charged with stealing fish when he was just 12 years old.

Stan Taylor did time in Pentridge Prison's notorious H-Division and was dubbed 'Wild Man' for his part in the 1972 prison riots. He was paroled in 1978 and by 1979 had been given a job with the Youth Council of Victoria working with troubled teens. He had even played small roles in a couple of long-running Australian television series including *Cop Shop* and *Prisoner*.

The big question for the Taskforce was: why had Stanley Brian Taylor visited the bomb house? Was he trying to talk the bombers out of their task, or was he involved?

Acting on information from Karl Zelinka's statement, Wayne Ashley was sent back to Haros Avenue on 20 May. The white weatherboard house had a concrete driveway beside it which led to a garage at the rear of the property. The entire concrete floor of the garage was swept for evidence. Apart from the lounge room which was carpeted, floors in the house were either floorboards or tiles. These too were swept and the dirt was bagged for later examination.

A Chux Superwipe similar to that found on the bomb timing device was found in the kitchen, and another under the house.

Two days later, Ashley and his team of crime scene examiners returned to examine the garage floor again. This time each crack in the concrete was examined, swept and diagrammed. Most of the evidence was handed over to Bob Barnes. In the search, they found rivets similar to the ones left on the bomb car and the Brock Commodore.

On the concrete in one of the corners of the garage, was an area where something had been spray-painted and the overspray had hit the concrete wall of the garage. This area was measured and photographed. A sample of the paint was taken for analysis. When compared, the overspray pattern was similar to the front grille of the Brock Commodore sitting in the police compound in Port Melbourne. The grill had been sprayed with silver paint.

Another connection between Zelinka's house and the bomb was found in a packet of 50 mm nails. These had identical tool marks to the nails hammered into the block of wood to set the timing device in place.

On 27 May, Peter Reed and his brother Steven Komiazyk were charged with the bombing of the Russell Street police headquarters and the murder of Angela Taylor. Both were remanded into custody. The charges against Komiazyk would later be dropped.

In an investigation like this, one breakthrough produces a domino effect. Taskforce detectives received information that the Minogue brothers were hiding out in the township of Birchip about 300km north-west of Melbourne.

All bomb-related raids after the Anzac Day shooting of Sergeant Mark Wylie, were carried out by members of the special operations group. The Taskforce would take no further risks with its members, and left the captures to their highly-trained SOG colleagues.

On 30 May, the Taskforce held a briefing at 2am at the St Arnaud police station and planned the raid carefully. Intelligence put Stanley Taylor at home at his house in Watchem Road, Birchip. Some SOG members assembled outside the house while others waited outside a house in Lockwood Street that belonged to Craig and Rodney Minogue. They patted a bull terrier guard dog which surrendered playfully.

Simultaneously, the SOG raided both houses. Operatives burst into Taylor's home and made the arrest without incident. Taskforce detectives followed them in after the house was secure. Stan Taylor was found in his bedroom.

With the six-hour interview rule still in place in Victoria, detectives had to get Taylor to the nearest police station and begin interviewing him without wasting any time. Back at the St Arnaud police station, detectives used a portable tape recorder to tape the interview. The only way they could interview their suspect for more than six hours, was to get an extension by a magistrate.

Stan Taylor was a softly spoken unassuming man who had fooled a lot of people in the small town where he had settled. He had invented a respectable past for himself and few of his new friends imagined that he had spent most of his adult life in prison, and no one questioned the LOVE and HATE tattooed across his knuckles. He was well-spoken and fit right in to his new community. Taylor used his ill-gotten gains to flash around the local footy club. Along with the Minogue brothers, Taylor spent a lot of time at the club. Craig Minogue even played a couple of games for them.

In a talkative mood, Taylor volunteered the name of the motel in Swan Hill where the Minogue brothers were hiding out. An SOG raid at 5am netted them without incident.

When news filtered through of the arrest of the Minogues at Swan Hill, the detectives used the police helicopter to fly Stan Taylor there, so the three suspects could be questioned at the same location. That way, detectives could easily compare notes.

The Swan Hill police station was conveniently located next to the courthouse. At the court, a magistrate asked Taylor if he agreed to an extension, and Taylor said he did. The interview continued in the Swan Hill CIB offices. Over the course of the interview, two extensions were granted by the magistrate.

Detectives were surprised Stan Taylor spoke to them at all; they expected him to 'no comment' his way through the interview. But Taylor was old school – he would admit to as much as he had to then try and blame everything on everyone else.

Sure, Taylor said, he'd been to the Haros Avenue house on the day of the bombing, but he'd left before and driven straight back to Birchip. He implied that Peter Reed and Craig Minogue were the ones most responsible for the bomb.

Later that morning, the Minogues appeared in the Swan Hill Magistrates' Court. In the interview room Craig, aged 23, gave detectives his name and address, and otherwise sat silently with a half-smile on his face. He was charged with nine offences in total including the murder of Angela Taylor and the attempted murder of Carl Donadio and Magistrate Iain West.

Rodney Minogue, aged 20, was held for further questioning. Unlike his brother, Rodney made what police referred to as a 'full and frank confession'. He told detectives that the bombing had been planned by Stan Taylor.

While the suspects were being questioned in custody, Wayne Ashley and his team searched for evidence at the two Birchip houses. Beginning at Watchem Road, the crime scene examiners searched inside and outside the neat white weatherboard house. Even though it looked like the house of a respectable middle-aged man, Ashley found small things that marked Taylor a crook. The number on the compliance plate of his Ford LTD parked under the carport, didn't match the chassis number. Along with the car, other items were taken and handed on to the Taskforce.

After the dawn examination of Taylor's house, the crime scene examiners went straight to the Lockwood Street home of the Minogue brothers which had been secured and guarded since the pre-dawn raid. The Minogues had two suspected stolen vehicles at their house.

Inside the house, the crime scene examiners found ammunition, a shotgun cartridge of the same brand found at Reed's house, and a loaded shotgun in one of the bedrooms. A sleeping bag lay on top of a mattress on the floor. Next to the bed was a Cold Power detergent box. Inside it, were three multi-frequency scanners, all of which were connected to a power-board which was plugged into an electrical outlet. In a nearby chest of drawers, they found two more scanners.

The Minogues too had been listening in on police frequencies. Since the scanners found in the raid on Peter Reed's house, radio silence had been adopted prior to all subsequent raids.

In another drawer was a book on Bull Terrier dogs. At the Lockwood Street house, the crime scene examiners noticed the bull terrier dog that the SOG had being playing with. Ashley gently removed some samples from the dog. The hairs would later prove to be consistent with the ones found on the bomb car rug.

It was in the kitchen that Ashley found what investigators had been looking for all along. Plugged into an extension cord and resting on the old kitchen bench was a high-speed engraving device. The spinning end of it looked to be the same size as the drill that had drilled out all the chassis numbers of the stolen cars and the serial numbers of the firearms found at other raids. It would have to be tested, but it looked promising.

Not only did the Minogues have evidence at their house, but police discovered that Craig Minogue had rented a storage garage in North Albury. The day after the Birchip raids and the arrest of the Minogues in Swan Hill, the crime scene examiners travelled to Albury to examine the storage unit. Police photographers recorded the clutter of furniture, boxes and tool boxes.

During the search, police found detonators and an explosives handbook. They also found a pair of blue-handled tin-snips, later found to be the ones that cut the wires on the bomb detonators as well as the detonators found at Peter Reed's house.

Sockets missing from a set located in the storage garage, were later found to have been used as shrapnel in the bomb.

Back at the forensic lab, Ashley used the engraving tool found in the Minogues' kitchen to drill into old firearms. He made casts

Russell Street bomber Craig Minogue
during the trial, in Melbourne, 1988.

of the patterns which he later proved were consistent with the other firearms, the Brock Commodore and the bomb car.

While the forensic team matched the evidence, detectives located a friend of Stan Taylor's. The friend admitted to taking part in the theft of gelignite and detonators from the Triconnel Mine, and described how Craig Minogue and Stan Taylor had tested the stolen detonators on a country property. He said he had also heard Craig, Taylor and Reed talk about blowing up the Russell Street police headquarters.

While awaiting trial in 1987, Craig Minogue joined seven other prisoners protesting against conditions in the maximum security Jika Jika division of Pentridge Prison. The prisoners sealed their doors and stacked bedding against them, and covered the windows in paper so warders couldn't identify the trouble makers. The men started a fire and ripped plumbing from the walls with the intention of breathing fresh air through the pipes. They badly miscalculated and five of the protesters perished in the fire. Craig Minogue was one of three prisoners to survive the Jika Jika fire. The section was quickly closed down.

The committal hearing for the suspects in the Russell Street bombing began in January 1988. There was so much forensic evidence, crime scene examiner Wayne Ashley spent four days in the witness box.

Standing in the Melbourne Magistrates' Court, a stone's throw from the scene of the crime, Ashley had a chance to study the four accused. Craig Minogue's hatred of the police was almost palpable. He was tall and his size was intimidating. Ashley reckoned that, of the two brothers, Craig wielded the power and Rodney was the master's apprentice. Peter Reed looked like the typical crook that he was; but Stan Taylor was harder to read. Occasionally, while Ashley was giving evidence, one or other of the accused would yell out, 'Liar!' The crime scene examiner tried to focus on the evidence, rather than the men accused of the bombing.

The trial proper began in March 1988. By this time, Stan Taylor was 51-years-old; Craig and Rodney were 26 and 23 respectively; and Reed was 31.

The evidence given at the trial suggested the bomb car was driven to Russell Street by Peter Reed and Craig Minogue. Stan Taylor allegedly followed in the stolen Brock Commodore. Once the bomb car was parked outside the south door of the Russell Street police headquarters, the Chux Superwipe was removed from the timing device and the bomb set.

One witness suggested that Taylor, Minogue and Reed had parked nearby and waited for the explosion.

When the bomb when off, said the witness, the bombers were thrilled.

On Tuesday 12 July, the accused arrived at the Supreme Court to hear their verdicts. As they entered the court room, they yelled out they were innocent.

Stanley Taylor and Craig Minogue were both found guilty of the murder of Angela Taylor and of causing serious injury to Iain West and Carl Donadio. Rodney Minogue was found guilty of being an accessory after the fact. The jury retired again to deliberate its verdict for Peter Reed.

On Wednesday 13 July, the packed courtroom awaited the Reed verdict. It came around 6pm. The jury found him guilty of the attempted murder of Steven Quinsee, and guilty of recklessly causing serious injury to Mark Wylie during the Kallista raid. It was then the jury returned a verdict of not guilty on all counts relating to the Russell Street bombing.

Peter Reed had been under police surveillance on the day the bomb went off. He had been followed to Haros Avenue where police believe the bomb was assembled. Because Haros Avenue is a dead-end street, the surveillance crew waited for his car to reappear from around a bend in the road. They were unable to park covertly and still have a view of the house. The surveillance team would have taken little notice of the two-tone Holden bomb car as it drove past. And if Peter Reed was in it, they didn't see him. So, because they saw him go to Haros Avenue and didn't see him leave, they became his alibi of sorts for the bombing.

As soon as the bomb went off, the surveillance headquarters at Russell Street was badly damaged, and all teams were recalled to the office. The team wasn't at Haros Avenue to see just who returned later on.

While the Taskforce detectives were elated at the convictions the previous day, the not guilty verdict for Reed was a crushing blow.

Taylor was given a life sentence, never to be released. Craig Minogue also received a life sentence, but the judge set a minimum term of 28 years. Rodney Minogue was convicted of being an accessory after the fact, but his conviction was quashed on appeal. At a re-trial in February 1990, Rodney Minogue was acquitted and released from prison. Peter Reed served nine years for his part in the raid shoot-out and was released in 1995.

The Jika Jika fire wouldn't be Craig Minogue's only difficulty in prison. The year he began his life sentence, another inmate, Alex Tsakmakis, was found beaten to death with gym weights hidden in a pillow case and used as a cosh. Minogue was found guilty of the killing and received a second murder conviction in 1988 to run concurrently with his bombing sentence.

Aside from the fatal fire which killed five inmates, and the coshing death of Alex Tsakmakis, Craig Minogue used his prison time productively. In 2005, he completed a Bachelor of Arts degree then did a PhD at La Trobe University.

When he applied for parole after serving his minimum sentence, a media campaign put pressure on the state government which then introduced laws to deny parole to anyone convicted of killing a police officer. The law could be applied retrospectively.

His legal support person declared: 'If the Andrews government was interested in community safety, the appropriate thing would be to enable the adult parole board to make a decision about Dr Minogue's level of risk to community.'

Joining Sisters in Crime Australia meant I regularly got to do criminally fun things with other writers of fact and fiction. Here I am with fellow True Crime writers Julie Szego, Robin Bowles and Kylie Fox.

21

STORYTELLER NOT EXPERT

There's a metamorphosis that happens to the writer who tells the stories of others. Along the way, we develop an expertise of sorts. When I heard the same stories of grief and resilience over and over, I began to truly understand ways in which people coped when the worst things happened.

I could also see that when people didn't do these things, they often didn't cope at all.

Everyone I met taught me something new and profound about life and death and all the stuff in between, so that when I faced death in my own family, I was perhaps more prepared than I otherwise might have been.

My sister-in-law Carole got breast cancer when she was 34. Very shortly after the diagnosis, she faced a mastectomy and chemo. I went up to Sydney to stay with her and my brother Andy and their two small children. Carole showed me the top of her scar but I didn't want to look too closely; a quick glance coupled with my overactive imagination and it looked to me like she'd been bitten by a shark.

One evening, the two of us sat at the table and talked long into the night.

'My biggest worry,' she said in her soft lilting accent – she was born in Manchester – 'is that if I died now, my boys would not remember me.'

It was a sobering thought. Carole was a devoted mother to her two boys, aged 3 and 5. She looked at me, searching for answers.

I don't know that I had much wisdom to offer her, but I did

---

know how to listen without shying away from these kinds of conversations. I'd been having them for years with people, most of them strangers, I interviewed.

We became experts of sorts, my family and I, about cancer stats: if the cancer doesn't return in five years, your chances of survival were much higher.

Carole recovered. Her children grew. And then, four years after her breast cancer, she got a pain in her hip. She went to the doctor and he took an x-ray. It was sent off for interpretation. Everything's fine, they said. You're just getting older, they said. Aches and pains are normal, they said.

Carole asked her doctor if he had noted on her x-ray that she'd had cancer before. She was a nurse; she knew these things were open to interpretation. No, he said. More tests. Then a diagnosis. Bone cancer – which is apparently survivable until it hits an organ. She lived with the pain and the treatment for another three years until it hit her liver in the October of 2006.

My sister got married that December, but Carole was too sick to travel down to Melbourne. Andy brought the boys who were then 10 and 12. At the wedding, George, the younger one, got upset because he missed his mum. I took him out to the foyer so we could ring her on my mobile. I don't know how much he understood about how sick she was. Hearing her voice settled him down again and we returned to the party. My heart broke in that moment, knowing there would be a time coming soon when he would miss his mum and he would not be able to call her.

And that moment came all too soon. Carole died on Friday 23 February 2007. She was 41. She was my age.

My entire family flew to Sydney to be with Andy and the boys. There was so much to do in the aftermath of Carole's passing. There was a funeral to organise and a Mass booklet to do. Being a Catholic primary school teacher *and* a writer meant that I was the best person for the job. As the family gathered from Melbourne and then Carole's family from England, I asked them for stories and memories so that alongside her booklet, I also put together the story of her life, using lots of photographs while we had access to them.

Being at a laptop during this time helped me to view it from my comfort zone – words were the way I coped and processed the world. Creating a beautiful funeral booklet for my sister-in-law was the last thing I could do for her. It was full of life and colour and was a tribute to her.

We all stayed in Sydney for over a week and then it was time to return to the real world. In grief, I was untested. I stayed strong for her boys; and in Sydney, there was so much to do. But privately, I couldn't think of Carole without my eyes filling with tears. There are no platitudes, no 'good-innings' comments that can be said for a woman of 41.

On the first day back at work, I got to school extra early. I was really worried that as soon as people started arriving and coming in to see how I was that I would crumble. My classroom was in a nook at the back of the school. I was sitting at my desk when I saw a woman appear at the door. It was one of my kid's mums, Leeanna. A sob rose in my chest as I went to the door. She hugged me, then held out a book on the stages of grieving.

'This helped me,' she said. She had lost someone close to her and we'd talked about grieving before.

I was forever grateful it was her at my door that day.

So what had years of crime writing taught me about grief? Mostly, it had taught me that everyone's grief is different.

I remembered Natalie Russell's mum, Carmel, telling me that she kept Nat's room as it was for years. She even set it up again after moving to a different house. She said it gave her comfort and she didn't understand people telling her to pack it up. I didn't either. If the room brought her daughter to mind, then why would anyone object?

I let myself go through the grief. The groundswell of feelings usually came on the long drive to work. I'd hit a certain spot in Glenferrie Road and I would spontaneously tear up. I'd hear the Green Day song, *Time of Your Life*, on the radio and I'd tear up. We had it playing on a loop after the funeral to accompany a photo montage of Carole having the time of her life.

Losing Carole made me miss my book deadline for *Crime Scene Investigations* which in turn also gave me the opportunity to dedicate the book to her: *This book is dedicated to my sister-in-law, Carole Burke (1965–2007).*

As I finished writing the book, I was sad and distracted and ill-equipped to deal with the changes the Victoria Police media department made to the access to information I had previously had. They began to use terms like 'intellectual property' in reference to their cases. There was also a growth in TV shows wanting access to police. This meant when I approached Victoria Police for permission to access their members for stories, they suddenly told me they were going to start charging; and writers would pay the same as TV shows with million-dollar budgets.

I only wrote one new story under these restrictions and it completely changed the way I wrote. Instead of interviewing a number of people, I compiled the bones of the story from files and research. I would then narrow down what I needed to ask police. I found honesty was the best policy. I would always tell police officers that the media department wanted to charge me by the hour, so I was conscious of their – my – time.

Without exception, people eager to tell their story would answer with a wink and we wouldn't watch the clock.

I never got a bill from VicPol so perhaps the people there saw how unfair it was to lump authors in with TV producers.

The truth was the profit from most crime books was a fraction of what people earn per annum in regular jobs. I always joked I'd make more per hour flipping burgers at McDonalds than from royalties. Readers everywhere are lucky writers are still prepared to write even though it usually does not give them a living wage. I think the latest figures, from 2018, puts the average income for a writer in Australia at about $11,000 per year.

Around 2007, I started going to events organised by Sisters in Crime Australia, the organisation dedicated to celebrating and promoting crime fiction and fact written by women. They hold an annual writing competition called the Scarlet Stiletto Awards. I took some long service leave that year and challenged myself to write a short story; up to 5000 words – of fiction.

The result was 'Side Window', a Kath-and-Kim-type take on *Rear Window*. The story was funny and it won a prize. Around this time, Carmel Shute, the Secretary of Sisters in Crime, invited me to do a comic debate: the Dicks versus the Dames. My debate partner would be Victoria Police Assistant Commissioner Sandra Nicholson, and our opposition consisted of male authors Robert Gott and Jared Henry. Our topic was: The female of the species is deadlier than the male.

Sandra and I met to discuss strategy and we came up with a winning argument: half a million people die each year from malaria which is carried by the *female* mosquito. Take that, Negative Team!

I wrote some classic lines: 'And you've got to admire Cleopatra – she's still known thousands of years later as the great queen of Egypt. And Caesar? He is best known for the salad named after him.'

After repeating my winning success in several comic debates, Carmel Shute told me I should write funny crime fiction. At her urging, I wrote a novel called *The Good, the Bad, and the Fugly*, but it didn't go anywhere with publishers. One day, I might put it up on Kindle and see if my funny crime fiction takes the world by storm.

A Dicks versus Dames debate in 2017 with fellow crime fiction writers: (from left) Sue Williams, Leigh Redhead, Robert Gott, Jock Serong, Angela Savage, Andrew Nette, and me.

I look back on this time and see that I was pushing at the boundaries of my writing to see what else I could write; testing the limits of my talent.

Around this time, the Bayside Libraries started a competition for local writers, and I was asked to judge. When I got the entries, I realised that there were a lot of people in the community who wanted to write, but many did not understand the basic principles of creating an effective story.

I pitched an idea to Bayside Libraries offering to run workshops and short courses to help people in the community. Libraries are a great vehicle for these because they have the budgets to supplement the author's fee and offer courses at a heavily subsidised price, or for free.

In the teaching of these courses, my author skills combined with my years in the classroom proved a popular combination. I regularly got 100% positive feedback on the post-course surveys and there were some people who did one course, and then enrolled every time I taught a new one.

The crossover was that the school where I worked at the time – the wonderful Genazzano FCJ College – capitalised on my ability in teaching English and moved me from generalist teaching in a Year 6 class to teaching English across Years 6, 7, and 8. I was in my element. I had always wanted to move into secondary education.

What an author brings to the English classroom is a complete passion for the subject. I live it. I breathe it. Every day. An author, after all, is a practitioner of everything taught in English classes. When I teach essay writing, I sell it to the kids as a new and magical superpower of persuasion. When I teach poetry, I tell the kids that poetry can touch your soul; it is beautiful language that can make you weep or sing for joy. And of course, all the poetic devices can be used in creative writing too.

A combination of the closing of the doors of the Victoria Police as a source of information, and my desire to expand the stories I told, led me inexorably to Rod Braybon.

Every writer at some point has people who approach them with the line: 'You should write my story – it's fascinating!'

Crime writers are no exception except we get more of: 'My next-door neighbour's cousin was beheaded. I heard the story and immediately thought of you!'

To which we reply, 'Er... thanks?'

Don't get me wrong, people's stories are always fascinating. To them. But the writer's gauge is a little different. We know publishers want a bestseller; they want stories that 10,000 people want to buy. So this broader appeal becomes the writer's filter. It's not the only filter though.

For me, if I'm going to spend a year writing a book, then it has to be a story that really grabs me.

Rod Braybon had been looking for a writer to write his life story. As often happens, another writer had been contacted but wasn't interested. Writers will offer projects they can't do to other writers and that is how I came to be sitting in my lounge room on the phone to Rod.

His story, he told me, had recently been featured on the news in an award-winning feature by television journalist Brendan Donohue.

Rod had lived part of his childhood in the notorious Salvation Army Boys' Home in Bayswater and had suffered terrible abuses at the hands of Salvation Army officers. He'd ended up a juvenile delinquent and, at 16 years old, had been sentenced to Pentridge Prison for stealing cars.

'Pentridge was like a bloody holiday camp compared to Bayswater,' Rod told me.

That was what hooked me. Pentridge was an awful place.

I knew that first-hand from a visit when I was in Year 11, doing legal studies at school. The teachers, in their wisdom, arranged for my class of sheltered Catholic school girls to visit Pentridge Prison to watch a play put on by the prisoners.

There was an exciting rumour that the guy in the main role was an axe murderer. Afterwards, we could chat to the actor-prisoners. A helpful young bank robber explained to my group the importance of stealing two cars when you rob banks – one to park outside as the getaway car, and one to park a couple of streets away for a quick change of cars to fool anyone in pursuit. Duly noted. I think he also told us the recipe for making illicit alcohol using potato peel and a bucket of water.

As thrilling as the visit was, we were certainly glad to leave the drab cold space with its clanging gates and lonely desperate men.

The fact that Rod Braybon considered this place a holiday camp was extraordinary.

I went to Rod's house to meet him and I could see straight away, the effect the abuse at the hands of the Salvation Army had on him. He was tall and powerful and still angry, 50 years later.

I agreed to write his story.

The whole experience was an honour.

For years, Rod had pushed the memories of his time at Bayswater to the very dark recesses of his mind. They were woken when the abuse was exposed in the media; and suddenly it all came flooding back in surround sound. He had a phenomenal memory for the smallest details. It was like he had locked them all in an air-tight box, then let them out again, fresh.

Over the year of Saturdays when we met, I documented Rod's horror story. I approached the Salvation Army to see if they would take us on a tour of the good work they did today. I wrote to them that it might help counter Rod's negative experience. They refused.

Like the Catholic church, which I'd written about in *Rockspider*, the Salvation Army responded not as a charitable organisation, but as a business. Letters to Rod were full of legalese.

Even his 'apology' letter went along the lines of:

> *Dear Braybon, if what you said happened did happen, we are very sorry...*

They might as well have flapped a bloody big red rag in front of a bull. The ignorance of organisations in the aftermath of child abuse never ceases to amaze me.

When Rod's book came out, I realised that in telling the story of one victim, I had told the story of many. I had so many people contact me to tell me the book helped them understand members of their own family who had been unlucky enough to spend time in Bayswater.

When we were writing the book, Rod described a beating he'd been subjected to where he was beaten so severely, he couldn't walk. He was taken to the Bayswater home for older boys and put in a subterranean cell for several days with bread and water and a tin can for a toilet. He received no medical treatment and no one checked on him more than once a day. He was still in primary school when this occurred.

Rod told me that beatings were regular at Bayswater. Some kids, he said, were carried off unconscious and never seen again.

'Do you think they died?' I asked.

It was not an unreasonable question. Beat small children unconscious with bits of wood – or in Rod's case, a tomato stake – and what are the odds that some of them never wake up? There were no check or balances in the 1950s. If a child was placed in a home, then disappeared, the homes would say they ran away – if anyone ever asked, that is. And if no one asked, it stood to reason, the homes would simply keep collecting the allowance for each child from the State, whether the child was there or not.

When the book came out, Rod took his allegations to the Cold Case unit. A couple of detectives were despatched to look into the rumours that bodies might be buried in the pristine bushland behind the Bayswater Boys' Home.

Nothing came of it.

To this day, I still wonder. If anyone has access to a cadaver dog and wants a nice piece of bushland to walk it through, I can recommend just the spot.

The Bayswater Boys' Home still stands today.
Rod and I took a trip there during the writing of his story.

22

SALVATION

When Rod Braybon read an article about child abuse in *The Age* newspaper, in an instant, things came flooding back – things that he'd forgotten; things that he'd pushed out of his mind and hidden in a Pandora's box of hurt. The Melbourne newspaper article was specifically about the abuse of children who were wards of the state decades earlier.

Rod Braybon was one of them.

Rod was in his early 60s and had spent half a century *not* thinking about what had happened to him as a young boy when he was shunted from one institution to another. And he especially spent those 50 years not thinking about his time at the notorious Bayswater Boys' Home run by the Salvation Army.

Even though most of the bad memories of his childhood were locked safely away, without realising it, Rod had felt the effects of them his whole life. Indeed the things that were hidden had become his master, because everything he had done in his adult life was done to counteract what had been done to him as a child. At the mercy of brutality, he sought power. Stripped of his rights, he found ways to protect himself. And when nothing in his life was how it should be, many of life's rules remained a mystery to him.

Rod's dad Richard was killed in 1950 in an accident at the Mount Hope Quarry in Cohuna where he worked to supplement the income from the family's dairy farm. He and two workmates had been concreting the floor of a shed. On one side of the shed, a large engine was being run-in and the workers had all been warned not to go near it.

Richard Braybon was operating the concrete mixer outside the shed, while one man wheeled barrows of concrete inside to the third man who was laying it. As far as anyone knew, Richard was supposed to work the mixer all day, but for reasons unknown to anyone, and contrary to orders, he entered the shed with a trowel in his hand and crawled on his hands and knees under the new engine's belt, which was about a metre off the ground. A worker saw him clearing some dirt out from underneath to prepare the area for concreting.

A sound alerted the two colleagues that something had gone wrong. According to their later statements to the Coroner, they both looked over and saw Richard lying on the ground with a small trickle of blood on his forehead.

One worker raced to find the foreman to turn the engine off. The foreman rushed into the shed and dragged Richard out from under the engine and carried him outside. He was taken to the Cohuna Hospital. Doctors later found him to be deeply unconscious and suffering from very serious brain injuries – a bolt from the machine had been driven into the back of his skull causing an inch-wide fracture. Surgeons operated, but found the injuries to the base of his brain too severe. They did what little they could.

A two-day vigil at the local Cohuna District Hospital drifted slowly toward the inevitable and Richard died with his beloved wife Peggy weeping by his bedside. He was 34 years old, and left behind his widow and eight children – Barry aged 10, Janice, 8, Rod, 6, Michael, 4, Stephen, 3, Geoffrey, 2, and the six-month-old twins, Sonia and Gordon.

Before his father's death, Rod and his school-aged siblings would walk the kilometre to the local school and do lessons with 40 other raggedy farm kids who only wore shoes for the duration of their classes. At the final bell of the day, shoes were stuffed into schoolbags and the children would take off, running through the paddocks to their farms and freedom. When they weren't doing farm chores, the sun-browned freckled-face kids leapt from ropes into the river or fished for yellowbelly, cod or redfin.

That joyous and carefree life, on a small dairy farm nestled into a bend in the river to the Cohuna Weir, came to an abrupt end. In the jostle that follows sudden tragic death and overwhelming grief, Peggy and her brood of youngsters left the farm, which had been the only home they had ever known. Peggy received £1500 in compensation and £160 was put in trust for each of the children for when they turned 18. She took her money and her family to start a new life in Shepparton.

But that didn't work out.

Richard had always been the disciplinarian in the family and without him, Peggy had neither the ability nor the inclination to keep her children in line. What's more, to cope with the hand fate had dealt her, she began seeking solace and male company at the local pub.

Left to their own devices, the Braybon children ran wild and soon came to the attention of the local police. The first time they were all picked up and locked in the police cells after throwing buckets of paint over their school principal's car.

The Braybon children's second trip in a paddy wagon came after some illicit pig riding.

One Saturday, Rod's Aunt Shirley and Uncle Gordon had arrived up from Melbourne in their swish car with their 8-year-old son, Denis. While the adults settled in for tea and cake and a natter, Barry, Janice, Rod and Mick set off to show Denis around Shepparton. When they wandered past a pig farm, Denis announced with authority of a city child, 'Pigs smell'.

'Nah, they don't!' challenged Rod.

'Everyone knows they do,' said Denis in his snide city voice.

And that was enough for Rod. He took off up the driveway of the pig farm, calling back something about proving Denis wrong. He was quickly followed by Barry, Janice, Mick and finally, Denis.

Running towards the sties, the children were careful to avoid the farmer, because farmers were always to be avoided when you were trespassing on their property.

Some of the pigs were loose in the paddock, snouts down, rooting around for food. Mud and pig poo oozed through the toes of the Braybon children, while Denis' highly-polished city boots were soon covered in grey-green sludge and the backs of his lily-white city legs were sprayed with mud.

When Rod spied some pigs penned up in yards, he quickly announced that those ones needed to be freed to join the others in the paddock. 'Let's ride them out!' he hollered, jumping the low concrete wall separating him from the pigs.

Rod climbed aboard the nearest pig who was lying on the concrete floor. He gave it a firm kick with his brown bare feet and the indignant pig immediately jumped to its feet, grunting and snorting. Barry opened the gates as everyone mounted a pig of their own, then he jumped on the boar. Soon, the five children all holding their pig's ears for dear life, were carried quickly down towards the paddock. It was hard to tell who was squealing more, the children or the pigs.

As soon as they hit the mud in the paddock, the pigs slid and the children all went flying. Both the pigs and the children soon resembled creatures from the Black Lagoon.

City Denis looked down in horror at his ruined clothes. Ironically, they now reeked, proving that he had been right; pigs did indeed smell. His cousins didn't care – they would all head for the river which would quickly take care of their dirty clothing.

In the ensuing laughter and glee, and the grunting and snorting as the startled pigs righted themselves, the children didn't hear the farmer approaching. They did, however, hear the gunshot as it boomed and echoed. For a second, even nature was silent.

The old Italian farmer stood nearby holding the biggest shotgun the children had ever seen. When the echo of the gunshot blast faded, the only sounds left were from indignant pigs, and the sound of Denis' city knees knocking together.

The face-off between the grey-green sludgy children and the angry armed farmer was interrupted by the arrival of a police paddy wagon pulling slowly into the driveway. The kids didn't know which was more frightening – the farmer with the shotgun, or the police.

As bad luck would have it, the police officer who climbed out was the same giant sergeant who had dragged them out of school after they painted Mr Dalgliesh's Holden. His bellow echoed like thunder, 'Not you Braybons again!'

'I'm only visiting,' whimpered Denis, anxious to distance himself from his criminal pig-riding cousins.

Despite his protestations, Denis was loaded into the paddy wagon, along with the rest of the children, as the angry Italian shook his fist and shouted that he wanted all the children charged. Rod pictured the frightening cells that they'd seen the week before and shivered. But the giant sergeant, for reasons of his own, didn't take the children back to the cells; he delivered them straight to Peggy's house instead.

As soon as the paddy wagon pulled into the driveway, Peggy and Aunty Shirley raced outside. Uncle Gordon limped along behind them. He had a club foot and wasn't as swift as the two mothers. The giant sergeant unloaded four of the muddied children, but left Barry inside the wagon. The four made a motley line, as they stood, eyes downcast in front of their angry parents. While Peggy didn't look surprised, Aunty Shirl and Uncle Gordon were ropeable.

When the sergeant confirmed who Denis was, he turned to Uncle Gordon and said, 'You'll get the paperwork on that one.'

Young Rod didn't understand what 'paperwork' meant and what it might mean for the rest of them. Were they going to get charged? Or put in jail. Paperwork did not sound like a good thing.

'You pack the car and I'll deal with him,' said Uncle Gordon. He grabbed muddy city-kid Denis and hauled him over to the garden hose by the scruff of his neck. Aunty Shirl scurried inside to get the picnic basket she'd brought, and took it to their swish city car. Uncle Gordon turned the hose on full-blast and before long, Denis appeared from underneath the mud.

'I'll deal with you later,' snarled Uncle Gordon, who limped on

Peggy Braybon

his club foot to the car and, without saying goodbye, screeched out of the driveway.

Meanwhile, the sergeant was talking to Peggy. 'You can have these three,' he announced, indicating Rod, Mick and Janice, 'but Barry's coming with me.'

Peggy nodded with a look that might have been relief. She could no more control Barry than turn back time and bring her husband up from the grave. The sergeant told Peggy to be at the courthouse on Monday and to bring all the kids with her.

Rod was too young to remain worried for long. All in all, it had been a pretty good day. Not only did he get to ride pigs, but going to court on Monday meant that he would miss school. Life couldn't get much better, especially when

Peggy didn't say anything about what they'd done. The children took turns in hosing each other, then their mother filled the old galvanised bath in the shed with warm water from the copper.

She bathed them all, and sent them to bed without any supper.

On Monday, the court took Barry away. Peggy counted her losses and moved the rest of the family to Braybrook.

It was there, two years later and after another incident in which the children broke into the local RAAF base, that Peggy made a decision that would alter their lives forever. She sent her children around the corner to their grandfather's house with a note. Peggy's father read the note, then drove the older kids to Russell Street police headquarters. He left them there without any explanation.

That was the day the Braybon children became wards of the state.

Janice was sent to a girls' home and the twins to a home for babies. The boys were separated, but Rod and Mick – aged eight and six – ended up together; and were placed in a string of boys' homes that were brutal and violent.

They had to learn how to look after themselves and each other. Being the elder, Rod had Mick's back – most of the time. There were occasions though, when he was simply unable to protect his little brother; and Mick would forever bear the scars from some things Rod was unable to prevent; like the time a worker at the Menzies Home for Boys drove a pitchfork through Mick's foot.

The brothers had been digging up carrots at the home, on Olivers Hill in Frankston, when the supervising officer sneered that they weren't digging deep enough.

'Here's how you do it,' he said, and grabbed Mick's pitchfork and thrust it into the dirt. Mick screamed blue murder as one of the large prongs pierced the arch of his right foot and impaled him into the ground.

'You stupid bloody fool,' said the man.

A lady from the kitchen came running and pulled the pitchfork out of Mick's foot. She untied her apron and wrapped it around the injury which had sprayed blood as soon as the pitchfork was removed.

Rod watched as his 10-year-old brother, using every fibre of his being, straightened his crumpled face back into a blank expression. Rod was helpless, but he understood completely. This was one lesson they'd learnt early: *feel no pain.*

If someone hurt you, you had to turn off the pain in your head, and hide it away. Rod and Mick had been caned and strapped and beaten often enough to understand the power struggle. A boy couldn't stop a belting, and he couldn't stop a pitchfork being driven though his foot, but he could call on every ounce of his inner-strength and show that it meant nothing.

After the pitchfork incident, Rod and Mick escaped from the Menzies Boys' Home – and, according to documents were caught on a boat on the Yarra. Rod has absolutely no memory of stealing a boat.

Other memories, he couldn't lose so easily.

On 7 May 1956 Rod and Mick – aged 12 and 10 – arrived at the Bayswater Boys' Home. It had been four years since they had first been dropped at the Russell Street police headquarters, and they were both older and a little wiser. The road leading up to this latest home was a dirt one, and the van travelled all the way to the front door of a rambling single-storey weatherboard building circled by a veranda.

There were orchards surrounding the place, and a little church across the road and down a bit from a school. It reminded Rod of the farm at Cohuna. As soon as the van stopped and the brothers got out, two men strode out the front door and across the veranda and stood before them.

'Welcome to Bayswater,' said one of the men. 'My name is Captain Francis. I'm in charge, and this is Lieutenant Haywood.' He gestured behind him to the second man, who was fat and bald and had eyes like a pig.

Lieutenant Haywood looked them up and down and a smile appeared on his face, but it wasn't a smile that Rod thought friendly. It was a smile that made him uneasy and wary. Both men wore strange uniforms, and their red hat-bands bore the words *Salvation Army*. The boys had never heard of the Salvation Army before.

The only things Rod and Mick brought with them to the Bayswater Boys' Home were the survival skills they'd honed in their four years of institutional living. They had lost everything, could count on no one, and used any opportunity they could to get back what was taken. They were good at sport and knew that they could use this to infiltrate groups of boys, which would give them extra protection. Aside from what they'd learnt, they brought the clothes on their backs, and a wary attitude mingled with a dash of devil-may-care.

They had given up hope that their mother would ever visit them, and after four years, they gave her little thought. All their energies went into surviving. They figured they were better off not having visitors anyway, as every kid who got a visit from their parents or relatives ended up spending the rest of the day blubbering.

Rod reckoned that visitors made you weak. They made you long for a life that you couldn't have; a life outside the walls of boys' homes where mothers cooked and fathers brought home wages. A life of warm fires and full bellies. And love.

As Lieutenant Haywood led the way, the boys looked around their new home. The main quadrangle, which had a basketball court in the centre, was framed by long weatherboard buildings. Rod had never played basketball. He hoped that this new home also offered footy and cricket – he was good at them.

Lieutenant Haywood took the boys into a room lined with stacks of shirts, jumpers, shoes, socks, and pants. By now, they knew the routine: strip off, put your old clothes in a thick paper sack, put on new set of clothes. The woman in the clothing store was introduced as Matron Fleming.

While they changed clothes, Matron examined their paperwork, entering details into a thick leather-bound ledger, and Lieutenant Haywood stood in the doorway and watched the boys change. Although privacy was a notion unfamiliar to the institutionalised boys, there was something about the way this man looked at them that made Rod feel most uneasy. Mick didn't notice.

After they were dressed, Lieutenant Haywood told them to play in the quadrangle until the other boys came back from school. They weren't offered any food.

'Don't leave the quad,' Haywood said in a voice they knew they had to obey. Rod and Mick always did what they were told – until they figured out the lay of the land. That was another thing they'd learnt.

The shower block, when they ventured in, was typical of all the places they'd been. The long row of showers were communal; and the toilets, separated by shoulder-high dividers that didn't reach the floors, had no doors and were spotlessly clean. Rod knew from experience that cleaning toilets was the number one punishment in institutions. Evidently the boys here got punished a lot.

The other children returned from school at 3.30pm. More than 100 boys marched silently into the quad, led by Lieutenant Haywood and followed by another officer. After they were mustered into a horse-shoe formation, the Lieutenant introduced Rod and Mick to the assembly.

'These are the boys who escaped from Menzies and stole a boat. That's why they are here.' Haywood's tone was nasty. 'They'll be in Dormitory 1.'

The introduction, designed to humiliate, had the opposite effect. Rod saw a couple of boys look at him and Mick with interest. He recognised the sparks in the eyes of boys who'd have an appreciation for boat stealing, escaping, and general mayhem. Rod was good at reading eyes. In places where children were marched and paraded and mustered and silent, for a good part of the day, the eyes were the only window to the soul.

After muster, all the boys followed Lieutenant Haywood single-file into the dining room. Rod and Mick were seated up the front, near the table of Hayward and the other officer, Envoy Collins.

Dinner times for Rod and Mick at other institutions had always been regimented and silent, but there was something different about Bayswater. Here, the single-file of boys walked past the servery, got their meal, then continued around the perimeter of the dining hall. The front boy led the line up the far aisle to the furthest seat, placed his plate on the table and stood behind the seat. The next boy followed. When that aisle was full, the next boy started the next aisle. Each boy seemed to know where he was to sit and when to start the next aisle. Only when every boy was standing behind his chair, did one of the officers give a signal.

'You can start grace,' he said, pointing at one of the boys. The boy began and was immediately joined by over a hundred other voices: *For what we are about to receive, may the Lord make us truly thankful, for Christ's sake, Amen.*

The boy who'd begun grace, and another, then left their places to get the officers' meals from the servery. Rod noticed that the officers ate different food to the boys. As plates of steak and roast vegetables were carried past him to the officers' table, he looked down at his own food. From his early years on the farm, he could tell that the stew in front of him was made of lamb flaps – the belly part of the lamb that his family had always fed as scraps to their dogs. Rod anticipated his stew would taste fatty and greasy, and he wasn't wrong.

Once the officers had been served, the boys all sat. Despite the quality of the food, all the boys tucked in with a vengeance, as if they were starving. Years in institutions had taught Rod that the plates of plain white bread on the table held exactly one slice each for each boy. He and Mick took their share and mixed their mashed potatoes with the stew until it was almost edible. The traditional sweet black tea was brewing in big cream-coloured enamel pots. Again, there was enough for one cup per boy.

At the end of the silent meal, everyone stood up and grace was said again: *We thank the Lord for the food we have received, for Christ's sake, Amen.* The entrance formation was repeated in reverse, plates were deposited at the servery, and the boys marched out into the quadrangle.

As soon as Rod and Mick got outside, they were allowed to talk for the first time since the others had returned from school. Rod knew that this initial meeting was crucial if he wanted to establish a place for himself and his little brother. He looked around for the boys who had locked eyes with him at the muster. He didn't have to wait long; they came to him. The spokesperson for the group, a 12-year-old solidly-built redhead called Bruce Brown, introduced himself.

'What are ya in fer?' he asked. Rod could spot a leader a mile off; notwithstanding the fact that Bruce, with his red hair and freckles, would've had to learn how to fight a long time ago.

Rod knew he had to join Bruce Brown and his band, so he explained his crimes. He was pleased to see that Bruce looked impressed and was full of questions. Rod embellished his stories to make himself, and Mick, sound good and rugged enough to join Bruce's group. It was important this young leader see their inclusion as vital; that they'd be better friends than foes.

'Yer part of our group,' announced Bruce at the end of their story. Rod was pleased. Their status had risen with his tales of escape and piracy on the high seas. Rod and Mick were used to fighting their way to the top; but this time, with one story, they were in.

'Ya need to watch out fer Haywood,' warned Bruce. 'We call him The Pig coz of his eyes. And watch Envoy Collins. He will only give ya a back-hander – but he'll tell Haywood if he sees ya do anything wrong. And Hayward issues the punishment. It's Haywood ya hafta watch.'

Getting the lowdown on the officers was another vital part of a new-home initiation. Soon the boys were bantering like old friends. Except Mick. He always let Rod do the talking.

At 6pm, all the boys were marched into a rec hall to listen to the news on the radio. They sat in rows and listened as the deep BBC voice droned on about a life outside their reality. After the news, Rod and Mick were shown to their dormitory. Between each dormitory, there was an officer's room and new kids always slept in the beds closest to the officer's bedroom.

Lieutenant Haywood was the officer for their dorm; so Rod and Mick were allocated beds, on either side of the door to his room. They changed into the second-hand flannel pyjamas they'd been issued, climbed onto their lumpy horse-hair mattresses and tried to adjust to their new beds.

As with all institutions there was silence, not even a whisper, as soon as the lights went out. All the boys in the dorm huddled under their starched sheets and thin blankets.

Rod took some time to think before he settled to sleep, and imagined that this place would be better than other places he'd been. Here – at least – there were no bars, no fences to keep boys in, and the officers seemed no better or worse than others he'd met. Their uniforms might have been Salvation Army, rather than the neat casual dress of guards at other places but, aside from Bruce's warning, there was nothing to suggest that the Bayswater Boys' Home would be any different from Turana, Glenroy, Menzies or the Andrew Kerr Memorial Home.

At only 12 years old, Rod was quite the authority on boys' homes. All the institutions operated on fear; and corporal punishment was used for any violation of the rules. Rod understood that the fear and beatings were designed to remove any willpower or independence, but the tactic had never worked with him. He had found a way to cope.

When he was being beaten – punched in the face or stomach, kicked while he was on the ground, or caned so hard that his backside felt like corrugated iron for a month – his mind fled to another place where pain didn't register; and where little boys could rise up against brutal men.

The violence and terror of all the homes had a different effect on Mick though. He had gone into his shell, and was no longer the carefree, happy-go-lucky kid he'd been on the farm. The pitchfork incident at Menzies had broken him, and since then Mick had backed off his involvement in everything. His eyes now darted this way and that, and he jumped at the slightest sound.

And so, on his first night at Bayswater, Rod relaxed in his lumpy bed. He was pleased to have gained the respect and friendship of Bruce Brown and his gang, and things were looking up. He reckoned that the prayers and hymns would be a small price to pay for the open space and fresh air, which worked on him like an elixir.

Being in tune with all such things, though, Rod had noticed one difference in this dormitory from all the others he'd slept in. The minute the boys, all of them, had hopped into the rows of beds, they ducked their heads all the way under their blankets. Rod had wondered why, but couldn't ask because speaking was forbidden.

It wasn't long before he heard music floating through the dark silence. It was a strange high-pitched music, the likes of which Rod had never heard before. He would later find out it was opera, and Verdi, but before he could even wonder too much, Lieutenant Haywood's door flung open.

There was a collective intake of breath and Rod could sense fear in the room as a golden light was cast over the dorm. He didn't know what was going on, but he instinctively sat up. Lieutenant Haywood came through the door and put one foot on the end of his bed.

'Braybon. In here,' he boomed. 'I've got some work I want you to do.'

No one else in the dorm moved a muscle. It was like all the other boys were holding their breath; they were like dead boys.

Rod knew better than to argue. The only times he'd been dragged out of bed before were for regular fire drills at other homes. So, outwardly compliant, Rod did as he was told.

The Lieutenant's room was a long narrow well-furnished space, with a nice-looking dressing table, a comfortable bed, and a table with chairs around it. Books and records lined shelves and a gramophone, on a low table, proved to be the source of the weird floating music. Haywood, who hummed along with it, walked over to the machine and turned the volume up even louder so that the high-pitched singers almost shrieked.

'Your job is to spit polish my shoes,' Haywood ordered.

Rod had polished shoes before, but watched obediently as Haywood, showed him how to do it. The officer spat on the toe of a black leather shoe, rubbed the spit in with an old cloth, then dipped the cloth into a small tin of black nugget and rubbed that in. He then lit a candle, held the toe of the shoe over the flame and as soon as the nugget began to melt, he withdrew it from the flame, spat on it again and rubbed it in. Once it began to shine, Haywood sat down, put the shoe between his knees and took up a long polishing cloth that might have once been the leg of pyjama pants.

Haywood's face reddened with the effort, but when the shoe shone like a mirror, he set it down and made Rod repeat the procedure with the other shoe.

Then he said, 'I'll show you how to set out my clothes for tomorrow.'

Lieutenant Haywood's voice had changed from a loud boom to something more normal, even friendly, as he walked over to his timber wardrobe. He chose a key from a bunch that usually hung on a chain from his belt – though not now because Lieutenant Haywood was wearing his pyjamas – and unlocked the two doors on either side. On the right, were shirts; on the left were trousers and jackets; all in the Salvation Army blue. There were some casual clothes too.

Haywood asked Rod to take a shirt, trousers and a jacket and to hang them on a single rail on the other side of the room. Once that was done, Rod turned and waited for his next instruction.

Without a word Haywood took a small jar of boiled sweets – black and white humbugs – from a shelf, removed one lolly and gave it to Rod, who popped it in his mouth. He could hardly recall the last time he had a lolly – possibly four years before when he and his brothers and sisters would go the milk bar or the movies on a Saturday, before their mother gave them up. It was the best thing he had tasted in years; Rod thought he was in heaven.

'Now I'll show you how to fold your pyjamas up in the morning so you don't get into trouble.' Haywood's voice was almost gentle.

Rod couldn't believe it. Not only was he sucking on a lolly, but now the officer was helping him avoid trouble. He wondered at Bruce's warning, because this bloke wasn't so bad after all.

Without hesitating, Rod took off his pyjamas. After years of communal showering and sharing dormitories, being naked in front of others was as natural as breathing.

Lieutenant Haywood took the pyjama top and pants, and showed Rod how to fold them by putting the seams on each leg together and then folding them so that they would have a seam down the middle. Then the legs were folded in half and in half again. Perfectly. The top was folded with similar precision. Rod watched in wonder. He was used to stuffing his pyjamas away in a drawer.

When Rod's pyjamas were folded and placed on the dresser, Haywood announced that he would show Rod how to fold *his* pyjamas.

Now this was odd. Rod saw naked boys every day, but he had never seen a grown man naked in his life. As he took them off, Rod thought Haywood's huge pyjamas looked like tents.

After the folding ritual was repeated, the man told the boy that he would teach him how to pray.

'Kneel at the end of the bed,' he instructed.

As Rod knelt by the foot of the bed, facing away from the Lieutenant, the music was turned up again, to screaming pitch. Without a word, Haywood came up behind Rod.

From that moment on, everything changed. For the boy who thought he knew his way around life, the experience of the fat, grunting man behind him – gasping and hurting him, tearing him, raping him – changed everything.

The attack was over in minutes. As Rod stumbled to his feet, he suddenly realised what the screaming music was for – it was to drown out the sound of boys screaming.

Dressed back in his pyjamas, Rod appeared in the lighted doorway for a moment before it was shut behind him and he was back in the dormitory. Haywood had turned the music off so there was no sound but the creaking and settling of the old timber building.

The red light that shone perpetually at night so that the room was never quite dark, illuminated 54 'sleeping' forms. Most boys remained with their heads under their blankets, but about half a dozen pale faces appeared and turned to look at him.

Rod was dazed; he couldn't understand what had just happened. But when he saw the faces of the boys, looking at him, he knew immediately that they all knew; what had just happened to him had happened to them too.

No one spoke, no one whispered. There were just the eyes. Horrified eyes. Scared eyes. Eyes that knew of the terror behind Lieutenant Haywood's door. Rod climbed painfully into bed, curled up into the smallest shape he could make, and squeezed his eyes shut. He shivered uncontrollably and his teeth chattered with shock. Then he slowed down his breathing.

Ever since he'd become a ward of the state, Rod had developed a skill that had served him well: the ability to fall asleep in an instant. It helped to block some things out completely, or at least leave behind whatever awful things had happened. No matter how bad things had been, he could close his mind and drift off to another place where little boys didn't get impaled by pitchforks, or flogged, or punched in the face by men, or have to kneel naked in prayer while someone did bad things to them.

He slept like a lamb.

The next morning, Rod woke to the pungent smell of urine. He hadn't wet the bed, but when he sat up he saw seven or eight boys stripping the sheets off theirs. He hadn't been in the dorm long enough yet to know that this was a regular occurrence the morning after a boy, any boy, had been taken into Haywood's room. The rest were too scared to get up to go to the toilet in case Haywood discovered they were awake and took them too.

Lieutenant Haywood, dressed in the uniform that Rod had laid out for him and looking immaculately groomed and clean, moved slowly down the aisle between the beds.

Eyes forward, Rod stood to attention, but he could sense the fear in the other boys. He dared not look at Haywood as the man strode the length of the dorm carrying a three-foot long cane which he flicked menacingly against his trouser leg. The sound of his whistle and then the slap made the boys flinch.

'Strip the beds!' Haywood's voice was so different from the gentler tone of the night before in his bedroom; it was back to being domineering and frightening.

The bet-wetters scrambled for their sheets while everyone else stood to attention.

'Mattresses on the rail!'

The seven boys grabbed their thin horse-hair mattresses, shuffled them out the door to the veranda and draped them over the railing to dry. They hurried back into the dorm and waited for Haywood's next order.

'Take off your pyjamas and get your sheets,' he shouted. The boys obeyed and then stood naked, trying to hold their reeking sheets and pyjamas as far out from their bodies as they could. They were marched out to the quadrangle to join those from other dorms who'd also wet their beds. Twenty boys stood naked and pale in the dewy morning, shivering with cold and humiliation.

Haywood left them there and returned to the dorm to order the rest of the children to make their beds and get dressed. He watched them strip and dress, and when that was over, marched everyone outside to the quad. Every resident of Bayswater was made to line up around the edge of the quadrangle, facing the naked boys.

Lieutenant Haywood and Envoy Collins looked at the boys with unveiled disgust.

'These filthy little animals can't even get up to go to a toilet,' Haywood spat. 'They will soon learn that it's better not to wet the bed than to give all this extra work to members of the Lord's Army.'

The guilty boys shivered in the cold for half an hour before the bed-wetters-are-wicked lecture was over and Haywood ordered them to march down to the shower block. There was complete silence among the other hundred residents, until the bed-wetters entered the shower block with Collins and Haywood who closed the door behind them.

The minute they vanished, there was a nervous buzz among the remaining boys. Rod listened to the talk. Boys who had wet the bed before, and who knew what happened, whispered with authority to the few who hadn't seen this before.

'They're gonna get a thrashing,' whispered one lad. Another muttered something about cold showers. 'It really kills when they get you with the cane when yer wet,' said another.

Within minutes, the sounds of swishing canes smacking against flesh could be heard from the shower block, followed by the screams of the boys, high-pitched and filled with terror and agony.

Every thwack and every endless scream jarred Rod's nerves and made him think over and over again: *I won't do anything that will put me there.*

Finally, the naked boys limped out of the shower block and scrambled to pick up their soiled sheets which had been left on the concrete path outside. This time Envoy Collins led the bizarre procession while Haywood, with a sick smile on his face, followed along behind looking at the boys' backsides.

Mick hid behind his big brother – *not looking, not looking*; but Rod looked on. And, as they marched back past, he knew the exact number of times each boy had been hit; he could count the vicious red welts left behind by the cane on their white backs and behinds.

Rod was horrified; the youngest boy among them was only about six, the oldest maybe 10. And without exception, they were wracked with sobbing; as if they'd been hurt so much they couldn't cry, but rather shook and sobbed from the very core of their being. At either end of the line, Collins and Haywood had similar smiles of satisfaction on their faces.

After the pitiful parade, everyone went into the dining room for breakfast. Rod's eyes darted around. He couldn't believe that the boys weren't kicking up a stink about what just happened. He saw fear in their eyes, but still couldn't believe they just accepted this behaviour. The Bayswater boys had clearly been belted into submission and were unable to help themselves.

Rod's mind raced with thoughts of the morning's violence, and of what had happened to him. It was Haywood's sickly smile that did it. Rod made a decision: he would report what had gone on the night before. He was certain that once Captain Francis knew that his lieutenant took boys into his room and did terrible things to them, Haywood would be removed from the home and no one would be hurt again.

After breakfast, the boys were allowed to mill around in the quadrangle and talk. No one discussed the naked boys and their beatings; the whole sorry thing wasn't even mentioned. It dawned on Rod then that it happened a lot.

He asked Bruce about it.

'Happens most days,' said Bruce with a shrug. 'Nuffin' you can do about it.'

'Well, I'm going up to see Francis,' said Rod.

Bruce shook his head. The look on his face was half disbelief and half-warning, but Rod turned so quickly he didn't take it in. Not then anyway.

Captain Francis, head of the Bayswater Boys' Home, was sitting on the steps of the veranda in the quadrangle, watching the boys.

'Oh, you're the new kid, Braybon,' he said, bluntly.

'Yes, Captain,' said Rod.

'What do you want?'

Rod was surprised by the tone of the man's voice. He had seemed different, nicer, the day before.

Nonetheless, Rod was on a mission. 'I wanna tell you about what happened last night with Lieutenant Haywood,' he began.

'What was it?' Captain Francis asked, his eyes narrowing.

Rod blurted everything in a rush. 'He called me into his room last night, and he made me fold his clothes, and clean his shoes and then take off my pyjamas and he showed me how to fold them so I wouldn't get into trouble…'

Francis' face turned red with fury and he spluttered, 'You filthy little animal! How dare you accuse a man of God, who has put so much work into you ungrateful urchins!' There was spittle flying from his mouth as he spoke.

Rod knew he had miscalculated. Badly.

Captain Francis leant over, grabbed a wooden tomato stake from the garden bed next to him and stood up. The stake hit Rod in the stomach before he even saw it coming. He doubled over, but recovered quickly and spun around to flee. Too late.

Captain Francis whacked him across the back of his knees with the stake and Rod's legs buckled. He dropped heavily to the ground, and lay there, as blows rained down on him. The only thing Rod could do was to try and protect his face with his arms. The rest of the body could take a beating; the head, not so much. And he was beaten relentlessly until a voice, an almost fearful Envoy Collins as it turned out, yelled: 'That's enough!'

The blows stopped and Captain Francis tossed the tomato stake back into the garden. 'Throw him into 48,' he said.

Collins grabbed Rod by his arm and dragged him to his feet. Even though he couldn't walk unaided, Rod was largely numb from the beating.

Collins hauled him into his Vanguard ute and drove for 10 minutes to a place with a sign out front that said: Salvation Army Youth Training Camp. Rod found out later it was the Bayswater No 1 Boys' Home for older boys; juvenile delinquents ordered by the court to serve time. Run as a dairy farm, Number 1 also had market gardens and the produce was sold in the community.

As Collins drove up the pristine driveway and parked at the entrance, the extent of Rod's injuries became apparent as feeling slowly returned to his body in a fiery throbbing. Collins led him through the office.

'Another one for 48,' he told the two officers they met.

'Your cell's empty,' said one of the officers without interest.

Collins led Rod downstairs to a semi-basement with a row of cells, unlocked the first door and shoved Rod into a tiny cell. The officer kicked a jam tin into the room and banged the door shut.

Rod heard a bolt sliding across the door and then a key turning, but the second the door had slammed he couldn't see anything. There was no light at all.

Apart from the jam-tin toilet, the room was completely empty. He eased himself down onto the cold wooden floor. The pain was so great it didn't leave room for much thinking, aside from: *I did nothing wrong.* It didn't even occur to Rod then that Captain Francis had started beating him before he'd even had a chance to tell him what Lieutenant Haywood had done.

Rod was left in the room all day and tried to sleep, as much as he could on the hard wooden floor, to escape his pain. After many hours, the door opened and Rod squinted against the weak light from the corridor.

Envoy Collins stood at the door and said matter-of-factly, 'Here's your dinner. You'll be here for a while.' The officer was holding a jug of water and two slices of bread. He had an old grey army blanket folded over his arm. He held them out and, from the floor, Rod reached up to take them. Collins stepped back out and shut the door. The bolt clanged into place.

Rod scoffed the bread and drank some water to wash it down. He was careful not to drink it all, and slid the jug over to the furthest corner away from him so that he didn't knock it over when he fell asleep. He doubted he would get anything more today.

Rod's entire body throbbed. He slid his hands gingerly over what he knew were welts. He had painful injuries everywhere, except his head which he had done his best to protect, and could only imagine what he looked like. Rod lay on the blanket and did his best to wrap the rest of it over him, but still shivered. Ironically, the coldness of the cell helped with the bruises and the welts.

The cell walls were thick and there wasn't a sound to be heard from the outside. Rod knew that also meant if he called out or needed medical attention, no one would hear him. Again, he used sleep to block out his reality.

Early the next morning, the door opened again and light flooded in. Rod held a swollen arm in front of his face, until his eyes became accustomed to the light. He was stiff and sore from a night on the wooden floor, and winced as the pain returned with wakefulness. He was able to stand when the door opened. Collins stood there with a bowl of porridge in one hand and a cup of black tea in the other. Rod took the bowl and sat back down.

'You'll be out tonight,' he said and closed the door.

Rod shovelled the porridge into his mouth. He ate so fast, he hardly tasted it and it was gone in moments. He savoured the sweet black tea which filled his stomach and warmed him. After he was finished, he stood up in the dark and tried to get his circulation going. He rubbed all his wounds vigorously and tried to move around the room as much as he could. He whiled away the time thinking – mostly about Mick. He knew Mick would be worried because he would've seen the flogging; all the boys were in the quad at the time. He hoped that Bruce would look after his little brother in his absence.

Over and over again, Rod said to himself: *this will never happen to me again; this will never happen to me again.*

Ideas flew through his mind, mostly about finding a way to keep himself safe and untouchable. But after that, he imagined exacting revenge on those who had hurt him.

Once, at Menzies, he'd led the other boys in a hunger-strike to protest about the weevils – the ones swimming in the porridge in their breakfast bowls. For three days, the same bowls of writhing porridge were served and re-served to the boys who refused to eat it. They were given nothing else. On the third morning, all 40 boys who had followed Rod in the protest upended their bowls on the floor. Their only punishment was that they had to clean the floors. The next meal was lunch and the boys were served as usual.

Rod had learnt several things over the porridge episode. A whole group is more powerful than one individual. And, if you stuck together, you could win. It also taught him that in the right conditions, even boys could be powerful.

Rod spent most of his time in solitary confinement lying on his side or his stomach because his backside was the sorest part of his body; but moving on the hard wooden floor hurt every time he did it.

After an endless stay in the 48 – which he finally figured meant 48 *hours* – Envoy Collins appeared at the door holding a mop and bucket. He told Rod to mop the cell and then take his jam tin down to the toilet block, empty it and rinse it with phenol. When Rod returned to the cell, he had to get down on his sore hands and knees and scrub the floor with a scrubbing brush. Generations of boys before him had made the circular swirls on the timber floors that Rod now followed. Collins watched his every move, without speaking.

Rod was good at scrubbing because ever since he entered boys' homes, he had been taught how to clean. Without exception, every institution was always spotless, courtesy of the labours of its young residents.

When the floor was finished, Rod got painfully to his feet and stood before Envoy Collins. The man cast his eyes around the floor, carefully inspecting every corner, and finally nodded.

Back at the Bayswater Boys' Home, Rod limped over to the boys who were playing in the quad in the late afternoon. The first to walk over to him was Bruce.

'Where's Mick?' Rod asked.

'In the gym,' said Bruce. 'Ya idiot, I tried to tell ya not ta say anything.'

'Don't worry about it,' replied Rod, rubbing a bruise on his arm. He and Bruce headed for the gym to find Mick.

'Has this happened before?' asked Rod.

'Yeah!' Bruce was emphatic. 'Happens all the time. Ya have ta learn ta keep ya mouth shut. I tried to tell 'em and I got the same.' Bruce paused and took a good look at Rod. 'Gees, ya got some welts,' he said.

Rod felt the pain, but had grown very good at removing himself from it. He just wanted to find Mick.

Inside the gym, Mick was practising with the calisthenics group. There was a huge fireplace in one wall of the gym and a roaring fire crackled and sparked. Rod felt the heat as soon as he entered and instinctively moved closer to it because the heat felt soothing to the welts on his legs.

Mick caught sight of his big brother and walked over. He didn't run or call out, because he too had learnt not to feel things too greatly. Sympathy is a sign of weakness. If you cared for something, you were vulnerable.

Mick's eyes flickered downwards to the welts on Rod's legs. He said gruffly, 'Glad ta have ya back'.

'From now on, we'll all have each other's backs,' declared Bruce. He turned and waved over the group of boys that Rod had met on the first day at Bayswater.

Bruce, at 12-and-a-bit, was the oldest in his gang; 10-year-old Mick was now the youngest. Standing by the warmth of the fire, a conversation took place that ended with a clenched-fist vow. From that moment on, the boys would look out for each other. If anyone was touched, the rest of the group would dish out vengeance. Of course, they were talking about protecting themselves against other boys. They knew there was nothing they could do about the officers.

That night, after dinner, Rod returned to his dormitory, and saw with relief that he and Mick had both been put in beds right down the other end, furthest away from Lieutenant Haywood's door. Two new boys had been given the beds near his room. Two brothers. Rumour had it that they were sent to Bayswater from the Box Hill Boys' Home for trying to escape.

Rod watched the brothers unpack their things, just like he and Mick had done a few days earlier, and made himself a promise to get to know them the next day. Not for a moment, though, did he think of warning them. He was flooded with feelings of relief that he was no longer near the door; and after the beating he had copped for trying to report Lieutenant Haywood to Captain Francis, it didn't enter his head to open his mouth again.

He had no doubt that if he spoke up again, he'd be beaten again; and the way he felt, he imagined another thrashing might kill him.

When Rod drifted off to a dreamless sleep that night, he put behind him any thoughts of the beating and also what Lieutenant Haywood had done to him.

Go with the flow. Don't upset the applecart. You can't win against the adults. Put it behind you. Sleep.

The next morning, Rod and Mick were moved to a different dorm. Their new leader was Envoy Collins.

After being allocated a new bed, Rod got ready for school, then stood again in stony silence with the others in the quadrangle for the bed-wetters' parade. When the whips and screams happened, Rod flinched and set his mind adrift so he didn't hear it. He thought of his boyhood farm; saw the river and the paddocks and, mostly, he felt peaceful. He pictured his father, his mother and his brothers and sisters at the dinner table, eating as much as they liked – fresh bread, roasted meat and vegetables, puddings – all smiling; all happy.

When the naked boys marched slowly past, their white skin covered in welts, followed by Haywood the grinning hyena, Rod didn't see them. Instead he imagined cows and tiny wriggling piglets and friendly farm dogs.

When he shook his head and came back to the reality of Bayswater, Rod blinked and looked around. Other boys were doing the same thing; he knew then he wasn't the only one who had learnt how to escape into imagination. The mind was a powerful tool – and Rod knew he could use his to escape, and he could use it to forget, and he could use it like a box, to put things into and then shut the lid. Tight.

By the time Rod left the Bayswater Boys' Home in 1959, just shy of his fifteenth birthday, he had been the victim of violent sexual assaults by both Lieutenant Haywood and Envoy Collins; in attacks that left Rod bleeding and vowing that no one would ever touch him again.

Four decades later, on 29 September 2000 – just after he met his soon-to-be third wife, Kath – Rod took her over to introduce her to his youngest brother Gordon. Gordon had suffered his own brand of hell – 12 years at the Salvation Army home in Box Hill – until Rod rescued him when he was still a teenager.

Sitting around over lunch, Gordon asked Rod if he'd read a certain article in *The Age* that day. The story took up a whole page and Rod read it in horror. It was about state wards who had been abused in orphanages from the 1940s to the 1970s.

Rod looked up and met Gordon's eyes. The brothers didn't need words. Even though they had been in different homes, Rod knew that Gordon had suffered too. When, as a 20-year-old, he'd gotten his baby brother out of Box Hill, Gordon had been timid and nervous. Although Rod knew all the signs, it wasn't a topic they had ever spoken about.

'Do you want to do something about this?' Rod asked him.

'Yes,' said Gordon, without hesitating. His voice was quiet but determined. 'They should be made to pay for what they've done.'

The two brothers' wives looked from Rod to Gordon, puzzled. Without explanation, Rod handed the article to Kath. She got halfway through it and had to put it down.

'But that wouldn't have happened to you?' she said. Kath only knew the strong man she had fallen in love with, and who was the centre of his family; the big fella, the fixer.

'Nah,' said Rod with a swell of bitterness he hadn't felt for years. 'What happened to us was much worse than what these kids went through.'

All appetites vanished and lunch was left unfinished.

Later, at home, Kath wanted to know what had happened. Rod still couldn't talk about it but told her he'd look after it. He had decided to ring the solicitor who was mentioned in the article.

Rod Braybon had never told a soul about what had happened to him – apart from Captain Francis who had beaten him; and the superintendent of Turana, after one failed escape attempt.

He and Gordon met with the lawyer, Angela Sdrinis from the firm Ryan Carlisle Thomas. She arranged for the brothers to see a psychiatrist. At the end of an emotional session, the psychiatrist told Rod that she had heard similar stories many dozens of times.

Angela Sdrinis had become a champion of the abused, and represented hundreds of ex-state wards. She had heard so many stories of violence and abuse that little shocked her any more. She agreed to represent Rod in his legal bid against the Salvation Army.

Memory is a funny thing and when Rod began to remember what had happened to him, the later assault by Envoy Collins was the one that came flooding back first. As for the initial rape by Lieutenant Haywood, it was almost as if the beating with the tomato stake had knocked it from his mind.

In 2005, when the brothers finally got $40,000 each

compensation from the Salvation Army, Rod had to sign a deed that stated:

> 'The Salvation Army denies liability to the claimant as alleged or at all' but 'in order to avoid the expense and inconvenience of litigation and so as to bring closure to the claimant's claim the parties have agreed to compromise the claim for the sum...'

In the claim of abuse, the rape by Envoy Collins was the only one Rod had mentioned.

It was the Salvation Army's letter of 'apology' that sparked off Rod's next battle. Nearly every paragraph contained cautious legal phrases like '*if what you say* happened', 'The Salvation Army *appears to have* betrayed that trust', and 'the experiences *that you say* you suffered'.

In their attempt to abdicate any and all responsibility, the Salvation Army had waved a red rag in front of a bull.

Rod decided to piece his life story together and as he worked on doing it, looking at the documents he'd received from Freedom of Information, he began remembering. And once the gates of memory opened, the process of remembering became a steady tide.

When he met other victims from Bayswater, Rod heard many of them mention Lieutenant Haywood.

That stopped him in his tracks. Another memory door opened and the attack on his first night came flooding back. Rod did not welcome it. But, like all the other things he'd recalled, he needed to remember in order to deal with it.

After all, it was this memory mechanism that had saved Rod in the first place. As a young boy, he'd found a way to protect himself by not remembering, but now he needed those memories in order to find justice.

Because of the Salvation Army's so-called apology letter, Rod couldn't rest. He decided to take on the State Government of Victoria. He believed that the State, which had an obligation to protect him as a ward of the state, had failed miserably.

Most other Australian states had set up funds to compensate

state wards in the same position as Rod and his siblings. But, while Victoria had made individual payments to victims, it had not set up a general compensation fund. That meant that each victim had to take individual action – and go through the pain and expense – to claim compensation from the government.

Obviously the big danger with that – for Rod and the other boys – was that the government has unlimited resources to fight these cases. If the government wins, they can get costs awarded against the victims; costs which could run into the hundreds of thousands of dollars.

Decades after these boys were neglected and abandoned by the

Rod Braybon in 2010

Government of Victoria, the men that they'd become could literally be bankrupted by the same government.

Rod Braybon, however, was happy to metaphorically raise his middle finger towards Spring Street. He reckoned that since the night Lieutenant Haywood raped him, he's had nothing to fear.

He also has right on his side, and he's the quintessential Aussie battler taking on the system. Most importantly, Rod knows a lot about bullies – the only way you beat them is to stand up to them. And the only way to win is if you have nothing to lose.

Although Rod knows the government will string him along and drag out the process, he reckons they will probably make him an offer. A big part of him doesn't want to take 'an offer'. Rod wants his day in court. He wants to parade hundreds of victims down William Street to the County Court and call them as witnesses.

At the end of the day, it is all about being heard. Being listened to. Rod wants the people of Victoria to hear his story, and those of all the other boys who are now damaged men.

In the lead up to the Pope's visit to Australia for World Youth Day in July 2008, the media exploded with suggestions that the Pope might apologise to victims of sexual abuse by Catholic clergy.

A number of people weighed in on the debate, including Bishop Anthony Fisher who said:

> Happily, I think most of Australia was enjoying [and] delighting in the beauty and goodness of these young people and the hope for us doing these sorts of things better in the future, as we saw last night, rather than dwelling crankily – as a few people are doing – on old wounds.

Dwelling crankily?

To victims such as Rod, comments and attitudes like Bishop Fisher's speak volumes about how many people see victims of this kind of abuse; and how authorities operate on a get-over-it mentality. Perhaps what Bishop Fisher and his ilk don't understand is that it is impossible to 'get over' something that has in fact *formed* you; made you exactly who you are. That would be like getting over yourself; which is indeed what many victims end up doing – by killing themselves to end the pain.

Talk of compensation means little to the state wards. No amount of money can buy back what was taken. Their entire lives have been shaped and damaged by their experiences of rape and violence; their sense of justice mangled by the indignities perpetrated by the very people who were meant to protect them.

How much is that worth? What price can you put on a lifetime of lost potential? How much did Australia miss out on because half a million of her children were brutalised as state wards?

Rod, who has always been the fixer, the fighter for the people, knows that his precedent will open the doors to other victims. But once this is over, he needs to stop fighting. He needs to focus on the rest of his life and see what he can make of it once this is finally put to rest.

Rod Braybon left the Bayswater Boys' Home on 2 November 1959. He left with little more than the clothes on his back and a loathing of the Salvation Army. In the half century since, not one Salvation Army collector has ever knocked on Rod's door. As if guarded by a higher – or perhaps lower – power, collectors have strangely kept away; perhaps with good reason. It was not that long ago that Rod's anger against the Salvos was palpable. Who knows what he might have done if a hapless officer walked innocently onto his property looking for a donation for the Red Shield Appeal.

But, the more Rod told his story and went public with what he had suffered, the more the anger was released, slowly, through a new pressure valve in his soul.

Indeed, one day when he was walking down a local shopping strip, a Salvation Army officer held a tin out in Rod's direction. Instead of making menacing gestures like he usually did, Rod reached into his pocket, pulled out a dollar and put it in the tin.

Perhaps that was the moment his healing truly began.

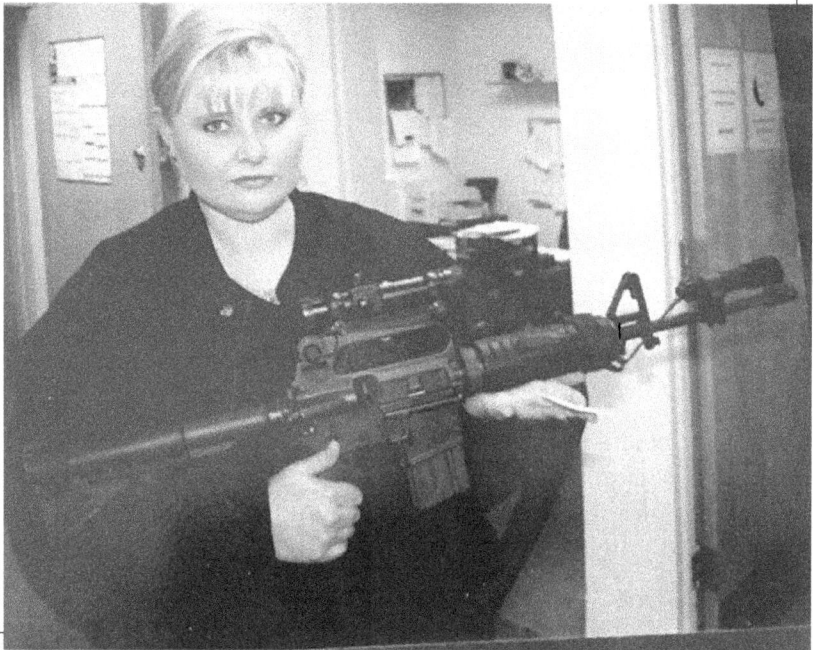

Crime writer uncomfortably holding enormous weapon.
I got the full tour of the Loveland Police Department.

23

MAKING CONNECTIONS

I met a man online when the internet was just new and didn't contain quite as many pitfalls it does now. His name was Wade and he was a retired US Special Agent for the Department of Defense. While Wade was sworn to secrecy about the work he'd done for the US government, he wanted to write a work of fiction that alluded to some of it.

For about a year, Wade would send me his work and I would make editing suggestions and send it back. When I planned a trip to the US, Wade invited me and my family to stay with him in Colorado.

Everyone I knew was certain he would turn out to be a serial killer; and I found out later that his adult children were likewise convinced I'd be the serial killer invited into their parents home. Luckily, none of us turned out to be serial killers, and we had an amazing time in Colorado.

Wade organised for me to do a ride-along with the local cops in the town where he lived – Loveland, Colorado – so I could write an article for the *Australian Police Journal*. When I arrived at the Loveland Police Department at our allotted time, I got a glimpse of the respect Americans have for writers. There were two officers on horseback, waiting ceremonially at either side of the front door to greet me. I was given a tour of the entire complex, then a SWAT team demonstration of storming the local high school – which wasn't far from the school shooting at Columbine. The high school was empty but the heavily armed men scared the bejeebies out of the cleaner. The Loveland Police

Department pulled out all the stops for me and my article. I was humbled by attention more worthy of a celebrity.

That was how I came to meet Patrol Officer Mike Halloran. Mike introduced me to the streets of Loveland on Halloween night. After the cuteness of kids Trick or Treating, they all go home to bed and the teenagers take over the night. On patrol, drunk people in costumes staggered along the street under the influence of alcohol and bad costume choices.

The one we stopped was a guy wearing red and black striped tights and a sheepish grin. He was overly polite causing officers from the three squad cars that attended to be suspicious of his intentions. He was joined on the footpath by his girlfriend dressed as a clown. He passed a sobriety test – a complex series of walking in a straight line and touching his nose – and was sent on his way.

Next stop were four ghouls in a white Mitsubishi. The two in the front looked reasonably sober but the two ghouls in the back looked drunk enough to require medical assistance. While the officers checked the licence of the driver, the two back-seat ghouls hung out their respective doors and vomited onto the road. As

Intrepid me with Colorado cop, Patrol Officer Mike Halloran.

the paramedics arrived to load the two passengers onto stretchers, female cries sounded from across the road: 'Oh my God! Oh my God!' and a devil in a short red costume and a pink fairy ran across the road. The girls hugged the ghouls and asked why the other ghouls were being loaded into an ambulance. The sober ghouls said that they had to go to hospital for observation coz they drank so much they might choke on their own puke.

Fun times.

I also learnt the possible origin of a band's name. Smashing Pumpkins is a Halloween tradition where drunk teenagers steal the Jack-o'-lanterns from people's porches and... er, smash them.

Don't ever let it be said that my learning curve doesn't sometimes swerve sideways.

Mike and I keep in sporadic touch with the odd email. When his boss, Sergeant Bob Shaffer, began using a method of lie-detection that required a forensic analysis of linguistics, Mike asked me if I'd be interested in writing a story about it. There was a man in Australia who'd studied with Shaffer that I could interview.

At the time I was a huge fan of *Lie to Me* – the TV show that focused on facial micro-expressions as indicators of truthfulness. I was fascinated to learn there were experts doing something similar with linguistics.

I duly met up with Bernie Kruger and wrote a story about forensic linguistic analysis. In the end, the police journal decided not to publish the story; perhaps because the science is in its infancy or perhaps it is because the use here isn't widespread. But listening to Bernie talk about the subtleties of language and how the smallest words can suggest the biggest things, it all made sense. I'll leave you to be the judge.

Australian-based SCAN expert, Bernie Kruger.

24

LIES BETWEEN THE LINES

How would you like to be able to tell if someone is lying? The TV show a couple of years back, *Lie to Me,* captured the public's fascination for people who can tell the truth from a lie. But can it really be done? Rather than using facial micro-expressions like on the TV show, there are a growing number of experts around the world who can spot a lie in the words themselves, rather than how they are spoken or which facial expressions accompany them. They are people trained in linguistics who are using their expertise in the forensic analysis of statements. This skill is being used increasingly as an investigative tool in police work.

Melbourne-based Bernie Kruger complete his initial training in statement analysis at a course called Scientific Content Analysis (SCAN), with the acknowledged guru in the area of statement analysis, Avinoam Sapir. As an intuitive youngster, growing up in crime-ridden South Africa, Kruger learnt to read people in the school yard and later studied to become a psychologist. Following a diverse career path from psychology to working in the computer industry, Kruger completed Sapir's linguistic analysis course in Arizona. And from that moment, he was hooked.

The way statement analysis works is that the expert understands how the brain functions when it is recalling an event. Think about how you would respond if someone asked you what you did yesterday. Your brain would quickly filter out non-important details like what you had for breakfast and how you cleaned your teeth, and you would list the more significant aspects of your day. If you wrote down what you did yesterday, there are hundreds of different things an expert may identify that could indicate if your account was deceptive or true. Once you know these things, they are easy to recognise; simple things like a change between past tense to present tense can sometimes indicate a switch from remembering to inventing, from recollection to deception.

On their own, linguistic clues seem pretty simple. One example is the use of pronouns. (Note: if too many years have passed since your high school grammar lessons, pronouns are the little words we use instead of nouns – he, she, my, his, hers.)

A man at a work dinner party might introduce his wife by saying, 'This is *my* wife.' The next day in the lunchroom with the lads, he might say, 'I'm taking *the* wife to a movie tonight.'

His use of 'the wife' instead of 'my wife' creates more of an emotional distance so he doesn't sound too sentimental. Using the understanding that pronouns can be very telling, a linguistic expert will look for these – or the lack of them – to flag sensitive areas in a statement.

Pronouns can be particularly revealing in accounts of sexual assault. There should be a strong separation in the account of the victim between herself and her attacker. Statement analysis experts would expect sentences like: *he forced me...he ordered me to...*

If a statement contains an overuse of the word 'we', it can suggest a connection between the two that may question the validity of the account: *when we got to the bedroom...when we were standing near the bed*; or perhaps suggest the victim knew her attacker.

The use of pronouns featured in a statement analysis in a American murder case. Darlie Routier claimed to have been attacked by an intruder who then stabbed her two young sons to death. The mother referred to her sons as 'the boys' rather than 'my boys'. It was one telling indicator, among many others, in her statement. Routier was convicted of their murder and is currently on death row.

Linguistic statement analysis can reveal the truth behind a story. The technique allows an investigator to examine the original words of anyone's spoken or written statement to determine which parts of their story are true and which are deceptive. It also helps identify hidden information in the person's subconscious mind. Even the starting point can be revealing.

When Darlie Routier was asked to write down her account of the event where the intruder had murdered her sons, she began her story earlier in the day when her husband arrived home from their shop accompanied by her sister.

Linguistic experts would immediately flag this starting point as significant and ask the question: *what is it about the husband, the sister or the shop that is significant?* Motive for Routier's attack on her children was purported to be that the family business had been in difficulty and she killed her two children so that she could maintain her lavish lifestyle.

Linguistic analysis can also be applied to emergency calls. Studies on 911 calls made by the FBI have revealed an interesting phenomenon. A normal person calling an emergency line begins with a cry for help along the lines of: *Oh my god! He's been hurt. Send an ambulance! Hurry!* Since perpetrators are often the ones to call emergency lines, an interesting difference was noted – their first utterance would not be a call for help, but rather an attempt to create a back-story.

Darlie Routier's call to 911 was particularly telling:

Operator:	911 What is your emergency?
Darlie Routier:	Somebody came here...they broke in...
Operator:	...ma'am...
Darlie Routier	...they just stabbed me and my children...

Studies of Routier's 911 call and her later statements typify the difference that a proper linguistic analysis can make. Note how her first words to the operator were to establish what had happened. Think about it – if someone you loved was stabbed by an intruder,

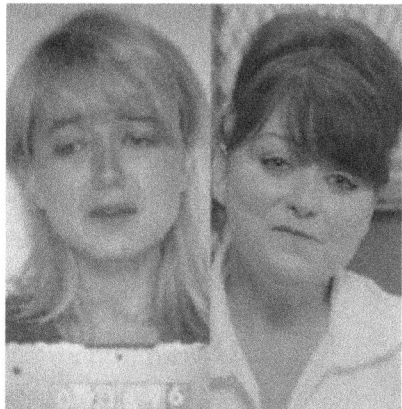

Darlie Routier, then and now. She was sentenced to death in 1997, and remains on death row in Texas.

what would your first words be to the operator? Would you waste time explaining what led to the event, or would you simply scream for them to send help to your dying children?

A second telling aspect in the Routier 911 call was the change between 'somebody' broke in – as in one person broke in, and in the next line, 'they' just stabbed… – implying more than one person. Experts also found the fact she said 'me' before she said 'my children' interesting as if they weren't her first concern.

Another interesting phenomenon that many police officers would be familiar with is the lack of emotion when someone is recounting a trauma. This is because in the midst of trauma, there is little time for emotion. If your child is hit by a car, you wouldn't waste a second standing by the side of the road accessing your emotional response.

Instead, you would rush to their side, scream for someone to phone for help, and be so focused on their well-being that there would be no time for emotion. That kicks in when things calm down and the adrenaline rush abates. The immediate aftermath of a traumatic event is about action, not emotion.

As such, the occurrence of emotion in a statement at times when it wouldn't normally be there, is also something that experts look for. If someone tries to cover up a crime in this manner, they can often include emotion all the way through their statement because they imagine that if they were truly the grieving innocent, that is how they would feel. To the expert, however, grief and the approximation of grief are very different.

Even though the Scientific Content Analysis course was mostly attended by law enforcement personnel, Bernie Kruger could see a wider application, and was particularly interested in exploring the way people tell their version of events and the way the brain accesses memory. Unlike many of the police on the course, whose interest was for grass-roots policing, Kruger wanted to understand the psychology behind the technique. He also knew that for this new investigative tool to be more widely accepted, there had to be academic support. Coupling his interest in psychology with his interest in writing computer programs, Kruger began to explore ways to further enhance the analysis.

Returning to South Africa with his new-found skills, Kruger set up a company and consulted on a number of cases. One case involved interviewing a maid after a home invasion where the woman of the house was shot. The maid had been polygraphed but the result was uncertain. After examining her written statement, Kruger concluded that there was no connection between the maid and the home invaders. Another case involved a truck driver caught with thousands of cartons of contraband cigarettes hidden among his cargo of wood. After analysing his statement, Kruger concluded that while the truck driver did indeed know what he was carrying, he was not involved in the racket.

The more Kruger used the techniques of statement analysis, the more he believed in its power to sort the truth from a lie. More recently, Kruger has relocated to Melbourne and uses his skills in the corporate world. He is keen to consult on statement analysis, and has an interest in cold case statements. Kruger works with no case background, preferring to get all of his information from the statements themselves. Recently, Kruger examined statements in a cold case from the 1980s without any background knowledge and came up with some startling conclusions based solely on his ability to read between the lines.

Not only does he use the techniques from his studies, but Kruger designs and refines computational linguistic techniques that will further analyse statements for their key and overlapping themes based on the number of mentions something is given in a statement. His analysis also indicates relationships and how strong they are between the statement giver and the people he or she mentions. As an investigative tool, it is exciting stuff.

Another person to attend the SCAN training was Sergeant Bob Shaffer from the Loveland Police Department in Colorado. Shaffer was an early fan of the techniques of statement analysis. Working at the suburban police complex in Loveland, Shaffer was assigned to recruit, test and hire new police officers. A friend of his had trained in linguistic statement analysis a few years earlier and recommended that Shaffer do the same. The friend explained that if an investigator could 'read between the lines' then he was always able to get a bigger picture – not only from applicants in the police recruitment office, but also in the broader context of interviewing witnesses and suspects. Shaffer signed up for the course thinking that the analysis skills might prove a novelty.

Exceeding his expectations, the training quickly taught Shaffer how to approach investigations in an entirely new way. He says, 'To become proficient at statement analysis, one has to throw traditional logic out the window and develop a new logic.' Indeed, one of his favourite cautions became: *Logic is the thought process by which we come to the wrong conclusions... with confidence.*

Sergeant Bob Shaffer completed his SCAN training course with Avinoam Sapir who recognised Shaffer's skill in statement analysis and later approached him to become a trainer. Shaffer completed a year-long mentoring program to refine his skills. At the end of the training he taught those skills to others for several years before starting his own business. His aim was to streamline training so that it would relate directly towards law enforcement personnel and the need-to-know practical aspects. Shaffer now trains police across the United States and says: 'Most of what officers do is listen to people talk; we might as well listen accurately. The technique that I teach people involves recognising words and phrases that people use multiple times every single day. It is simply learning a unique way of interpreting what people say.'

So what is this new technique that so impressed the cop from Colorado – and thousands since? Shaffer says that the ability to see beneath the actual words is an important skill for police officers who rely on other people for information. If they don't have the best tools to determine the reliability of that information, then they are at a disadvantage. Used strategically, the analysis of a suspect or a witness statement allows investigators to ask the right questions in the follow-up interview.

Ideally, a witness would write their account before they were interviewed. Their statement would then be analysed and any points of deception or sensitivity would be identified. From there, the interviewing detectives would develop a guideline for the interview before the questions even started.

Sometimes statement analysis will put the analyst in opposition to the investigating officers. Shaffer says that the technique, 'demands that the analyst initially ignore the superficial story that the author offers, and to look below the surface at the underlying, subconscious processes that generated the story, to cut through the clutter and reveal the reality and truth behind their story.'

Put simply, Shaffer says statement analysis 'determines whether or not a story was generated from a person's memory (truthful) or from other sources (deceptive). When a story is the result of someone recalling completely from memory, it takes on specific traits and characteristics. When a story is altered or misrepresented (deceptive), it takes on different and easily identified traits.'

Another aspect identified by statement analysis is when a story is based on truth but becomes deceptive when the author omits critical or incriminating information. Statement analysis identifies the linguistic signals that indicate when a story is missing critical information intentionally left out. The story may contain the truth, but not the whole truth.

For police professionals like Shaffer, the proof is in the pudding. The more it is used, the more widely accepted it will become as law enforcement professionals see for themselves. And a wider use means that practitioners hone their skills. Studies have shown that the polygraph and statement analysis are similar in accuracy. Indeed, Shaffer believes that statement analysis has benefits over the polygraph.

'Polygraph accuracy can be a delicate thing,' he says, 'being subject to environmental factors such as the subject's health and comfort levels, distracting outside noises, counter techniques by the subject and is limited to having to be conducted in very a controlled environment. In contrast, statement analysis can be conducted anywhere at any time. Another benefit is that when the author writes his or her statement, they do so without knowing that their statement will be subjected to examination, so the level of cooperation is usually much greater.'

Additionally, for US law enforcement, equipping a polygraph examiner costs around $6000 and requires three months of training. Shaffer's graduates needs only a $3 set of highlighters and five days of training.

A couple of years back, Shaffer made state-wide news when a detective asked for his assistance in two sexual assaults by a gang of three men. The women were randomly targeted and after five months and a quarter of a million dollars in funding, a taskforce had failed to identify the perpetrators. Shaffer examined the taped interviews of the victims to see if there was another layer of information that might help police.

In a strange turn of events, Shaffer saw strong evidence that the victims were not truthful. He submitted his report to the taskforce with suggestions as to how to approach the women to find the truth. The two quickly confessed. The first 'victim' had fabricated her story and it had been reported in the newspapers along with her description of her 'attackers'. The second 'victim' had narrowly escaped being caught in an affair by her husband and latched on to the story she'd read about in the newspapers, claiming the same men had attacked her.

Another statement Shaffer found deception in was that of a store clerk who had told police she had been the victim of an armed robbery. According to her story, a man came into the store, held her at gunpoint and stole money.

Shaffer explains: 'The analysis revealed she was deceptive and had probably staged the robbery. It also revealed that she likely knew the "robber" and was likely to have a romantic attraction to him. The investigator followed up on the information from the analysis and revealed within a couple days that it was indeed staged and that she had conspired with her boyfriend to commit the crime.'

Another case involved suspected arson. After a suspicious house fire, the homeowner gave a statement explaining his theory that faulty wiring had set off a defective natural gas system. Shaffer analysed his statement and not only could he see that the homeowner was deceptive, but that he'd actually started the fire. The analysis also pinpointed to within a five-minute window when the man had done it. Using Shaffer's information, the investigators got the man to confess in a follow-up interview. From fire to confession took under a week. This kind of case can take weeks to solve, if it is solved at all. This is another benefit to statement analysis – a better, faster solve rate.

These examples are just the tip of the iceberg of statement analysis, but show how simple it can be to begin to get a different meaning from statements.

While there has been some criticism in academic circles about the lack of research consolidating the forensic linguistic analysis principles, Bernie Kruger wants to change that. Coming from an academic background, Kruger realised that for statement analysis to become an accepted method of investigation, it had to have academic support. Having completed his Master's Degree in Applied Linguistics, Kruger hopes to bridge the gap between the practical applications of statement analysis and the academic research needed to give the field the credibility that other investigative tools enjoy.

In order for statement analysis to gain more acceptance, Sergeant Bob Shaffer knows that there must be a governing body to certify instructors, and an organisation overseeing the quality control. He believes there needs to be a validation of the accuracy of the process – just like it took for the polygraph to become accepted in the United States. He has also seen the value of the word-of-mouth endorsement that comes from people who have been trained in and see the value of this investigative tool.

Both Shaffer and Kruger would like to see statement analysis techniques employed as widely as possible. According to Shaffer, there is considerable research to attest to the validity and accuracy of statement analysis. The techniques are used by the FBI as well as countless local, federal and international investigative agencies in the United States.

The benefits to statement analysis are not just in law enforcement. As Kruger has proved with utilising his skills in the corporate world, there are no limits to the ability to spot deception. These skills would prove invaluable to lawyers, prosecutors, private investigators, and human resources personnel.

Winnie, Armchair Dog Detective,
expert in detecting armchairs.

25

GOING TO THE DOGS

I'll never forget the day I got my first dog. He was my 10th birthday present. After much family discussion, we named him Scarper. I'd used the World Book Encyclopedia to research dog breeds and we'd settled on a miniature Schnauzer. The wait for a puppy to be ready seems like years when you are 10, but I'm sure it wasn't that long. While he was growing old enough for us to be able to collect and bring home, I knitted him a blanket.

Being a dab hand at the needles with several rainbow-coloured scarves to prove it, I had the bright idea to knit a big chunk of green knitting (in plain for those readers who care) until the chunk was the same size as a bunny rug left over from the infanthood of one of my many siblings. Once my knitting matched the rug, I cast off and got one of mum's friends who had a sewing machine to sew the two together.

Armed with by double blanket, we set off in the car to collect my puppy. The long drive to wherever the puppy lived was one filled with dreams of my dog. In my imagination, he would be just like Timmy from the Famous Five novels. He would bark at burglars, snarl at smugglers, and generally be obedient and adorable at all other times. He would follow me around and probably collect my slippers and grin at me. Just like Timmy.

The naiveite of a 10-year-old knows no bounds.

At first glance, Scarper was perfect. Tiny. Soft. Snuggly. But the World Book Encyclopedia had skipped over the bit about puppies having razor sharp teeth and a propensity to piddle. In the car. On the way home. Twice.

Instead of my loyal canine servant doing my bidding and joining me on adventures, I became used to the call: *Vik! Scraper's done a poo!* Even though the whole family wanted to share the dog, anything he excreted was all mine.

Scarper made short work of his lovingly-knitted blanket. I think he cut his big-boy teeth on my neat rows of knitting. He piddled, he skidded, he didn't fetch, and he humped things. (That too was not covered by the bastards at World Book.)

Scarper established me firmly in the camp of the loving dog owner who had no clue about how to actually control or train a dog. To be fair, I was only 10 and *The Dog Whisperer* hadn't been invented yet. But still.

Fast-forward to Winnie, my surprise Mother's Day present from my daughter whose secret intention, I suspect, was to get another dog. Winnie was a tiny, arrogant, aloof Moodle and quickly established herself to be the leader of our human pack. She was soon joined by Muffin who was the complete opposite – a loveable little doofus who thinks she's much bigger than she is, especially when she confronts dogs twice her size in the park. Walks with Winnie consisted of me following my weaving Moodle wherever she wants to go and usually ending with the lead tangled around my legs.

The flipside to Winnie was that she is *my* dog. Or perhaps, I am *her* human. Everywhere I go, she is there. Whatever I eat, I have to give her some (she had a very forceful glare) and whenever I sit down, she wants to sit on my lap and have her tummy scratched. Over the years, despite our dogged devotion to watching *The Dog Whisperer*, Winnie gets no better.

Having an affinity with my naughty fluffballs meant I jumped at the chance to write a book on the Victoria Police Dog Squad, when an editor at Penguin asked if I was interested.

I thought: *is the Pope Catholic?*

(I'm pretty sure he still is for now.)

And certainly, with my two little fluff-balls, I felt I had the necessary street cred. My brief was to go out to the Dog Squad, interview handlers, and write stories about heroic dogs.

While I'm confident about my ability to fashion anything into a story, I did wonder if I would be able to capture the personalities of the dogs. Turned out I had nothing to worry about. The police dog handlers all seemed to have a clear favourite dog. They were amazing bunch of people who love the work they do and love talking about their dogs – which was just as well because aside from some deep barking, the dogs remained quite tight-lipped about their work.

When I was interviewing one of the handlers, he said that while the police dogs were highly trained and motivated, they still had their 'Squirrel!' moments.

I'd seen the film *Up* and knew exactly what he was talking about.

I've met the best people during my career of true crime,
and some of them have four legs.

Here I am at the launch of *The Dog Squad* with
Victoria Police Dog Squad officers:
Senior Sergeant Shaun McGovern, Sergeant Bob Carter,
Sergeant Michelle Dench and her police dog partner, PD Archer.

The dogs in the animated movie are fitted with collars which allow them to speak. Most of the time, they are articulate and focused, but every now and again, their heads will all snap to the side and one would yell, 'Squirrel!'

So the officer was telling me that in the real world even the most highly trained dog could still act on its instincts. To me, that just made them more human... er... for dogs.

One story that didn't make it into the book was when one of the police dogs (who shall remain nameless) was called in to work a siege. A man had been reported firing a gun inside his house. Police surrounded the house and they could hear the gunshots going off. Things finally fell silent, and when nothing was heard from inside for a while, the waiting police reckoned the man was either asleep or had perhaps used the gun on himself. With much caution, two police dog handlers and a dog were sent into the house. They made their way quietly down the hallway, checking each room.

The rumours that I make people laugh are apparently true.
The audience at the book launch of *The Dog Squad* found something very funny. In the foreground here, are two Helens and a John: Helen Cooper, Helen Burke (my mum) and John Burke (my dad).

They found the gunman in one of the bedrooms, snoring and peacefully asleep on a double bed. One handler made his way around to the gunman's side of the bed, while the other knelt on the vacant side of the bed, both ready to grab the guy.

The handler's weight on the bed made the spare pillow flip forward.

The brave police dog jumped up on the bed and grabbed the pillow. He snatched it away and jumped back down onto the floor for a play, biting and shaking the pillow, oblivious to the wrestling match that was taking place on the bed as the two handlers grappled with the gunman. The dog shook the pillow, jumping around happily. With one fluffy paw, he held a corner of it down then clamped his powerful chompers onto the opposite corner. He jerked his head up and ripped the pillow to shreds. Pieces snowed down on the arrest.

The capture tally for the night: one gunman, one pillow. But I'm not supposed to tell this embarrassing story so forget you ever heard it.

The dogs I met were extraordinary. Their human handlers were just as amazing and I loved every minute writing *The Dog Squad*.

It was hard to pick just one story from the collection, but I chose 'On the Track of Escaped Criminals' about the dog and handler who assisted in the capture of escaped prisoners Peter Gibb and Archie Butterly.

Most off-duty cops have their own chew toys.

Police Dog Archer, of the Victoria Police Dog Squad, at the launch of the book *The Dog Squad* in which he features.

26

Sniffing Out Escapees

As a police dog handler, you spend countless hours training the dog to be the best they possibly can be. There are nights where you are tired or it's cold or raining and you think to yourself, I'll just let it go tonight, but you really do need to put the effort in because that training can mean the difference between coming home from work or not coming home.

— Sergeant Trevor Berryman (Dog Squad)

In 1988 police officer Trevor Berryman had been in the force for seven years, mostly working general duties in Prahran. For a couple of years, Trevor had volunteered as a police puppy walker. Police puppy walkers cared for a German shepherd pup for around 10 months, and the Berryman family were on their third police puppy.

They received regular visits from members of the Dog Squad, who gave them instructions on how best to socialise and develop the puppies in their care. The puppy walking program included walking the potential police pups at all times of the day and night, and introducing them to as many different environments as possible. The puppies needed to get used to being in different places: shopping centres, police stations, bushland, the beach. As the pups needed to be socialised, each police puppy quickly became part of Trevor's family – that is, until they had to be handed back to the squad.

So when a vacancy at the Dog Squad came up, Trevor jumped at the chance. What attracted him to the squad was the thought of catching offenders even if they didn't leave behind typical evidence such as DNA or fingerprints. Dogs didn't need such forensic evidence. They worked on scent and scent alone.

Trevor was chosen from around 40 applicants. After many years in the squad, he can look back with hindsight and see that he ticked all the boxes. He was young and fit, and he had a good operational background. Dog Squad members worked one-up – which meant they were on their own with their dogs – so they had to have their wits about them.

As soon as he accepted the position, Trevor was given his first dog: a long-haired shepherd called Boss. The dog lasted just 12 months in the squad, because he had a growing aversion to slippery floors. This condition was not uncommon in dogs, but what began as a mild annoyance grew to be so bad that Trevor was unable to search buildings with slippery floors or even lino. Trevor and one of the trainers at the squad worked on the problem; they tried several tactics to help the dog overcome his fear, but he continued to balk at slippery floors.

Boss was retired and given to a police officer who was looking for a pet. While Trevor was disappointed, he was a little relieved too; handlers and their dogs had to be fit and ready for any situation. It was embarrassing that Boss couldn't complete some jobs simply because they involved a slippery floor.

In the Dog Squad, there was never much time to lament the loss of an old dog before a new dog arrived. For Trevor, the new one was a short-haired German shepherd called Shamus. Right from the beginning, every exercise that Shamus did showed that he had far greater skill than Boss. Shamus was a natural police dog; he had perfect obedience, and his desire to track and search was extraordinary.

On Friday 12 March 1993, Trevor attended a job that turned out to be one of the most dangerous of his career. He had worked till 4am, and had only grabbed a couple of hours of sleep before getting a call-out at 9am.

On the previous Sunday, dangerous criminals Peter Gibb and Archie Butterly, had escaped from the Melbourne Remand Centre.

What made front-page news all week was the fact that Gibb and Butterly had been aided in their escape by prison officer Heather Parker, who had fallen for the dubious charms of Peter Gibb; her beau had prior convictions for manslaughter and armed robbery.

The two had begun a relationship when Gibb was held in the Melbourne Remand Centre and Parker worked there as a prison officer. When prison colleagues noticed the growing intimacy between the guard and the crook, Heather Parker was transferred.

Undeterred, she visited Gibb in prison and smuggled in a small piece of explosive, which Gibb and Butterly used to blow out a window. The two escaped by climbing down knotted bed sheets to La Trobe Street below, where they met Heather Parker in a getaway car loaded with firearms.

The escape was not smooth sailing. Archie Butterly fell during the climb from the window and injured his ankle. Then their getaway car was pursued by a quick-thinking prison officer who hailed a taxi to follow them. They crashed the getaway car, stole a motorcycle, and then crashed that too. Butterly sustained internal injuries in the collision and needed medical attention.

The escapees were stalled again by a police divisional van on Southbank Boulevard. A shootout followed, and Senior Constable Warren Treloar was gunned down. As Treloar lay on the ground with serious bullet wounds in his chest and arm, the escapees stole his police revolver, jumped into the police divisional van and fled the scene.

Escapee, Peter Gibb, circa 1993.
He died in 2011.

A state-wide alert was issued, and every police officer in Victoria was on the lookout for the fugitives. And so was the public. Not long after the police shooting, Gibb and Butterly were seen getting into a car, which was later found to belong to Heather Parker.

Parker and the two fugitives made a brief stop at the Latrobe Regional Hospital so that Butterly could be treated for his injuries.

They next surfaced on Wednesday 10 March, at the old Gaffneys Creek Hotel near Jamieson, where Parker and Gibb had a meal in the pub before retiring. By the next morning, the Gaffneys Creek Hotel was a smouldering ruin and the three fugitives had vanished.

Butterly was well known for torching stolen vehicles; it was suspected that the escapees had torched the room they'd stayed in to destroy any evidence that they had been there. The fire had spread through the whole pub.

When questioned by police, locals recognised the fugitives' pictures. It was thought that they were still in the area. And that was where the police dogs came in.

When Trevor Berryman got the call, his brief was to make his way to Jamieson and work with officers from the Special Operation Group to locate Parker, Gibb and Butterly.

Another handler, John Murray, and his dog Rebel joined Trevor and Shamus as they systematically searched farmhouses and outbuildings around the area. Given that the fugitives had showed no hesitation in gunning down police officers, the dog handlers wore ballistic vests.

It wasn't as nerve-racking as it might sound. The heavily armed SOG operatives at their backs, and the nose of the dog at the front, made the job a little easier. And there was no time for any trepidation; the handlers had to give the dogs their total concentration. The smallest shift in behaviour could signal that the dog had sensed something, so the handlers had to be able to read the subtleties of these alerts. Sometimes it would be a slight difference in pull on the tracking line, or a raise of the head.

Shamus was a head raiser.

The police found nothing on the first day of the search. The two handlers checked into a local motel around midnight, while the dogs stayed in the cars.

Back on deck at 6am, the team of police officers pushed through their exhaustion and continued searching. Local police had set up roadblocks and checkpoints around the area and were handing out flyers with descriptions of the fugitives. Around midday, a local man approached one of the checkpoints and reported that when he was fishing in the Goulburn River nearby, he had seen a car parked off-road with a camouflage net over it.

While John Murray and Rebel continued searching outbuildings, Trevor and Shamus went with the SOG to the camouflaged car. If the car belonged to the escapees and was camouflaged rather than abandoned, there was a likelihood that they would return to it. And if they did, police could be hiding close by.

From the car, Trevor cast Shamus on his 10-metre tracking line to see if he could pick up a scent. Nose to the ground, Shamus sniffed around and quickly alerted.

'He's got a track,' Trevor told the two SOG operatives. It was the first time during the search that police had been close.

The bush was dense, and tangled prickly blackberry bushes added to the challenge. But while Trevor and the two SOG officers battled their way through, a very excited Shamus powered ahead, tail wagging. The dog loved a search; to him it was all a big fun game.

'Good boy! Good boy!' Trevor encouraged Shamus as the dog pushed on.

They followed the scent for around half a kilometre before Shamus suddenly stopped in a small clearing surrounded by dense bush. The dog raised his head.

'He's got something,' Trevor said in a quiet voice.

One of the SOG members moved in front of Trevor and Shamus, and one stayed behind. Part of their job now was to protect the handler and his dog. And, more importantly, their big black Steyr semi-automatic rifles were much more powerful that Trevor's police-issue handgun.

Then all hell broke loose in a hail of bullets. The fugitives were firing on them!

An old colleague had once told Trevor that if anyone ever shoots at you, 'just move'. Remembering the sage advice, Trevor picked up Shamus and dived into the closest bush. The blackberry prickles didn't even register as the police officer huddled with his dog. Under gunfire, he quickly went over his tactical options. He could stay put and keep Shamus with him, or send the dog to try and take down the offenders.

The second option was not the best, under the circumstances, because if he released Shamus with an order to take down the shooters, the dog wouldn't differentiate between the SOG members returning fire and the fugitives. Unless directed towards a particular person, police dogs will take down anyone in range.

The three police officers were well and truly under fire – so close, in fact, that Trevor could hear the sonic cracks of the gunfire breaking the sound barrier. Trevor had lost sight of the SOG officers; he worried that they might have been taken down in the original burst of gunfire. He couldn't see them because the gunfire had filled the air with thick smoke. The earthy eucalyptus smell of the bush had been replaced with the acrid smell of gun powder.

It would only have been a couple of minutes since Trevor dived into the blackberries with Shamus, but it felt a lot longer. Then he heard the low voice of one of the SOG officers. 'I've been shot in the leg,' he said matter-of-factly.

'Are you still good to continue?' asked the second SOG bloke, appearing from behind a tree, dripping wet. He had emptied his magazine in the return fire, then jumped into the river to reload underwater, out of firing range.

'Yep.'

Not long after it began, the hail of bullets stopped; the officers could hear shouting further down the river.

Shamus was as excited as a pup, tail wagging madly. In training, a gunshot signalled play. He thought he was going to catch some crooks and he was very happy about it, but Trevor held on to him.

Regular police radios were useless in the thick bush, but the SOG had internal communications and they were able to call for backup. Trevor and his colleagues got the report that the head of the SOG, Bruce Knight, had arrested Heather Parker and Peter Gibb. Archie Butterly wasn't with them.

'Stay where you are,' one of the SOG guys told Trevor.

For the next half-hour Trevor and Shamus remained in the blackberry thicket while heavily armed SOG members swarmed the area to search for Butterly. Until he was found, the threat was very real; he could come up from anywhere and ambush the searchers.

After the immediate area around Trevor was cleared, an SOG operative pointed to Shamus. 'Can we use him to find Butterly?' he asked.

Trevor explained that Shamus could do it if he was kept on the

Heather Parker under arrest after police caught her and Peter Gibb trying to cross the Goulburn River, in the bush 175km from Melbourne.

lead – there were too many people around with guns for the excited police dog. Trevor would have to take Shamus right into the area where the SOG thought Butterly was hiding.

With much manoeuvring through spiky blackberry bushes, Trevor and Shamus scrambled to higher ground, making their way cautiously to where the gunfire had originated. Trevor let the dog out on the 10-metre line. After a few moments, Shamus alerted – there was someone in nearby bushes.

'There's someone here,' Trevor told the SOG.

The dog was excited. It was his turn. This was what he had trained for. Once the nod was given for the dog to go for it, Trevor issued the command: 'Subdue!' The handler dropped the tracking line and Shamus took off like a shot, disappearing into the bush to face whatever lay behind it.

The bush moved and rustled. 'Good boy! Good boy!' Trevor called.

Shamus growled, which meant he had located someone. But while there was a lot of growling, which would be accompanied by biting, there was no human sound.

Trevor recalled the dog, and he came leaping out of the bush. Trevor could see a significant amount of blood on Shamus' honey-coloured chest. He knew it didn't belong to Shamus because the dog was bounding around, happy as a clam.

'He's in there and he's either dead or very badly injured,' Trevor told the waiting SOG.

Trevor gave Shamus lots of pats and praise, then cautiously checked his dog for injuries – just in case.

While the SOG officers closed in, Trevor and Shamus withdrew; their work was done. In a culvert, the SOG found Archie Butterly dead – a single gunshot wound to the head. Beside him lay the stolen police revolver.

While police combed the scene for evidence, Trevor returned to Jamieson Police Station to hose the blood off his dog. The exhausted handler was offered a ride back to Melbourne on the police helicopter. Shamus and Trevor, strapped into harnesses, made it back to Melbourne in half the time it would have taken them to drive. A couple of beers at the pub later on and that was about it.

Heather Parker and Peter Gibb both received 10-year prison sentences for their crimes. Parker's sentence was reduced by half on appeal.

Trevor and the two SOG officers received awards for their involvement in the search, and Shamus got his picture in the newspaper. The lady who had donated Shamus saw the picture and sent Trevor a beautiful letter saying how proud she was.

> Dear Senior Constable Berryman,
>
> It was with pride and delight that I read in the morning paper what a good police dog, Shamus is – as I am the person who gave Shamus to the Dog Squad.
>
> He must be a fine looking dog now – as he will be seven this year. I have only seen him once since I gave him to the Dog Squad. His first handler brought him to see me at the hospital where I worked and where Shamus, as a pup, spent a lot of time. That was great. I really would love to see him again, but I understand that he is a police dog, but I still do think of him as my dog!
>
> One favour I would ask is a photo of him. I was promised and promised a photo and never received one. I feel a little bit let down over that. Anyway, I'm so glad he's turned out tops. He was a lovely pup and young dog.
>
> All the best and keep safe,
>
> (Miss) Margaret O'Malley

Trevor took Shamus over to Moe and spent the day with his proud first owner, much to her delight.

With my friend Sandra Nicholson, a 35-year veteran of
Victoria Police, and recently retired at the rank
of Assistant Commissioner.

27

SATURDAYS WITH THE SKULL

I make Christmas puddings. When my work as a teacher breaks up for the Christmas holidays, I select a day, mark it in my diary, and that day becomes Pudding Day. It starts early. Fruit soaked fat with brandy is added to brown sugar, loads of eggs, mixed spice and treacle and flour and stirred together. The lumpy brown mess is poured onto floured calico circles, tied tightly with string, then dropped into huge pots. The next seven hours requires a slavish devotion to topping up water from the boiling kettle and stirring the bobbing desserts as the smell of Christmas puddings fills the house.

Pudding day has become a bit of a tradition. Friends drop in and make their own puddings and savour the glorious smell. We eat lunch and chat. At the end of the day, half a dozen puddings rest their warm bottoms on a wire rack, the calico replaced by shiny foil, each adorned with a Christmas ribbon.

For those who can't come to pudding day, I drop their puddings off. And that is how I came to be sitting on a balcony of an apartment near the city having lunch with my friend (and one-time debating partner) now-retired Assistant Commissioner Sandra Nicholson. This pudding was for her orphans' Christmas, filled with friends whose families, like hers, were too far away to meet on the day.

I'd just finished writing *The Dog Squad* and I complained to Sandra that I needed to find a new topic to write about. Writers without a work in progress are liable to do crazy things like re-paint the house, or hand-sand wooden floors, or if there's a circus that needs joining, watch out.

'You should write a book about Brian,' Sandra said.

'Brian who?' I asked.

'Brian Murphy. The Skull. He was my old boss back in the 80s.' Sandra got up from her chair, disappeared inside to her bookshelf, and returned with a book called *The Skull* by journalist Adam Shand. She handed it to me. The cover was red with a picture of a bald man in dark glasses on it. The subtitle was: *Informers, hitmen and Australia's toughest cop.*

I have to admit, informers and hitmen are not my favourite topic, but I had recently dabbled in the dark side of organised crime in my writing which I had previously left to the male writers of underbelly fame. It's my observation – and I could be wrong – that female true-crime writers tend to pick stories that are more people-focused. Male crime writers have more shooting.

'This was written by a journalist,' said Sandra, 'but Brian always wanted to tell his own story.'

I told Sandra that I would read *The Skull* to get a feel for Brian's story, and let her know if I was interested, then she could put me in touch with Brian.

In my writing, I like to explore resilience – how do people survive and thrive after catastrophic things happen to them? I like to see what makes people tick, what motivates them. This is why, more recently, I'd moved towards biography; although crime still remains at the heart of my work. Any great story needs an explosion at the start: something that happens to start the ball rolling, something that makes the characters learn and grow. Crime is the perfect inciting event.

I took the book, and left Sandra with the pudding.

I was intrigued with *The Skull* more for what it didn't say than what it did. Adam Shand had done a fine job creating the rogue that Brian Murphy was as a copper, a dashing man, fast with his fists, breaking the rules and getting the bad guys in the end. But I got the sense that Brian spooked Shand; got under his skin. The journalist admitted that the first time he met Murphy, the retired detective told him something in confidence that if it got out, Brian would know he was the source.

'If you tell anyone what I've told you, you will be walking on stumps,' Brian told him.

I marvelled at this testing. I've seen it before – often in the classroom among little kids – it means: *can I trust you?* with a bit of: *you'll be sorry if I can't* – thrown in for good measure.

In bloke code – of which I am mostly ignorant – it clearly meant something else. I wondered if Adam Shand wrote the book a tiny bit worried at this perceived threat.

By the time I reached the final page, I wanted to meet Brian. There was a lot of *what* he had done, but not so much *why* he had done it.

My interest always lies in the method behind the madness.

I told my parents that I was thinking of writing about Brian 'The Skull' Murphy, and Dad's response was surprising.

'I met him once,' he said. 'He was the scariest bloke I ever met.'

Huh? How did my chartered accountant dad rub shoulders with The Skull? Turned out, tax brought them together. One of Dad's friends was The Skull's nephew. When the Murphys needed an accountant, the nephew recommended Dad. Mostly, though, he met with Brian's wife Margaret. She would drop the paperwork into the office and tell Dad the latest Skull stories.

'I'll never forget,' said Dad, shaking his head as if he still couldn't believe it, 'she told me that Brian had caught someone breaking into the house next door. When the bloke came at him with a screwdriver, Brian aimed a gun at the dirt near his feet, but accidentally shot the bloke in the foot!'

For an accountant from the suburbs, this was as exciting as neighbourly relations got. I made a mental note to ask Brian about the time he shot the thief next door. After reading Shand's book and its declaration that The Skull had shot 40 people – none of them fatally – in the course of his career, I suspected that in the case of neighbourly shooting Brian's aim had been deliberate.

Brian 'The Skull' Murphy lived at an address that just by sitting quietly immovable in Middle Park for the last hundred or so years, had moved in location from undesirable to highly-desirable. It's a family home with stained glass windows and the high ceilings. It is here that Brian met me at the door. For a writer, I'm not particularly good at describing people and have wondered in idle moments if I could describe members of my own family to a police artist with any accuracy.

My first impression was that Brian reminded me of my dad; around the same vintage, give or take half a dozen years. But there is something recognisable in men that age. Politeness, a ruddy glow to their cheeks, a lack of hair, a gait swayed by a dodgy hip. It only took me a moment to understand that Brian would never do to me what he did to Adam Shand; there would be no veiled threats. A gentleman doesn't do that to a lady. Just like my dad wouldn't.

And because I trusted my dad, and because I trusted the judgement of my friend Sandra Nicholson, I felt an immediate fondness for Brian 'The Skull' Murphy.

We started writing over summer. Brian was 82 and sharp as a tack. His memory for times and dates was phenomenal. But writing someone's story takes patience and a fair bit of wrangling. Because

Brian 'The Skull' Murphy and I, with two of his newest fans, Emily Webb and Meshel Laurie from the *Australian True Crime* podcast.

I work full time as a teacher, I have honed my writing skills to an economy necessary for me to write a book every year or two. When I interview my subjects, I type as they talk. This means that after three or four hours with The Skull, the day's story is largely written, and I don't have to duplicate the time later by transcribing from notes.

It's also an incredibly good way of keeping your subject on track. If you're in the middle of typing a story about the first time he arrested someone, and he veers off on a tangent, you can quickly bring him back as your fingers hover over the keyboard waiting to resume the story.

With a project like ours, there always needs to be a rapport. What did I have in common with The Skull? We were both Catholic (he practising, me not), knew people in common, and were interested in some of the same crimes; but there was something else. He was a natural-born storyteller and so was I. We both understood that words spoken in just the right way at just the right time can change lives.

After the book was finished, I took long service leave in 2016 and decided to enter the Horne Prize essay writing competition. The essay had to be on some aspect of Australian life, and 3000 words or less, so every word had to count. I had just written Brian's book which at one point had blown out to 138,000 words and needed to be wrangled back to 90,000 or so. The craft needed to tell a story in so few words as the competition allowed, would challenge me to write in a very different way.

My essay took over a month and it absorbed me in a way I hadn't been absorbed for a long time. It didn't win the prize, but that didn't matter. I was proud of it and loved that it allowed a different form of expression.

Brian 'The Skull' Murphy was perfect for a story about Australian life. His childhood was the quintessential one with heaps of kids, strict parents and peril everywhere. He was always in strife. I wanted to capture the wild child who turned into the wild cop.

Brian 'The Skull' Murphy

28

AUSTRALIAN LIFE (AND DEATH)

There existed last century an absolute unwavering respect for certain people in the community. Coppers, by and large, had it. So did bank managers, scout masters, priests, and nuns, or *current buns* as they were called back then – but only when they were out of earshot.

But respect is a funny old thing. Last century – before the war (any one, take your pick; we're not fussy) – dictionaries declared: **respect**, *noun*, a feeling of deep admiration for someone or something elicited by their abilities, qualities, or achievements.

But those dictionaries were lying through their etymological teeth. Respect was not given to people you liked or trusted; it was usually given as a result of fear. Fear that the fat bank manager would refuse you a loan. Fear that the long arm of the law might reach out and cuff you over the back of the head. Fear the priest would condemn you to Hell with a fiery sermon about keeping your own hands away from your own front bottom. Fear that if you didn't conjugate your French verbs correctly, Sister Marie-France would whack you over the knuckles with her cane. That, my friend was respect: **respect**, *noun,* the deep feeling of fear you develop towards people with power over you who might wallop you without a moment's notice.

Our little essay begins back in the 1930s when a small boy called Brian looks up at a nun who is just about to give him a piece of her mind. His crime? He got a little over-excited after a school Mass when the grand priest comes up to say hello. When the priest bends forward to pat him on the head, Brian touches the priest's silken robes, and before he can stop himself, he is twirling irresistibly into their folds. The priest laughs. The nun didn't. Hence her tirade as soon as the priest is out of earshot.

Brian watches the nun's chin as she waffles endlessly about respecting the priests, and finally says, 'You need to shave. Your whiskers are getting long.'

There are gasps all round. The unspeakable has happened. Someone has told the truth.

When his mother finds out what Brian has done, she drags him halfway to the local orphanage before calming down enough to take him home. *Never disrespect the nuns!* she cries, wagging her finger in his face. The message is reinforced again later, when his father gets home.

An old man now, Brian sits at his dining room table. He is bald. His head is scarred. At his next birthday, he will turn 84.

He hasn't given in to aging, but his body gives things away, the dirty rotten traitor: the heavy hip that sways his walking; the scars and patches of skin that hid cancers until they were discovered then removed then replaced with Frankenstein-like stitches. But his blue eyes twinkle beneath the burden of age, and he's quick with a joke.

He offers tea that he knows his wife will make with lots of enquiries about milk and sugar and would you like cake with that?

Once settled with Nescafe, his brew of choice, Brian begins talking about the good old days. His name was still Brian back then, but on the streets, he was known as Mr Murphy, or more commonly, The Skull. Photos from a box of mementos show a dashing young policeman, scrubbed, polished and ready for duty. In some pictures, he is standing between his parents, grimacing their pride the way people did in photos back then because pride goeth before a fall and all that.

The beaming young man wanted to fight for truth and justice, and to be a hero like the coppers he'd seen as a child. Those officers of the law would ride their bikes where angels feared to tread, breaking up drunken brawls outside pubs while raggedy kids watched and dreamed of being just like them.

'Things were simpler back then,' says Brian over a biscuit he shouldn't be eating because of his blood sugar levels.

In those simpler times, freckled-faced and keen as mustard, he never imagined he'd one day stand in the dock for killing someone. No indeedy, he didn't. But in life, sometimes you get lemonade and sometimes, you get lemons.

If what occurred on Friday 26 March 1971 was translated into a recipe – as so much is these days on TV with bake-offs are disguised as high drama – it might read like this:

1 cup of Painters and Dockers

3 tablespoons of 1970s protesting mentality

500g of alpha-male policing methods

A sprinkling of Henry Bolte's hang-em-high politics and, finally, a dollop of nuns

Boil for a decade in a pressure cooker, then be careful when you open the lid.

On that Friday in March, Brian is busy. Someone had knocked off thousands of dollars of leather jackets the night before and he is on the case. Good detectives like Brian know the likely suspects straight away. The biggest one is Ray Chuck Bennett, professional bad guy; not yet a Great Bookie Robber, but he will be, you just wait.

Brian is out and about, burning shoe leather when he hears over the police car radio that two uniformed coppers have picked up another volatile offender: Neil Stanley Collingburn.

Brian has seen Collingburn arc up before. He is the type of cocky young bloke who will react to the slightest prodding. At the same time, Brian knows that if he is treated respectfully,

Collingburn can be kept in line. Brian found that out one day when he was asked to take the young buck home and search his house. On the way there, in the police car, Collingburn pleaded that Mr Murphy not search his baby's room. She's been sick, he says. And if the cops wake the baby, there'll be hell to pay with the Missus.

Brian did the eye-contact thing; made Collingburn promise there was nothing untoward in the baby's room. 'I swear Mr Murphy. There's nothing there.'

Then Brian did the man thing and took his word for it. The baby wasn't disturbed and something was created that day. It could've been trust or it could have been respect, but it was never labelled because in those days, real men didn't label things that mattered.

Nonetheless, when Brian hears the radio report of Collingburn and some mates being picked up, he radios the arresting officer, Carl Stillman.

'It's Brian Murphy, here mate,' he says. 'They're all dangerous blokes. Painters and Dockers. Be careful when you're dealing with them. If Collingburn gets you down, you won't get back up.'

In the crackle of Stillman's response, Brian hears the tone of another young buck, a man who knows more than him, a man who can get the better of Neil Stanley Collingburn and his crim mates.

Pride goeth before a fall, indeed.

As serendipity – that fickle mistress – would have it, later that day Brian is walking past an office at the Russell Street police headquarters when he hears a commotion. He rushes in and sees the cocky officer Stillman on his back, more turtle than rooster, and Collingburn looming over him with fists and boots. Brian grabs Collingburn and slams him into a chair and things and policemen are soon right way up again.

But all is not well.

Stillman has kicked upwards when he was on the floor and kicked a good blow into Collingburn's middle. Right where his duodenum is. Duodenums, as a rule, don't like being kicked, and Collingburn's ruptures in protest. And thus begins a slow leak into other parts of Collingburn that prefer their own company, and take umbrage at the trespassing fluids.

Soon, the young crim doubles over with pain and is taken begrudgingly to the nearest hospital – a Catholic one; with nuns who have vowed to live in poverty, chastity, and obedience – but never subservience. No siree, Bob.

So, when Neil Stanley Collingburn makes the fatal error of greeting them with the standard: *Fuck off, ya black crows*, these feisty sheilas push his trolley to the back of the room *where you can stay till you have learnt some manners, young man.*

Collingburn grumbles his way to a slow death as the leakage in his middle becomes gangrenous, and by the time the doctor examines him, it's too late. He's a goner. A victim of narcissism, bravado, a policeman's boot, and nuns.

Brian knows nothing about anything until he gets a death threat over the phone a couple of days later. *Ya bastard*, says the threatener, *you're dead!*

'What the hell are you talking about?' asks Brian. But he soon learns. Bosses come a-running; a huge protest march appears like magic outside the Russell Street police headquarters.

Who killed Collingburn? they chant, then provide their own answer: *The police killed Collingburn!* And so it goes. The marchers throng down Russell Street with their chanting and their placards.

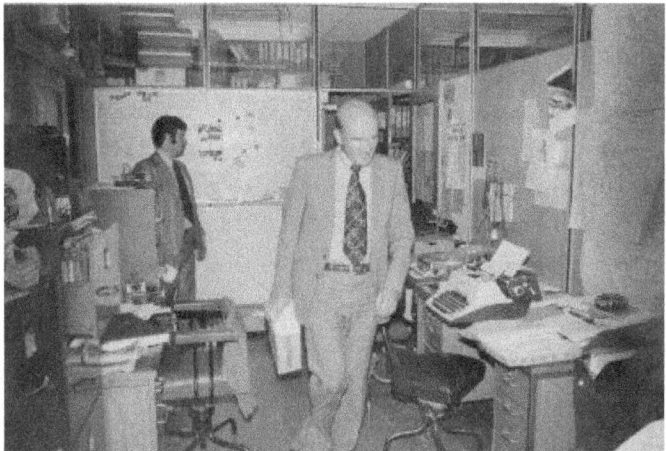

The Skull in his natural habitat.

The bosses look panicked. 'You'd better go out the back way,' they tell Brian. 'They're out for blood!'

Brian isn't a leaving-out-the-back-way kind of fellow. And so he steps out the front door of Russell Street and takes in the crowd. *Who killed Collingburn? The police killed Collingburn!* Some of the beefy tattooed men carry a coffin just in case people missed the bit about Collingburn dying. Brian senses the spirit of the mob – its dire message is being delivered by a rather festive bunch. He waves to them and smiles. They wave back and smile. Hail fellow, well met.

An inquest sends Brian and the other officer, the kicker, Stillman to trial. The coppers' story is that Collingburn started it. The crim witnesses say the opposite as crim witnesses do: brutal police officers Murphy and Stillman went on a stomping rage, shouting, *The Bash Is On!* rampaging around the small office with much smashing of heads into filing cabinets and stomping up and down on middles like trampolines; leaving the public with two choices: Murphy and Stillman are innocent, or they're dirty rotten lying lunatic bash-artist murdering copper pigs.

Thus begins a crazy trip down the rabbit hole. A detective – big bloke, bully – visits Brian to investigate. Brian smells a rat; he's a detective too, after all. He knows the drill. This guy's not kosher.

On a hunch, he gets his undercover mates to follow the big bloke who goes from Brian's place to the Police Club, gets smashed off his nut, and weaves his car all the way home in the dead of night. Brian's pals later describe how the big drunk spills himself out of his car, face-plants in his driveway and falls asleep right then and there. The version the court hears has less beer in it: *Your Honour, after interviewing the accused, I returned to the Russell Street police headquarters to type up my statement...*

During this difficult time, Brian and his family attend Mass at the local Catholic church each Sunday, just like they always have. Kind parishioners arrive early and clean off graffiti left by the riff-raff about Brian rotting in hell and such like. During the trial, Masses all around Australia are offered up for a not-guilty verdict for the Good Catholic Copper.

On the morning of the verdict, Brian takes aside the eldest of his children for The Talk. 'If I don't come home,' he says with tears in his eyes and a catch in his voice, 'you need to take care of Mum and the little ones.'

After a tense wait, the jury declares him innocent.

That night, Brian receives cards and letters from nuns, priests, Catholics, and normal people from all over the country. And the following morning, Brian and his wife are invited to the local convent for a celebratory breakfast with the nuns who make a lovely spread, and toast his success with cups of tea. *Nuns?* I hear you say as your brain synapses fire, making connections that raise your eyebrows. But, Dear Reader, quieten your suspicions. Keep reading; nothing to see here.

So where does respect fit in to all of this? you ask. Because naturally, a sad story is here for a reason. Surely, the young man can't die in vain.

Let's give it a good Aussie crack. The definition about respect being feelings of admiration for someone with good qualities is the one we use now. The other definition about respect being the fear of someone who might wallop you has changed – this is now called something else.

Bullying.

Which is quite a different thing entirely.

What we do know is this: Neil Collingburn had neither – no respect for the law who might wallop him, and no respect for the nuns who might save him.

Stop the victim blaming, you cry!

And rightly so. Don't kick the poor dead chap while he's down, lying on the stainless steel table with a boot-shaped bruise in his post-mortem middle. He's been kicked sufficiently, thank you very much. But what if he shook off the mortal coil and went floating out into The Great Beyond, what might he know now? What can he see with his God's Eye view? Does he slap his frosty forehead and say: 'Oh! I get it now. What a wally I was!' and realise that a bit of respect towards both coppers and nuns might have saved his life? Or would he still weigh it all up and think it was more important to try and gain the upper hand, show his superiority, grandstand, puff out his chest, my muscles are bigger than yours, I'm not afraid of no nuns.

But he should have been afraid.

And so, Gentle Reader, the pendulum has swung, as pendulums always do because that's their job both as a metaphor and as a swinging thing. Respect is gaining momentum. Gaining street cred.

We respect Obama because he's a fine chap and he hasn't cheated on his wife, or avoided taxes, or called women fat or boasted about groping them. And he has normal hair. The one who might take his place stands at podiums to convince us to give him our respect, but he's building on very spongy ground indeed.

And our politicians fare no better. We love them until they're voted in, then we fire off barbs in the press and on social media: ooh she can't do the job, she's a sheila; he's got big ears and wears budgie smugglers, get rid of him!

#dontblamemeIdidn'tvoteforthem!

Brian 'The Skull' Murphy, back in the day — as they say.

And we do this until our Prime Ministers pass the use-by date of their short shelf life and then we get a new one and do the same thing. No respect for the office, I say.

[Aside: #confusion – can we respect an office if it doesn't respect us? Can an *office* be disrespectful? Don't look here. We don't know.]

Brian finishes his coffee and takes another biscuit. 'Things look different through old eyes,' he says. But he is still torn between the old ways and the new, is still caught on the notion that certain people deserve respect without having to earn it.

'Should be a given,' he says. 'People don't respect the police any more, but who do they call when things turn pear-shaped?' – that old hairy chestnut (the *question*, not Brian).

Do the old days look different through old eyes? Do things viewed in sepia, twist back till they bite their own backsides?

Brian respected female police officers so much he didn't like working with them; he reasoned that if the shit hit the fan, his instinct would be to protect them first, rather than tackle the threat. His respect for justice and his own safety meant that over his career, 40 men felt the sting of his bullets, and countless more, the thud of his fists.

'Better to be judged by 12 than carried out by six,' he says.

So what do we know about respect after a wander along its labyrinthine pathways? Not much. This essay has no answers; she is not your bitch.

'But what's the take-away here?' cry modern business types who like their learning in catch-phrases. 'What's the meme?' beg the long-of-hair and short-of-attention-span.

Here's your takeaway; here's your meme: *Life is short. Keep your duodenum away from boots. Always respect nuns.*

Author's note: this was written before Donald Trump was voted president, in the innocent days when any thought of a victory for him was laughable. #sigh

29

PhDs and Podcasts

In 2017, something lovely happened. One of my best friends, Annemarie Casey, nominated me for a Kilbreda College Past Pupil of Distinction award. We both darkened the doorways of Kilbreda back in the 1980s, pushing at the boundaries, and discovering who we were and deciding who we would become. When I got the letter inviting me to the event, I had no idea that Annemarie had taken the time to write an account of my contribution to the world of writing. I was incredibly moved.

Fast forward to the awards night at Kilbreda. The profiles of all the nominees including mine were read out, then the four inaugural inductees were announced. One of the inductees was Dr Mayumi Purvis who started at Kilbreda five years after I finished. Mayumi is a criminologist and private consultant and an Honorary Fellow at the University of Melbourne School of Social and Political Science in criminology. Her field of expertise is working with sex offenders and training others in this area.

When Mayumi gave her acceptance speech for the award, she spoke about how amazed she was that I was in the audience. She had read my book *Rockspider* as a young woman and been so moved by it that she decided to dedicate her professional life to working with sex offenders – some of whom I'd written about – to try and make a positive difference.

Hearing Mayumi describe the profound difference *Rockspider* had made in her life my first thought was: *That is so cool!* It was perhaps the most difficult book I've written. The subject matter was traumatic, and even though I'm usually quite stoic as an author, this one gave me nightmares. I remember thinking if this book could help even one child, or one victim, then it would be worth it. Mayumi told me that she had gone on to train over a thousand people in the field of working with sex offenders and they would have gone on to influence thousands more.

So, beyond my wildest dreams, *Rockspider* had make a difference. A huge difference.

It's hard to describe the feeling of making a life-altering difference in someone's life. It's not the first time I've heard how my books have changed lives. I'm delighted when people come up to me after author talks and tell me that they became a cop or an investigator after reading my books.

Around 2017 lots of my writer friends began enrolling to do their PhDs, and the idea began to take seed that maybe that was my next step. A Creative Writing PhD would help me develop my next project and give me academic cred. (I also really liked the berets PhDs got to wear at graduation and Dr Petraitis had a certain ring to it.)

A friend, Dr Kelly Gardner, who earned her PhD back in 2014, gave me excellent advice. She told me to take things slowly and enjoy the learning experience a PhD had to offer. The advice was

My very own co-PhDers, long-time friends and fellow published writers , Amra Pajalic and Kimberley Starr.

Once a Copper: The Life and Times of Brian 'The Skull' Murphy.

timely because for writers, deadlines make everything rushed. If I took time to smell the roses, I could enhance the PhD experience.

It's important to understand, I had no idea how to do a PhD. But I trusted myself as a learner. I knew I'd figure it out.

My natural idea was to write a non-fiction book, but I soon set that aside. I could write non-fiction with one hand tied behind my back (which would slow down my typing rate, but still). Over the years, I had dabbled with fiction. I'd always written stories for the kids I taught. I'd written a funny kids' story called *Sergeant Warrior and the Case of the Budgie Smugglers* which allowed me to indulge my comedic writing, but publishers weren't interested in it. I decided to up the ante in my PhD learning challenge – I'd write a crime novel. Fiction. Make stuff up. For adults.

In 2017, when I enrolled to do the PhD, my calendar was pretty free. A long period stretched ahead where I pictured myself going to Uni, studying in the library, and maybe discussing existentialism in the quad.

The journey turned out a little different.

Once a Copper came out in early 2018, but it was finished before that, so my writing time was my own. Over the Christmas school holidays, my friend and fellow true crime writer, Emily Webb, invited me to go on the *Australian True Crime* podcast which she hosted with Meshel Laurie. I was slow to the podcast thing and agreed without giving it much thought.

I had listened to Rachael Brown's *Trace* podcast and loved it; and years ago, I had seen the actual Homicide file on the case and the crime scene photos, I remember, were brutal. The mystery of the case was expertly captured in *Trace* and the revelations it contained prompted the Victorian Coroner to reopen the investigation into the 38-year-old cold case death of Maria James who was stabbed to death in the back of her Melbourne bookshop in 1980.

In preparation for my interview with Emily and Meshel on *Australian True Crime*, I listened to a couple of episodes of their podcast show. The crime chats were compelling.

Emily asked if we could talk about my first book, *The Phillip Island Murder*. The book had been out of print for years, but people occasionally still contacted me about it, usually as bamboozled about the mystery as the rest of us.

Around the same time, Anna Priestland, a researcher for another podcast called *Casefile* got in touch. Anna told me that *Casefile* had a million listeners around the world! She wanted to do the Phillip Island case too. I told her that *Australian True Crime* had just done the case, but Anna explained that *Casefile* covered stories differently. They researched the case themselves and an anonymous reader, nicknamed 'Casey' narrated it. Anna assured

I joined podcasters Emily Webb from *Australian True Crime* (l), Rachael Brown, *Trace*, and ex-Homicide detecive Charlie Bezzina on a public true crime panel where we talked about how podcasts are changing the landscape of crime reporting and investigating.

me that both podcasts would complement each other. I met with Anna and was not surprised to see the mystery get under her skin too. Pretty soon, the Phillip Island murder mystery became *Case 80: Beth Barnard*.

In the meantime, publisher and good friend, Lindy Cameron, and I were preparing a new edition of *The Frankston Murders* to come out for the 25th anniversary. I rang Lindy and told her that if the Phillip Island book was getting worldwide exposure through the podcast world, we needed to at least have an e-book edition for people to be able to buy. If they loved the podcast, then lots would be interested in reading the bigger story. Lindy and I put in a lot of hours getting the book ready in time. We nearly made it. *Casefile* went to air and we got the e-book out the next day; closely followed by a new print edition – because some people still prefer paper.

Another fortuitous conversation took place in January 2018. I had lunch with a teaching colleague, Aimee Shackleton who has gone onto marvellous things in the world of IT and e-learning. Aimee is a huge advocate for the power of social media. I didn't usually have time to devote to social media beyond my own personal Facebook page where I mostly posted things that make me laugh or had funny animal pictures in them – sometimes all at the same time. Aimee explained how she used Twitter to expand her profile and how authors could too.

I took this advice onboard and when the avalanche of social media followed both true crime podcasts, I interacted with those interested in my story. I set up a Facebook author page and invited people to like it. For me, it was the first time in 25 years of writing that the spotlight truly fell on me. All my writing career, I've pushed interest away from me. The stories were what was interesting; not me. But something shifted in my thinking. My understanding of the world, and the wisdom I've gained from doing this kind of writing *was* of interest.

True crime and the people who tell true crime stories are interesting. When I do author talks, I mostly spoke about cases, but no there was a huge interest in me – the story behind the story.

In July 2018, I did a talk at Robinsons Book Store in Frankston. I'd just released *The Frankston Murders: 25 years on* and was asked to do an author talk at the bookshop that had launched the original book back in 1995. After the talk, my mum, Helen (who never seems to tire of coming to my author talks), together with my publisher Lindy Cameron and her mother-in-law (also called Helen) and I all went for coffee and cake at the wonderful Twisted Sista Café just down from Robinsons.

We got talking about the Frankston case, and the conversation turned to Baby Jake – Debbie Fream's 12-day-old baby left motherless after her murder. Even though he had just turned 25, he would be forever cast in our collective psyche as 'Baby Jake'.

I interviewed Jake over the phone for the 25th anniversary edition and had been profoundly moved by his story. The young man had fallen on hard times. He was finding it hard to get workand accommodation. He was trapped by his circumstances.

'Maybe you could do a fund raiser,' my mum said.

Lindy's eyes lit up. 'We could set up a GoFundMe page for Jake. To give him a leg-up,' she said.

And an idea was born.

I loved the plan but was acutely aware that Jake was a proud person and I would need to gently suggest the idea to him.

I'd felt bad because Carmel and Brian Russell had asked me to

Carmel and Brian Russell have also been featured on the *Australian True Crime* podcast, to talk about the heartbreaking murder of their daughter Natalie.

(l-r) Emily Webb, Brian Russell, Meshel Laurie, me. (f) Carmel Russell

ask Jake if he would like to join them to visit the track – now named Nat's Track – on Natalie's 25th anniversary. I hadn't put the idea to Jake because he had recently become homeless and it seemed insensitive at the very least to suggest he travel from South Australia to Melbourne when he couldn't put a roof over his head. But, if we started a fund-raising campaign, maybe we could raise enough to fund a trip over for him.

Spending my entire adult life writing about inhumanity, I understand that humanity is the counterpoint. The only way to fight inhumanity is to do as much good as you can.

Neither Lindy nor I have spent any time in corporate corridors or in high-finance places but sometimes, motivation is more important than knowledge. We had already had a huge response to the talks I planned to do at the Frankston RSL to commemorate the 25th anniversary of the crime that had touched so many in the area. The first one had booked out in a couple of days. Nearly 300 tickets were sold and the RSL asked if I would repeat the talk the following week. Those 300 sold out quickly too. A local woman called Kate, who ran the Frankston Community Noticeboard on Facebook – a page with a huge local following – had offered to promote my talks and also asked if she could organise a tribute to commemorate the anniversary.

So over coffee and cake at the Twisted Sista Cafe, our idea was born. We would set up a GoFundMe page and see how many people we could enlist to promote it. There's something about affirmative action that warms the heart and quickens the step.

After getting the go-ahead from Jake Blair who agreed that if a fundraiser could help him get somewhere to live and some furniture, and could help him get his driver's licence, he would be really happy.

I secretly hoped for much more than that.

Debbie's anniversary was on 8 July and I waited, on the night before, for the clock pass midnight, to announce the idea on my Facebook author page. I'd posted an earlier teaser and was humbled that people waited up to hear my midnight news. One woman, Sheryl, even set her alarm so she wouldn't miss the announcement.

There was a groundswell of community love and support and I felt the sky was the limit to what we could achieve.

I did another podcast with *Australian True Crime* – this one about the Frankston Murders. I spoke about finding Baby Jake and how he had fallen on hard times. When it went to air, a guy called Ryan messaged Emily Webb and said he had a construction company and offered Jake work. When I got the email in the small hours of Sunday morning, I forwarded the offer straight to Jake. After the podcast, a number of people got in touch to offer Jake a job. One woman even offered him an overseas trip to help with trafficked people in a non-profit organisation – an experience she felt might be of benefit to Jake. Another person was the child of a murdered mother and offered to reach out to Jake. Generosity is boundless.

Because contact with Jake was sporadic while he tried to find a place to live, I constantly worried whether I was doing the right thing. I knew some of what he had suffered, and the last thing I wanted was to make things worse for him. Some reactions from people in his circle when he did an interview with Megan Norris for the *Australian Women's Weekly* had not been positive, and I didn't want to further add to his woes.

25-year-old 'Baby' Jake made it to Melbourne to join the Russells for their 25th anniversay memorial at Nat's Track.

When I told him we had raised enough money to fund a trip to Melbourne for the anniversary, he told me that he wanted to come, but knew it would be a really hard thing to do. I didn't want to push him into anything that could cause further pain, but I really believed that if he came to Frankston and stood in his mother's heartland, he would be surrounded by people who already held him dear in their hearts, the Russells included.

Even when Jake said he was definitely coming, I didn't book his accommodation until he texted me that he was on the road. Finally, on Sunday 29 July, late in the evening, he texted me that he and his girlfriend, Mini, had made it to a petrol station near my house – our pre-arranged meeting place. I hopped in my car, quickly drove around and pulled up next to theirs. He jumped out as soon as he saw me. I got out too.

'I need a hug,' I said, warmly embracing Baby Jake after seven months of texting and talking and messaging. He was finally here. I drove and they followed me, all the way to Frankston and once they checked into their motel, the three of us went out for dinner.

'How are you feeling?' I asked Jake.

'It's so great to be here,' he said, looking around at the streets of Frankston. He had never been back after his mother was taken.

I told him how dear he was to the people of Frankston and how generous they had been in the Baby Jake campaign. He could hardly fathom the generosity. Growing up so far away from the events that had so changed the course his life, he never imagined that a whole community could know and understand how this had affected him.

'I know you're 25,' I told him, 'but tomorrow, you're going to be Baby Jake to everyone you meet.'

He smiled. He knew.

It was so amazing to finally meet this articulate young man. I felt such a strong connection to him and knew that orchestrating this visit had been the right thing to do.

The next day, I left work early to attend the memorial at Nat's Track. Kate from the Facebook Frankston Community Noticeboard had promoted the memorial to give all the people who needed it, a place to go and express their sorrow for the victims of the crime that had shaken the suburb to its core. I picked up Jake and Mini and we drove to the track.

It was lovely to see that my urge to hug Baby Jake when I first met him was duplicated by everyone who met him on the day. I took him around and introduced him to all the people who began gathering. I didn't do a headcount, but it looked like 150 people. The wind blew bitterly and the clouds threatened, but the weather held.

Before we arrived, Carmel and Brian Russell had walked up the track to pay their respects to Natalie. They were flanked by family. As they appeared coming back down the track, I walked Jake up to meet them. When I first broached the idea of him coming to Melbourne, Jake told me he didn't know if he'd be able to hold it together when he met the Russells.

'If you can't,' I told him, 'they, of all people, would understand.'

And when they met, it was like they had known each other always; and in some ways, they had.

One of the highlights for me was the small army or orange-clad SES workers who turned up to pay their respects. Led by Brian McMannis, who'd left his own birthday party all those years

Jake and I, with members of the SES who turned up to mark the anniversary of Natalie's death. Some of them were there 25 years ago, searching for her along the track that now bears her name .

ago to search for Natalie, they marched as one to the memorial. Among them was the SES member who had found Natalie's body. He got to meet Carmel and Brian Russell for the first time. Carmel hugged him and thanked him for finding her daughter.

It was an afternoon of sadness and strength; the two go hand in hand.

On Sunday 4 August, I did a fund-raising talk and donated the $800 in ticket sales to the Baby Jake fund. The way the community came together and helped out was amazing. The Frankston Pines Football Club offered the venue for free. Local woman, Gail Ak organised the event; her friend Mel set up the booking page; and on the day, another friend, Jane made cupcakes for the crowd. Their friend Leon offered his AV services for free. It was a fabulous occasion and once again, the audience was spellbound by the story of the Frankston murders all those years ago.

Afterwards, people offered to sign any future petitions to keep Denyer in jail. So not only did we raise money for Jake, but we also raised awareness on the sentencing – which was our original purpose of releasing the 25th anniversary edition of *The Frankston Murders*.

Adding to the excitement of the year, *Once a Copper* was longlisted for the Ned Kelly Awards, and Brian 'The Skull' Murphy and I had been contacted by a producer who wanted to option the book for a film project.

I did more publicity than I had done in years, and people started to recognise me, which I was not used to. That's not entirely true; I've often been recognised in public, but it was usually: 'Are you Mrs Petraitis who taught me in Grade 3?'

This new recognition was a whole other thing. The first time it happened, I was at Southland in the men's department shopping with my dad to buy him a birthday present. A man approached me and said, 'Are you Vikki Petraitis the crime author?'

Doing half a dozen podcasts had given me more recognition than all the books I'd written over 25 years. Add social media to the mix where people can easily interact with authors, and the world changes. Social media – which didn't exist when I began writing – gave readers a way of connecting and giving much-appreciated positive feedback.

In the cross-pollination of life, students I taught years ago also connected. I had never sought validation for my writing or my teaching, but messages like this are certainly humbling: 'Thanks again Mrs P. I've taken a great interest in crime over the last 10 years, and I love your writing. Grade 6 was one of the best years of my life.' And: 'I love reading your books. I always lose myself in the story which is as it should be.'

Around this time, I did an author talk at the beautiful Geelong Library. At the end of the talk, I took questions from the audience. One man said, 'Cops get PTSD. Are you at risk of it as a writer since you write about some pretty horrendous stuff?'

I was about to be flippant like I usually am, but then something occurred to me. I've helped so many people over the years process what has happened to them by helping them write their stories. Wasn't that what I did? Processed things by writing about them? Writing about them until they made sense? Beginning, middle, end. Good vs evil. Just deserts.

For writers, everything becomes a story in the end. Years ago, I was in a difficult situation at work. After working at a school for just a year, I needed to move on. It was a really toxic environment; one person in a position of power at the school was making everyone else suffer. I could've made up some excuse for my departure: it's too far from home, or (to steal a line from Gilmore Girls) my leg is haunted; but instead

I thought that whatever happened in that moment

would become a forever story I might tell at a dinner party. So, what did I want that story to be? Making my excuses and bowing out? Or having a conversation with the person and saying exactly how I felt? I chose the latter and I'm glad I did. Makes a much better story.

Maybe I process life like that. I can't control the way other people treat me, but their treatment of me becomes *my* story. And I'm a storyteller.

And so dear reader, after having four books released in the last year and a half (including this one), it is time to turn my head firmly towards my PhD in Creative Writing. My first work of fiction is shaping up well. It's crime, of course, and I get to fictionalise and explore all the things that have affected me over 25 years of writing true crime.

Naturally, I'm exploring sexual abuse because it has been a recurring theme in my writing. But it's more than that. Over the years, I've seen the treatment of female victims as an area of great concern. Still, today, we get headlines that blame women: *Woman raped for refusing threesome* suggests that it was her fault when actually, she was raped because two men decided their need to sexually use her forcefully without any regard for her as a human being was worth more than her consent.

A lot of women I know have experienced gender inequality; doors shut to them because they are women. The older you get, the more you see opportunities automatically offered to men. The gender pay gap is still very real and it shouldn't be. I see women still carrying the bulk of the emotional load at home, the organisational load with men still 'helping'.

I see the silencing of women, the lack of female voice at the very time we need to be shouting from the rooftops. I have experienced misogyny. Men less qualified than I am, have made a point of telling about how unqualified I am. It would be funny if it wasn't so serious.

Misogyny is exquisitely subtle in some instances, and in others, it's whack-in-the-face overt. Once, in conversation with a man I'd just met, we were talking about reading and writing. As part of the conversation, I said, 'I'm doing a PhD in Creative Writing and I've written 14 books.'

'It's not a competition,' he said like a snarky child.

I raised an eyebrow and said, 'Well, unless you've written 15, it really isn't.'

Researching my PhD, I've come across some truly worrying statistics. Eight out of ten women aged between 18 and 24 have been harassed on the street, which means – unless there are just a few men working as full-time street harassers – that a huge percent of men think it's okay to harass women.

And we all know, when women are not treated equally and respectfully it contributes toward the violence committed against them.

Conviction rates in rape trials are still appallingly low which means the law doesn't serve victims and there is little guarantee of justice. The rise in just the reported incidents of domestic violence is disturbing. While the fact that 71 women were killed by violence – in nearly every instance by their male partners – in 2018 (and another 22 by June 2019) is terrifying.

Solutions all seem to revolve around what women can do to keep safe, but rarely how we can stop men from raping, and beating and murdering.

Indeed, the affront too many men feel when the subject is raised shuts down conversation – that is the superpower of affront.

So, for me, writing is about always moving forward, looking for the next thing to capture my attention. Writing is about connecting with others. Writing is about teaching people. It's about helping other people tell their stories. And it is always about learning.

In stories, a hero can only be a hero after they face hardship and are knocked down but get back up again, time after time. Challenges that buffet us, also build us.

It is true in stories and it is true in life.

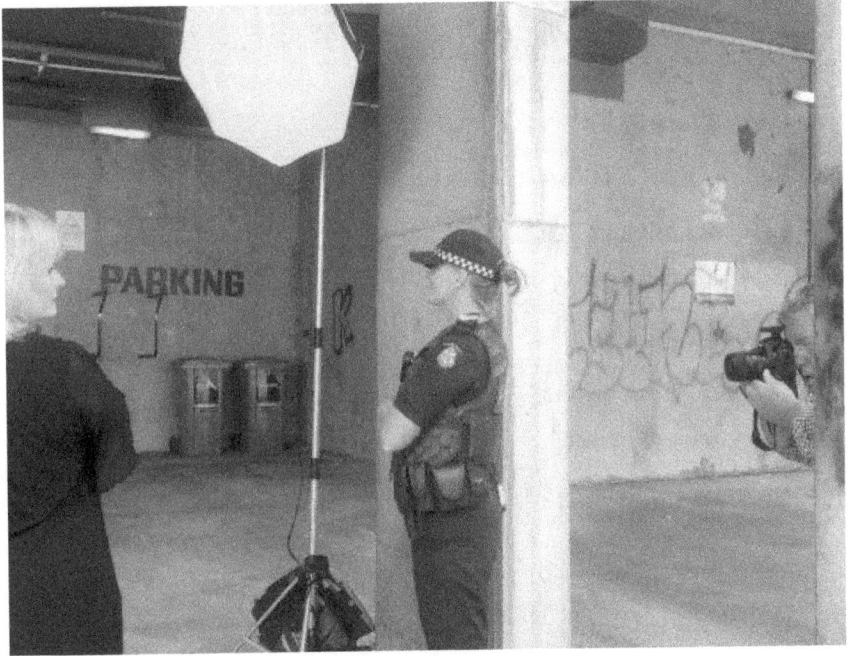

A photo of the photo shoot for the fabulous cover of
Inside the Law: 25 years of true crime writing.

That's Darren McNamara, my brother-in-law and professional
photographer lurking professionally behind the pillar; and the
police woman is real, but anonymous.

This photo was taken by my publisher, Lindy Cameron, on her
mobile phone. The difference between this and the cover image
says a lot about using professionals.

Photo credits

Darren McNamarra: Cover image; and p 442

Carmel Shute, founding member, Secretary, & official photographer of Sisters in Crime Australia: pp 180, 183, 218, 22, 254, 257, 286, 289,336, 341, 396, 397, 398, 408, 424, 436

Peter Ward: p 142

Simon O'Dwyer, *The Age* newspaper: p 146

Peter Lorimer: p 203

Chris Pavlich: p 206

News Ltd: p 299, 324

Graham Crouch p 332

Amra Pajalic: p 426

Lindy Cameron: p 439

CPSIA information can be obtained
at www.ICGtesting.com
Printed in the USA
BVHW071926230619
551754BV00001B/10/P

9 780648 293712